CW00767675

December 19, 1989

With Best Regards
to
Dr. S. Durai Raja Singam —

I deeply appreciate your kind words of interest and encouragement since the beginnings of this book.

Indira Peterson

13 Burnett Avenue
South Hadley
MA 01075
U.S.A.

With Love and kisses to Selva
from father
Durai Raja Singam
and a
Happy Birthday
Dec. 1990

Poems to Śiva

PRINCETON LIBRARY

OF ASIAN TRANSLATIONS

Poems to Śiva

The Hymns of the Tamil Saints

Indira Viswanathan Peterson

PRINCETON
UNIVERSITY PRESS

Published by Princeton University Press, 41 William Street,
Princeton, New Jersey 08540
In the United Kingdom: Princeton University Press, Guildford, Surrey

Library of Congress Cataloging-in-Publication Data

Tēvāram. English.
Poems to Śiva.
(Princeton library of Asian translations)
Translated from Tamil.
Bibliography: p. Includes index.
1. Śiva (Hindu deity)—Prayer-books and devotions—English. 2. Śaivism—Prayer-books and devotions—English. 3. Śiva (Hindu deity)—Prayer-books and devotions—Tamil—History and criticism. 4. Śaivism—India—Tamil Nadu. I. Peterson, Indira Viswanathan, 1950– . II. Title. III. Series. BL1218.2.T4813 1989 294.5′43 88–22470

ISBN 0–691–06767–8

Publication of this book has been aided by a grant from the Paul Mellon Fund of Princeton University Press

This book has been composed in Linotron Sabon

Clothbound editions of Princeton University Press books are printed on acid-free paper, and binding materials are chosen for strength and durability. Paperbacks, although satisfactory for personal collections, are not usually suitable for library rebinding

Printed in the United States of America by Princeton University Press, Princeton, New Jersey

Designed by Laury A. Egan

For

my parents

CONTENTS

ILLUSTRATIONS AND MAP

15. Verses from the *Tēvāram* (Appar IV.196) inscribed on the wall of Tiruvāṉmiyūr temple. Photo by the author

PREFACE

As a child, I lived for a year with my grandmother in Mylapore, the old brahmin quarter of the city of Madras. The house was located on one of the four streets which form the square enclosing the ancient temple of Śiva Kapālīśvara. In that year and in that place began my acquaintance with the *Tēvāram*, the hymns of three Tamil Śaiva poet-saints. Every evening at the temple I heard the clear, sweet voice of the hymn singer rise in song above the voices of the devotees worshipping at the shrine. The words were in Tamil, my mother tongue; they spoke eloquently of deep emotion, of sacred places, of God in beautiful landscapes. I was enchanted. In 1978 and 1979 I returned to Tamilnadu to study the performance and cultural milieu of the *Tēvāram*, as groundwork toward a translation of the hymns. This book is the result of that research and my work on the translations over a period of seven years.[1]

My thanks go to the institutions whose generous support has made this book possible. Amherst College gave me a Miner Crary Memorial Research Fellowship (1978) to record the *Tēvāram* hymns in India; I received a Research Fellowship (1979–1980) from the National Endowment for the Humanities to study the performance tradition of the *Tēvāram* in India; and Mount Holyoke College gave me a Faculty Grant (1984) to help me complete the manuscript. I am grateful also to the following for their assistance: Yvonne Nicholson, for typing the first draft; Lee Weissman, for the loan of the *Civastalamañcari*, which helped me identify some of the ancient shrines associated with the *Tēvāram*; cartographer Roy Doyon, for executing the map; and Elizabeth Gretz, for skillful copyediting. It has been a pleasure to work with Margaret Case, my editor at Princeton University Press. Her excellent editorial advice and suggestions have made this a better book in every way.

Lalgudi M. Swaminathan, *ōtuvār* at the Kapālīśvara temple in Madras, and Ñāṉacampanta Ōtuvār, of the Caṭṭaiṉātar temple at Cīrkāḻi, initiated me into the world of *Tēvāram* singing. Their beautiful voices and superb rendering of the hymns have truly enriched my understanding of the *Tēvāram*. I also wish to thank the *ōtuvārs* I interviewed and recorded in Tanjavur, Tiruvārūr, Maturai, Tiruvāṉmiyūr, Tarumapuram, and at the

[1] A cassette tape of selections from *ōtuvār* performances of the *Tēvāram* hymns is available from the author. Readers interested in obtaining a copy should write to Indira Peterson, Committee on Asian Studies, Mount Holyoke College, South Hadley, Mass. 01075.

1979–1980 conference on *paṇ* research in Madras for sharing genrously of their time and talent.

His Holiness Caṇmuka Tēcika Ñāṉacampanta Paramācāriya Cuvāmikaḷ of the Tarumapuram Ātīṉam and members of the Ātīṉam center in Tarumapuram and Madras gave their gracious and enthusiastic support to my venture. I spent several delightful and informative days with Vēlāyuta Ōtuvār's class of young trainees at Tarumapuram.

I have gained in insight from discussion and exchange of ideas with the following scholars in India at various stages of my study: K. Veḷḷaivāraṇaṉ, François Gros, K.K.A. Venkatachari, V. A. Devasenapathy, P. S. Somasundaram, P. Cuntarēcaṉ, B. Natarajan, and N. R. Murukavēḷ. My particular thanks to François Gros and the Institut français d'indologie for supplying excellent photographs for the book from their archives in Pondicherry, and for delivering them to me in record time.

I owe a special debt of gratitude to George L. Hart III, A. K. Ramanujan, and Barbara Miller, colleagues and mentors, eminent scholars and translators in the field, who read the translations in draft versions. The translations have benefited greatly from their suggestions and advice, their keen sense of poetry, and their high standards of translation.

David Reck has long been my colleague, friend, and partner in the study and performance of South Indian music. Always encouraging me in my study of *Tēvāram* performance, he helped prepare and house at Amherst College the tapes that I made in 1978 and 1979 in India. Gary Tartakov of Iowa State University has followed the progress of this book from its inception and has generously contributed a photograph from his personal archives. John Carman, Dennis Hudson, Alan Babb, Glenn Yocum, Vidya Dehejia, Norman Cutler, and David Shulman have all shared their ideas on Tamil *bhakti* and encouraged me in my work; my thanks to them. Thanks also to *Tēvāram* fans Durai Raja Singam, Leila Diraviyam, and N. R. Damodaran for their help and encouragement.

My parents, R. Viswanathan and Jaya Viswanathan, have aided and encouraged my work in every possible way, at every step of the project. Other members of my extended family in India—uncles, aunts, and cousins—opened their homes and hearts to me in Madras and South India: Mr. and Mrs. S. S. Sundharesan, the late Dr. V. Srinivasamurthy, Mr. and Mrs. V. Sankar, Mr. and Mrs. S. Krishnamurthy, and Mr. and Mrs. A. N. Jagannatha Rao.

My husband, Mark, has participated, kindly and cheerfully, in every aspect of the making of this book: discussing my work, subjecting draft translations to a clear-eyed reading, teaching me the intricacies of word-processing. Above all, his love, friendship, and encouragement have sustained me through the most frustrating moments and deepened the many joys of writing and translation. My daughter, Maya, was born at the same time that I began the first draft. I hope that someday, when she reads this book, she will appreciate the study that engaged her mother's mind during the time that she grew from an infant into a little girl.

I am pleased at last to be able to acknowledge my debts of gratitude to all of the people and institutions who have helped me in my work on the *Tēvāram* hymns. I know that they will share my joy at seeing the book in print.

A NOTE ON TRANSLITERATION

Wherever names of major figures in pan-Hindu mythology and culture occur, I have used the standard transliteration for the Sanskrit: e.g., Śiva, Bhagīratha, *rāga*, Viṣṇu. The names of figures, places, and concepts occurring exclusively in Tamil culture and religion, including the majority of the place names in the *Tēvāram* hymns, have been transliterated according to the system provided in the *Tamil Lexicon* (University of Madras, 1936): e.g., Campantar, *akam*, Iṭaimarutūr. When referring, in a general context, to monuments and place names in common usage in contemporary Tamil, I have adopted the popular, nonscholarly transliteration: e.g., Chidambaram, Kaveri, Tamilnadu.

NOTE: Masculine names and epithets ending in *-ṉ* in Tamil substitute *-r* for the final *-ṉ* in plural and honorific forms. E.g., Campantaṉ, Campantar (honorific); *pattaṉ*, *pattar* (plural/honorific). In the case of honorifics, the usage is contextual.

GUIDE TO TAMIL PRONUNCIATION

Vowels

a	like *u* in *but.*	e	like *e* in *pet* or *bench.*
ā*	like *a* in *father.*	ē*	similar to *a* in *cake.*
i	like *i* in *it.*	ai	like *i* in *pipe.*
ī*	similar to *ee* in *keep.*	o	like the first *o* in *potato.*
u	like *u* in *put.*	ō*	similar to the *o* in *open* or *oak.*
ū*	similar to *oo* in *coop.*	au	like *ow* in *fowl.*

*The asterisked long vowels are purer than their English counterparts and closer to Italian vowels.

Consonants and Nasals

k (guttural) like the English *k*; the nasal *ṅ* is used with *k*: e.g., *maṅkai.*

c (palatal) similar to *ch* in *chalk*, but unaspirated; the nasal *ñ* is used with *c*: e.g., *neñcu*. The following sounds that have come into Tamil from Sanskrit are also represented by *c*: (palatal) *ś*, pronounced "sh"; and *s*, similar to the English *s*: e.g., *civaṉ* (Śiva), pronounced as "S(h)ivan" or "Sivan."

ṭ a retroflex sound, pronounced with the tongue curled back so that it touches the roof of the mouth; *ṇ* is the retroflex nasal: e.g., *toṇṭar.*

t (dental) similar to *t* in French or Italian; the nasal *n* is used with *t.*

p like the English *p*; the nasal *m* is used with *p.*

Tamil consonants are pronounced without the slight aspiration that is characteristic of the pronunciation of similar consonants in English.

Semivowels

y, r, l, and v similar to their English counterparts; the *r* is rolled.

ḻ similar to the American *r*, as in *American* or *first.*

ḷ pronounced as a retroflex sound.

ṟ AND *ṉ*

In origin, *ṟ* and *ṉ* are closer to alveolar sounds than *r* and the other nasal sounds of Tamil; however, *ṟ* and *r* are almost indistinguishable in contemporary pronunciation; the combination *ṟṟ*, as in *Ciṟṟampalam*, is pronounced like *tr* in *country.*

Special Rules

Initially (i.e., at the beginning of a word) and between vowels, *c* is pronounced like the English *s*.

Between vowels, *k*, *ṭ*, *t*, and *p* are voiced, and pronounced as *g* or *h*, *ḍ*, *d*, and *b*.

Following a nasal, *k*, *c*, *ṭ*, *t*, and *p* are voiced, and pronounced as *g*, *j*, *ḍ*, *d*, and *b*.

Thus *Campantar* is pronounced as *Samban'dar*, *Cuntarar* as *Sun'darar*, *Caṅkam* as *Sangam*, *akam* as *aham*, *Murukaṉ* as *Murugan*, *Añcai* as *Anjai*, and *pātam* as *pādam*.

Doubled consonants are given full value and held longer. E.g., Ka*cc*i is pronounced as "kac(h)c(h)i."

Sounds from Sanskrit

In addition to *ś* and *s*, the following Sanskrit letters have been incorporated into Tamil orthography and the sound system of Tamil:

ṣ the retroflex sibilant, as in Viṣṇu.
kṣ the combination of *k* and *ṣ* as in Kṣēttirakkōvai.
j like english *j*.
h like English *h*.

The voiced sounds of Sanskrit (*g*, *d* etc.) are represented by their unvoiced counterparts (*k*, *t* etc.) in Tamil.

Tamil has no true counterparts for the aspirated sounds (kh, gh, etc.) of Sanskrit.

PART ONE

Introduction: Poetry and Religion in the Songs of the Tamil Śaiva Saints

South India: Sacred Places Associated with the *Tēvāram*.

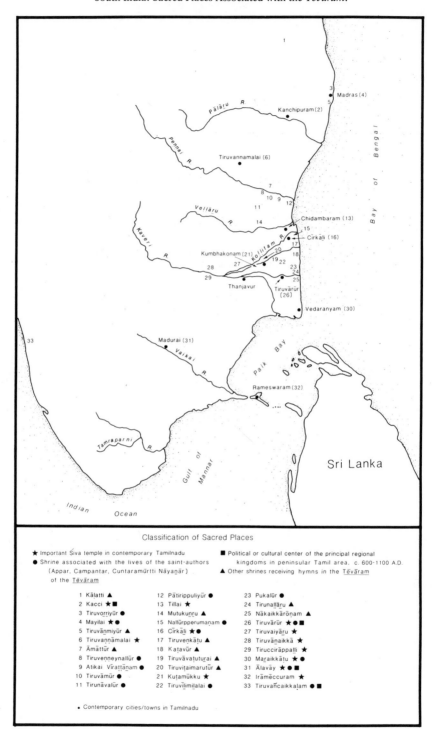

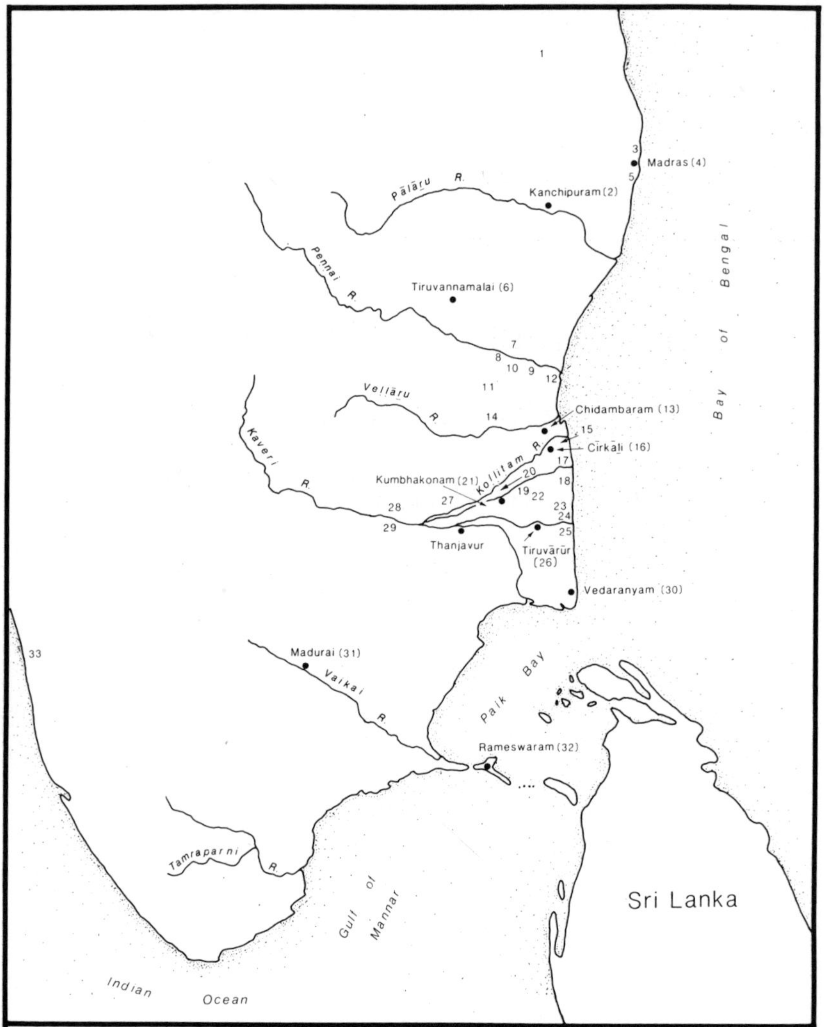

Classification of Sacred Places

★ Important Śiva temple in contemporary Tamilnadu

● Shrine associated with the lives of the saint-authors (Appar, Campantar, Cuntaramūrtti Nāyaṉār) of the Tēvāram

■ Political or cultural center of the principal regional kingdoms in peninsular Tamil area, c. 600-1100 A.D.

▲ Other shrines receiving hymns in the Tēvāram

1 Kālatti ▲
2 Kacci ★■
3 Tiruvoṟṟiyūr ●
4 Mayilai ★●
5 Tiruvāṉmiyūr ▲
6 Tiruvaṇṇāmalai ★
7 Āmāttūr ▲
8 Tiruveṇṇeynallūr ●
9 Atikai Vīraṭṭāṉam ●
10 Tiruvāmūr ●
11 Tirunāvalūr ●
12 Pātirippuliyūr ●
13 Tillai ★
14 Mutukuṉṟu ▲
15 Nallūrpperumaṇam ●
16 Cīrkāḻi ★●
17 Tiruveṇkāṭu ▲
18 Kaṭavūr ▲
19 Tiruvāvaṭuturai ▲
20 Tiruviṭaimarutūr ▲
21 Kuṭamūkku ★
22 Tiruvīḻimilalai ●
23 Pukalūr ●
24 Tirunaḷḷāṟu ▲
25 Nākaikkārōṇam ▲
26 Tiruvārūr ★●■
27 Tiruvaiyāṟu ★
28 Tiruvāṉaikkā ★
29 Tirucciṟāppaḷḷi ★
30 Maṟaikkāṭu ★●
31 Ālavāy ★●■
32 Irāmēccuram ★
33 Tiruvañcaikkaḷam ●■

• Contemporary cities/towns in Tamilnadu

CHAPTER 1

The Study of the *Tēvāram*

The poems translated in this book are Tamil hymns of devotion to the Hindu god Śiva.[1] The poets, Tiruñāṉacampantar (popularly known as Campantar or Ñāṉacampantar), Tirunāvukkaracar (Appar), and Cuntaramūrtti (Cuntarar), lived between the sixth and eighth centuries A.D. in the Tamil linguistic-cultural region of India. They are celebrated as the principal saint-leaders or Nāyaṉār ("leader, master") of the Tamil Śaiva sect (see illus. 1).[2] The collection of the three saints' hymns, entitled the *Tēvāram*, serves as the primary scripture for Tamil Śaivas.

To study the *Tēvāram* is to study more than a text. In understanding the meanings and contexts of the saints' hymns we move closer to an understanding of the religion, world view, and values of the people of Tamilnadu, where nearly every village has a temple to Śiva and every temple is linked to the lives and songs of the saints. The *Tēvāram* also guides us into the world of classical Tamil civilization, for it is heir to the rich and sophisticated tradition of classical Tamil poetry, while the melodic setting of the hymns gives us clues to the ancient musical system of the Tamils.[3]

The Tamil regional cults of the worship of Śiva and Viṣṇu, which arose

[1] Śiva is one of the three supreme gods of the classical Hindu pantheon. The worship of Śiva and Viṣṇu forms the basis of the broad division of Hindus into the Śaiva and Vaiṣṇava sects.

[2] Tamil is the language of the Tamil community of the present-day state of Tamilnadu in South India and of ethnic Tamils who live elsewhere. Tamil is the oldest representative of the Dravidian group of languages, which is distinct from the Indo-Aryan family of languages represented by Sanskrit and most of the languages of North India. For a general history of Tamil culture, see K. A. Nilakanta Sastri, *The Culture and History of the Tamils* (Calcutta: Firma K. L. Mukhopadhyay, 1964). In Tamil, the Tamil Śaiva saints are also collectively known as the "Nāyaṉmār" (the Tamil plural of *nāyaṉār*).

[3] Except for early inscriptions, the earliest documents we have of Tamil civilization are the anthologies of sophisticated classical poetry from the age of the Caṅkam ("academy") (A.D. first-third centuries). In *The Poems of Ancient Tamil: Their Milieu and Their Sanskrit Counterparts* (Berkeley: University of California Press, 1975), George L. Hart III discusses this literature in its cultural and historical context.

and flourished between the fifth and ninth centuries A.D. and later grew into the Tamil Śaiva and Vaiṣṇava sects, were among the first cults devoted to *bhakti*, a popular religion of emotional devotion to a personal God, which eventually permeated the Hindu tradition in all its aspects.[4] The hymns of the Nāyaṉārs and the Āḻvārs, the early Tamil Śaiva and Vaiṣṇava saints, may be credited with many "firsts": they are the first literary expression of emotional *bhakti*; the first sizable corpus of full-fledged "religious" poems in Tamil;[5] and the first Hindu sectarian scripture in a vernacular language.[6] The *Tēvāram* claims distinction in other ways as well, particularly in the ease with which it straddles diverse categories in Indian religion, literature, and culture: "Sanskritic" and vernacular domains; classical and popular literature; universal and local themes in *bhakti* and the Hindu religious tradition; scripture and popular

[4] The Sanskrit term *bhakti*, meaning "partaking (of God), participation, loving devotion," derived from the root *bhaj-*, has been broadly applied both to a type of religiosity and to the popular movements through which devotional religion spread in India. The idea of *bhakti* in the sense of "devotion to a personal god" is present in early Hindu philosophical texts in Sanskrit that predated the Tamil *bhakti* cults by several centuries, most prominently in the *Śvetāśvatara Upaniṣad* and the *Bhagavad Gītā* (A.D. first-second centuries). Textual and iconographic evidence from the early Christian era also points to the existence of devotional cults involving image worship, a practice that was not part of the theism of the early Vedic religion. However, the emotional devotionalism of the Tamil cults was a new development in Hinduism. On early *bhakti* religion, see Thomas J. Hopkins, *The Hindu Religious Tradition* (Encino, Calif.: Dickenson, 1971), chs. 5, 6, 7. For a general introduction to *bhakti* religion and poetry, see A. K. Ramanujan, *Speaking of Śiva* (Baltimore: Penguin, 1973) and idem, *Hymns for the Drowning: Poems for Viṣṇu by Nammāḻvār* (Princeton: Princeton University Press, 1981). On the evolution of emotional *bhakti*, see Friedhelm Hardy, *Viraha-Bhakti: The Early History of Kṛṣṇa Devotion in South India* (Delhi: Oxford University Press, 1983).

[5] Although the classical Tamil poems were deeply imbued with the indigenous Tamil view of the sacred, religion is not their primary concern. The earliest Tamil works with an explicitly religious focus are the *Paripāṭal* and *Tirumurukāṟṟuppaṭai*, two late classical texts (A.D. sixth-seventh centuries). Addressed to Tirumāl (Viṣṇu) and the Tamil hill-god Murukaṉ, these early poems qualify as *bhakti* literature. On *bhakti* in the two classical texts, see Ramanujan, *Hymns*, pp. 109–17. For a discussion of the poetry of the Śaiva saint Kāraikkāl Ammaiyār and the three Vaiṣṇava poet-saints who preceded the authors of the *Tēvāram*, see Norman Cutler, *Songs of Experience: The Poetics of Tamil Devotion* (Bloomington: Indiana University Press, 1986).

[6] The hymns of the four Vedas (Rig, Sāma, Yajur, and Atharva; 1200–800 B.C.), which are in Vedic Sanskrit, are considered to be *śruti*, "revealed" (lit., "heard") literature and the highest scripture of the Hindus. Within Hinduism, until the rise of the popular *bhakti* cults and sects in the South, all sacred texts were written in Sanskrit, the "language of the gods" (*deva-vāṇī*). The use of Pāli and Prakrit (vernacular dialects related to Sanskrit) for religious literature was one of the innovative and revolutionary strategies of Buddhism and Jainism, the two great popular religions of ancient India, which rose in opposition to brahmanical Hinduism around the sixth century B.C. The hymns of the Tamil saints are thus the first Hindu religious literature to be written in a language other than Sanskrit. See my discussion of the *Tēvāram* as the Tamil Veda in Chapter 4 below.

song; written and oral texts; the celebration of tradition and the poetry of an innovative movement; and personal and communal religion.[7] In Part One I have sought to present the text in its multidimensional richness, to locate it in as many of its contexts as possible. I have tried not only to inform the reader in regard to the religious settings and significance of the saints' hymns but also to give a sense of the ways in which Tamil Śaivas experience these religious poems. In the process, I have explored the broader issue of the role of sacred texts, and of poetry in particular, in Tamil *bhakti*.

Among the regional languages of India, Tamil alone had an early classical civilization, religion, and literature of its own, quite distinct from the Indo-Aryan heritage of Sanskrit and brahmanism. Although the indigenous Dravidian civilization of the Tamils was progressively "Sanskritized" by early contact with the brahmanical civilization of the North, it retained its distinctive character even as late as the period of the Tamil Śaiva saints. As the first literary expressions of a popular and regional religious culture in Hinduism, the *Tēvāram* hymns reflected many features of Tamil culture, and differed in many respects from the authoritative sacred texts of the Great Tradition, composed in Sanskrit, the classical language of the brahmanical civilization. At the same time, they provided a powerful new synthesis of the values of brahmanical Hinduism and those of the indigenous Tamil civilization, affirming, celebrating, and transforming both traditions.[8]

The *Tēvāram* is not only the document and expression of an important moment, a turning point in the history of Hinduism and of Tamil regional culture, but a broader cultural phenomenon, one that has been "a great living, moving force" in the lives of the Tamils.[9] Like other formative or fundamental religious texts, the *Tēvāram* has transcended and transformed its literary, religious, and cultural contexts, itself becoming an important, continuing context for Tamil Śaiva religiosity. In its capacity as the scripture of the Tamil Śaiva sect, this text has had a life of its own and has functioned as a symbol and motivator of sectarian and communal

[7] I use the term "Sanskritic" broadly, to refer to those aspects of Indian culture and civilization that are primarily associated with the Sanskrit language and pan-Hindu civilization, especially in relation to early brahmanical Hinduism.

[8] A. K. Ramanujan discusses the contrasts between Sanskrit texts and vernacular *bhakti* texts in Ramanujan, *Speaking of Śiva*, pp. 37–48, 134–39. Frits Staal has demonstrated the complexity of the process that has been called "Sanskritization"; he points out that this is in fact a two-way process in which vernacular and Sanskritic elements continually influence each other. J. Frits Staal, "Sanskrit and Sanskritization," *Journal of Asian Studies* 22, no. 3 (May 1963): 261–75.

[9] Kamil V. Zvelebil, *Tamil Literature*, in *Handbuch der Orientalistik*, Zweite Abteilung, *Indien*, ed. Jan Gonda, Band 2: *Literatur und Bühne*, Abschnitt 1 (Leiden/Cologne: E. J. Brill, 1975), p. 32, note 19.

identity. Indeed, crossing the boundary of the strictly "religious," it has played an important part in shaping the ethnic-national consciousness of the Tamils as a whole. The study of the *Tēvāram* calls for a synchronic as well as a diachronic approach: the former, in order to study the poems in their "historical moment" and to trace their career through the history of Tamil Śaivism; the latter, in order to understand the great symbolic value of the *Tēvāram* for practicing Tamil Śaivas today.

The *bhakti* lyrics of the Nāyaṉārs differ in many respects from the poetry of the saints of later *bhakti* cults in other regions of India.[10] Appar, Campantar, and Cuntarar have more in common with their Tamil Vaiṣṇava counterparts and the later Tamil Śaiva saint Māṇikkavācakar, but there are significant differences here as well.[11] The importance of the *Tēvāram* for the study of *bhakti* can hardly be stressed enough. Yet the slim volume of selected translations offered by Kingsbury and Phillips in 1921 remains the only translation available to the English-speaking world.[12] The size and specialized nature of Dorai Rangaswamy's study of Cuntarar and his poems prevent it from becoming an accessible introduction to the hymns of the three saints.[13] The *Tēvāram* needs to be translated and described in context at least in order to clarify the history of *bhakti*

[10] Eleanor Zelliot notes some of these differences in her essay on regional *bhakti* cults. Zelliot, "The Medieval Bhakti Movement in History: An Essay on the Literature in English," in *Hinduism: New Essays in the History of Religions*, ed. Bardwell L. Smith (Leiden: E. J. Brill, 1976), pp. 143–68.

[11] The Śaiva Nāyaṉārs and the Vaiṣṇava Ālvārs were contemporaries, fellows, and rivals in the great religious movement that swept over the Tamil region in the sixth, seventh, and eighth centuries A.D. The similarities of vision are reflected in a shared vocabulary and imagery. For an excellent treatment of the Tamil poet-saints as members of a single religious and poetic universe, see Cutler, *Songs of Experience*. In addition to the early *bhakti* saints, Cutler also deals with the later saints Māṇikkavācakar (Śaiva) and Nammāḻvār (Vaiṣṇava). Glenn E. Yocum treats the contrasts between the two traditions in "Sign and Paradigm: Myth in Tamil Śaiva and Vaiṣṇava *bhakti* Poetry," in *Structural Approaches to South India Studies*, ed. Harry M. Buck and Glenn E. Yocum (Chambersburg, Pa.: Anima Books, 1974), pp. 184–206. Again, on the devotionalism of Māṇikkavācakar (A.D. ninth century?), consult Glenn E. Yocum, *Hymns to the Dancing Śiva: A Study of Māṇikkavācakar's Tiruvācakam* (New Delhi: Heritage, 1982).

[12] F. Kingsbury and G. E. Phillips, *Hymns of the Tamil Śaivite Saints* (Calcutta: Association Press; London: Oxford University Press, 1921). The authors provide translations of 79 out of the 8,284 stanzas of the *Tēvāram*. None of the hymns has been translated in its entirety.

[13] M. A. Dorai Rangaswamy, *The Religion and Philosophy of Tēvāram; with Special Reference to Nampi Ārūrar (Sundarar)*, 4 vols. in 2 books (Madras: University of Madras, 1958–1959). In the most recent edition of the *Tēvāram* hymns, François Gros has written an excellent introduction to the study of the text. Gros, "Introduction: Toward Reading the *Tēvāram*," in *Tēvāram: Hymnes Śivaïtes du pays tamoul*, vol. I: *Ñāṉacampantar*, ed. T. V. Gopal Iyer, general editor: François Gros, Publications de l'Institut français d'indologie no. 68.1 (Pondicherry: Institut français d'indologie, 1984), pp. xxxvii–lxviii.

religion and literature. As the poetry of exemplary "leaders" whose lives and ideas have been, and continue to be, a powerful influence on the Tamils, the hymns of the Nāyaṉārs ought to be made accessible to all who are interested in Indian civilization. This introductory essay and the translations that follow in Part Two represent my contributions toward that goal.

CHAPTER 2

The Making of the *Tēvāram*: The Text and Its Context

At the time of the rise of Tamil *bhakti*, the Tamil linguistic-cultural area covered most of peninsular India south of the hill of Vēṅkaṭam, and roughly corresponded to the region made up of the three Tamil kingdoms of the Caṅkam classical age, ruled by the Pāṇṭiya (Pandya), Cōḻa, and Cēra kings.[1] In this region, such basic elements of brahmanical Hinduism as the Vedas and Vedic sacrifice, the Vedic-brahmanical gods, and the veneration of brahmins as specialists in the sacred had already become part of Tamil religion and culture; at the same time, aspects of the earlier indigenous religion played an important part in the shaping of Tamil Śaivism and Vaiṣṇavism.[2] Buddhism and Jainism, the great "heterodox" religions of India, had also come early to the South and flourished in the Tamil region.[3]

The age of the three ancient Tamil kingdoms came to an end around the third century A.D. Little is known about the history of the region in

[1] The three ancient Tamil kingdoms or *nāṭus* were: Cōḻanāṭu, with its old capital at Uṟaiyūr; Pāṇṭiyanāṭu, with Maturai (Madurai) as its capital; and Cēranāṭu, with the city of Vañci as its capital. For the early history of these kingdoms, refer to Nilakanta Sastri, *Culture and History*. The names of the kingdoms continued as designations for later kingdoms and macro-regions in the Tamil region. On the subdivisions of the Tamil region, see Burton Stein, *Peasant State and Society in Medieval India* (Delhi: Oxford University Press, 1980).

[2] On the Sanskritization of the early indigenous culture of the Tamils, see Hart, *Poems*, ch. 4. Hart points out that though the Caṅkam poems do show the influence of "northern" religion, ideas, and customs, Sanskritization was much more pervasive in the post-Caṅkam age, when Buddhist and Jain influences were strong, as reflected in the fifth-century epic *Cilappatikāram*. The indigenous Tamil currents in *bhakti* religion are discussed in Glenn E. Yocum, "Shrines, Shamanism and Love Poetry: Elements in the Emergence of Popular Tamil Bhakti," *Journal of the American Academy of Religion* 41, no. 1 (March 1973): 3–17.

[3] K. A. Nilakanta Sastri, *Development of Religion in South India* (Madras: Orient Longmans, 1963), gives a general account of Buddhism and Jainism in South India.

the three centuries that followed, except the rise of the Pallavas, a non-Tamil dynasty that ruled from the city of Kanchipuram.[4] The Pallava Mahendravarman I (seventh century) was the first ruler powerful enough to be able to establish a measure of stability in Tamil India.[5] Poet, artist, and builder of the first rock-cut temples in South India, Mahendravarman was a great patron of the arts and local cultural activity.[6] However, like the imperial Guptas of the North, the Pallava ruler identified more with the Great Tradition connoted by Sanskrit, the enduring language and symbol of pan-Indian civilization, than with the "local" classical tradition of the Tamils.[7] Buddhism and Jainism were the dominant religions in Mahendravarman's kingdom. According to tradition, the king himself practiced Jainism until his friend, the saint Appar, persuaded him to convert to Śaivism.[8] It was in this atmosphere that the Tamil Śaiva and Vaiṣṇava *bhakti* movements blossomed.

Bhakti was a popular religion of intimate relationship with a gracious God, and the new *bhakti* devotionalism was characterized by ecstatic modes of expression. Under the leadership of poet-saints who sang songs of passionate and total devotion for their God not in Sanskrit but in Tamil, their mother tongue, people from every segment of Tamil society gathered to form devotional communities that cut across caste, sex, and other hierarchies of orthodox Hinduism.[9] In all these respects the early Tamil *bhakti* cults were models for the regional *bhakti* movements that followed them. The Tamil movement is better characterized, however, as a movement toward communal solidarity than as an expression of social protest. Although many later *bhakti* movements arose primarily as reactions against the Hindu "orthodoxy" and the established forms and practices of brahmanical Hinduism, the early Tamil *bhakti* cults saw themselves as the champions of the Hindu tradition and, more important, of a

[4] On the Pallavas and Kanchipuram, see T. V. Mahalingam, *Kāñcīpuram in Early South Indian History* (New York: Asia, 1969).

[5] According to Nilakanta Sastri, *Culture and History*, p. 19, the Kalabhras who preceded the Pallavas were "evil rulers" and "an enemy of civilization." On the life and achievements of Mahendravarman I (A.D. 580–630), consult Mahalingam, *Kāñcīpuram*, ch. 4.

[6] The rock-cut temples are in Mahabalipuram.

[7] The Gupta emperors (A.D. 320–540), who ruled from Ujjain in North India, were great patrons of Śaiva and Vaiṣṇava cults, and initiated the great age of temple building in Hinduism. On the relationship between Sanskrit and the civilization of the imperial Guptas, see Daniel H. H. Ingalls, "Kālidāsa and the Attitudes of the Golden Age," *Journal of the American Oriental Society* 96, no. 1 (January-March 1976): 15–26; on Mahendravarman and the Gupta patterns, see Ramanujan, *Hymns*, pp. 104–6. Mahendravarman was an accomplished writer in Sanskrit and wrote the Sanskrit play *Mattavilāsa*.

[8] Mahalingam, *Kāñcīpuram*, p. 75.

[9] On these characteristics of *bhakti* religion see Ramanujan, *Speaking of Śiva*, pp. 19–48, and *Hymns*, pp. 115–26, 150–57. In his discussion, Ramanujan brings out the intimate relationship between *bhakti* as personal religion and the idea of the "mother" tongue.

Tamil Hindu religion, one that was truly harmonious and continuous with the Tamil religious and cultural past. It is clear from the hymns of the Nāyaṉārs and Āḻvārs that the "enemy" was not brahmanical Hinduism, or Sanskritic religious modes, but Buddhism and Jainism, which were seen as alien to Tamil culture, defined by the new cults as an intrinsically Hindu culture.

Campantar devotes a verse in each of his hymns to invective against Buddhist and Jain monks, and Appar rails against the Jains who had led him away from Śaivism. The lives and poems of these two saints indicate a shift in the role of Jainism and Buddhism in the Tamil region. The two heterodox religions had been in the mainstream of Tamil culture in the early centuries of the Christian era. Jain and Buddhist authors and thinkers had made great contributions to Tamil literature. Iḷaṅkōvaṭikaḷ, the author of the Tamil national epic *Cilappatikāram*, was a Jain monk.[10] This fifth-century author celebrated the land of the three Tamil kingdoms and portrayed the Hindu, Jain, and Buddhist religions as coexisting harmoniously in the Tamil region. Less than two hundred years later, Campantar condemns the Jain and Buddhist monks of his time as corrupt rogues who speak neither good Tamil nor the Sanskrit language but mutilate both, babbling in the Prakrit dialects; and he speaks with deep revulsion of the Jain ascetic practices of nudity, tonsure, and abstaining from bathing and cleaning the teeth. Burton Stein has convincingly argued that such hostility reflects the ethos of a newly formed cultural and ideological alliance between the brahmins and peasants of the Tamil plains region. It is also likely that the *bhakti* saints were reacting to groups of Jain and Buddhist monks who had recently arrived in the Tamil country from the Kannada and Telugu areas in the northern part of the peninsula, and who were truly strangers to the Tamil language and culture.[11] The hagiographical accounts, and some of the *Tēvāram* hymns themselves, suggest that the *bhakti* cult leaders had to compete with powerful Jain and Buddhist monks to gain and retain royal support for their religion. Finally, though it can be argued that the ascetic temper of the two heterodox religions was largely confined to the monastic life and that

[10] In his epic Iḷaṅkōvaṭikaḷ celebrates the Cōḻa, Pāṇṭiya, and Cēra kingdoms.

[11] Stein, *Peasant State*, ch. 2. C. V. Narayana Ayyar makes the point about "alien" Jains in *Origin and Early History of Śaivism in South India* (Madras: University of Madras, 1939, 1974), ch. 10. Basing his theory on epigraphical and other evidence, he suggests that the opponents of the *bhakti* saints were Jains who had migrated to the Tamil region from the Kadamba and Western Calukya kingdoms situated to the north of Tamilnadu, and had acquired the support of kings and chieftains in the Tamil region in the sixth century. For further details, see P. S. Somasundaram, *Tirujñāṉasambandhar: Philosophy and Religion* (Madras: Vani Pathippakam, 1986), pp. 209–11. For some reasons for the decline of Buddhism and Jainism in Tamil India after the sixth century, see Kamil Zvelebil, *The Smile of Murugan: On Tamil Literature of South India* (Leiden: E. J. Brill, 1973), pp. 194–97.

they were closer to the Hindu *bhakti* cults in lay practice, there is nothing in early Jain and Buddhist devotional religion that comes close to the sensuous, often erotic, aestheticism of early Tamil *bhakti*, its exaltation of the personal, ecstatic experience of God, and its exuberant expression of love.[12] These *bhakti* characteristics were uniquely bound, on the one hand, with ritual religion and on the other, with the classical culture and aesthetic of the Tamils.[13] The mythology and cultural contexts of the Hindu gods were more congenial to the spirit of a new personal religion in the framework of Tamil civilization than Buddhism and Jainism could be. The *bhakti* saints' aversion to the two heterodox religions was based as much on aesthetic as on doctrinal grounds.

The importance given to the temple and ritual worship in the *Tēvāram* hymns highlights the most striking feature of early Tamil *bhakti*. Many later *bhakti* sects protested against or detached themselves from image, temple, and ritual worship.[14] By contrast, the Tamil cults were closely associated with the teaching and ethos of the large body of ritualistic literature called the Āgamas and Tantras, which developed along with the spread of theism, image worship, and temple worship in Hinduism.[15] From the age of the poet-saints to the present, the temple or shrine has occupied a central position in the literature and practice of Tamil Śaivism and Vaiṣṇavism.[16] The Śaiva Āgamas give detailed expositions of ritual practice in connection with temple worship; they also provide a comprehensive description of devotional acts in a fourfold system that is relevant

[12] A. K. Ramanujan rightly points out that the popular, vernacular, communal, and devotional aspects of the Tamil Hindu *bhakti* cults probably owe more to devotional practice in Jainism and Buddhism in South India than has been acknowledged. See Ramanujan, *Hymns*, pp. 126, 140, 142–46.

[13] For a detailed discussion of Campantar in relation to Jainism and Buddhism, see Somasundaram, *Tirujñāṉasambandhar*, ch. 5.

[14] Ramanujan describes the medieval Vīraśaiva sect as rejecting both the "great" and the "little" traditions of Hinduism (*Speaking of Śiva*, pp. 22–31). He notes that the rejection included classical belief systems, superstitions, image worship, the caste system, and the Vedic ritual, as well as local sacrifices of lambs and goats (p. 30).

[15] For a succinct exposition of the role of the Āgamas in Śaiva religion, see Jean Filliozat, "The Role of the Śaivāgamas in the Śaiva Ritual System," in *Experiencing Śiva: Encounters with a Hindu Deity*, ed. Fred W. Clothey and J. Bruce Long (Columbia, Mo.: South Asia Books, 1983), pp. 81–86. Jan Gonda, *Medieval Religious Literature in Sanskrit*. A History of Indian Literature, vol. II, fasc. 1 (Wiesbaden: Otto Harrassowitz, 1977), contains a detailed historical survey of the Āgamas and related literature.

[16] On the role of the temple in South Indian religion, see Burton Stein, ed., *South Indian Temples: An Analytical Reconsideration* (Delhi: Vikas, 1978), especially the essay by Friedhelm Hardy, "Ideology and Cultural Contexts of the Śrīvaiṣṇava Temple," pp. 119–51. M. A. Dorai Rangaswamy discusses the centrality of temples in the Tamil Śaiva cult in bk. 1, ch. 1 of *The Religion and Philosophy of Tēvāram*. David Shulman, *Tamil Temple Myths: Sacrifice and Divine Marriage in the South Indian Śaiva Tradition* (Princeton: Princeton University Press, 1980), is an excellent study of the meaning of the temple in Tamil religion.

to our understanding of early Tamil devotional religion as described in the *Tēvāram* and forms the framework of Tamil Śaiva philosophy as later formulated by the Śaiva Siddhānta.[17] The literature of the Āgamas is an important link between the exoteric and esoteric aspects of Tamil *bhakti*. It is this Āgamic flavor that sets the religion of the Nāyaṉārs and Vaiṣṇava Āḻvārs apart from the devotionalism of even the more traditionalist of the later *bhakti* saints in other regions of India.[18]

Tirumuṟai: The Canonization of the *Tēvāram*

In the *Tēvāram* hymns we have the earliest literary evidence of a vigorous popular Tamil *bhakti* cult centering on Śiva.[19] The poet-saints portray Śiva as the *bhakti* God whose grace ends his devotees' karma. We hear of Appar, Campantar, and Cuntarar traveling with fellow devotees from all castes and walks of life to worship and sing of Śiva at the many shrines that dotted the Tamil countryside, especially along the banks of the river Kaveri. Kings who had been seduced by "the false doctrines of the heretic Jain and Buddhist monks"[20] are rescued and brought back into the fold of "Tamil" religion, thanks to our poets, who defeat their opponents in public debate and establish the superiority of Śaivism over all other creeds. We get glimpses of the lives of the three saints as well as of other Śaiva devotees, who "dance, weep, worship him, sing his [the Lord's] feet."[21] Above all, we get a vivid impression of a growing Tamil Śaiva community whose members are united by their passionate love for Śiva and his shrines.

Even within the Tamil Śaiva literary tradition, the *Tēvāram* songs are distinguished by their pervasive orientation to shrines and sacred places. The poet-saints dedicated nearly every one of their hymns to a temple of Śiva. Together, Appar, Campantar, and Cuntarar sang hymns to Śiva as the god of shrines situated in 274 sacred places (*pati*, *talam*). Of these, 269 are South Indian shrines the saints visited in their pilgrimages; the remaining shrines belong to the Himalayan regions in the North, which are associated with the pan-Indian myths of Śiva. The Nāyaṉārs concen-

[17] Tamil "*caiva cittāntam*."

[18] Aspects of ritualistic *bhakti* can be found in the devotional compositions of the composers of South Indian classical (Carnatic) music in the eighteenth and nineteenth centuries. See Indira V. Peterson, "The *kṛti* as an Integrative Cultural Form: Aesthetic Experience in the Religious Songs of Two South Indian Composers," *Journal of South Asian Literature* 19, no. 2 (Fall-Winter 1984): 165–79.

[19] There are few references to Śiva in classical Tamil literature, though such early works as the *Puṟanāṉūṟu* do refer to him and his myths: see Hart, *Poems*, p. 56, and Narayana Ayyar, *Origin and Early History of Śaivism in South India*, ch. 7.

[20] Campantar I.75.10 (Poem 54).

[21] Appar V.177.8 (Poem 204).

trated their travels in the Cōḻa country (Cōḻanāṭu), singing hymns at 190 shrines in this segment of the Tamil region; the rest are distributed among the regional divisions of Pāṇṭināṭu (14 shrines), Toṇṭaināṭu (32), Naṭunāṭu (22), Koṅkunāṭu (7), and the Cēra area, later known as Malaināṭu (1). Two hymns are devoted to shrines in the northern part of the island of Sri Lanka (Īḻam), and one to Tirukkōkarṇam in the Tulu country. By unifying the many sacred places of Śiva through a network of pilgrimages and hymns, the three saints created a Śaiva "sacred geography" for the Tamil land.[22]

The history of Tamil Śaivism in the three hundred years following the activity of the poet-saints is literally carved in stone and inscribed on copperplates and palm leaves.[23] This was the great age of Tamil Śaivism as the "official" religion of the Tamils, and of the completion and compilation of the canonical texts of Tamil Śaivism. The Pallava successors of Mahendravarman I and the Tamil Cōḻas who consolidated their power in the Tamil region in the tenth century were great patrons of the Tamil *bhakti* groups.[24] The Cōḻas, in particular, favored Śaivism and gave royal support to the institutions and practice of Tamil Śaivism. In their time, the agricultural region watered by the river Kaveri, the birthplace of Tamil Śaiva *bhakti* and the area once ruled by the Cōḻa kings in the Caṅkam age, again became the political heartland of the Tamil land, and the great Śaiva temple and cult centers of Tiruvārūr and Tillai (Chidambaram) in the Kaveri Delta replaced Pallava Kanchipuram as centers of political as well as sacred power. The political map of the Tamil region

[22] For a list of shrines and sacred places that are repeatedly invoked in the *Tēvāram* hymns, see Appendix A in this volume. Some of these sites are shown on the map of important sacred places associated with the *Tēvāram* (p. 2, above). On sacred geography in the hymns of Appar, Cuntarar, and Campantar, see George W. Spencer, "The Sacred Geography of the Tamil Shaivite Hymns," *Numen* 17 (1970): 232–44. Spencer provides an analysis and detailed maps of the range and distribution of the *Tēvāram* shrines. He points out that the densest clustering of shrines is found in the contemporary district of Thanjavur (Tanjore) in Tamilnadu. Ka. Veḷḷaivāraṇaṉ, *Paṉṉiru tirumuṟai varalāṟu: Mutal ēḻu tirumuṟaikaḷ* (Annamalainagar: Annamalai University, 1972), gives a complete index of the 274 *Tēvāram* shrines. For the sacred geography of the hymns of the Tamil Vaiṣṇava saints, consult Katherine K. Young, *Beloved Places (Ukantaruḷiṉanilaṅkaḷ): The Correlation of Topography and Theology in the Śrīvaiṣṇava Tradition of South India* (Delhi: Motilal Banarsidass, 1984); and Hardy, *Viraha-Bhakti*.

[23] The rock-cut temples of Śiva are rich in cult-related sculpture and inscriptions. We have copperplate inscriptions from this period, and manuscripts were traditionally made of palm leaves. On Pallava and Cōḻa epigraphy, see T. N. Subramaniam, ed., *South Indian Temple Inscriptions*, 3 vols., Madras Government Oriental Series no. 157 (Madras: Government Oriental Manuscript Library, 1955–1957).

[24] On the Pallavas and Cōḻas as patrons of *bhakti*, see Mahalingam, *Kāñcīpuram*, and K. A. Nilakanta Sastri, *The Cōḻas*, 2nd ed., rev., 2 vols. in 1 (Madras: University of Madras, 1955).

was now identical with the sacred-cultural map outlined by the early saints through their pilgrimages.[25]

The *Tēvāram* saints and their hymns had a lasting impact on the temple, the center of Tamil *bhakti* culture. The Cōḻa kings enlarged and rebuilt extant Śiva shrines and built great structural temples in stone, particularly in the places visited by the Nāyaṉārs, now called *pāṭal peṟṟa talam*, "a place sung by the saints."[26] The prefix *tiru-* (sacred, auspicious; from Sanskrit *śrī*, "auspicious") was added to the names of the shrines visited by the Nāyaṉārs: thus Ārūr became Tiru-v-ārūr, and Aiyāṟu, Tiru-v-aiyāṟu.[27] The Cōḻas also perpetuated the institution, begun by the Pallava kings before them, of employing singers to sing the hymns of the Nāyaṉārs during ritual worship in the temples; similar endowments were made and continued by private citizens. The exquisite Cōḻa temple bronzes and stone sculptures of this period closely reflect the devotional spirit and imagery of the *Tēvāram* in their depiction of the mythology of Śiva. (See illustration section.) The Nāyaṉārs themselves became a part of the iconography and ritual complex of the temple.[28]

Both temple iconography and the inscriptions of the Cōḻa period reflect a well-established cult of the veneration of the saints in the Tamil Śaiva tradition. Sixty-two of these Nāyaṉārs—including Appar and Campantar—were first named together in a *Tēvāram* hymn of Cuntarar, called "List of the Holy Devotees" (*Tirut toṇṭat tokai*); the final list of the "Sixty-three" (*Aṟupattumūvar*), whose lives are narrated in the definitive twelfth-century hagiography of Cēkkiḻār,[29] includes Cuntarar himself.

[25] On the significance of the *Tēvāram* shrines and the saints' pilgrimages in Tamil Śaivism, see Indira V. Peterson, "Singing of a Place: Pilgrimage as Metaphor and Motif in the *Tēvāram* Hymns of the Tamil Śaivite Saints," *Journal of the American Oriental Society* 102, no. 1 (January-March, 1982): 69–90.

[26] *Tiru-* is also prefixed to names of persons, objects, and texts associated with the *bhakti* God: e.g., Tiru-nāvukkaracar (a name of the saint Appar), *Tirut toṇṭar purāṇam* (Cēkkiḻār's *Lives of the Holy Devotees*). For information on the Cōḻa temples associated with the *Tēvāram* hymns, see S. R. Balasubrahmanyam, *Early Chola Temples* (Delhi: Orient Longman, 1971); idem, *Middle Chola Temples* (Delhi: Thomson Press, 1975); and idem, *Later Chola Temples* (Delhi: Mudgala Trust, 1979).

[27] Consult the inscriptions cited in Dorai Rangaswamy, *Religion and Philosophy*, 1: 18, 22–24; Nilakanta Sastri, *Cōḻas*, pp. 6, 555, 637–38, 642; and Balasubrahmanyam, *Early Chola, Middle Chola,* and *Later Chola Temples*, passim.

[28] For developments in the iconography of Śiva in Cōḻa times, consult Douglas E. Barrett, *Early Cola Architecture and Sculpture, 866–1014* (London: Faber, 1974), and Balasubrahmanyam, *Early Chola, Middle Chola,* and *Later Chola Temples.* Dorai Rangaswamy, *Religion and Philosophy*, Bk. 2, offers a detailed discussion of the image of Śiva in Cuntarar's hymns and the iconography of the Pallava temple of Kailāsanātha in Kanchipuram. On the iconography of the saints, see Balasubrahmanyam, op. cit. Events connected with the lives of the saints are ritually commemorated in Tamil Śiva temples.

[29] The *Periya purāṇam* (Great Story) or *Tirut tontar purāṇam* (Story of the Holy Devotees).

Eventually, the three *Tēvāram* poets were honored as the "First Three Saints" (*mūvar mutalikaḷ*) of the Tamil Śaiva sect. In yet another configuration, the three poets, along with the later (ninth century?) saint Māṇikkavācakar, the author of the *Tiruvācakam* ("Sacred Utterances"), are known as the "Preceptors of the Faith" (*camayakuravar*) or simply, "the Four" (*nālvar*).

Two centuries separate Cuntarar from Appar and Campantar; all three poets speak of saints who lived before them. Yet the tradition saw fit to unite the three saints in the concept of the "First Three Saints"—pioneers and leaders, gifted poets who shared a common sensibility and vision.[30] In the eleventh century the hymns of these three poets were compiled in seven volumes, later to be collectively designated the "Tirumuṟai" ("Sacred Tradition," "Sacred Text"), and revered as the primary scripture (*maṟai*) of the Tamil Śaiva sect. Though the collective title "Tēvāram" ("a text related to ritual worship"?) was given relatively late (the sixteenth century?) to the Nāyaṉārs' hymns, Tamil Śaivas have always looked upon them as a single "text."[31]

The story of the canonization of the *Tēvāram* is told in a fourteenth-century work, the *Tirumuṟaikanta purāṇam* (The Story of the Discovery of the Tirumuṟai).[32] According to the *Purāṇam*, the eleventh-century Cōḻa king "Apayakulacēkaraṉ" asked the poet Nampi Āṇṭār Nampi of Nāraiyūr to reveal the hymns and lives of the Śaiva saints to the world.[33] Guided by the deity Gaṇeśa (son of Śiva and god of Beginnings), Nampi discovered the *Tēvāram* hymns in manuscript form, half-eaten by white ants, in a sealed room near the golden hall of the great Śiva temple in Chidambaram. Having compiled these hymns of Appar, Cuntarar, and Campantar into seven books (Books I–VII of the Tirumuṟai), Nampi set out to recover the lost musical tradition of the songs. The scholar finally managed to reconstruct the melodic and rhythmic aspects of the hymns

[30] Cuntarar himself declares: "(I saw the Lord) who loves the hymns in which I repeat / all that melodious Ñāṉacampantaṉ / and Nāvukkaracar, King of Speech, / have sung of him in their good Tamil songs" ("nallicai ñāṉacampantaṉu nāviṉukkaracarum pāṭiya naṟṟamiḻmālai colliyavē colliy ēttukappāṉai . . . ," (*Tēvāram* VII.67.5; Poem 261).

[31] "*(Tiru)muṟai*" corresponds to the Sanskrit term *āgama*, "(sacred) tradition." Zvelebil (*Tamil Literature*, 1975, p. 134) points out that "the term *(tiru) muṟai*, meaning (holy) book," is rather late, occurring "for the first time in Cēkkiḻār's *Periya purāṇam* (ca. 1135 A.D.) . . . and in the inscriptions of the age of Kulottuṅga III (1178–1218)."

[32] A work attributed to the fourteenth-century Śaiva teacher Umāpati Civam, this narrative can be found in editions of the *Periya purāṇam*. The dating of the second half of the *Purāṇam*, which deals with the compilation of Books VIII–XI of the canon, appears to be later than Nampi. See the discussion in Zvelebil, *Tamil Literature*, 1975, pp. 134–35.

[33] Identifying "Apayakulacēkaraṉ" as Kulottuṅga III (A.D. 1070–1122), Zvelebil, *Tamil Literature*, 1975, p. 134 places Nampi Āṇṭār Nampi in the period A.D. 1080–1100.

with the help of a female descendant of the musician who had accompanied Campantar on his travels.

The story of the "discovery" of the *Tēvāram* hymns in written form and the reconstruction of their ancient musical modes (*paṇ*) suggest that prior to the eleventh century there may have been a break in the oral tradition through which the *Tēvāram* hymns were transmitted.[34] The recovery legend itself may have been molded in its present form in order to serve symbolic as well as practical purposes: it establishes the authenticity of the *Tēvāram* hymns as "revealed" scripture, attested by miraculous communications from Gaṇeśa and by Śiva himself;[35] it suggests that the poetic output of the early saints had been of greater magnitude than what is actually available to us;[36] and it celebrates the role of the Cōḻa monarch as the great patron of Śaivism, and of Chidambaram (designated simply as "The Temple" [*kōyil*] in later editions of the hymns), as the greatest center of Śaivism.[37]

The seven books of the *Tēvāram*, also known as the "Complete Canon" (*aṭaṅkaṉmuṟai*), form the bulk of the primary sacred texts of Tamil Śaivism. Though Nampi Āṇṭār Nampi could not have been the editor of the remaining five books of the Tirumuṟai, it is most likely that the compilation of the entire canon took place between the eleventh and thirteenth centuries.[38] Books VIII–XI of the Tirumuṟai are made up of

[34] The later oral and musical tradition is discussed in detail in Chapter 4 below.

[35] According to the *Tirumuṟaikaṇṭa purāṇam*, at the king's request that the lost hymns of the saints be recovered, Nampi Āṇṭār Nampi worshipped his chosen deity, Gaṇapati or Gaṇeśa in his persona of Pollāppiḷḷaiyār of Tirunāraiyūr. The deity revealed the location of the hymns—the sealed room in Chidambaram temple—to Nampi. Upon further prayers from Nampi, Gaṇapati revealed the termite-eaten manuscripts to the king and the scholar. Later, a heavenly voice (Śiva himself?) commanded Nampi to learn the tunes of the hymns.

[36] It is said that termites had eaten a large number of hymns and that the hymns compiled by Nampi consisted only of the remaining hymns. Fabulous figures are quoted for the actual output of the saints. At least in the case of Cuntarar, it is quite likely that his hundred hymns (a nice, round figure) represent only part of his composition. The legend of enormous numbers of writings being lost and subsequently recovered, but only in part, is a recurrent motif in the Tamil literary tradition, the most famous of such accounts being the legend of the three classical *caṅkam*s or academies, from whose literary works only a portion is said to have survived great floods or tidal waves. A detailed analysis of the "Caṅkam" legend may be found in Zvelebil, *Tamil Literature*, 1975, pp. 55–61. A closer parallel (in particulars and in time period) to the Śaiva legend is the legend of the Tamil Vaiṣṇava *ācārya* (teacher) Nāthamuni's recovery of the entire collections of the 4,000 hymns of the Āḻvārs. See the account in Ramanujan, *Hymns*, p. xiii, and Zvelebil, *Tamil Literature*, 1975, pp. 152–55.

[37] On the rise of Chidambaram as the center of Tamil Śaivism, see B. Natarajan, *The City of the Cosmic Dance: Chidambaram*, Southern Art Series 2 (Delhi: Orient Longman, 1974).

[38] Cf. the arguments in Dorai Rangaswamy, *Religion and Philosophy*, 1: 20–21. For a list of the works contained in the twelve Tirumuṟai texts, see Zvelebil, *Smile of Murugan*, pp. 188–89, and for short accounts of these works, see Zvelebil, *Tamil Literature*, 1975, pp. 134–38, 142–51.

hymns (Books VIII, IX, and XI); the *Tirumantiram*, a mystical-philosophical text (Book X); and hagiographical poems (Book XI).[39] The canon was completed in the twelfth century, with the composition and grand, public canonization of the *Periya purāṇam* (The Great Story), Cēkkiḻār's narrative of the lives of the sixty-three Nāyaṉārs, as the twelfth book of the Tirumuṟai.[40] For Tamil Śaivism the age following the *Periya purāṇam* was characterized by the rise of *maṭams* and *ātīṉams*, great centers of sectarian learning and administration.[41] The sectarian leaders and teachers who were attached to these religious centers were typically ascetics who came from both brahmin and Vellala (a high-ranking peasant caste) backgrounds; between the thirteenth and sixteenth centuries they produced the large body of primary texts and commentaries in Tamil that makes up the literature of the Śaiva Siddhānta, the philosophical system of the Tamil Śaiva sect. Though the Siddhānta philosophy has definite connections with the philosophy of other Śaiva sects such as the Pāśupatas and Kashmir Śaivas,[42] the particular form of doctrine expounded in the fourteen treatises of the "lineage of teachers" (*cantāṉācāriyārkaḷ*) is unique to Tamil Śaivism.[43] According to the Śaiva Siddhānta there are three ultimate reals: *pacu* (Sanskrit *paśu*, the individual soul), *pati* (the Lord, Śiva), and *pācam* (Sanskrit *pāśa*, fetter, the bondage of *karma*). Through a fourfold, four-stage hierarchical path of "devotion"—of acts of service, worship, spiritual discipline, and ultimate knowledge, acti-

[39] The poems of Nampi Āṇṭār Nampi on the lives of Appar and Campantar are included in Tirumuṟai XI.

[40] The dramatic narrative of the canonization of Cēkkiḻār's hagiographical poem is told in the *Cēkkiḻārnāyaṉār purāṇam*. Zvelebil, *Tamil Literature*, 1975, pp. 178–81, provides a summary.

[41] On the early history of sectarian *maṭams* (Sanskrit *maṭha*) in the Tamil area, see Nilakanta Sastri, *Development of Religion*, pp. 117–18. The Tamil Śaiva *maṭams* at Tiruvoṟṟiyūr and Tiruvāvaṭutuṟai have a very ancient history and probably date at least from the time of the Nāyaṉārs.

[42] On the early Śaiva sects, often collectively referred to as the "Pāśupata" sects, see R. G. Bhandarkar, *Vaiṣṇavism, Śaivism and Minor Religious Systems* (Strasbourg: Karl J. Trübner, 1913), pp. 115–19. Although the many "Pāśupata" sects differed in practice, they seem to have shared in common the doctrine of the three categories of *paśu*, *pati*, and *pāśa*. Like Śaiva Siddhānta, the philosophy of Kashmir Śaivism is closely related to the Āgamas: see J. C. Chatterji, *Kashmir Shaivism* (Srinagar, 1914). On the Kāpālikas, see David N. Lorenzen, *The Kāpālikas and Kālāmukhas: Two Lost Śaivite Sects* (Berkeley: University of California Press, 1972).

[43] On Śaiva Siddhānta philosophy and theology, see: V. A. Devasenapathy, *Śaiva Siddhānta* (Madras: University of Madras, 1958); Mariasusai Dhavamony, *Love of God according to Śaiva Siddhānta: A Study in the Mysticism and Theology of Śaivism* (Oxford: Oxford University Press, 1971); and K. Sivaraman, *Śaivism in Philosophical Perspective: A Study of the Formative Concepts, Problems and Methods of Śaiva Siddhānta* (Delhi: Motilal Banarsidass, 1983). The first two authors deal with Śaiva Siddhānta as expounded in the Tamil canon; Sivaraman uses a number of sources in Sanskrit.

vated at each stage by the Lord's grace (*aruḷ*)—the soul is liberated from bondage.

Devotion is at the center of Tamil Śaiva religion, as the focus of the Āgamas and worship at the Śiva temple, as the theme of the songs and lives of the saints, and as the basis of the Siddhānta philosophy. Devotion, expressed in act and attitude, continues to be the most important religious activity for Tamil Śaivas; and these devotees continue to hold that the symbolism and meanings of devotion are best realized though the hymns of the saints. Among the canonical texts of Tamil Śaivism the average Tamil Śaiva is likely to know well only three: the *Tēvāram*, Māṇikkavācakar's *Tiruvācakam*, and the *Periya purāṇam*, all connected with the devotional spirit of the early "leaders" (Nāyaṉmār), each beloved for the special and unique way in which it articulates that spirit. Chapter 3 and 4 study the particular ways in which the *Tēvāram* functions as a "textbook" of Tamil Śaiva devotion.

CHAPTER 3

The Poets and Their Poems

The Three Saints

The dates of the three *Tēvāram* poets and the factual details of their lives continue to be a matter of controversy.[1] It appears most likely that the lives of Appar and Campantar overlapped, and that they lived between A.D. 570 and 670. The most plausible date for Cuntarar is the end of the seventh and the beginning of the eighth centuries. Quite apart from considerations of factual accuracy, for Tamil Śaivas Cēkkiḻār's *Periya purāṇam* hagiography is the most authoritative account of the lives of the sixty-three Nāyaṉārs. In this brief summary of the lives of the *Tēvāram* saints, I have followed Cēkkiḻār's narrative.[2]

Appar was born Maruṇīkkiyār, a Śaiva Vellala, in the town of Tiruvāmūr. In his youth he converted to Jainism, took the name Tarumacēṉar (Sanskrit "Dharmasena"), and became the head of a Jain monastery in Tiruppātirippuliyūr. Afflicted by painful abdominal disease, the Jain monk turned to his sister Tilakavatiyār, a devout Śaiva, for help. She convinced him to put his faith in Śiva. Tarumacēṉar appealed to Śiva, was miraculously cured, and underwent a dramatic conversion. He poured out his devotion to his Lord in melodious Tamil hymns. Angered by the poet's devotion to Śiva, the Jains persecuted and tortured him, but he emerged unscathed from all his trials and succeeded in reconverting the

[1] The question of the dates and relative chronology of the *Tēvāram* poets is discussed in Zvelebil, *Tamil Literature*, 1975, pp. 138–44, and by F. Gros in his Introduction to Gopal Iyer, ed., *Tēvāram*, vol. I, pp. xl–xlvi. According to Zvelebil's account, Campantar's mention of the Pallava general Ciṟuttoṇṭar, who destroyed the Chalukya capital of Vātāpi in A.D. 642, gives us some idea of his date. Appar is presumed to have been a contemporary of the Pallava king Mahendravarman I (A.D. 580–630) and is placed between 570 and 677. Cuntarar is seen as a contemporary of the Pallava king Narasimhavarman II (A.D. 690–710?).

[2] Without, of course, claiming factual and historical accuracy for this hagiographical narrative. In its blend of fact, legend, and archetypal motifs, Cēkkiḻār's work is typical of Hindu narratives of saints' lives.

Pallava king to Śaivism. Hailed as a saint, he spent his long life (of over eighty years) traveling from one Śiva shrine to another in Tamil countryside, singing hymns in each sacred place. In iconography, the saint is often portrayed holding the hoe (*uḻavārap paṭai*; see illus. 1 and 3) with which he cleared the temple courtyards of weeds and grass—an image appropriate both for the Tamil Śaiva ideal of humble service (*toṇṭu*) and the Vellala farmer's attachment to the land. The saint's eloquence earned him the name Tirunāvukkaracar ("King of Speech," Sanskrit *vāgīśa*), but he is popularly known as Appar, a name he acquired because the young Campantar is said to have affectionately addressed him as *appar* ("my father").

Campantar (pronounced SAMBAN'DAR), whose popular name is a shortened version of Ñāṉacampantar or Tiruñāṉacampantar ("He who is related to the Lord through [divine] wisdom"), was a child prodigy who began composing hymns when he was "barely weaned."[3] Born a brahmin in Cīrkāḻi, a coastal town near Chidambaram on the mouth of the Kaveri, Campantar is said to have mastered Vedic learning by age three, when he miraculously received the gift of sacred poetry from Śiva himself. From then on, the child-saint embarked on a career of incredible religious activity. Accompanied by crowds of fellow devotees, Campantar made four great pilgrimages to the Śiva shrines in the Tamil region. At every shrine he composed melodious Tamil hymns in various complex meters and rhythms. A Pāṇar musician called Tirunīlakaṇṭayāḻppāṇar accompanied Campantar on his journeys and set his hymns to *paṇ* tunes. The many stories of the miraculous powers of Campantar's hymns suggest that the poet's followers must have written down his songs soon after he had spontaneously sung them at the shrines.[4] In the iconography, Campantar is a child, sometimes holding the golden cymbals (*tāḷam*) that Śiva himself gave him to keep his tender hands from getting sore while keeping time (*tāla*) to the hymns (see illus. 1 and 2; in the latter he holds the divine cup of wisdom).

Campantar himself speaks of having defeated Buddhist and Jain monks in debate and having reconverted the Pandyan king of Maturai (Madurai) to Śaivism. The life of this saint who is credited with many miracles had

[3] Campantar refers to himself thus in *Tēvāram* III.297.1 ("pāṉal vāy oru pālaṉ"; Poem 228). The great Vedanta philosopher and pan-Hindu religious leader Śaṅkara (eighth century?) refers to Campantar as the "Tamil child" (*drāviḍaśiśu*) in one of his hymns (*Saundaryalaharī* 76).

[4] In hymn III.345 (Poem 231), Campantar refers to manuscripts when he speaks of the praises of Śiva that emerge unhurt when they are cast into the flames. According to the hagiographical tradition, this hymn alludes to Campantar's triumph over the Jains who challenged him to cast the name of his god into fire and thus prove the name's indestructibility. See Part Two, Section 4 below.

an appropriately miraculous ending. Campantar's parents had arranged the marriage of their adolescent son to take place in Tirunallūrpperumaṇam. At the time of the wedding, however, Śiva appeared as a great blaze of light and invited the saint to join him. The gracious deity included the bride and the entire wedding company in Campantar's final union with God.

Nampi Ārūrar or Cuntaramūrtti, affectionately called Cuntarar (pronounced SUN'DARAR; "the Handsome One") by Tamil Śaivas, was born a Śaiva brahmin in Tirunāvalūr on the river Peṇṇai. On Cuntarar's wedding day, Śiva appeared at the assembly and claimed him as his devotee and bondservant. The saint received Śiva's grace in Tiruveṇṇeynallūr. Cuntarar lived mainly in the great Śaiva center of Tiruvārūr (hence the name Nampi Ārūrar, "Prince of Ārūr"), but like the other saints, made pilgrimages and composed hymns at various shrines. His hymns are full of autobiographical material, especially in connection with his marriages to the temple dancer Paravai in Tiruvārūr and the Vellala woman Caṅkili in Tiruvoṟṟiyūr. The saint mentions kings and local chieftains as his friends and benefactors, the Cēra king Cēramāṉ Perumāḷ and the Pallava feudatory Naraciṅka Muṉaiyaraiyaṉ among them. Cuntarar is said to have ascended to heaven on a white elephant, accompanied by his friend, the Cēra king. The contrast between Cuntarar's life and personality and those of the other two *Tēvāram* authors is brought out in the iconography, where he is depicted as a handsome, well-dressed, princely young man, often in the company of his wives (see illus. 1 and 4).

The Text

Like other terms connected with the hymns of the Nāyaṉārs, the word *tēvāram* is of obscure etymology and was applied quite late to the first seven books of the Tirumuṟai. Citing the use of the word in Pallava and Cōḻa inscriptions, Dorai Rangaswamy argues that the word originally connoted "private ritual worship" and eventually came to be applied to the early hymns because of their many associations with temple worship.[5] The significance of the term cannot be fully understood, however, without reference to its musical and devotional associations in the *Cilappati-*

[5] See the discussion in Dorai Rangaswamy, *Religion and Philosophy*, 1: 27–35. Somasundaram, *Tirujñāṉasambandhar*, p. 12, rightly notes that the so-called earliest use of the term *tēvāram* for the hymns of the three saints—in the *Ēkāmparanātar ulā* of the fourteenth-century poet Iraṭṭaiyar—is in reality a continuation of the older usage, "private worship." The first unambiguous application of the term to the corpus of hymns as we know them is in the *Aruṇaikkalampakam* of a later poet, Caiva Ellappa Nāvalar, who refers to the "beautiful sacred hymns of the *Tēvāram* and *Tiruvācakam* [of the three poets and Māṇikkavācakar]."

kāram epic. Veḷḷaivāraṇaṉ and others rightly point out that *tēvāram* must be related to the word *vāram*, which is used in the sense of "a song addressed to a deity" in this classical poem.[6]

The *Tēvāram* corpus consists of 796 hymns composed by Campantar, Appar, and Cuntarar.[7] The 383 hymns of Campantar are contained in the first three books of the Tirumuṟai, Appar's 313 songs constitute Books IV–VI, and the seventh book consists of the 100 hymns of Cuntarar. The many terms by which the poets themselves refer to their songs relate to different aspects of these hymns: structure, as in the term *pattu* (decad, ten verses); musicality, as in *pāṭṭu* (song); and connections with the Tamil language and literature, as in *tamil̲ pattu* (ten verses in Tamil). *Patikam* (verse, poem, song, from Sanskrit *padya*, verse) is the word that has been consistently used to denote the hymns throughout their history.[8] The individual hymn has ten or eleven verses. The verses are four-line stanzas with a refrain.[9] The last verse in Campantar's and Cuntarar's *patikam*s forms a coda or signature verse, in which the poet includes his name and speaks about himself, the nature of his song, and the benefits of singing or listening to it.[10] Though Appar does not include his name in the final verse of his hymns, he uses the myth of the demon-devotee Rāvaṇa as his unique closure motif and "signature." A similar thematic pattern distinguishes Campantar's hymns from those of the other Nāyaṉārs: he devotes the eighth, ninth, and tenth verses of his *patikam*s, respectively, to the myth of Rāvaṇa, that of Śiva as the cosmic *liṅga*, and to the denunciation of the Jains and Buddhists.

The language of the *Tēvāram* hymns is considerably different from that

[6] *Vāram* and *tēvapāṇi* songs are mentioned several times in the Araṅkēṟṟukātai of the *Cilappatikāram*; the reference of particular interest to us is in lines 136–37, "vāram iraṇṭum varicaiyiṟ pāṭap / pāṭiya vārattu īṟṟiṉ niṉṟicaikkum." See the discussion in Veḷḷaivāraṇaṉ, *Paṉṉiru tirumuṟai varalāṟu*, pp. 35–43, and Somasundaram, *Tirujñāṉasambandhar*, ch. 1.

[7] The number goes up to 797 with the inclusion of a recently discovered hymn (attributed to Campantar) inscribed on the wall of the temple at Tiru-viṭaivāy in Thanjavur (Tanjore) district.

[8] In the early inscriptions that record endowments for the singing of the hymns in temples, the Nāyaṉārs' songs are called *tiruppatiyam* (sacred song). The most likely origin for the term is the Sanskrit *padya* (poem). Less plausible are the popular etymologies that derive *patikam* from Sanskrit *pathika* (traveler), hence "pilgrim song," and from Tamil *pattu* (ten), hence *patikam*, "a poem of ten stanzas." See Dorai Rangaswamy, *Religion and Philosophy*, 1: 15–18. See below for further discussion of the association of the hymns with the Tamil language.

[9] Some of Campantar's hymns have complex stanzaic patterns that deviate from the four-line model. Aspects of poetic form in the *Tēvāram* hymns are discussed in Chapter 5 below.

[10] Such coda verses, called *phalaśruti*, are also a standard feature of classical sacred texts and devotional works in Sanskrit. The final verse in Campantar's poems is called *tirukkaṭaikkāppu* ("the final sacred protection" or "sacred closure"); this was also the name applied to Campantar's hymns themselves. See Dorai Rangaswamy, *Religion and Philosophy*, 1: 31.

of the poems of the Caṅkam classical age and is in many ways closer to the literary Tamil of later centuries. The form of the hymns is also new to Tamil poetry. The Tamil Śaiva hymns are "true" songs, in contrast to the classical poems, which appear to have been recited as well as sung, as indicated by *akaval* ("to call, recite"), the name of the principal meter of the classical poetry, and by the classification of bards into musicians (*pāṇar*, etc.) and nonmusicians (e.g., *akavunar*).[11] The Nāyaṉārs combined the basic metrical patterns of Tamil verse with prosodic principles largely new to Tamil poetry, creating a large number of new "musical" meters, as well as a new song form, the *patikam*, with its ten stanzas and refrain, eminently suited to the spirit and themes of the new religion of *bhakti*.

Several features of the *Tēvāram* tradition draw attention to the musical nature of the *patikams*. The traditional arrangement of the hymns in manuscripts and printed editions is the *paṇmuṟai*, or "arrangement according to the musical modes." The hymns were set to music in 23 of the 103 *paṇ* scale-types of ancient Tamil music, and were once sung to the accompaniment of the ancient Tamil stringed instrument, now extinct, known as the *yāḻ*.[12] Though the ancient tunes have not survived, the musical dimension of the hymns plays an important role in the Tamil Śaiva apprehension of them; it is also the key to a clear understanding of their metrical and rhythmic aspects. Since at least the eleventh century the oral tradition of the professional singers of the hymns in the temples has been the principal means for the preservation and transmission of the saints' poems as songs.[13]

Themes and Strategies

In *bhakti* hymns, the inner state of the "I" of the poems becomes prominent for the first time in Indian religious poetry.[14] Yet the expression of the personal relationship between God and self is only one of the concerns

[11] See K. Kailasapathy's discussion of the *akaval* meter in classical Tamil poetry, in *Tamil Heroic Poetry* (Oxford: Oxford University Press, 1968), pp. 110–11. On the many types of bards, singers, and performers in classical Tamil civilization, see Hart, *Poems*, ch. 6.

[12] The legend of Campantar's musician-companion suggests that, like the Caṅkam poets, the *Tēvāram* saints were accompanied by *pāṇar* musicians. One of Campantar's hymns is called "*yāḻ-murippaṉ*" ("a tune which is beyond the capacity of the *yāḻ*"). The *yāḻ*—which is now extinct—and aspects of ancient Tamil music are described in the epic *Cilappatikāram*. On the *yāḻ*, see Swami Vipulānanda Cuvāmikaḷ, *Yāḻnūl: A Treatise on Ancient Tamil Music* (Tanjore: Karantai Tamil Sangam, 1974). See Appendix B below for a list of the twenty-three *paṇ* scale-types used in the *Tēvāram*. For further detail on the subdivision of these *paṇs* according to the rhythmic structure of the hymns, see Veḷḷaivāraṇaṉ, *Paṉṉiru tirumuṟai varalāṟu*, pp. 453–552.

[13] See my discussion of *ōtuvār* performances, Chapter 4 below.

[14] See the discussion in Zvelebil, *Smile of Murugan*, pp. 199–202.

of the early Tamil saints. Their hymns are poems of praise as well as love, celebrations of cult and community as well as God. The themes of the hymns are closely connected with ritual and communal worship at the temple. The poets saw their songs as formal "offerings of song" or "garlands of verse" (*pāmālai*, *nāmālai*) offered in place of "garlands of flowers" (*pūmālai*),[15] which formed part of the ritual milieu of the temple. In venerating the songs as sacred texts and officially incorporating the *Tēvāram* into the temple ritual, Tamil Śaiva tradition only affirms this view. The hymns are public poems in other ways as well. Appar, Cuntarar, and Campantar address some hymns to Śiva, some to themselves, others to their fellow devotees; many poems assume the Tamil Śaiva community as witness.[16] The poets paint an affectionate portrait of Tamil Śaiva religion, which is expressly designed to move the hearts of the listeners to greater devotion to Śiva. The many poetic images of Śiva and the descriptions of the settings of devotion, exemplary devotees, and devotional acts all serve this end.

The Names of the Lord: The Hymns as Poems of Praise

As composers of songs praising God, the Nāyaṉārs were working within two separate traditions of praise poetry, one arising from indigenous Tamil cultural roots and the other from the brahmanical cultic heritage of Śaiva religion. The saints' adoption of the classical Tamil genre of the poet or bard's praise of his king is no mere literary borrowing but gives insight into the very nature of God and the *bhakti* relationship as conceived in early Tamil Śaivism. Reserving the discussion of this aspect of the poems to the detailed consideration of the Tamil cultural contexts of the *Tēvāram* below, let us turn first to the Sanskritic heritage of the hymns.

The poems of the Nāyaṉār Kāraikkāl Ammaiyār (A.D. fifth century?) are the earliest examples we have of Tamil hymns exclusively addressed to Śiva.[17] In the Tamil literature that preceded the *Tēvāram* authors, Śiva has no "indigenous" persona comparable to Viṣṇu as Māyōṉ, the pastoral god of the late classical Tamil poems, who is a blend of features from

[15] The poets, and others after them, refer to the hymns by these words. See also Appar IV.103.3 (Poem 213), in which he refers to the hymn as "the ornament (*paṭimakkalam*) of Tamil song."

[16] On varieties of rhetorical structure in Tamil *bhakti* hymns, see Cutler, *Songs of Experience*, ch. 1. Cutler points out that even poems that are framed as interior monologues may have a public dimension.

[17] See Karavelane, ed. and trans., *Chants dévotionnels tamouls de Kāraikkālammaiyār*, Publications de l'Institut français d'indologie, no. 1, new edition (Pondicherry, 1982).

indigenous and Sanskritic religion.[18] In terms of subject matter and some formal characteristics, as well as in terms of their function as sacred utterances in a ritual context, the *patikams* are closely associated with early Sankrit *stotra* ("praise poem") hymns. The primary function of the Vedic hymns, the earliest religious literature in Sanskrit, is praise of the gods in the context of the sacrificial ritual.[19] Many features of the Vedic hymns are carried over into the early Sanskrit *stotra*s that are addressed to the gods of the classical pantheon and found in longer sacred texts such as the *Bhagavadgītā* and other portions of the epic *Mahābhārata*, as well as in "secular" poems by court poets such as Kālidāsa (A.D. fourth century) and Bhāravi (sixth century).[20] In their simplest form these hymns are catalogues of the names, epithets, and attributes of the deity.[21] *Tēvāram* verses such as this one by Campantar have many stylistic affinities with the early Sanskrit litanies:

> My heart can think of nothing
> other than the brahmin who is the Veda,
> he who bears the white moon
> on his pure, matted red hair,
> God who is both man and woman,
> the Supreme Lord
> who dwells in the beautiful shrine
> of holy Ēkampam in Kacci.
>
> Campantar II.148.1 (Poem 15)

Such phrases as "who bears the white moon / on his pure, matted red hair" in Campantar's verse are counterparts to the compound epithets in Sanskrit hymns. The parallelism of grammatical endings in the phrases describing Śiva in the Tamil verse (maṟaiy*āṉai* mācilāp puṉcaṭai malkuveṇpiṟaiy*āṉai* . . .) is also a standard feature of the Sanskrit *stotra* and gives a sonorous regularity to the hymn. Many of Appar's hymns in the

[18] On the Tamil cult of Māyōṉ-Viṣṇu, see Hardy, *Viraha-Bhakti.*

[19] See Zvelebil's discussion of the Vedic hymns in relation to Tamil *bhakti* hymns: Zvelebil, *Smile of Murugan*, pp. 201ff.

[20] E.g., the praise of the Goddess (Durgā), *Mahābhārata*, Book 4, ch. 6; *Bhagavadgītā* XI.36ff.; the hymn to Viṣṇu in Kālidāsa's *Raghuvaṃśa* X.16ff.; the hymn to Śiva in Bhāravi's *Kirātārjunīya* XVIII.22–43.

[21] E.g., the *Viṣṇusahasranāma-stotra* ("Hymn of the Thousand Names of Viṣṇu") in the *Mahābhārata*: "He who is of the form of the Universe and is all-Pervasive, who is of the form of Sacrifice. . . . The Terrible, the Multi-headed, the Tawny One." In the translation of V. Raghavan, *The Indian Heritage: An Anthology of Sanskrit Literature* (Bangalore: Indian Institute of World Culture, 1956), pp. 422–24. On the magical power of sacred names, see Jan Gonda, *On Names and the Name of God in Ancient India*, Verhandelingen der Koningklijke Nederlandse Akademie van Wetenschappen, Letterkunde, Nieuwe Reeks, vol. 75, no. 4 (Amsterdam, 1970).

long *tāṇṭakam* meter, which make up the sixth book of the Tirumuṟai, are cast in this paratactic framework; Appar VI.301.1 ("vāṉavaṉ kāṇ"; "See the god! / See him who is higher than the gods!"; Poem 20), which I have analyzed in detail below in relation to the performance of the saints' hymns, is a good example of the type.

Within the Śaiva tradition, one Sanskrit *stotra* stands out as the most influential model for the *Tēvāram* hymns: this is the *Śatarudrīya* ("The hundred names of Rudra") hymn in the *Yajur Veda*.[22] This ancient litany is addressed to Rudra-Śiva, the Vedic prototype of the classical Śiva Mahādeva. It enumerates the hundred names and epithets of the god, describing him, praising his deeds, and invoking his grace in verses such as these:

> Obeisance to the primal cause, salutation to Rudra (that melts misery), . . . salutations to the blue-throated and the white-necked, supplication to the wearer of the *kaparda* locks [matted hair], . . . homage to the mountain-lord . . .

and

> Oh! Rudra! make us happy here and grant bliss hereafter. To you that diminishes our sins we offer our respects. With your goodwill we shall enjoy the happiness and the negation of misery vouchsafed to us by our father prajapati Manu.[23]

There are a number of reasons for citing the *Śatarudrīya* as the most likely source of inspiration for the *patikam* as "*stotra*." In the first place, the *Śatarudrīya* is the most complete early catalogue of the names, deeds, and attributes of Śiva; the later *stotra*s to Śiva are but classical elaborations of the imagery of this hymn.[24] Second, this litany has had a very important role in Śaiva ritual in both the Vedic and the Āgamic traditions, whence the likelihood of the hymn being a direct influence on the Nāyaṉārs. The *Śatarudrīya* or "Rudram" is the principal Vedic text used to accompany important Āgamic temple rites and, in particular, the *abhi-*

[22] On the *Śatarudrīya*, see C. Sivaramamurti, *Śatarudrīya: Vibhūti of Śiva's Iconography* (Delhi: Abhinav, 1976); J. Gonda, "The Śatarudrīya," in *Sanskrit and Indian Studies: Essays in Honor of Daniel H. H. Ingalls*, ed. M. Nagatomi, B. K. Matilal, J. M. Masson, and E. C. Dimock, Jr. (Dordrecht: D. Reidel, 1980), pp. 75–91; and J. Bruce Long, "Rudra as an Embodiment of Divine Ambivalence in the *Śatarudrīya Stotram*," in *Experiencing Śiva*, ed. Clothey and Long, pp. 103–28. Of the two recensions of this hymn, the text as it occurs in the Taittirīya Saṃhitā of the Black (*kṛṣṇa*) Yajurveda is used in South India; see Sivaramamurti for the text and translation.

[23] Sivaramamurti, *Śatarudrīya*, pp. 21, 28.

[24] Ibid., and Gonda, "Śatarudrīya."

ṣeka (bathing/anointing) ritual for the image of the deity in the temple.[25] When the saints speak of the tradition of Vedic chant and Sanskrit sacred formulae (mantra) being used in the temple ritual of their times, the reference is surely to the *Śatarudrīya*, which continues to be the most important Sanskrit text used in major temple festivals and processions as well as in the daily rites.[26] Lastly, the *Śatarudrīya* is of particular significance to Tamil Śaivas, since it is in this text that the five-syllable sacred formula (*pañcākṣara-mantra*) "namaḥ śivāya" (Hail Śiva!), the supreme sacred formula (mantra) in Tamil Śaiva doctrine, appears for the first time.[27]

Seeing Śiva: Image and Vision in the Hymns

The catalogue of Śiva's attributes is only one of the many forms the *Tēvāram* hymns take; the images of Śiva in the saints' hymns are more expansive, detailed, and stylized than those evoked by the phrases in the *stotra* literature. Appar, Campantar, and Cuntarar were innovative poets who molded elements of the classical poetry of both Sanskrit and Tamil to create a sophisticated literary genre as well as a new kind of religious expression. Again, it is convenient to look at the Sanskritic context of the hymns at this point. It is in the areas of subject matter, certain formal characteristics, and autonomy of content that the *patikam* verse resembles the descriptive verses that are typical of Sanskrit *kāvya* court poetry. Like the *kāvya* stanza, in four short lines the *Tēvāram* verse often presents a suggestive, sharply defined descriptive vignette, which, though it is part of a sequence of ten or eleven verses, can be understood and enjoyed in isolation.[28] And yet, despite so many similarities, the intent and the effect of description in the Tamil Śaiva hymns are quite different from that in Sanskrit court poetry, especially in its later manifestations.

Śiva's appearance and his mythic deeds are favorite subjects for description in the *Tēvāram*; in the saints' hymns we find poetic counterparts for the many iconographic depictions of Śiva that we find in Śiva temples. The images and myths of Śiva and Viṣṇu are also popular subjects with Sanskrit court poets who, like the Tamil saints, lived in a *bhakti* culture in which the gods, temples, and image worship were emphasized.[29] The

[25] Consult Gonda, "Śatarudrīya," and Long, "Rudra," for a description of the use of this hymn in Śaiva ritual.

[26] Personal observation in Tamilnadu.

[27] In the eighth *Anuvāka* of the Taittirīya version. See Sivaramamurti, "Śatarudrīya," p. 1, and Long, "Rudra," p. 106.

[28] For an introduction to the *kāvya* stanza and Sanskrit court poetry and poetics, see Daniel H. H. Ingalls, *An Anthology of Sanskrit Court Poetry: Vidyākara's Subhāṣitaratnakoṣa*, Harvard Oriental Series, vol. 44 (Cambridge Harvard University Press, 1965).

[29] Ibid., introd., and translation sections 1–6.

earliest iconographic descriptions of Śiva in *kāvya* poetry are found in the court epics and plays of the fourth-century poet Kālidāsa and reflect a vision harmonious with that of the *Tēvāram* poets.[30] The majority of such verses in Sanskrit poetry are later than the Tamil hymns, however, which suggests the possibility of the influence of the Tamil hymns and hymnists on Sanskrit poets even outside the sphere of explicitly "devotional" literature.[31] The contrast between these Sanskrit poems and the Tamil stanzas reveals the particularity of the vision of Śiva in Tamil *bhakti*. It is instructive to compare the treatment of the popular theme of the dance of Śiva in a *Tēvāram* verse and a Sanskrit poem dating from the seventh century or later, composed by a poet from a different region in India.

> May the god of tangled locks protect you,
> at whose dance of madness in the fullmoon twilight
> the golden mountain sways with leaping woods,
> as sway the sun and moon, to the rhythmic motion;
> as if the earth, of head resplendent,
> with hair and earrings flying,
> did nod in admiration.
>
> Sanskrit poem from an eleventh-century anthology; trans. D.H.H. Ingalls[32]

The point of the Sanskrit verse is the "image" (*alaṃkāra*: trope, figure of speech, conceit) of the earth nodding in admiration at Śiva's dance, an image that must be appreciated through the gradual comprehension of each of the iconographic comparisons made in the poem—head: the golden mountain (Mount Meru, at the center of the universe); flying hair: leaping woods; flying earrings: the sun and the moon. The religious conception of Śiva forms the basis and enriches the meaning of the poem; yet the cleverness of the conceit is more central to the aesthetic of the stanza than the "religious" idea on which the figure of speech is based, namely, the cosmic nature and power of Śiva's dance. This is quite in keeping with the purpose of Sanskrit court poetry, which was to offer intellectual and aesthetic stimulation to an audience of connoisseurs of poetry.[33]

[30] See in particular the invocatory verses to Kālidāsa's three plays, and the *Kumārasaṃbhava*, an epic poem on the marriage of Śiva and the Goddess Pārvatī in Barbara Stoler Miller, ed. and trans., *Theater of Memory: The Plays of Kālidāsa* (New York: Columbia University Press, 1984); and *The Origin of the Young God: Kālidāsa's Kumārasaṃbhava*, translated, with annotation and an introduction, by Hank Heifetz (Berkeley: University of California Press, 1985). See also Barbara Stoler Miller, "Kālidāsa's Verbal Icon: Aṣṭāmūrti Śiva," in *Discourses on Śiva*, ed. Michael W. Meister (Philadelphia: University of Pennsylvania Press, 1984).

[31] Most of the *kāvya* stanzas describing the Hindu gods in an "iconographic" mode in the (eleventh century) *Subhāṣitaratnakoṣa*, an early anthology, date from the seventh and eighth century or later. See Ingalls, *Anthology*.

[32] *Subhāṣitaratnakoṣa* 52, in Ingalls, *Anthology*, p. 79.

[33] Ingalls, *Anthology*, introd. Also see the discussion in Edwin Gerow, *A Glossary of In-*

When our Lord who is both end and beginning
dances to the deep sound of the *mul̠avam* drum,
holding blazing fire in the hollow of his hand,
as the mountain's daughter watches,
the Gaṅgā's murmuring stream with foaming waves
flows over the cool crescent moon.
He who smears his body
with ash from the burning-ground
is our Lord who dwells
in Vēṭkaḷam's fine town.

Campantar I.39.1 (Poem 30)

In contrast to the Sanskrit poet, Campantar presents an image of Śiva's dance that, though rich in iconographic and sensory detail, is devoid of fanciful figures of speech and poetic conceits. The iconography of the poem is thoroughly realistic, for it corresponds in every respect with specific sculptural conceptions of Śiva's dance. The poem is meant to conjure up a precise "icon," a concrete image, of Śiva in the hearer's mind. When the Tamil Śaiva poet wishes to describe Śiva as the god who bears the moon on his crown, he says simply: "crowned with the pure white crescent moon," or "who bears the white moon on his pure, matted red hair," or "crowned with the white moon / bright as beaten silver leaf. . . ."[34] The conceits that are commonplace in Sanskrit court poetry, such as the poetic fancy that the moon looks "as if it were a sprout that grew / under the daily waterings of Ganges / from out the white skull of his diadem,"[35] and that "the new moon like a minnow / dives and surfaces"[36] in the river Ganges that flows through Śiva's matted hair, are alien to the *bhakti* hymns.

In the final analysis, neither iconographic accuracy nor simplicity of expression is an end in itself for the poet-saint. What matters is that all description be framed in the perspective of the devotional vision, which renders these Tamil poems different from both kinds of Sanskrit poetry with which they are allied. Tamil *bhakti* requires that God be perceived—by poet and reader or listener—through the lens of passionate love, personal involvement. In most *Tēvāram* hymns the *bhakti* point of view be-

dian Figures of Speech (The Hague: Mouton, 1971), pp. 70–74. According to Gerow (p. 72), the aim of the Sanskrit poet is "a richness of intelligibility which is at first overwhelming."

[34] "Tūveṇ mati cūṭi" (Campantar I.1.1; Poem 183); "mācilāp pun̠caṭai malkuveṇ pir̠aiyān̠ai" (Campantar II.148.1; Poem 15); and "veḷḷit takaṭan̠n̠a veṇpir̠ai cūṭi" (Appar IV.113.1; Poem 2).

[35] Ingalls, *Anthology*, p. 78.

[36] Ibid. Other themes that invite comparison between the Sanskrit and Tamil verses: the description of Śiva as the cosmic *liṅga* (e.g., Ingalls, *Anthology*, no. 48), and the descriptions of Śiva's head and hair (Ingalls, *Anthology*, nos. 40, 53, 55).

comes an integral part of the content of the poem. As an illustration, let us consider a verse by Campantar that begins with what appears to be a straightforward iconographic description of Śiva:

> He wears a woman's earring on one ear;
> riding on his bull,
> crowned with the pure white crescent moon,
> his body smeared with ash from the burning-ground,
> he is the thief who stole my heart. . . .
>
> Campantar I.1.1 (Poem 183)

The description of Śiva as androgyne (Ardhanārīśvara) and bull rider proceeds in what might be called a purely "objective" manner almost to the end of the second line of the stanza, where the phrase "the thief who stole my heart" ("eṉṉ uḷḷaṅ kavar kaḷvaṉ") occurs, altering our perception of the foregoing images of Śiva. Everything about the god—his androgynous form, the bull on which he rides—becomes beautiful, attractive, enchanting, in an intimate, emotional sense, because he is conceived of as the artful lover who has seduced the saint. "Thief who stole my heart" is a common expression in Tamil,[37] indicating the speaker's fond, teasing, love relationship with the "thief"; it also belongs to the conventions of classical Tamil love poetry, as illustrated in a poem in the *Kuṟuntokai* anthology. The poem, in which a woman speaks of her clandestine love-making with a man who might betray her in the future, begins:

> Only the thief was there, no one else.
> And if he should lie, what can I do?[38]

It is not enough to note that Campantar suggestively uses the allusion to human sexual love and to conventions in classical Tamil love poetry in his description of Śiva; if this were all, the *Tēvāram* verse would be no different from many Sanskrit poems that use erotic imagery in contexts of devotion.[39] The crucial difference in the Tamil *bhakti* poem is that whatever effect the phrase in question might have on readers in terms of a purely literary aesthetic—be it in the Sanskrit or Tamil tradition—their surest and deepest response is to what they perceive as the saint's personal and genuine love for Śiva, the sincerity of his emotion as indicated by the poetic phrase. What makes the *bhakti* poem valuable and effective is the

[37] As also in Sanskrit and other Indian languages. It is an expression frequently used to describe Krishna, the butter-thief and archetypal lover in Hindu mythology.

[38] Kapilar, *Kuṟuntokai* 25, translated by A. K. Ramanujan, *The Interior Landscape: Love Poems from a Classical Tamil Anthology* (Bloomington: Indiana University Press, 1967; Midland edition, 1975), p. 30.

[39] Ingalls, *Anthology*, pp. 21ff., discusses a Sanskrit poem in which the poet uses erotic imagery in conjunction with the Śaiva myth of the three cities of the demons.

projection, in various ways, of what the audience sees as the saint's own personal feeling and experience onto his descriptions of God and of devotion itself. Look at Appar's description of Śiva's dance:

> If you could see
> the arch of his brow,
> the budding smile
> on lips red as the *kovvai* fruit,
> cool matted hair,
> the milk-white ash on coral skin,
> and the sweet golden foot
> raised up in dance,
> then even human birth on this wide earth
> would become a thing worth having.
>
> Appar IV.81.4 (Poem 29)

In this verse subjective adjectives such as "sweet golden foot" (both "sweet" [*iṉittam uṭaiya*] and "golden" [*poṉ-*] are terms of endearment in Tamil) color the descriptive portion of the verse, so that the conclusion—"then even human birth on this wide earth / would become a thing worth having"—rings true, impressing the reader with the force of personal conviction. Such personal nuances are foreign to the aims and aesthetic of *kāvya* poetry, which is essentially an impersonal aesthetic focusing on the interplay of language and imagery.[40] Although personal emotions and stances may be portrayed in Tamil love poetry (e.g., affective words like "sweet" and "thief" do appear in the dramatic monologues of the classical poems), they do not correspond to the feelings of any real person.[41] Impossible in both the Sanskrit and the Tamil classical traditions are poems such as the verse in which, abandoning all "realistic" description, the poet speaks of Śiva in purely subjective terms, calling him "the gorgeous gem, delicious honey, milk, / the sweet taste of sugar cane, clear sugar syrup, / precious gem, the sound / of flute, drum, cymbals, and lute, . . ." (Appar VI.243.1; Poem 25). The aesthetic of description in the *Tēvāram* is an aesthetic of personal experience and feeling.[42]

The Tamil Śaiva poet aims at "imaging" Śiva, in the sense of *directly* presenting an intimate and specific experience of his Lord, a task that steers him away from using such "poetic" intermediaries as wit, paradox, or complex figure, which might distance the reader from the *bhakti* experience. The saints sought to move their listeners to devotion and pro-

[40] On the impersonality of *kāvya* poetry, see Ingalls, *Anthology*, pp. 22–27.

[41] On the use of "dramatis personae" in Caṅkam love poetry, see Ramanujan, *Interior Landscape*, pp. 112–15.

[42] Ramanujan (*Hymns*, p. 162) speaks of *bhakti* poetics as a "new poetics" of "personal feeling whether aesthetic or not." See his discussion, *Hymns*, pp. 161–64.

tested, like George Herbert, against all "fictions" that intervene: "Must all be veiled, while he that reads, divines, / Catching the sense at two removes?"[43] The poets of the Tamil hymns seek to help their fellow devotees to see (*kāṇ-*) Śiva, to approach him (*naṇṇu-*, *nāṭu-*, *aṇuku-*, *cēr-*), and to melt in love for him (*uruku-*, *neku-/nekku-*, *kaci-*).[44] Their description of Śiva focuses on visual images and the act of seeing. Vision (Sanskrit *darśana*) is of paramount importance in establishing intimate contact or communion with the divine in Hinduism, and finds its fullest expression in the traditions of image and temple worship, which are fundamental contexts of *bhakti* in Tamil Śaivism.[45] The poet-saint acts as the "seeing eye,"[46] recording the vision or image of Śiva for readers "to see" for themselves. Undistracted by "quaint words and trim invention," by thoughts that "burnish, sprout, and swell, / Curling with metaphors a plain intention, / Decking the sense as if it were to sell," the reader finds in the poet's love "a sweetness ready penned,"[47] which melts his heart to love. Generations of Tamil Śaivas have acknowledged that this is the primary function of *bhakti* poetry. Māṇikkavācakar's *Tiruvācakam* is prized for its affective qualities; the Tamil belief that it has the power to move all but the stoniest hearts is embodied in the popular saying, "No words can move him who does not melt upon hearing the *Tiruvācakam*" ("tiruvācakattiṟku urukātār oru vācakattiṟkum urukār").

The Tamil saints find many meanings in the myth that narrates how Viṣṇu and Brahmā arrogantly declared their superiority over Śiva and then were humbled by their failure to perceive Śiva's cosmic form as the flame-liṅga in its entirety. One interpretation of this myth is that none but those who love God can see him, and only through his grace can they obtain a vision of him. It follows, then, that only those who love Śiva can, having seen him, describe him. In the Tamil Śaiva view, an "objective" description of Śiva is meaningless; the only true image of God is that which is seen in the poet-devotee's loving eye.

[43] George Herbert, "Jordan (1)," in *Seventeenth-Century Prose and Poetry*, ed. Alexander M. Witherspoon and Frank J. Warnke (New York: Harcourt Brace and World, 1929; 2nd ed. 1963), p. 849.

[44] E.g., Appar VI.301.1 (Poem 20): "See the god! / see him who is higher than the gods!" and Campantar III.307.1 (Poem 144): "those who melt with love / and flow with tears as they chant (his name)" The notion of "melting" is central to the devotion and poetry of Māṇikkāvacakar. See Yocum, *Dancing Śiva*, pp. 168–73.

[45] For an excellent exposition of the idea of "seeing the divine" (*darśana*) in Hinduism, see Diana Eck, *Darśan: Seeing the Divine Image in India* (Chambersburg, Pa.: Anima, 1981), esp. ch. 1.

[46] Appar speaks of Śiva himself as the devotee's "eye" (*kaṇ*): Appar VI.229 (Poem 28), Karukāvūr *Tirut tāṇṭakam*.

[47] Herbert, "Jordan (2)," in *Seventeenth Century Prose*, ed. Witherspoon and Warnke, p. 854.

The Tamil Roots of the *Tēvāram*

According to the canons of *Caṅkam* literature, poetry was classified into two basic categories, "interior" (*akam*) and "exterior" (*puṟam*), corresponding to the classification of human experience itself.[48] With their closely interwoven themes of ceremonial praise and intimate love, the Tamil Śaiva songs do not belong strictly to either of the classical genres. Nevertheless, the majority of the poems have greater affinities to the *puṟam* (public) rather than to the *akam* (interior) genre. A number of factors account for this, all ultimately stemming from key ideas in Tamil civilization.

Of the two kinds of poetry, *akam* poems, which are love poems, deal with "idealized types, rather than historical persons,"[49] and landscape types rather than specific places. In contrast to this impersonal, interior poetry, "*puṟam*, the so-called 'public poetry,' is allowed names, places, expression of personal circumstances in a real society, a real history, and freedom from the necessities of poetic convention both in *uḷḷuṟai* (implicit metaphor) and in the landscapes. Thus it is the 'public' *puṟam* poetry that becomes the vehicle of personal expression and celebration of historical personages."[50] As poets expressing personal sentiment, praising a real God who manifests himself in particular places, and celebrating a particular community, the *Tēvāram* saints are heir to the *puṟam* tradition.

Local Hero: Some *Puṟam* Themes in the *Tēvāram*

The mode of royal praise in the saints' hymns was not simply grafted onto a religious genre but was a natural development from ideas about kingship and the sacred in the classical civilization. The Nāyaṉārs' model for the image of Śiva was the Tamil "king" or local ruler, who was considered to be "the central embodiment of the sacred powers that had to be present under control for the proper functioning of society."[51] The cult of temple worship in Tamil country after the Caṅkam age shows clear evidence of the transference of the idea of the king with sacred power to the deity in the temple.[52] As George Hart points out, "words that meant

[48] See Ramanujan, *Interior Landscape*, Afterword, for an introduction to the poetics of *akam* and *puṟam* in classical Tamil poetry.

[49] Ibid., p. 104.

[50] A. K. Ramanujan, "Form in Classical Tamil Poetry," in *Symposium on Dravidian Civilization*, ed. Andrée F. Sjoberg, publication no. 1, Asian Series, Center for Asian Studies, University of Texas at Austin, general editors: Edgar C. Polomé et al. (Austin and New York: Jenkins, 1971), p. 97.

[51] Hart, *Poems*, p. 13.

[52] Discussed in the following essays: Hardy, "Ideology and Cultural Contexts"; George L. Hart III, "The Nature of Tamil Devotion," in *Aryan and Non-Aryan in India*, ed. Madhav M. Deshpande and Peter E. Hook, Michigan Papers on South and Southeast Asia, no.

king in ancient Tamil now denote God. For example, *iṟaivaṉ* ('he who is highest') used to mean king but is now generally applied to the supreme deity, while *kōyil* ('king's house' or 'palace') now means temple."[53] Certainly, the *Tēvāram* poets address Śiva most often by such words as *kō*, *kōmāṉ*, *perumāṉ*, *iṟaivaṉ* (king, ruler), *nampi* (prince), and *īcaṉ*, *pirāṉ*, *empirāṉ* (our lord, master). The king is only one of the persons and objects in which sacred power manifests itself for the Tamils. Particular places—landscapes, natural phenomena, human settlements—can themselves be loci of the sacred. The "divinities" of the ancient Tamils were indwellers of such sacred places.[54] Again, the *bhakti* cult of sacred places is an extension of this idea of sacred loci, for the shrine or town where Śiva manifests himself is such a place.[55] The simplest formula for the refrain in the *Tēvāram* hymns is a phrase identifying Śiva as a "god of the place," the "dweller" or "lord" of a particular shrine, for instance, "aṇṇāmalaiyār" (Lord of Aṇṇāmalai) in Campantar I.69 (Poem 80). Śiva is the "king" who dwells in Aṇṇāmalai, Paḻaṉam, and other Tamil places. Appar, Campantar, and Cuntarar are bards who praise him, asking him for grace, even as the Caṅkam poet would praise his lord, hoping to be rewarded with gold and gifts.[56] In order to fit into the indigenous conception of the divine, Śiva had to become a local hero, an indweller of particular places.

In *puṟam* war poems, the poets sing of the heroic deeds and exploits of their kings. The Nāyaṉārs, too, speak of the mythic deeds of Śiva in heroic terms, merging his cosmic persona with his local identity, as in this verse in which Śiva who destroyed the three cities (*tripura*) of the demons—in a well-known myth of great antiquity—is identified as the local lord of the hill-shrine of Aṇṇāmalai:

> The Lord of the gods,
> the spouse of beautiful Umā,
> he who once bent his bow of war

14 (Ann Arbor, Michigan: Center for South and Southeast Asian Studies, 1979), pp. 11–33; and A. K. Ramanujan and Norman Cutler, "From Classicism to Bhakti," in *Essays on Gupta Culture*, ed. Bardwell L. Smith (Columbia, Mo.: South Asia Books, 1983), pp. 177–94.

[53] Hart, *Poems*, p. 13.

[54] Rajam Ramamurti offers a new formulation for the idea of localization: "a site was so independent of the divinity— . . . that it could precede or survive their presence." Rajam Ramamurti, "On the Themes of Divine Immanence and Localization," *Tamil Civilization*, Quarterly Research Journal of the Tamil University, Thanjavur (September 1983): 73–76.

[55] See Yocum, "Shrines, Shamanism."

[56] Cuntarar asks Śiva himself for gold: *Tēvāram* VII.46 (Poem 256). See my discussion of this motif in Indira V. Peterson, "In Praise of the Lord: The Image of the Royal Patron in the Songs of Saint Cūntaramūrtti and the Composer Tyāgarāja," in *Patronage in Indian Culture*, ed. Barbara Stoler Miller (Princeton: Princeton University Press, forthcoming).

to set fire to the three cities,
is the Lord of Aṇṇāmalai,
on whose slopes
waterfalls bring large pearls and gems
gathered in forest tracts
by gypsy hunters with long bows.
Campantar I.69.5 (Poem 80)

The process of localization is taken a step further in the mythology of the "Eight Heroic Deeds." According to the Tamil Śaiva tradition, like the battles of the Tamil kings, Śiva's cosmic acts of destruction, such as the destruction of the three cities and the burning of the Love-god (Kāma), were actually performed in the Tamil countryside, especially in the Kaveri Delta region. Eight myths are designated the Eight Heroic Deeds, and the places where these deeds took place are collectively known as Aṭṭavīraṭṭāṉam, "the shrines of the Eight Heroic Deeds." The eight myths and the Vīraṭṭāṉam shrines have a prominent place in the *Tēvāram*.[57]

Involving Śiva in the origin myths of his shrines is another strategy adopted by the Tamil Śaivas to make him their own god.[58] For instance, the Nāyaṉārs allude in their hymns to the claims of several temples of having been the sole survivors of the great cosmic flood because Śiva manifested himself at that shrine to save it at the time of the flood.[59] The Tamil country also became the locale for Śiva's wanderings as a beggar, riding on his bull, and the stage for his many dances. The local and regional flavor of the poems is further enhanced through the frequent references to events in the poets' own lives and devotional careers as well as those in the lives of other Tamil devotees, both historical and legendary, some of whom were contemporaries of the *Tēvāram* saints. Such allusions are interwoven with descriptions of exemplary Śaiva devotees who appear in the Sanskrit epics and Purāṇas. Thus the stories of the well-known Tamil saints Kaṇṇappar and Caṇṭīcar may be juxtaposed in a verse or hymn with the Sanskrit epic myths of the austerities with which Arjuna and Bhagīratha propitiated Śiva. In all these ways Śiva Mahādēva ("the great god") manifests himself in the *Tēvāram* as a true hero of *puṟam* poetry, a local chief ruling over particular Tamil towns and landscapes, performing

[57] The term "Vīraṭṭāṉam" is added to the names of these towns, beginning with (Tiruv-) Atikai Vīraṭṭāṉam. For a list of the eight shrines and the myths associated with them, consult Appendix C.

[58] Such myths were elaborated in the Tamil *talapurāṇam* (local myth, myths of the place) genre from the sixteenth century on. See Shulman, *Tamil Temple Myths*.

[59] See, e.g., Campantar I.75.2 (Poem 54), Campantar I.53.4 (Poem 107), Campantar I.131.9 (Poem 108), and Campantar III.376 (Poem 109).

acts of heroism and largesse to protect and favor his Tamil "subjects" and being praised by his devoted bards, the *Tēvāram* saints themselves.

TAMIL LANDSCAPES, TAMIL LOVE

Bhakti connotes not only "devotion," in the sense of reverence, attachment, and loyalty, but "love" (Tamil *aṉpu, kātal*) in all its dimensions. The Śiva of the Tamil hymns is not just an awesome, transcendent, brahmanical deity and the manifestation of sacred power on the Tamil model; he and his devotees are bound to each other by a powerful mutual love. The intimate nature of this relationship comes across in the many images and terms of endearment with which the saints address their God: "my pearl," "my honey," "my treasure." Even while picturing Śiva as king and master, the Nāyaṉār sees him as related to his devotees by the closest and most significant kinship ties in the Tamil family: the Lord is the devotees' father (*attaṉ, appaṉ, tantai*), mother's brother (*māmaṉ, ammāṉ*), even mother (*tāy, ammai*). Poems in which the Lord is portrayed as the lover are rare in the *Tēvāram*, although there is an undercurrent of erotic mysticism in many poems in which the saint laments his separation (*viraha*) from God. Whatever the kind of love the saint wishes to portray, he draws on the tradition of the classical Tamil *akam* poetic genre, which constitutes the literature of the interior, the literature of all intimate love relationships.

The most striking feature of *akam* poetry is its system of landscapes.[60] The tradition classifies love between man and woman into five phases (*uri*), each of which is associated with, and takes place in, a particular landscape type in the Tamil region. In the classical poems, landscape elements suggest and symbolize aspects of human love: for instance, the *kuṟiñci* (hill) landscape relates to lovers' union; *mullai* (forest), to patient waiting and domesticity. Landscape forms an important, though not essential, part of the descriptive repertoire of the Tamil saints. In many *patikam*s Campantar and Cuntarar self-consciously use *akam* landscape conventions in a way that brings out both the affinities and the differences between *akam* and *bhakti* poetry. Let us compare a Caṅkam love poem with a verse of Campantar, in which similar landscape elements are used:

WHAT SHE SAID
Once: if an owl hooted on the hill,
if a male ape leaped and loped

[60] See Ramanujan, *Interior Landscape*, pp. 105–12, for a concise introduction to the idea of landscape in Tamil poetry. A more detailed account can be found in A. K. Ramanujan, *Poems of Love and War: From the Eight Anthologies and the Ten Long Poems of Classical Tamil* (New York: Columbia University Press, 1985).

out there on the jackfruit bough in our yard
my poor heart would melt for fear. But now
in the difficult dark of night
nothing can stay its wandering
on the long sloping mountain-ways
of his coming.

Kapilar, *Kuṟuntokai* 153; trans. A. K. Ramanujan[61]

Tiruvaiyāṟu is the place
where the female ape, in fright
leaps up on a branch to look for rainclouds,
taking for thunder the roll of drums
when women dance, going around the shrine
where the Lord dwells who delivers us from fear
when the five senses wander out of their cages,
and cease to function,
the phlegm rises, the reason fails,
and we are afraid.

Campantar I.130.1 (Poem 76)

In the classical poem we overhear the interior monologue of a speaker who is identified as the "heroine." The situation or phase of love is lovers' union, a topic associated with the hill landscape (*kuṟiñci*). The theme of this particular poem is the emotional landscape that surrounds the maturing of a young girl through her love for her man, a hero who comes from the hill country. The suggestive use of images and features conventionally appropriate to the mountain landscape—the owl hooting on the hill, the ape on the jackfruit tree, night, the hero's mountain path—is the principal means by which the meanings of the poem are brought to the reader. The suggestions are multiple; for instance, not only is the noisy male ape in the heroine's yard an obstacle to the clandestine meeting of the lovers in the heroine's own home at night, he is a counterpart of the hero himself, symbolizing him as the strong but somewhat insensitive man who initiates the innocent virgin into a world of powerful sexuality.[62] The process of the "virgin's progress from abstraction to experience"[63] is made vivid to the reader through the phenomenon of " 'Inscapes' . . . of the natural scene" repeating "the total action of the poem."[64]

Turning to Campantar's verse, we see that the *Tēvāram* poet does not

[61] Ramanujan, *Interior Landscape*, p. 64.

[62] Hart, *Poems*, p. 167, cites another classical poem where the image of the male ape is used in a similar manner.

[63] Ramanujan, *Interior Landscape*, p. 109.

[64] Ibid., pp. 109–10.

strictly adhere to the classical conventions of time, place, and voice, or of landscape elements. The town of Tiruvaiyāṟu, situated in the Kaveri Delta region, is not in a mountain-landscape setting, of which the ape is a "native element." The rainy season is properly associated with the *mullai* or "patient waiting" phase of love. The verse itself is not an interior monologue; the poet-persona is speaking to an implied audience, his fellow devotees. Lastly, the shrine of Śiva and the ritual activities of the devotees are as important for the affective impact of the poem as the landscape elements. However, the two poems are also similar in important respects: the natural description in both poems is firmly grounded in reality;[65] landscape is used in both to suggest emotional states; and in both cases the emotions evoked are fear and love.

The function of the imagery in the classical love poem is "to arouse the complex interplay of suggestions."[66] Like Kapilar (the author of the *akam* poem), Campantar, too, uses the descriptive elements of his verse in suggestive ways. The female ape who leaps up "in fright" is implicitly compared to the mind of the devotee, which is confused and gripped by fear (of karma and rebirth) at the moment of death.[67] The ape is skillfully integrated into the temple scene by the device of the animal's mistaking the sound of drums for thunder. The description of the dancing devotees naturally leads to mention of the temple and the deity who dwells within, the god who delivers the devotee from fear when his mind, like the monkey, leaps about in ignorance and uncertainty. Yet the suggestions in the *Tēvāram* verse are not "bottomless."[68] This poem has a "solution," its diverse images unambiguously converge on a point: the image of Śiva as the god who delivers his devotees from fear. The classical poem is clean and spare in design; yet, while no explicit comparisons are made, every aspect of the landscape is linked to the heroine's interior state in suggestive relationships of increasing complexity. In Campantar's poem, on the other hand, the links that lead the reader to progressive awareness of the comparison between the natural and inner "scenes" are presented in a linear manner, leading to the clarity of the total effect.

From the point of view of classical Tamil poetics, Campantar's poem would be an inferior example of the use of suggestion in poetry. However, from the *bhakti* point of view, his verse is highly successful, if only for the fact that it felicitously brings together several aspects of Tamil *bhakti* religion—the interior and exterior aspects of the devotional relationship,

[65] On realism in classical Tamil poetry, see Ramanujan, "Form in Classical Tamil Poetry," p. 91.

[66] Hart, *Poems*, p. 196.

[67] The conception of the mind as a monkey is a common one in the Tamil tradition.

[68] In contrast to the Caṅkam poems, which, George Hart suggests, have suggested meanings that cannot be "tied down; there is no one correct solution" (Hart, *Poems*, p. 163).

Śiva as local god and transcendent deity—in the emotional setting of classical Tamil poetry. And that, indeed, is the saint's primary concern. The conventions of *akam* love poetry were more directly relevant to Tamil Vaiṣṇava *bhakti* lyricism, which focused on the classic lover-god Visṇu-Krishna, and some of the Vaiṣṇava Āḻvārs used the *akam* tradition with greater versatility and depth than the Nāyaṉārs.[69] Appar, Campantar, and Cuntarar use the *akam* world primarily as an instrument and context with which to evoke the Tamil cultural past in a very general way, through association and allusion. The purpose of this evocation is to establish the link between landscape and love that is essential to the Tamil world view.

In one aspect of landscape description the Nāyaṉārs are in harmony with both *akam* and *puṟam* poets. The lush beauty and abundance of the agricultural landscape of the banks of the Kaveri and of the many hills and wooded regions of the Tamil countryside are both a characteristic of the *akam* and *puṟam* traditions, where the bard evokes the richness of his hero's lands by means of natural description,[70] and an observable fact for the population of the Kaveri region. The Tamil Śaiva cult was born, and flourished in, the Kaveri Delta, the richest rice-growing region in Tamil country. The focus on the lore and landscape of the legendary river Kaveri had a particularly strong appeal for the Cōḻa rulers and the peasantry of this area:[71]

> Let us sing the feet of the tridentbearer,
> the Lord who dances with ringing anklets,
> and loves his abode
> where his loving devotees praise him,
> Kāṭṭuppaḷḷi on the Kaveri
> who rushes down in many gurgling streams,
> washing sandal- and aloe wood
> with soft sounds onto her banks.
>
> Campantar I.5.4 (Poem 75)

[69] The Vaiṣṇava saint Nammāḻvār devoted 270 verses in the *Tiruvāymoḻi* and the whole of his *Tiruviruttam* to *akam* themes. The woman Āḻvār Āṇṭāḷ wrote two important poems in the genre of women's songs involving *akam* themes: the *Tiruppāvai* and *Nācciyār tirumoḻi*. Among the Śaiva poets, Māṇikkavācakar stands out for his successful use of *akam* themes in the *Tirukkōvaiyār*.

[70] See, for instance, the poet Kapilar's poem on the legendary Caṅkam chieftain and patron Pāri: *Puṟanāṉūṟu* 109, in Ramanujan, *Love and War*, pp. 142–43.

[71] The ancestral myths of the Cōḻas connected them to the Kaveri River and its delta region, particularly in the area covered by the present day Tanjore (or Thanjavur) district. The first part of the epic *Cilappatikāram*, set in the Cōḻa realm, contains an ode to the Kaveri.

In such descriptions, Appar, Campantar, and Cuntarar at once express their own deep love of this land and strike a sympathetic chord in their audience. Poet, God, king, and community are united by their love for the Tamil countryside.

ŚIVA AS TAMIL GOD

The three *Tēvāram* poets express a self-conscious love of the Tamil language and poetry. They refer to their hymns as Tamil songs in a number of expressions: *tiruneṟiya tamiḻ* ("sacred Tamil"), *tamiḻ mālai* ("garland of Tamil verse"), *tamiḻ pattu* ("Tamil decad"), "*tamiḻ*" ("Tamil, a literary work in the Tamil language"). Campantar speaks of the tunes of their hymns as "Tamil musical modes" (*paṇ*), and Appar laments: "[I have] never failed to sing you in melodious Tamil songs" ("tamilōṭicai pāṭal maṟantaṟiyēṉ," IV.1.6; Poem 234). In this respect, the Tamil saints represent an ancient tradition in which the Tamil language is seen as the very manifestation of "sweetness, pleasantness and correctness."[72] In effect, they also affirm the sacrality of the Tamil language and *paṇ* music by identifying both with Śiva. Their Śiva is a chanter of the musical (Sāma) Veda, and a lover of music. He loves to listen to the songs of his devotees: "He listens, and takes delight in their songs" (II.42.4). The Lord is himself an expert singer of *paṇ* music (*"paṇṇiyal pāṭaliṉāṉ,"* I.108.6); a fine player on the lutelike *vīṇā* (*"icai vīṇai pūṇar,"* I.279.6; *"vīṇai tāṉ avar karuviyō"* VII.33.5); and a connoisseur of all the arts (*"ceḻunaṟ kalai terintavar,"* III.338.4). Finally, Śiva is art itself; he *is* the Tamil language and *paṇ* music. Cuntarar calls Śiva "the seven notes of music, / the fruit of my song" ("*ēḻicaiyāy icaippayaṉāy*," VII.51.10; Poem 249). Campantar sings of the Lord who is "the *paṇs*, the seven notes of music, and the many sounds of the Tamil language" ("*paṇṇum patam ēḻum palavōcait tamiḻ avaiyum*," I.11.4), and Appar sees Śiva as "Sanskrit of the North and southern Tamil and the four Vedas" ("*vaṭamoḻiyun teṉṟamiḻu maṟaika ṇāṉkum*," VI.301.1; Poem 20). The last reference is representative, and is significant for the way in which it juxtaposes the Vedas and the Sanskrit language with Tamil. With the religion of the Vedas and Purāṇas the Tamils accepted the ideas of Sanskrit as the sacred tongue and the Vedas as *śruti*, "revealed" scripture. Appar and his fellow poets gave the Tamil language, and hymns in Tamil as well as Tamil music, equal status with the sacred "northern" language and its scriptures. These are only some of the ways in which the saints proclaim their own and their God's special love for the Tamil cultural heritage, the language and literature of which

[72] Zvelebil, *Tamil Literature*, 1975, p. 53. *Tamiḻ* refers not only to the language but to literature in Tamil, classified into "three types" (*muttamiḻ*): *iyal* (verse and prose, meant for recitation); *icai* (musical composition, song); and *nāṭakam* (drama).

continue to be the most powerful symbol of cultural identity for the Tamils.[73]

With the evocation of the Tamil tongue the *Tēvāram* poet-saints complete for their readers and listeners the portrait of a religion of love that is quintessentially Tamil in character: love of a Tamil king-hero-god whose presence and acts are "placed" in beloved Tamil landscapes, love expressed through the images and animated with the spirit of a treasured classical literature, and love that is articulated in the language that symbolizes and connotes all of the above.

Ritual, Service, and Love: Portrait of a Community

Aṭiyār: The Community of Servants

We are slaves to no man,
nor do we fear Death.
Hell holds no torments for us,
we know no deceit.
We rejoice, we are strangers to disease,
we bow to none.
Joy alone is ours, not sorrow,
for we belong forever
to Śaṅkara, who is the supreme Lord,
our King who wears the white conch earring on one ear,
and we have reached
his beautiful, flower-fresh feet.
Appar VI.312.1 (Poem 240)

Although many hymns of the three *Tēvāram* poets bear the imprint of the author's unique personality, attitudes, and experience, especially in the verses that directly deal with the intimate aspects of his relationship with Śiva, we also hear a strong collective voice. The emotional stances and themes in the poetry of the three saints are remarkably similar and are expressed in shared vocabulary and imagery. The hymns are products of the individual saint's personality and experience interacting with a shared Tamil Śaiva vision of devotion to Śiva. Once again, the communal

[73] The Drāviḍa Muṉṉēṟṟak Kaḻakam, a modern political party whose platform is a separate ethnic-national identity for the Tamils, sees the Tamil language and its unique literary and cultural heritage as the foundation of this identity. The state formerly known as Madras has been renamed "Tamilnadu" (land of the Tamils). On contemporary Tamil political-cultural movements, see Robert L. Hardgrave, Jr., *The Dravidian Movement* (Bombay, 1965).

dimension of Tamil Śaiva *bhakti* comes to the fore; saint and community come together in the ideal of the "the devotee."

In the vocabulary of the *Tēvāram*, and of later Tamil Śaivism, the devotee is an *aṭiyār*, a servant; literally, "one who is at the feet." To the saints, their fellow devotees are *nantamar*, *namar* ("our people"), or simply *nām* ("we"), as in the well-known verse of Appar quoted above. At one level, the Nāyaṉārs included all worshippers of Śiva in "the community of devotees" (*aṭiyār kūṭṭam*): not only people who exclusively adhered to Tamil Śaiva cultic practice but also members of other Śaiva sects, even the Kāpālikas and "Viratis, men of bizarre appearance, who wear garlands of skulls,"[74] whose extreme ritual and ascetic practices were abhorrent to the followers of *bhakti* religion. At a more specific level, especially in the affectionate references and addresses of the poet-saints to their fellow devotees, the term *aṭiyār* seems to denote only those who worshipped and served Śiva in the new mode of passionate, emotional devotion.

ACTS OF LOVE

The conception of the ideal *aṭiyār* must be understood in the context of the totality of acts and attitudes that the *Tēvāram* poets consider "devotional." In the Nāyaṉārs' hymns, devotees express devotional feeling in spontaneous, unstructured ways that are characteristic of emotional *bhakti*:

> O devotees who have joined our group
> out of love,
> dance, weep, worship him,
> sing his feet,
> gather at Kuraṅkāṭuturai,
> place of our Lord!
> Appar V.177.8 (Poem 204)

However, the devotees also engage in structured, ceremonial acts, acts of ritual worship:

> Kaṭavūr Vīraṭṭam's Lord
> is like sweet sugar cane
> to those who become the madman's devotees,
> who rise at dawn to bathe, to gather fresh flowers,
> and lovingly offer them in worship,
> lighting lamps and burning incense for the rite.
> Appar IV.31.4 (Poem 86)

74 Appar IV.21.1 (Poem 98).

The activities described in this verse are part of "*pūjā*," the ritual mode of worshipping and honoring divine images and personages in Hinduism.[75] Though ritual was the core of the Vedic religion, image worship was not part of it, and the emphasis was not on the relationship between deity and worshipper but on the proper performance of ritual itself, the sacrifice being seen as "the principal manifestation of reality."[76] The *pūjā* ritual combines many non-Vedic ideas with a similar emphasis on ritual purity and the power of ritual. In the South Indian temple, pūjā is performed by priests according to Āgamic prescriptions.[77] The devotees in the Nāyaṉārs' hymns support temple ritual and perform private and communal *pūjā* rites that are open to all.

The Nāyaṉārs are well aware that ritual, by its very definition, holds the possibility of degenerating into mechanical piety, devoid of the emotion and spontaneity that is the essence of *bhakti* religion. Yet they view acts of ritual worship as an essential expression of emotional *bhakti*. When we consider the associations of sacred power and beauty that Śiva's concrete manifestations and his abodes hold for Tamil Śaivas, it is not surprising that acts of ritual offering and service which take place in these contexts are invested with great emotional and aesthetic significance. The Nāyaṉārs' conception of ritual is itself derived only in part from the brahmanical legacy of Tamil Śaivism; it has popular, communal, and ecstatic dimensions that have their roots in indigenous Tamil religion, perhaps in such customs as the communal dances in which men and women celebrated the Tamil god Murukaṉ and were possessed by him.[78] Certainly, in the early Tirumāl and Murukaṉ *bhakti* texts, devotees are depicted as practicing an ecstatic and communal devotionalism focused on pilgrimage, worship at particular shrines, and ritual.[79] In the religion of the Nā-

[75] On the *pūjā* ritual, in addition to Eck, *Darśan*, see Joanne P. Waghorne and Norman Cutler, in association with Vasudha Narayanan, eds., *Gods of Flesh, Gods of Stone: The Embodiment of Divinity in India* (Chambersburg, Pa.: Anima, 1985). See especially Paul B. Courtright's "On This Holy Day in My Humble Way: Aspects of Pūjā," pp. 33–50, and Vasudha Narayanan's essay on the image of God in Śrīvaiṣṇava theology: "Arcāvatāra: On Earth as He Is in Heaven," pp. 53–66.

[76] Hopkins, *Hindu Religious Tradition*, p. 21. On the Vedic ideal of ritual, see ibid., ch. 2.

[77] On *pūjā* in the South Indian Śiva temple, see J.W.V. Curtis, "Space Concepts and Worship Environment in Śaiva Siddhānta," in *Experiencing Śiva*, ed. Clothey and Long, pp. 87–101.

[78] Ecstatic dancing, shamanism, and sacrifice are described in classical works such as the *Tirumurukāṟṟuppaṭai* and *Cilappatikāram*. For details, see Hardy, *Viraha-Bhakti*, pp. 131–42, 230–31, and app. 7.

[79] *Paripāṭal* 19 contains a fine, detailed description of a Pāṇṭiya pilgrimage from Maturai to Tirupparaṅkuṉṟam. The *Tirumurukāṟṟuppaṭai*, as its title indicates, is a "guide to Murukaṉ," a guide for pilgrims who wish to visit the god in his shrines in the Tamil region.

yaṉārs, ritual is also a personal and sensuous mode of experiencing the beauty and glory of God:

> Hands, join in worship,
> strew fragrant flowers
> on the Lord who binds
> the hooded snake around his waist!
> Hands, join in worship!
>
> Of what use is the body
> that never walked around
> the temple of Śiva,
> offering him flowers in the worship rite?
> Of what use is this body?
>
> Appar IV.9.7, 8 (Poem 197)

For Appar, Campantar, and Cuntarar, ritual is beautiful. It is an important component of *bhakti* as aesthetic experience. Ritual is an essential means for expressing one's love for the Lord; it can be as emotionally charged as dancing or singing. Lastly, it consists of acts of offering and service, the ideal way of life for the true devotee.

RITUAL AND SERVICE IN THE LIVES OF THE SAINTS

In the Nāyaṉārs' depiction of the ideals for devotees and devotion we get a vivid image of the paradox inherent in early Tamil devotion. In addition to ritual worship, the poet-saints celebrated and cherished many aspects of traditional religion and culture associated with the brahmin elite and the aristocracy. Campantar describes himself as the "Kavuṇiyaṉ" (a Tamil brahmin of the Kauṇḍinya *gotra*, I.8.11), "Ñāṉacampantaṉ, well versed in the four Vedas" (*nāṉmaṟai ñāṉacampantaṉ*, I.4.11), and praises the brahmins (*antaṇar*) of Tillai (modern Chidambaram) as "men who have conquered cosmic evil / through sacred learning / and the tending of the sacred fire" (I.80.1; Poem 102).[80] Such conservatism is explained by many factors: the Āgamic roots of Tamil Śaiva religion, the fluidity of class relationships in the Tamil society of the time, and the closeness of brahmin and Vellala in the Tamil social hierarchy.[81] And yet

[80] "Kaṟṟāṅkeriyōmpik kaliyai vārāme ceṟṟār. . . ." The Pallavas and Cōḻas made gifts of entire villages (*brahmadeya*, "gift to brahmins") to brahmins. Chidambaram is one of the most important among these brahmin settlements; Cuntarar begins his list of devotees with "those who serve the brahmins who live in Tillai [Chidambaram]."

[81] From the earliest times, there have been several kinds of brahmins in the Tamil area, each showing various degrees of assimilation to the indigenous culture (Hart, *Poems*, pp. 51–56). In contemporary Tamilnadu, Smārta brahmins claim superiority over Ādiśaivas (Tamil Śaiva brahmins) and *kurukkaḷ* (priests). See Charles J. Fuller, *Servants of the Goddess: The Priests of a South Indian Temple* (Cambridge: Cambridge University Press, 1984),

the saints' hymns are full of images of a "communitas" within which social hierarchy is radically overturned.[82] The poets assert that unswerving devotion to Śiva overrides all other affiliations and markers of identity and is the supreme criterion for respect, friendship, and communal consciousness among the Tamil Śaivas. Appar puts it eloquently:

> Were they to offer me both treasures
> of Kubera's world,
> and give me earth and heaven itself to rule,
> the wealth of decaying mortals
> would be as nothing to me,
> when those who gave
> were not single-minded devotees
> of our great Lord.
> But the leper with rotting limbs,
> the outcaste, even the foul *pulaiyaṉ*
> who skins and eats cows,
> even these men, if they are servants
> of him who shelters the Ganges in his long hair,
> I worship them,
> they are gods to me.
>
> Appar VI.309.10 (Poem 211)

The key to the paradox lies in the ideal of "service" (*aṭimai*, *toṇṭu*) itself, which is the highest qualification for becoming an *aṭiyār*. *Cariyai* (acts of service and attendance, from Sanskrit *caryā*, conduct) and *kiriyai* (Sanskrit *kriyā*, deed, [ritual] act, rite) constitute the first two aspects of religious activity in the fourfold classification of the Āgama ritual texts; they are also the types of action that form the subjects of the Nāyaṉārs' description of service. Acts of service that involve manual labor or indirectly contribute to the worship of Śiva—for instance, digging wells near Śiva's temples, gathering flowers, or tending to the lamps intended for the *pūjā* ritual—are classed under *cariyai*. Ritual worship, with an emphasis on devotional attitudes, is classed under *kiriyai*.[83] The metaphysical bases of the Āgamic classification are fully developed in the Śaiva Siddhānta texts,

ch. 3. However, in the Tamil region (Vellala) Mutaliyār, Piḷḷai and certain other nonbrahmin caste groups have enjoyed rank and prestige equal to that of brahmins. In some social and ritual contexts, the Vellalas have greater power, authority, and status than the brahmins. On the high status of peasant communities in the Tamil area, see Stein, *Peasant State*.

[82] "Communitas" is Victor Turner's term in *The Ritual Process: Structure and Anti-Structure* (Chicago: University of Chicago Press, 1969).

[83] Dhavamony, *Love of God*, pp. 234–37, gives a clear description of the four paths as explained in Aruṇanti's *Śivañāṉacittiyār*. The various Śaiva Siddhānta authors differ on the precise demarcation between *cariyai* and *kiriyai*; however, they agree on the point that *kiriyai* involves a formal, ritual component combined with an attitude of devotion.

in which *cariyai*, *kiriyai*, *yōkam* (Sanskrit *yoga*, contemplative discipline), and *ñāṉam* (Sanskrit *jñāna*, knowledge), are hierarchically organized, each one taking the soul a step closer to its release from the bondage of karma. Although sincere devotion is the guiding principle behind each of the modes or stages in this hierarchy, *cariyai* and *kiriyai* are lower, preparatory modes of religiosity, with *ñāṉam*, the knowledge of the true nature of the relationship between the soul (*pacu*) and the Lord (*pati*), being the highest instrument of release.[84] This is where the emphasis of the poet-saints is different. Though the poets are aware of technical distinctions among the four modes, they do not speak of a hierarchy of devotional acts. They focus instead on *cariyai* and *kiriyai* and portray manual labor and ritual worship as modes that encompass the meanings and benefits of discipline and knowledge. The Nāyaṉārs also suggest the meanings of service chiefly through their portrayal of exemplary devotees, and in personal and emotional terms, rather than in terms of proper behavior.

The Tamil devotees cited as exemplars in the Nāyaṉārs' *patikam*s are true "servants," either by serving Śiva directly or by serving his devotees. Naminanti kept the lamps in the Tiruvārūr temple burning with water when they ran out of oil; the Pāṇṭiya queen Maṅkaiyarkkaraci and her minister Kulacciṟai humbled themselves in the service of Śiva's devotees; men, women, and even animals—like the rat who kept the lamps burning in Maṟaikkāṭu shrine, and the spider who built a canopy for Śiva's image out of thread from his own body—lovingly perform the ritual worship of Śiva at risk to their bodies and lives. Kaṇṇappar and Caṇṭīcar, the two Nāyaṉārs whom the *Tēvāram* poets repeatedly invoke as exemplary *aṭiyār*, epitomize the unique blend of qualities that characterize the Tamil Śaiva ideal: great concern for the proper performance of ritual worship, and a passionate, all-consuming, personal love for God, before which all rules and laws of conduct and ceremony crumble.[85] Kaṇṇappar was a low-caste hunter who broke all the rules of ritual purity when, making ritual offerings of meat and other forbidden things, he lovingly worshipped an image of Śiva that he found in a forest shrine.[86] The great power of his love for Śiva was proved to the world by the Lord himself. While engaged in worshipping his God, the devout hunter readily dug out his own eyes to replace the eyes of the image, which Śiva had caused to

[84] Dhavamony, *Love of God*, pp. 118, 215, 268–70. G. Subrahmaniya Pillai, "Introduction and History of Śaiva Siddhānta," in *Collected Lectures on Śaiva Siddhānta: 1946–1954* (Annamalainagar: Annamalai University, 1965), pp. 50–51.

[85] Caṇṭīcar is also known as Caṇṭēcar. Kaṇṇappar's life is the subject of several hagiographical poems in addition to Cēkkiḻār's account in the *Periya purāṇam*.

[86] Consult the summaries of these lives and commentaries on the significance of the lives, in Yogi Suddhananda Bharati, *The Grand Epic of Śaivism* (Tirunelveli/Madras: South Indian Saiva Siddhanta Works [hereafter SISSW] Publishing Society, 1970).

bleed in order to test the sincerity of Kaṇṇappar's devotion. In an equally remarkable act of devotion, the brahmin boy Caṇṭīcar cut off with an axe the foot of his own father when he tried to stop his son from ritually bathing a *liṅga* that he had lovingly fashioned with earth. The lives of Kaṇṇappar and Caṇṭīcar contain the central themes of the lives of the sixty-three saints as told in Cēkkiḻār's *Periya purāṇam*.[87] The list of these Nāyaṉārs includes men and women; kings and peasants; brahmins; a potter, a cowherd, and a hunter, all members of low castes; and even a *pulaiyaṉ*, a person who handles unclean objects like animal skins and is therefore an outcaste.[88] A number of the Nāyaṉārs spent their lives engaged in serving at Śiva's shrines. Some provided flowers, sandalwood, incense, and other materials required for the ritual; others performed acts of service at the shrine—lighting lamps, sweeping the courtyards, serving as musicians and priests; yet others, like Queen Maṅkaiyarkkaraci, served other devotees. As in the stories of Kaṇṇappar and Caṇṭīcar, the dramatic moment in the lives of these other Nāyaṉārs occurs when they commit an extraordinary act—of self-sacrifice or the sacrifice of those who are dear to them—in order to preserve the integrity of their service to God or his devotees. These acts can be staggeringly gruesome, as exemplified by Kaṇṇappar's plucking out his eyes or Caṇṭīcar's cutting off his father's foot. In each case, the sacrificial act, epitomized in the shedding of blood, which is considered to be a pollutant in the context of the Āgamic worship ritual, reveals the spontaneous, passionate, emotional devotion that underlies the Tamil *bhakti* ideal of ritual.[89] The value of the ritual act is measured not by its conventional propriety or by the status of the person performing it but by the utter sincerity and passion with which it is performed.

EXPERIENCE AND EXPRESSION IN THE POETRY OF THE SAINTS

> Joy alone is ours, not sorrow,
> for we belong forever

[87] It is not clear from the earliest narratives of the Kaṇṇappar legend, including the account in the *Periya purāṇam*, whether the image that Kaṇṇappar worshipped was an aniconic or anthropomorphic image of Śiva. The image might have been a *mukha-liṅga*, a *liṅga* with a face or faces. In the later sculptural tradition Kaṇṇappar is usually shown worshipping a *liṅga* image. On this point, see Narayana Ayyar, *Origin and Early History*, pp. 163–64. On the *mukha-liṅga*, see Stella Kramrisch, *The Presence of Siva* (Princeton: Princeton University Press, 1981), ch. 7.

[88] On the caste composition of the group of sixty–three Nāyaṉārs, see Zvelebil, *Smile of Murugan*, pp. 192–93.

[89] See George Hart's formulation of the tension between the concern for propriety and the respect for sincere emotion as exemplified by the acts of the Nāyaṉār Ciṟuttoṇṭar, in "The Little Devotee: Cēkkiḻār's Story of Ciṟuttoṇṭar," in *Sanskrit and Indian Studies*, ed. Nagatomi et al., pp. 217–36.

to Śaṅkara, who is the supreme Lord, . . .
and we have reached
his beautiful, flower-fresh feet.
Appar VI.312.1 (Poem 240)

For the *Tēvāram* poets and their community, "to serve" Śiva, simply to *be* an *aṭiyār*, is both the means and the end of the religious life. To be an *aṭiyār* is to commune with Śiva through love; to be an *aṭiyār* is also to bring out the love that is within, to express it in every way. Emotional *bhakti* is deeply concerned with the private, interior nature of human religious experience. It is, at the same time, the most exuberantly expressive kind of personal religion in the Hindu tradition. The Tamils celebrate the poetry of the saints as the perfect embodiment of both aspects of emotional *bhakti.*

The three great poets stand in an interesting relationship to the rest of the Nāyaṉārs. Compared to the violent and spectacular crises that are characteristic of the lives of the other saints, the pattern of the poet-saints' lives seems almost humdrum. Yet it is these poets who, along with their fellow poet Māṇikkavācakar, became the Camayakurus, "Preceptors of the Tradition." They were the men who literally led their fellow devotees around the Tamil countryside, seeking communion with their God in every temple. They were more dynamic as cult leaders and more prolific in their literary activity than any other Nāyaṉār poet before them. These achievements in themselves are enough to account for the high status that Appar, Cuntarar, and Campantar have earned in the Tamil Śaiva tradition. Yet their veneration in the cult ultimately rests on a well-defined premise: the special significance of poetry as a religious mode in Tamil Śaivism. Cēkkiḻār, who aims at elucidating the essential significance of the life of each Nāyaṉār as a model of devotion to Śiva, explores this very theme in his narrative of the lives of the *Tēvāram* saints.[90] The basic pattern of Cēkkiḻār's account of the lives of these three Nāyaṉārs is provided by the recurrent descriptive themes of the saint's journey to a shrine and the composition of a particular hymn at that shrine. The hagiographer tirelessly records the circumstances under which each poem was composed, dwelling on the emotional aspects of the scene, as in this description of Appar's acts upon arriving at the temple of Śiva in Vīḻimiḻalai:

He approached and entered the temple
where the Lord who has the golden mountain for his bow
dwells in delight.
He circumambulated it,

[90] We may discern this meaning in Appar's famous line: "eṉ kaṭaṉ paṇi ceytu kiṭappatē" ("my task is only to serve"), Appar V.133.9 (Poem 172).

prostrated himself at the sacred courtyard,
entered the presence of the three-eyed god,
bull rider crowned with matted red hair.

Then he fell at his feet,
rose, sobbed out . . .
He folded his hands in adoration,
and praised the Lord's feet;
his deep love melted in a stream,
the flood from his eyes gushed out
and spread over his body.

Standing thus he sang a garland
of words of praise:
"Those who do not belong to the red-haired god
are trapped in the path of Evil"—
this Tāṇṭakam poem
which shows us the way to our release.
When he had sung,
his ceaseless love welled up stronger, . . .
and he still praised
that jewel-mountain with the golden form
in Vīḻimiḻalai of beautiful streams.[91]

In the imagery of this sequence of verses, and others similar to it, the intense desire to see and experience the Lord, which draws the saint to a particular temple, itself becomes an overflowing expression of love that physically manifests itself in torrential tears and, verbally, in a flood of poetry. Poetry is the *bhakti* experience made palpable. The hymn is the embodiment of the unification of emotion and ritual, interior (*akam*) and exterior (*puṟam*)—the experience of love, and its expression; in this lies the value of the hymns for Tamil Śaivas.[92] In their hymns the three saints articulated the entire range of Tamil Śaiva religious experience. Tamil song, the saints' medium of expression, makes that experience accessible to their fellow devotees, across space and time, with a remarkable vividness and immediacy. So powerful and vital is the link between the Nāyaṉārs' love for Śiva and their expression of that love, that all Tamil Śaivas may participate—"to participate" is one of the primary meanings of the root from which *bhakti* is derived—in that love relationship simply

[91] *Periya purāṇam* 5.21 (Tirunāvukkaracunāyaṉār Purāṇam), verses 252–54.

[92] I have explored this idea in detail in: Indira V. Peterson, "Lives of the Wandering Singers: Pilgrimage and Poetry in Tamil Śaivite Hagiography," *History of Religions* 22, no. 4 (1983): 338–60.

by adopting the paradigmatic expressive mode, by singing the *Tēvāram* songs:

> Moved by intense love for Śiva
> Ñāṉacampantaṉ, the Tamil poet
> from Pukali of pure streams,
> worships in song
> the Lord who dwells in Ārūr of paddy fields
> where beautiful waterlilies bloom.
> He who can recite these ten verses
> and listen to them
> will wipe his life clean of sorrow.
>
> Campantar I.105.11

The power of the saints' songs has indeed moved generations of Tamil Śaivas to treasure and to love them, to know and sing and listen to them. The sequence of identifications made by the poet-saints, that love of Śiva is the love of Tamil places, Tamil landscapes, the Tamil language and music, ends with the inclusion of the *Tēvāram* hymns, the songs of the Nāyaṉārs, as the final element. The text becomes a symbol for the *bhakti* experience in its entirety: Love of the *Tēvāram* hymns is love of Śiva.

CHAPTER 4

The Lives of a Text: The Role of the *Tēvāram* Hymns in Tamil Śaivism

> By all means, let us, with regard to anything, know how it became; but let us study further how and what it went on becoming. The study of history must in large part be the study of creativity.
>
> —Wilfred Cantwell Smith[1]

In a continuous tradition going back at least to the time of the recovery of the hymns, the *Tēvāram* has remained the fundamental instrument for Tamil Śaivas in their personal, communal, and ritual worship of Śiva. Devotees and professional hymn singers sing and recite the hymns, in informal as well as ceremonial settings. The *patikam*s can be heard in homes, temple courtyards, concert halls, and festival processions. Holy men sing them on city streets and country roads.[2] The rise in popularity of other gods and cults, as well as the "secularization" of modern Tamil life, appear to have in no way diminished the affectionate regard in which Tamil Śaivas hold the three Nāyaṉārs and their songs.

The institution, established in Pallava and Cōḻa times, of employing specialists called *ōtuvār* ("one who chants or sings") to sing selections from the Tirumuṟai texts during the worship ritual and on other public occasions, continues in major Śiva temples in the Tamil region. In many shrines, the "song of the place" (*talattup patikam*) is inscribed on the

[1] "The Study of Religion and the Study of the Bible," *Journal of the American Academy of Religion*, 34, no. 2 (1971): 131–40, at p. 135.

[2] Kingsbury and Phillips, *Hymns of the Tamil Śaivite Saints*, p. 63, tell us that in Madras "there used to be a beggar . . . who recited it [Appar's poem "ariyāṉai antaṇartam . . ."], and it alone, all day long."

walls of the temple (see illus. 15).[3] The myths and personages celebrated by the Nāyaṉārs, and the poets themselves, are an integral part of Tamil temple iconography. In the temple, the words, images, and sounds of the *Tēvāram* surround the Tamil Śaivas.

The hymns of the three saints have been, and continue to be, at the center of the Tamil Śaivas' consciousness as a religious community. Just as the *Tēvāram* helped forge a new cultural and communal identity for the Tamils in the age of the Nāyaṉārs, its veneration as "The Tamil Veda" (*tamiḻmaṟai*)—the term used by the twelfth-century hagiographer to refer to the hymns[4]—played a crucial role in helping the Tamil Śaivas maintain a distinct, and distinctly Tamil, sectarian identity. This latter function of the text must be seen in the context of major developments within the Tamil Śaiva sect, and in religion in Tamil India, from the twelfth century to the present.

The Tamil Veda:
The Hymns as Sectarian Scripture

Bhakti cults sprang up all over India in the wake of the Tamil devotional movements. In South India, forces of religious syncretism and sectarian development were simultaneously at work in the period that followed the age of the Nāyaṉārs. On the one hand, the great Sanskritic philosophers and sectarian leaders of the South wrote definitive interpretations of the Sanskrit sacred texts, covering both *śruti* ("revealed literature," "the literature of the Vedas and Upaniṣads") and *smṛti* ("traditional" sacred texts such as the *Bhagavad Gītā*);[5] on the other, emotional *bhakti* was fully incorporated into the brahmanical and traditionalist segment of South Indian society, especially in the Tamil region. Thus, while brahmanism of the pan-Indian type flourished with renewed vigor, emotional devotion to Śiva or Viṣṇu was no longer a phenomenon peculiar to the "vernacular" cults. During this time, Tamil Śaivism established itself as a separate sect, mainly on the basis of the Śaiva Siddhānta philosophy.

Unlike the philosophers of the non-Tamil Hindu sects, and of the Tamil Vaiṣṇava sect, the authors of the Siddhānta texts wrote primarily in Tamil; the fourteen fundamental treatises (*cittānta cāttiram*) of the tra-

[3] The discovery of a *patikam* attributed to Campantar inscribed on a wall at the Tiruviṭaivāy temple shows that this must have been a practice of some antiquity. In many Tamil temples today, the hymn is painted on the walls of the inner courtyard of the temple.

[4] E.g., *Periya purāṇam* 6.319: "paṉṉu tamiḻ maṟaiyām patikam."

[5] Śaṅkara, Rāmānuja, and Madhva were the outstanding figures in this group. Rāmānuja was the great teacher of the Śrīvaiṣṇava sect.

dition are in Tamil.[6] Because of this the Siddhānta philosophy did not get wide recognition outside the sect, as did the Sanskrit philosophical writings of the other sects, and remained in large measure the internal possession of the community of Tamil Śaiva intellectuals.

Many factors contributed to the differences in emphasis between the poets and the professional philosophers in Tamil Śaivism. While the Siddhānta philosophers shared in the Nāyaṉārs' world view and their concern with ritual and temple worship imbued with devotion, they rarely established a direct connection between the emotionally charged poems of the saints and their own doctrinal writings, in which they expound the nature of soul, God, bondage, and release. The link between the two lineages of teachers (*kuru*, *ācāriyār*), the poets and the philosophers, remained a tenuous one. Though the theologians treated the saints' hymns with the reverence due scripture, they did not connect the two streams of thought through commentaries. Among the sacred texts of the Great Tradition, the Siddhānta philosophers placed greater emphasis on the philosophy of the Āgamas than on the fundamental scriptures of the orthodox tradition.[7] In all the above features the Tamil Śaiva philosophers stand in marked contrast to their Tamil Vaiṣṇava counterparts, the theologians and philosophers of the branch of the Vaiṣṇava sect that developed out of the *bhakti* cult of the Āḻvārs. Several of the great Ācāryas of the Śrīvaiṣṇava sect wrote in Sanskrit,[8] but they developed a comprehensive exegetical system in which the poetry and theology of the Āḻvārs were directly connected to their own formulations of doctrine. Through a number of powerful arguments, the Ācāryas established the authority of the words and ideas in the *Tivviyap pirapantam* hymns of the Āḻvārs as being equal to that of the Vedic literature. The resultant philosophy, flowing out of the two streams of "scriptural" tradition, the Tamil and the Sanskrit, was called the "ubhayavedānta" or "the philosophy of the two Vedas or Vedic traditions."[9] These differences between the Tamil Śaiva

[6] This, in spite of the fact that several of the sectarian teachers, both brahmin and Vellala, were Sanskrit scholars. Some of the Śaiva Siddhānta philosophers also wrote works in Sanskrit (Sivaraman, *Śaivism*; Natarajan, *City of the Cosmic Dance*, ch. 12), and as Stein (*Peasant State*, pp. 230–40) and Zvelebil (*Tamil Literature*, 1975, pp. 250–51) point out, because of their orientation toward Sanskritic ritual and doctrine, and the connections with sects in other regions, the Tamil Śaiva sectarian centers were actually centers of Sanskritization.

[7] J. Estlin Carpenter clearly states the Tamil Śaiva position: The Siddhānta philosophers see both the Vedas and Āgamas as emanating from the Lord and therefore true, but not of equal value. "The Vedas are more general . . . ; the Āgamas are the more special, suitable for advanced believers. . . . Revelation is . . . progressive." *Theism in Medieval India* (1921; reprint Delhi: Munshiram Manoharlal, 1977), p. 359.

[8] E.g., Yāmuna, Rāmānuja.

[9] Expounded in a large body of commentaries and subcommentaries, written first in Sanskrit, and later in an amalgam of Sanskrit and Tamil, called *maṇipravāla* ("mixture of ruby

and Vaiṣṇava sects are closely related to the differences that developed in their cultural milieu and caste orientation after the era of the poet-saints, the Śaivas becoming predominantly Vellala and the Vaiṣṇavas, predominantly brahmin.

From the Cōḻa period on membership in the Tamil Śaiva cult stabilized, being composed predominantly of prosperous nonbrahmin peasant castes who ranked high in the regional caste hierarchy.[10] The nonbrahmin Vellalas had always played an important part in the cult's leadership. Appar and many other Nāyaṉārs were Vellalas. The Siddhānta philosophers also came from both brahmin and Vellala caste backgrounds.[11] The heads of the Tamil Śaiva sectarian *maṭam*s, which flourished in the fourteenth century and earlier, have traditionally been Vellalas.[12] As for the lower castes among the Tamil nonbrahmins, though they have traditionally professed allegiance to Tamil Śaivism, their ritual and worship activity, as well as their mythology and lore, have centered more on local and tutelary deities than on the major Hindu gods.[13] Thus throughout the history of the Tamil Śaiva sect, Vellala agrarian communities have formed the sect's core constituency and leadership.

As prosperous landowners and farmers, Tamil Śaivas have always given economic support to the major Śiva temples in the Tamil countryside, and have been able to shape and influence the administration and ritual system of these temples.[14] However, since their inception, Tamil Śaiva sectarian centers and communities have been involved in a complex economic and social power relationship with royal patrons as well as with the brahmin elites of the region.[15] In the last two centuries, especially in the Kaveri Delta, where both brahmins and Vellalas have traditionally

and coral"). On this literature, see K.K.A. Venkatachari, *The Maṇipravāla Literature of the Śrīvaiṣṇava Ācāryas: 12th-15th Century A.D.*, Anantacharya Research Institute Series no. III (Bombay: Anantacharya Research Institute, 1978).

[10] See Chapter 3, note 81 above.

[11] Meykaṇṭār (thirteenth century) was a Vellala; Aruṇanti and Umāpati Civam were Tamil Śaiva brahmins. See Zvelebil, *Tamil Literature*, 1975, ch. 10.

[12] On the lineages of teachers associated with particular *maṭam*s, see Zvelebil, *Tamil Literature*, 1975, pp. 206–7.

[13] See Burton Stein, "Temples in Tamil Country, 1300–1750 A.D.," in *South Indian Temples*, ed. Stein, pp. 11–45.

[14] For instance, the Tamil Śaiva *maṭam* centers ("Ātīṉam," administrative centers) at Tarumapuram, Tiruvāvaṭuturai, and Tiruppaṉantāḷ have power and control in the major Śiva temples in Tamilnadu. For the history of the Tarumapuram Ātīṉam and its holdings, see A. Kaliyāṇacuntara Tēcikar, "Tarumaiy ātiṉak kuruparamparai varalāṟu," *Makākumpāpiṣēka viḻā malar* (Tarumapuram: Vaidyanāthasvāmi Devasthānam, 1970), pp. 338–466.

[15] The patterns of sectarian and caste-group alliance and competition, involving royal patrons, have been analyzed for the South Indian Vaiṣṇava case in Arjun Appadurai, *Worship and Conflict under Colonial Rule: A South Indian Case*, Cambridge South Asian Studies 27 (Cambridge: Cambridge University Press, 1981), ch. 2.

been powerful, Smārta brahmins have vied with Tamil Śaivas for ideological influence in the temple.[16]

As early as the age of the Nāyaṉārs, and certainly by the age of the Siddhānta philosophy, a large number of Tamil brahmins had adopted the syncretistic philosophy and practice known as Smārta traditionalism.[17] Moving away from sectarian polarities, they not only adopted the worship of all the major deities of Hinduism but combined their strongly Sanskritic religious orientation with aspects of Tamil Śaiva and Vaiṣṇava devotionalism and the ascetic philosophy of Śaṅkarācārya. Apart from this eclecticism, the Tamil Smārtas identify themselves as Śaivas, and worship in Śiva temples. The Smārtas accept the singing of the *Tēvāram* songs as part of the Āgamic heritage of their religion and celebrate the presence and lore of the Tamil Śaiva saints as part of the history and iconography of the Tamil Śiva temple. In this sense, the Nāyaṉārs and their hymns are not simply the exclusive sectarian scripture and property of the Tamil Śaiva community. Yet they continue to have a unique symbolic significance for Tamil Śaivas. Today, in the context of worship in the temple, the Tamil Śaiva sense of sectarian identity is expressed primarily through their attitude toward the saints and the Tirumuṟai hymns.

Consider the attitude of Tamil Śaivas to the performance of the *Tēvāram* in private worship and ritual. When Tamil Śaivas worship at the subsidiary shrines[18] in which various aspects of Śiva are depicted within the Śiva temple, they sing or recite selections from Tamil sacred literature, especially from the *Tēvāram* and the *Tiruvācakam*. At the same shrines, the Tamil brahmins and affiliates of other sects prefer to use late Sanskrit devotional *stotras*, *nāmāvalīs* (litanies of the names of the deity), and other Sanskrit texts.[19] When the *ōtuvār*s sing the Tamil hymns at the end of the *pūjā* ritual, the Smārta brahmin worshippers regard this practice as one of many items in the ritual and attach no special significance to it. To the Tamil Śaiva worshippers, on the other hand, the part played by these hymns in ritual is a point of great doctrinal significance, legitimizing and confirming their belief that Śiva loves the offering of Tamil song equally with the Sanskrit mantras. This was certainly the view held by the Nā-

[16] The Pallava-Cōḻa institution of *brahmadeya* ("gift to brahmins") villages, especially in the Kaveri Delta, has resulted in concentrated areas of brahmin power in the Tamil region. On Smārta power and influence in the Tanjore district, see Peterson, "The *kṛti*."

[17] On the rise of the Smārtas, see Hopkins, *Hindu Religious Tradition*, ch. 7, and Nilakanta Sastri, *Development of Religion*, pp. 60–61.

[18] Ranging from recesses and niches in the inner walls of the main building, to separate auxiliary shrines, depicting forms of the central deity or of other divinities, saints, and devotees. See K. V. Soundara Rajan, *South Indian Temple Styles* (Delhi: Munshiram Manoharlal, 1972), p. 15, app. A.

[19] The authors of most of these Sanskrit works are South Indian Smārta brahmins. See Gonda, *Medieval Religious Literature*, ch. 14.

yaṉārs themselves: "My Lord who wears the cool *koṉṟai* blossom / rules in Acciṟupākkam . . . / where Tamil and Northern words join his feet" (Campantar I.77.4).[20]

The difference in Tamil Śaiva and Smārta attitudes toward the Tamil hymns of the saints is dramatically brought out in their apprehension of the singing of these songs at great ceremonial occasions, such as festival processions. At Śiva temple festivals a special image (Sanskrit *utsavamūrti*, festival image) of Śiva, appropriate to the particular festival, is taken out in procession around the temple.[21] Brahmins, chanting passages from Vedic literature, especially the *Śatarudrīya* hymn,[22] lead the procession; crowds of devotees follow; a group (*kōṣṭi*) of *ōtuvār*s singing the *Tēvāram* forms the rear of the procession.[23] Although it would be difficult to determine the date of this particular arrangement of elements in the procession, we have descriptions, in the saints' own hymns and in later literature, of such festival processions that included brahmins, devotees, and singers of the saints' hymns.[24] Contemporary worshippers offer their own interpretation of the disposition of the Vedas and the *Tēvāram* in relation to the deity in the procession. According to the Smārtas and the brahmin reciters of the Veda, the Vedas take "first place" as the primary scripture; their position at the head of the line reaffirms the supremacy of the Vedas as *śruti* (revealed literature), crucial to the proper performance of the ceremony, and the superiority of the brahmins as the top-ranking group in the caste hierarchy. Smārta worshippers see the *ōtuvār*s and the *Tēvāram* as a subsidiary element of the ceremonial complex, rightly placed at the end of the procession.[25] The Tamil Śaiva devotees explain the relative placement of the texts differently: the *ōtuvār*s walk at the end of the procession, since the hymns of the saints are the final and most accessible embodiment, in the form of mantras, of the essence of the Vedic mantras and of the Āgamas, which are the word of Śiva himself.[26] Even more significant is the fact that the Tirumuṟai is sung simultaneously with the Veda, an act that affirms their sectarian view that the *Tēvāram* hymns

[20] "tamiḻc colum vaṭacolun tāṇiḻaṟ cēra / ammalark koṉṟaiy aṇintav emmaṭikaḷ / acciṟupākkama tāṭci koṇṭārē."

[21] The following description of recitation patterns in such a procession is based on my observation of the Pradoṣa-Pūjā (Twilight Ceremony) procession at the Kapālīśvara temple, Mylapore, Madras, and the Ārudrā (Tiruvātirai) Festival procession at the Marundeeswarar temple in Tiruvāṉmiyūr in July 1978 and December-January 1979.

[22] See my discussion of this hymn in chapter 3 above.

[23] The *ōtuvār kōṣṭi* at the Mylapore temple, in July 1978, consisted of two singers.

[24] E.g., Appar IV.21 (Poem 98); a description of the Tiruvātirai festival in Tiruvārūr.

[25] Discussion with Smārta brahmin worshippers and Vaidika brahmin priests (*cāstirikaḷ*) at the Kapālīśvara temple, Madras, July 1978.

[26] See note 7 above.

are equal to the Vedas as scripture and mantra.[27] Again, the words of the Nāyaṉārs themselves are cited in support of this equation, which is very much a part of the Tamil Śaiva sectarian consciousness. The idea that the *Tēvāram* is a Veda (*maṟai*) is deliberately inculcated in the *ōtuvār*s themselves when they are being trained for their profession at the training schools run by Tamil Śaiva sectarian institutions connected with temples.[28] *Ōtuvār* trainees are taught to recite the *Tēvāram* through a process of memorization and repetition very similar to that of Vedic recitation. Since the teaching of musical compositions in India is normally an oral tradition, it is natural that the *Tēvāram* songs are taught orally. But the *ōtuvār* trainees are continually reminded that they are initiates, like students of the Veda, and that they are memorizing the Tamil Veda through the techniques of Vedic *adhyayana*.[29] The insistence on "Vedic" status, especially in such detail, is no doubt motivated in part by the desire of Tamil Śaivas to give their religion impeccable credentials as a full-fledged sect with a proper primary scripture. Rivalry with the Śrīvaiṣṇavas, whose teachers have been eminently successful in relating the Sanskrit-Vedic tradition to Tamil Vaiṣṇava doctrine and practice, may also have been a factor in this development. Ironically, the Tamil Śaivas only accept the Vedas as revealed scripture, without attaching fundamental doctrinal significance to them; as we have seen, the Āgamas and the Tirumuṟai take pride of place in this respect. Since the Tamil Vaiṣṇava theologians directly integrated the ideas of the Vedas and *smṛti*s with the songs of the Āḻvārs and the Sanskrit theology and philosophy of Rāmānuja, the non-brahmin as well as the brahmin members of the Śrīvaiṣṇava sect can di-

[27] Discussion with *ōtuvār*s and Tamil Śaiva devotees at the Kapālīśvara temple, July 1978. The simultaneity of the Vedic and *Tēvāram* singing was brought home to me in the process of recording the two performances on tape at the Pradoṣa Pūjā festival in July 1978. Having started out by recording the *ōtuvār*s at the rear of the procession, I moved on to the brahmins reciting the *Śatarudrīya* at the head of the line. While recording the latter, I could not hear the *Tēvāram* singing at the end of the long line of people; however, I could see that the *ōtuvār*s continued to sing even as I was listening to the brahmins.

[28] I visited the "Tēvāra Pāṭacālai" (school for *Tēvāram* singing) run by the Tarumapuram Ātīṉam near Māyavaram, Tanjore district, in July 1978 and observed the methods of teaching and learning used in the school. Vēlāyuta Mutaliyār, a retired *ōtuvār*, instructed fifteen boys, ranging from five to fourteen years in age, in memorizing and singing the Tirumuṟai.

[29] Not only the technique of instruction but also the patterns of *gurukulavāsa* ("living with the guru during the years of instruction") at the *Tēvāram* school were modeled on those of the Ātīṉam's school for Vedic study (*adhyayana*), which was situated next door to the *Tēvāram* school. Memorization and the oral nature of the hymns were emphasized, though the book containing the seven Tirumuṟais was always kept in front of the teacher. The boys memorized the words and the rhythmic and melodic patterns of two to three hymns per day. On Vedic recitation, consult Alain Daniélou's notes to his recording of Vedic recitation in Daniélou, *Vedic Recitation and Chant: The Music of India*, record no. 6, UNESCO collection, *A Musical Anthology of the Orient*, Kassel/Basel: Bärenreiter.

rectly relate their devotionalism with both the Vedas and the Tamil songs of their saints. The Tamil Śaiva situation is different, in that, though devotees can think of the Vedas and the Tirumuṟai as being equal in scriptural sanctity, they cannot emotionally identify with the Vedic *śruti* ("heard," primary scripture) literature, whose direct relevance to the unique sectarian scripture has not been clearly communicated to the average worshipper by the sectarian teachers.[30]

The Tamil Śaiva view of the performance of the Tirumuṟai gives us insight into the manifold function of these songs as the sacred literature of their sect. As the "Tamil Veda," the Tirumuṟai is the only formal part of Tamil temple worship and ritual that is of exclusive doctrinal significance to Tamil Śaivas as followers of the four poet-teachers. It is also the only ceremonial text that—for the reasons given above—draws from them the kind of emotional response that the Vedas inspire in the Tamil brahmins. At the same time, unlike the Sanskrit Veda—and more like the *smṛti* and *stotra* literature—the *Tēvāram* and *Tiruvācakam* are not bound to ritual functions or restricted to ritual specialists;[31] as song-offerings, they are directly available to Tamil Śaiva devotees as the means for their personal worship of Śiva. Further, the songs are looked upon not merely as mantras to be recited but as the literature of the saints' experience, to be experienced by all Tamil Śaiva devotees. The songs of the saints are freely accessible to all Tamil Śaivas: since the content of the hymns, as described above, has become the center of Tamil Śaiva experience, and since the structural contours of the language of the *Tēvāram* continue to remain functionally close to the literary and spoken idioms of the Tamils, the hymns are intelligible to the average Tamil even after thirteen centuries. To this day, devotees directly consult the words of the saints for guidance in various situations, and sing them when they seek personal inspi-

[30] In Śrīvaiṣṇava temple processions, the position of the Vedas and the hymns of the Āḻvārs is the reverse of the Śaiva case; here the singers of the hymns walk before the image of the deity, while the Veda reciters follow after. Śrīvaiṣṇavas see this as a symbolic representation of the *ubhayavedānta* ("two Vedas") doctrine. Although some Śrīvaiṣṇavas interpret the position of the Tamil hymns as indicating their priority in the hierarchy of texts, the Vedic *śruti* literature continues to play a central role in Śrīvaiṣṇava doctrine, ritual, and culture. On the recitation of the hymns of the Āḻvārs at the "festival of the recitation of the sacred texts" (*adhyayanotsava*) see Paul Younger, "Singing the Tamil Hymnbook in the Tradition of Rāmānuja: The *Adyayanotsava* Festival in Śrīraṅkam," *History of Religions* 20, no. 2 (February 1982): 272–93. In the Tamil Śaiva case, in the centuries of sectarian development after the Nāyaṉārs the Vedic literature progressively lost the direct affective value we see it as having in the poetry of the saints. If anything, in this tradition the hymns of the saints completely take over the symbolic value of the Veda. See the discussion in Ramanujan, *Hymns*, pp. 130–32.

[31] This is one of the ways in which Zvelebil distinguishes between the function of the Vedic and the Tamil Śaiva *bhakti* hymns in their respective cults. Zvelebil, *Smile of Murugan*, p. 201.

ration or comfort as well as devotional experience.[32] In this way the Tirumuṟai simultaneously functions as *śruti* and *smṛti*, mantra and *stotra*, classical and popular song, and ceremonial and personal scripture for the Tamil Śaivas, bringing together categories usually kept separate in Great Traditional Hinduism.[33]

The Singer of Hymns: Performance as Interpretation

The vividness and emotional appeal of the Tirumuṟai hymns and the direct access the Tamil Śaivas have to them have rendered learned commentaries and traditional interpretive devices a matter of interest mainly to Tamil Śaiva intellectuals. Yet there is a special tradition in which the songs are interpreted for all Tamil Śaiva devotees: this takes place in the performance of the songs by *ōtuvār*s.

According to Tamil Śaivas and scholars the institution of the *ōtuvār* is now in danger of extinction. Research in the musicological aspects of the *Tēvāram* has established that the musical tradition of the hymns—itself an eleventh-century reconstruction—has undergone major changes in the recent past.[34] The rapid and tremendous developments that took place in the courtly and authoritative tradition of South Indian classical music (Carnatic music) from the sixteenth to the nineteenth centuries have obviously had a great influence on the music of the *Tēvāram*, so much so that the *paṇ* tunes of the hymns have been irretrievably lost, having been replaced by Carnatic *rāga* scales.[35] In 1977 and 1978 I went on a pilgrimage to the *Tēvāram* temples, following the paths of the Nāyaṉārs and recording the singing of the *Tēvāram* hymns at these places.[36] I found a small but living tradition of *Tēvāram* performance by *ōtuvārs*: flourishing in popular shrine centers and *Tēvāram* temples such as Madurai and Ti-

[32] Notes are provided in modern printed editions of the *Tēvāram* regarding the efficacy of consulting, studying, and reciting specific *Tēvāram* hymns in specific situations in one's personal life: desire for marriage or children, a death in the family, bad health, financial loss. In this context, Tamil Śaivas use the *Tēvāram* very much as many Christians use the Bible. For some examples, see Veḷḷaivāraṇaṉ, *Paṉṉiru tirumuṟai varalāṟu*, preface, p. i.

[33] *Bhakti* songs continue to play this integrative role in South Indian culture. On the similar function of the devotional *kṛti* in Carnatic music today, see Peterson, "The *kṛti*."

[34] Consult the Proceedings of the *Paṇ* Research Conferences (1949–1968): Lē. Pa. Ka. Irāmanātaṉ Ceṭṭiyār, ed., *Paṇ ārāycciyum ataṉ muṭivukaḷiṉ tokuppum*, comp. M. Periyacāmit Tūraṉ (Madras: Tamiḻ Icaic Caṅkam, 1974). I attended the *Paṇ* Research Conference in Madras in December 1979.

[35] Note, however, that the *Tēvāram* hymns continue to be sung in a style that is different from that of Carnatic music.

[36] Among the major temples I visited were Kapālīśvarar (Madras), Marundeeswarar (Tiruvāṉmiyūr), Tiruvārūr, Cīrkāḻi, Ekāmranātha (Kanchipuram), Kuṃbheśvara (Kumbhakonam), Māyavaram, Vaittīśvaran Kōyil, Maturai (Mīṉākṣi-Cokkanātar), Brihadīśvara (Tanjore), and Tiruvaṇṇāmalai.

ruvārūr, barely sustained in more obscure shrines, and in Madras, an important center of Tamil culture, enthusiastically supported by large Tamil Śaiva audiences in public concerts organized by the *tamiḻ icai* (Tamil music) revival movement, itself a part of the larger Tamil revival movement in Tamilnadu.[37] The following account of the contemporary performance tradition is based on the observations made during my two trips.

The responsibility of the *ōtuvār*, the member of a caste of religious artists,[38] is to sing hymns from the Tirumuṟai during daily rituals and ceremonial occasions at the temple. The typical *ōtuvār* is recruited for the job as a young boy of seven or eight and apprenticed under a teacher at one of the Tamil Śaiva *maṭam* centers.[39] In his years at the *tēvāra pāṭacālai* (*Tēvāram* school) the boy memorizes the hymns of the *Tēvāram* and *Tiruvācakam* and selections from the other Tirumuṟai books, and learns the techniques of musical performance.

Today, the *ōtuvār* in the Tamil Śiva temple stands just outside the *garbhagṛha* (inner sanctum) of the temple during the two or three daily *pūjā* rituals performed by the brahmin priests (*arccakar*, *kurukkaḷ*).[40] At the end of the (sixteen) ceremonial honors (*ṣoḍaśopacāra*) extended to the deity during the *pūjā*,[41] the *ōtuvār*, in accordance with the injunction of the Āgamic ritual manuals, which states: "Then, following the ceremony, there should be singing in the Dravida language,"[42] sings two or more selections from the Tirumuṟai texts. There is a convention, of uncertain date, that at least on especially auspicious days the *ōtuvār* should sing verses from the *Pañcapurāṇam* ("The five poems"), which consists of the *Tēvāram*, *Tiruvācakam*, *Tiruvicaippā*, *Tiruppallāṇṭu* (from Book XI of the Tirumuṟai), and *Periya purāṇam*.[43] Normally, even in this special performance pride of place is given to the *Tēvāram* and *Tiruvācakam*. The *Tēvāram* singing of the *ōtuvār* is, as we have seen, part of temple ritual, but it is not tied to ritual contexts alone, nor is it prescribed that a specific song be sung on a specific day.[44] In the freedom of choice, the *ōtuvār* takes

[37] See Chapter 3, note 73 above. The Tamiḻ Icaic Caṅkam is the nucleus of the "Tamil music" movement.

[38] It is not clear whether the *ōtuvār*s are a separate subcaste among Tamil Śaivas. Boys from various subcastes train to become *ōtuvār*s. Fuller (*Servants of the Goddess*, p. 38) says that *ōtuvār*s belong to the Veḷḷāḷar or Śaiva Piḷḷai (Vellala) caste.

[39] The Tarumapuram class I observed was typical in these respects.

[40] On the hierarchical structure of this arrangement, see Fuller, *Servants of the Goddess*, pp. 38–39, 47–48.

[41] On these ceremonial honors, see ibid., pp. 12–14.

[42] Quoted in Dorai Rangaswami, *Religion and Philosophy*, 1: 4.

[43] The *Tiruvicaippā* and *Tiruppallāṇṭu* are tenth- and eleventh-century hymns included in Tirumuṟai IX. Today, as always, the *Tēvāram* and *Tiruvācakam* selections continue to be the most popular and well-known pieces.

[44] However, hymns associated with specific ritual occasions and events in the saints' lives are sung at the appropriate times.

the first step toward freedom of interpretation. The ancient Tamil scale-types (*paṇ*) were associated with particular times of day and particular moods; when the classical *paṇ* modal system was strictly followed, the choice of hymns must have been guided by the need for singing in the appropriate *paṇ*.[45] Within recent memory, however, the only restriction on the selection of *patikam*s has been that the *ōtuvār* should sing at least one *Tēvāram* verse dedicated to Śiva at the particular temple where the performance takes place. Once the *ōtuvār* has chosen the hymns, he has a choice of styles in which to sing his selections, a choice that, as we shall see below, has interpretive implications.

In singing the *Tēvāram*, the singer may select two or more verses from a hymn and render them in a set tune developed from a particular *rāga* scale and regulated by a cycle of beats called *tāla*, sometimes keeping time with hand-cymbals (*tāḷam*).[46] This rendering is done in a simple, straightforward manner. The *ōtuvār* may attempt a few original grace notes, ornaments, and flourishes, but the basic melody is simple, and the melodic pattern itself has been fixed by tradition and learned by rote.[47] Most devotees know the tunes of the most popular hymns. However, the *ōtuvār*s also perform the hymns in a sophisticated, free-form, individualized singing style called the *viruttam* or *cuttāṅkam* style; the devotee's appreciation of the *ōtuvār* as a specialist in *Tēvāram* singing rests largely on the singer's ability to perform in the *viruttam* style. Appar's hymns in the Tiruviruttam, Tirunēricai, and Tāṇṭakam genres (based on the *viruttam*, *nēricai*, and *tāṇṭakam* meters, respectively) are always sung in the *viruttam* style, in *rāga*s assigned to each genre (rather than to each hymn).[48] It is not clear whether the option of singing all of the *Tēvāram* hymns in the *viruttam* style is an ancient practice or a more recent application of the Tiruviruttam and Tāṇṭakam performance style to the entire corpus.[49] Whatever the case may be, the *viruttam* style itself is considered to have ancient connections with the hymns of the saints, and it is known today as the style that is truly characteristic of *Tēvāram* singing. The uniqueness of both styles of *Tēvāram* singing in their traditional form is illuminated when we consider them in relation to the style of rendering classical songs

[45] Particular *paṇ*s were also associated with particular types and tunings of the *yāḻ*. Campantar mentions the time of day in relation to the *paṇ* in some of his hymns.

[46] The nature of rhythm in the hymns is discussed below in this chapter.

[47] Typical of the oral tradition of learning songs in Indian music. There is no written notation for the *Tēvāram*, as has been developed for Carnatic song-texts in the last few centuries.

[48] According to the *Tirumuṟaikaṇṭa purāṇam* (39), the Tirunēricai and Tiruviruttam songs are to be sung in the *paṇ* Kolli. No *paṇ* is specified for the Tāṇṭakam genre.

[49] Interview with Lalgudi Swaminathan, Ōtuvār at the Kapālīśvara temple, Mylapore, Madras, July 1978.

in Carnatic music, and the influence that the two traditions have had upon each other.

Rāga (melodic framework) and *tāla* (beat cycle) are standard features of songs in the ancient musical system of India.[50] More precisely defined, "A rāga is not a tune, nor is it a 'modal' scale, but rather a continuum with scale and tune as its extremes. Many rāgas can share the same intervallic structure, that is, the same scale type . . . ; at the same time any number of compositions or improvisations can be in the same rāga."[51] *Tāla* "is not simply rhythm; rather, in the general and abstract sense a tāla is a fixed and cyclically repeated time-span for music, articulated into segments by beats of the hand or a percussion idiophone."[52] The *rāga* tunes in which the *ōtuvār*s sing the hymns can be seen as contemporary "equivalents" of the ancient *paṇ*s, which were Tamil variants of the pan-Indian *rāga* concept, but the use of *tāla*, a fixed beat cycle on the model of Carnatic music, is a departure from the original conception of the rhythmic aspect of the hymns. In studying the metrical and musical aspects of the *Tēvāram* songs, we find a critical difference in the way in which text, tune, and rhythm are related in the Carnatic song and the *Tēvāram patikam*. Whereas in the Carnatic song, a metrical or non-metrical text is "set" to a *rāga* tune and fit into one of a few standardized cyclical beat patterns (*tālas*),[53] the metrical pattern of the *Tēvāram patikam* itself acted as the rhythmic framework of the hymn; equally important, this metrical pattern also indicated the tune, the melodic mold, in which the line of text would be sung. This coincidence of patterns of meter, tune, and beat in the *patikam* was called *kaṭṭaḷai* (rule).[54] In the musical (*paṇmuṟai*) systematization of the *patikams*, the hymns were grouped, first according to their *paṇ* and, under each *paṇ*, according to *kaṭṭaḷai*-pattern. For instance, the *Tirumuṟaikaṇṭa purāṇam* points out that hymns 1–22 in Book I of the *Tēvāram* are sung in the *paṇ* Naṭṭapāṭai,

[50] For definitions of *rāga*, *tāla*, and other features of Indian music, consult essays I ("The region, its music and music history," pp. 69–91) and II ("Theory and practice of classical music," pp. 91–141) by Harold S. Powers on the music of India, under the entry "India, subcontinent of," in *The New Grove Dictionary of Music and Musicians*, edited by Stanley Sadie (London: Macmillan, 1980), 9: 69–141.

[51] Powers, essay II, in *New Grove Dictionary*, 9: 98.

[52] Ibid., 9: 118.

[53] See Peterson, "The *kṛti*," and Indira V. Peterson, "Sanskrit in Carnatic Music: The Songs of Muttusvāmi Dīkṣita," *Indo-Iranian Journal* 29 (1986): 183–99.

[54] Scholars of Tamil literature and music have a poor understanding of *kaṭṭaḷai*. Some assert that it is nothing more than a metrical pattern; others suggest that it is a pattern of beats independent of the meter of the poem Irāmanātaṉ Ceṭṭiyar, ed., *Paṇ ārāycciyum*, pp. 114ff.). Powers, essay I, in *New Grove Dictionary*, 9: 75, defines *kaṭṭaḷai* more precisely: "they [the *Tēvāram* hymns] are grouped according to melodic types called *paṇ* and specific times called *kaṭṭaḷai* (mould)." The rhythmic aspect of *kaṭṭaḷai* needs to be clarified. See my suggestions below.

and have eight *kaṭṭaḷais*.[55] This is just another way of saying that these hymns in a particular *paṇ* are classified under eight set "tunes" that coincide with eight distinct beat patterns. To this day, *ōtuvār*s memorize the hymn tunes with the aid of *kaṭṭaḷai* patterns, and till recently, hand-cymbals (*tāḷam*) were used to mark out *kaṭṭaḷai* beat patterns, and not autonomous *tāla* beat cycles.[56]

The *viruttam* style of singing the *Tēvāram* presents a contrast to the *kaṭṭaḷai*-based style I have just described. The improvisatory technique of *viruttam* singing is not actually taught to *ōtuvār* trainees; throughout their student career *ōtuvār*s listen to creative *viruttam* performances of the hymns by older *ōtuvār*s, until they feel ready to perform on their own. The *viruttam* performance is entirely improvisatory and "free" in terms of melodic form; though the verse is sung in a specific *paṇ* or *rāga*, there is no fixed tune or melodic pattern to which the text is "set." The *rāga* functions as no more than a skeletal outline or framework of contours and limits for melodic exploration. In these respects, this technique resembles a type of improvisatory singing that is characteristic of all *rāga* music: the *ālāpana* or free-form exposition of a *rāga*.[57] There is also a significant difference. The *ālāpana* technique of South Indian classical music is concerned with melody alone, whereas the effect of the *Tēvāram* style depends on the ways in which the "mold" of rhythm, tune, and text is broken. In *virutta*m singing, there is much improvised ornamentation and asymmetrical repetition of melodic and textual phrases. There is no regular rhythm; the boundaries of *tāla* and meter are completely ignored.[58] The textual line is violated in many ways. The *ōtuvār* may repeat one line of the verse many times and quickly glide over others. He may dwell on a single word; he may move back and forth among widely separated lines of the text, so that they fall out of their original sequence and rearrange themselves in new ways. A single stanza from a *patikam* can

[55] *Tirumuṟaikaṇṭa purāṇam*, verses 33–43. Verse 35: "coṉ ṉaṭṭapāṭaikkut tokaiy eṭṭuk kaṭṭaḷaiyām."

[56] In performances of Carnatic music, singers use hand-cymbals only when they sing Tamil devotional hymns.

[57] On *ālāpana* or *ālāp*, the improvisatory technique through which a *rāga* is elaborated, see Powers, essay II, in *New Grove Dictionary*, 9: 107ff. *Ālāpana* is basically "improvisation with the elements of a *rāga* and within its structural framework," creatively using melodic motifs and "rising and falling phrase types" (p. 107).

[58] *Ālāpana* refers only to the exposition of *rāga* with no text or beat component. In both South and North Indian music, there are various types of melodic and rhythmic improvisation in the context of a composition (*nibaddha*, lit., dependent), and therefore regulated by *tāla* (e.g., *pallavi* and *niraval* techniques in Carnatic music). Thus the free textual-melodic improvisations of the *ōtuvār* fall midway between the canonical categories of "dependent" and "independent" melodic improvisation.

thus be elaborated for as long as ten or fifteen minutes.[59] The entire performance is characterized by freedom of expression and discursiveness enlivened by a sense of drama.

The specific function of improvisation in *Tēvāram* singing must be examined in the context of the history and associations of the word *viruttam* in Tamil poetry. *Viruttam* is the Tamil form of Sanskrit *vṛtta*, a term used in Sanskrit for meter in general and especially for meters based on the number of syllables in a line (*akṣara* or "syllabic" meters), as opposed to those based on the duration of syllables in the line ("moric" meters, measured in *mātrā* or syllabic instants).[60] In Tamil poetry the term *viruttam* was first used to designate a variety of meters that developed out of earlier classical meters such as *kali* and *akaval*.[61] The new meters, though basically governed by the rules of classical Tamil prosody, were also influenced by Sanskrit prosodic principles.[62] The Nāyaṉārs and Āḻvār poets were the first Tamil poets to make extensive use of these so-called Viruttam or supplementary meters.[63] From the tenth century on, the term *viruttam* has been specifically applied to a particular type of meter that became the standard vehicle for narrative poetry, especially epics and Purāṇas, in Tamil.[64] Thus historically the Tamil word *viruttam*, when applied to a metrical form, has been associated with Sanskrit meter and Sanskrit narrative and lyric poetic genres (*kāvya*) as well as with Tamil devotional hymns.

To understand the application of the term *viruttam* to a style of singing, we must turn to musical performance styles in the musical- and dance-drama traditions of South India, in which epic and mythological plots are retold or enacted; to folk as well as classical forms, ranging from the stylized Yakṣagāna of Karnataka to the Terukkūttu "street drama" of Tamilnadu.[65] Although these dramatic musical traditions differ from each

[59] An elderly afficionado of *Tēvāram* singing told me that he had heard *ōtuvār*s elaborate a verse for as long as half an hour.

[60] For definitions of these meters in Sanskrit poetry, see V. S. Apte, *The Practical Sanskrit-English Dictionary*, 3rd ed., rev. and enl. (Delhi: Motilal Banarsidass, 1965), app. I (Sanskrit Prosody).

[61] Kamil Zvelebil, *Tamil Literature*, in *A History of Indian Literature*, ed. Jan Gonda, vol. X, fasc. 1 (Wiesbaden: Otto Harrassowitz, 1974), p. 97.

[62] Ibid., pp. 101, 105, 108–19. See Chapter 5 below.

[63] A. Chidambaranatha Chettiar, *Advanced Studies in Tamil Prosody* (Annamalainagar: Annamalai University, 1977), pp. 115–21.

[64] E.g., the *Periya purāṇam* and Kampaṉ's (thirteenth century?) *Irāmāvatāram*.

[65] Other genres include the Kuṭiyāṭṭam of Kerala, the Telugu-Tamil Bhāgavatameḷa, and the Tamil Nāṭakak Kīrttaṉai. On these types of theater, see Kapila Vatsyayan, *Traditional Indian Theater: Multiple Streams* (New Delhi: National Book Trust, 1980) and Balwant Gargi, *Folk Theater of India* (Seattle: University of Washington Press, 1966).

other in important ways, they are similar in their employment of both fixed and "free" recitative and musical styles in the rendering of the song-texts that accompany the dance and mime.[66] Songs that are replete with *tāla* and fixed melodic patterns alternate with lyric stanzas that are sung or recited, either entirely in free form—i.e., without observing rhythmic boundaries—or at least in a style sharply differentiated in rhythm and structure from the other songs. In these regional dramatic traditions, both the stanzaic form and the style in which such stanzas are sung is known as *viruttam*. According to Balwant Gargi, the *viruttam* form is used in these dramatic genres primarily for narration.[67] His description of the occurrence of the *viruttam* style in the Terukkūttu ("Street drama") of Tamilnadu is representative: "The chanting (*virutham*) precedes every song. . . . The *virutham* is usually set in the same *rāga* as the song and leads to the next situation in the play. The singer chants the words to underline the meaning, sums up the situation, and makes the audience understand clearly the progress of the story. This breaks the monotony of the singing."[68] Also, these *viruthams* are "verses without rhythmic beats, half chanting, half singing, like the *alaap* [Carnatic *ālāpana*] of a classical melody."[69] The alternation of snappy, highly structured songs with slower, unstructured melodic performance that unfolds "in slow motion, like the rising of smoke"[70]—or, as one writer suggests in explaining the name of one of Appar's hymn-types (Nēricai), "like the continuous and flowing humming of bees"[71]—makes for a sharp contrast in texture, a change of pace, a momentary pause in the action. In the folk theater, it is the narrative associations of the *viruttam* meter (Sanskrit *vṛtta*, *itivṛtta*, *vṛttānta* all mean event, narration) that predominate, and the *viruttam* portions of the performance are used mainly for narrative purposes. Again, though the *viruttam* verses are performed at a slower tempo, in the context of the play they function as straightforward, highly compressed summaries of "events" and information, turning our attention to the themes and actions, which are then elaborated and interpreted in a leisurely manner in the songs that follow. This stylistic contrast in the musical drama is probably traceable to the influence of the Sanskrit *Gītagovinda* (twelfth century), the earliest known dramatic-musical poem, in which *kāvya*-style lyric stanzas are placed at the beginning of cycles of

[66] See Gargi, *Folk Theater*, chs. 8, 9.
[67] Ibid., pp. 158–59.
[68] Ibid., p. 136.
[69] Ibid.
[70] Ibid.
[71] Veḷḷaivāraṇaṉ, *Paṉṉiru tirumuṟai varalāṟu*, p. 410.

songs composed in musical "moric" meters and set to *rāgas*.[72] In the *Gītagovinda* the *kāvya* verses "function as independent grammatical and esthetic entities. Most of them are narrative verses identifying the singer of a song or elaborating its context."[73]

Which of the characteristics and functions of the *viruttam* style are featured in the *ōtuvār*'s performance? The stanza sung in *viruttam* style certainly creates a change in the tempo and texture of the *Tēvāram* performance. Yet, although a verse in this free style does function as a pause, it rarely has narrative connotations. The *ōtuvār* does not compress or summarize a body of information in the *viruttam*; instead, he explores and expands the stanzaic microcosm. Far from urging us to move on to the next song, he invites us to dwell on, to savor, every word and phrase in the *viruttam* text. The nonlinear elaboration of the text, with its complex repetitions, disposes words and meanings in ever-changing patterns, like fragments of colored glass in a kaleidoscope. In these respects the *viruttam* verse in a *Tēvāram* performance is like the few *kāvya* verses in the *Gītagovinda* which are "relatively independent of the story and serve primarily to reinforce the esthetic atmosphere of the poem. Such verses may be recalled and enjoyed like miniature paintings from an album."[74]

In the context of the *Tēvāram*, the *viruttam* style is more closely related to the religious *stotra* verse in Sanskrit than to the epic or narrative stanza. This is borne out in the performance tradition of Carnatic music today, in which the hymns of the *Tēvāram* and *Tiruvācakam* and Sanskrit *stotra* stanzas (called *culokam*, from Sanskrit *śloka*, "a verse") are the only lyric texts that are performed without *tāla*, in the elaborate *viruttam* style. In *Tēvāram* performances, the *viruttam* style has devotional and aesthetic functions; it has a deeply reflective, expansive, trance-inducing quality, and it is an essentially interpretive style.

My experience of several *viruttam*-style performances of the *patikam*s by *ōtuvār*s leads me to believe that the *ōtuvār*'s selection, his repetitions and rearrangements of the text, his elaboration and ornamentation of particular lines and phrases in text and melody, all constitute his interpretation of the text—in his role of religious professional and artist—and help reveal particular aspects and nuances of the hymn to his audience of devotees. In the context of the *pūjā* ritual, with its constraints of time and hierarchy, the *ōtuvār*'s *viruttam* singing tends to be prefunctory. In festival processions, the *ōtuvār kōṣṭi* (the chorus of *ōtuvār*s) parallels the large group of brahmins reciting the Veda at the head of the procession and,

[72] See Barbara Stoler Miller, *Love Song of the Dark Lord: Jayadeva's Gītagovinda* (New York: Columbia University Press, 1977).

[73] Miller, *Love Song*, introd., p. 9.

[74] Ibid.

like them, contributes to the general din and spectacle that characterize such events. Here the *ōtuvārs* sing in groups of two or more, sometimes in unison, sometimes adopting an antiphonal style; the rhythmically and melodically bound song form is more suitable than the *viruttam* for this group singing. It is in "public" performances of the *Tēvāram*, outside of the context of *pūjā*, that the *viruttam* style comes into its own. Like the pan-Indian Paurāṇika who narrates and interprets stories from the sacred epics and Purāṇas in public places, and especially in the temple, the *ōtuvār* in Tamil Śiva temples regularly sings the *Tēvāram* hymns in the capacity of a specialist-performer of sacred texts. In twentieth-century practice, in the more prosperous and prominent Śiva temples in Tamilnadu, the *ōtuvār* may be found seated, of an evening, on a porch (*maṇṭapam*) or courtyard of the temple, giving a leisurely rendering of hymn texts, mainly in the *viruttam* style.[75] In such a performance the *ōtuvār*, like the Purāṇa narrator (Paurāṇika) or temple dancer, becomes a truly creative religious artist.

An Ōtuvār Performance

To give an idea of the nature of the *ōtuvār*'s performance of the *Tēvāram* hymns, a brief description and analysis follows of a performance of Ñāṉacampanta Ōtuvār of the Caṭṭaiṉātar Śiva temple at Cīrkāḻi, birthplace of the Nāyaṉār Campantar, and shrine to which the saint dedicated over seventy hymns. With the singer's permission, I recorded this informal performance at the Cīrkāḻi temple in July 1978. Ñāṉacampanta Ōtuvār (see illus. 14) had finished his ritual duties for the morning *pūjā* and was seated on the temple porch, singing hymns from the *Tēvāram*, as some devotees casually strolled by, and others gathered around him to listen. Of the ten selections he sang over a forty-minute period, four were in the *viruttam* style.

In my translation of Ñāṉacampanta Ōtuvār's *viruttam* selections, given below, I have marked and underlined phrases and lines that the performer highlighted through repetition, musical ornamentation, and other stylistic strategies. For one selection, Appar VI.301.1 ("vāṉavaṉ kāṇ"), I have given a detailed analysis of performance style and emphases. Square brackets indicate particular emphasis, which involves a great deal of repetition and musical ornamentation, and connections not found in the text. The italicized lines and phrases were repeated and ornamented as units.

[75] These texts consist of the *Tēvāram*, *Tiruvācakam*, and the *Tiruppukaḻ* of the fifteenth-century Murukaṉ devotee Aruṇakirinātar.

1.
If you ask:
"What is the town
of him who holds the battle-axe
in his hand?" the answer is:
"Kaḻumalam, where flags flutter
on the gateways of tall mansions,
this great town
where herons gather in canals in the fields,
and bees, drunk on honey from their beloveds' lips,
cling to every flowering palm."
Appar IV.83.1[76]

2.
[*This Tōṇipuram,*]
beautiful with [*enduring life,*
and *grandeur*, and *justice*,]
[*once floated*]
on the rising waves of the cosmic flood—
The flower-[feet of Kaḻumalam's Lord]
who burned the triple city with his arrow
rule us forever.
Appar IV.82.6[77]

3a.
[*My Lord who is ambrosia to me*,]
the Lord who is dear to all who seek him,
he who holds fire in his hand,
skullbearer who flayed the huge killer elephant,]
god with the poison-stained throat,
is the great god who lives
in Piramapuram
of fragrant groves.
Campantar II.176.1[78]

[76] The repeated phrases are as follows: *maṭaivāyk kurukiṉam*, "herons in canals in the fields"; *pāḷai piritoṟum*, "on every flowering palm"; *vaṇṭiṉaṅkaḷ peṭaivāy matuvuṇṭu*, "bees, drunk on honey from their beloved's lips"; *pērātirukkum*, "cling"; *perum patiyē*, "great town."

[77] Repeated phrases: *it tōṇipuram*, "this Tōnipuram"; *nilaiyum perumaiyum nītiyum*, "enduring life, and grandeur, and justice"; *cāla aḻakum uṭaittāy*, "having much beauty [beautiful]"; *aṉṟu mitanta*, "once floated"; *nantammai āḷvaṉavē*, "rule us."

[78] Repeated phrases: *empirāṉ eṉakkamutam āvāṉum*, "my Lord who is ambrosia to me"; *taṉṉaṭaintār tampirāṉ, "the Lord who is dear to all who seek him"; kampamā kariy uritta kāpāli*, "skullbearer who flayed the huge killer elephant."

3b.
He who gives blessings to his devotees,
the Lord who is the ultimate truth,
the king who dwells in stone-walled Piramapuram—
[*Campantaṉ*] once attained him.
[*Those who know these ten verses*] of the poet
are *blessed*,
and [*will have riches*,]
and [*enjoyment of every kind*.]
Campantar II.176.11[79]

In the following more detailed analysis of Appar VI.301.1 ("vāṉavaṉ kāṇ" [Poem 20], a Tāṇṭakam verse dedicated to the shrine at Civapuram), three versions are given: (a) a free translation, (b) a literal translation, with text; and (c) a transcription, with translation, of the rendering by Ñāṉacampanta Ōtuvār in July 1978. There are minor differences between (b) and (c) in the Tamil; these occur because the Tamil in (b) follows the printed text, and the Tamil in (c) follows the rendering I recorded by Ñāṉacampanta Ōtuvār. Punctuation in the Tamil text is my own. Roman numerals indicate the beginning of clauses or sentences in the Tamil text, most of which cross the boundary of the Tamil metrical "line." Arabic numerals in (b) indicate the beginning of "lines" in the four-line stanza.

4A. FREE TRANSLATION

I
See the god!

II
See him who is higher than the gods!

III
[See him who is Sanskrit of the North
and southern Tamil and the four Vedas!]

IV
See him who bathes in milk and ghee,

V VI
see the Lord, see him who dances, holding fire,
in the wilderness of the burning-ground,

[79] Repeated phrases: *campantaṉ*, "Campantaṉ"; *moḻipattum ivai vallār*, "those who know these ten verses"; *poṉṉaṭaintār*, "will have riches"; *pōkaṅkaḷ palav aṭaintār*, "will have enjoyment of every kind"; *puṇṇiyarē*, "they are blessed."

VII
see him who blessed the hunter-saint!

VIII
[See him who wells up as honey
in the heart-lotus of his lovers!]

IX
[See him who has the unattainable treasure!]

X XI
[See Śiva!] See [him who is our treasure
here in Civapuram!]

4B. TEXT AND LITERAL TRANSLATION

I II
1 vāṉavaṉ kāṇ; vāṉavarkku mēlāṉāṉ kāṇ;
The sky-dweller see; him gods-higher-than-who-is, see;

III
vaṭamoḻiyun teṉṟamiḻu maṟaika ṇāṉkum
the northern language, southern Tamil and the Vedas four,
IV
2 āṉavaṉ kāṇ; āṉaintum āṭināṉ kāṇ;
him-who-is, see; in the five (products) of the cow, who bathes, see

V VI
aiyaṉ kāṇ; kaiyil aṉalēnti āṭum
the Lord, see; in-hand fire-holding, who dances,

VII
3 kāṉavaṉ kāṇ; kāṉavaṉukk aruḷ ceytāṉ kāṇ;
him of the burning-ground wild, see; to the hunter, who granted grace, him see;

VIII
karutuvār itayattuk kamalatt' ūṟum
those who love (him), in their heart-lotuses welling up as

IX
4 tēṉavaṉ kāṇ; ceṉṟaṭaiyāc celvaṉṟāṉ kāṇ;
honey, him see; the unattainable treasure who holds, him see;

X XI
civaṉ avaṉ kāṇ; civapuratteñ celvaṉṟāṉē
Śiva, him see; in Civapuram, him who is our treasure, that very one.

4C. TRANSCRIPTION

I. vāṉavaṉ kāṇ. See the god.

II. vāṉavarkku mēlāṉāṉ kāṇ. See him who is higher than the gods.

III. vaṭamoḻiyun teṉ ṟamiḻu maṟaika ṇāṉkum āṉavaṉ kāṇ. See him who is Sanskrit of the North and southern Tamil and the four Vedas.

III. vaṭamoḻiyun teṉ . . . nāṉkum āṉavaṉ kāṇ. See him who is Sanskrit . . . and the four Vedas.

IV. āṉaintum āṭiṉāṉ kāṇ. See him who bathes in milk and ghee.

V. and VI. aiyaṉ kāṇ; kaiyil aṉal ēnti āṭum kāṉavaṉ kāṇ. See the Lord. See him who dances, holding fire, in the wilderness of the burning-ground.

VII. kāṉavaṉukk aruḷ ceytāṉ kāṇ. See him who blessed the hunter-saint.

VIIIa. karutuvār . . . Of his lovers, . . .

VIIIb. itayattu . . . in the heart, . . .

VIIIc. kamalattu ūṟum tēṉavaṉ kāṇ . . . in the lotus, who wells up as honey, him see.

VIII. karutuvār itayattuk kamalatt' ūṟum tēṉavaṉ kāṇ. See him who, in the heart-lotus of his lovers, wells up as honey.

IX. ceṉṟu aṭaiyāc celvaṉṟāṉ kāṇ. See him who has the unattainable treasure.

IX. ceṉṟu aṭaiyāc celvaṉṟāṉ kāṇ. See him who has the unattainable treasure.

X. civaṉ avaṉ kāṇ. See Śiva.

XI. civapurattu eñ celvaṉṟāṉē. See him who is our treasure here in Civapuram.

IX. ceṉṟu aṭaiyāc celvaṉṟāṉ kāṇ. See him who has the unattainable treasure.

XI. civapurattu eñ celvaṉṟāṉē. See him who is our treasure here in Civapuram.

III. vaṭamoḻiyun teṉṟamiḻu maṟaika ṇāṉkum āṉavaṉ kāṇ. See him who is Sanskrit of the North and southern Tamil and the four Vedas.

XI. civapurattu eñ celvaṉṟāṉē. See him who is our treasure here in Civapuram.

VIII. karutuvār itayattuk kamalatt' ūṟum tēṉavaṉ kāṇ. See him in the heart-lotus of his lovers, wells up as honey.

IX. ceṉṟu aṭaiyāc celvaṉṟāṉ kāṇ. See him who has the unattainable treasure.

X. civaṉ avaṉ kāṇ. See Śiva.

XI. civapurattu eñ celvaṉṟāṉē. See him who is our treasure here in Civapuram, that very one.

In each of their hymns, the three poet-saints of the *Tēvāram* focus on particular aspects of the range of Tamil Śaiva religious themes that are articulated in their poetry. In his performance the *ōtuvār* brings out the nuances of these selected images. In different selections, Ñāṉacampanta Ōtuvār dwelt upon and highlighted different themes from the hymns: the grace of Śiva ("the flower-feet"; selection 2); the heroic deeds of Śiva ("the skullbearer who flayed the huge killer elephant," 3a); local myths ("This Tōṇipuram . . . once floated on the . . . cosmic flood," 2); *akam* landscapes ("where herons gather in canals in the fields," 1). Of all the pieces that he rendered in the *viruttam* style, the *ōtuvār* performed Appar's "vāṉavaṉ kāṇ" (selection 4) with the highest degree of stylistic elaboration. "Vāṉavaṉ kāṇ" is the first verse of a patikam in the long Tamil *tāṇṭakam* meter, of which Appar was one of the earliest and best exponents; hymns in this meter are usually sung in the *viruttam* style.[80] As is typical of Appar's Tāṇṭakam verses, "vāṉavaṉ kāṇ" consists of a series of relatively short sentences. The verse also contains a concentration of major *Tēvāram* themes. In his rendering of this hymn, through such strategies as the repetition of entire phrases, melodic ornamentation, rhythm changes, and alteration of the sequence of "lines," Ñāṉacampanta Ōtuvār chose to highlight four themes: those embodied in lines III, VIII, IX, and XI in the transcription. What motivated the particular emphases in this performance? The creative fantasy of the artist? The demands of an ancient musical tradition and style? A devotee's response to the saint's lyrics? Though each of these factors contributed to the singer's selection, the overarching consideration was his task, as a religious artist, of fulfilling the expectations of his religious community and tradition.

As I listened to Ñāṉacampanta Ōtuvār and others like him, in temples and homes and concert halls, the role of the *ōtuvār* in the transmission of the meanings of the *Tēvāram* hymns became increasingly clear to me. In the singer's unique rendering of such songs as "vāṉavaṉ kāṇ," I saw a subtle balance between artistic virtuosity and the spirit of *bhakti*; between the creative artist's freedom of interpretation and the religious specialist's veneration of the intended meanings in the saint's song. Patterns of audience response, the devotee's perceptions of the *ōtuvār*'s singing, and the *ōtuvār*'s own view of it all contribute to our understanding of the specialist's performance.

[80] See my discussion of meter in the *Tēvāram* hymns in Chapter 5 below.

He who can recite these ten verses
and listen to them
will wipe his life clean of sorrow.
Campantar I.105.11

Like the *Rāmāyaṇa* and other popular sacred texts of Hinduism, the *Tēvāram* hymns command from their "readers" absolute faith in the power and efficacy of the text as an instrument of devotion. The signature verses of the Tamil hymns are particularly influential in that their description of the transformative, experiential power of the hymns is ascribed to the saints themselves and not to the anonymous "tradition."[81] Although no canonical distinction is made between the devotee's recitation of the *Tēvāram* in private worship and his listening to the hymns when performed by *ōtuvār*s in ritual and informal contexts, there is a felt difference in the two experiences.

As the performer of a sacred text, especially of a "Veda," the *ōtuvār* takes great pains to enunciate clearly and to render faithfully the words of the Nāyaṉārs. Yet unlike the non-specialist devotee, the religious artist feels free, indeed compelled, to rearrange the text and to render it with varying highlights in every performance. The *ōtuvār*s are largely unacquainted with the intricacies of Tamil Śaiva theological and philosophical texts. They confine their expertise to an avowedly nonintellectual, artistic appreciation and interpretation of the Tirumuṟai, the primary texts of the tradition. As one *ōtuvār* put it, "I am not a scholar; all I know are the words of the saints."[82] What do the *ōtuvār*s see as their primary function? In the words of Lalgudi Swaminathan, the *ōtuvār* of Kapālīśvara temple in Madras, "To render faithfully the words of the saints; to serve at the *pūjā* ritual."[83] Whether he sings the hymns in pre-set melodies and rhythms or in the freer *viruttam* style, the *ōtuvār* sees his performance as being "faithful to the words of the saints," and himself as the vehicle or medium for those words. The audience of devotees shares in this view.

Despite the efforts of such organizations as the Tamiḻ Icai Caṅkam to play up the merits of *Tēvāram* singing as a musical genre worthy of the "secular" concert stage, the majority of listeners at a Tirumuṟai public concert tend to be the same devout Tamil Śaivas who listen to the *ōtuvār*

[81] Some scholars are of the opinion that the *phalaśruti* verses in the *Tēvāram* hymns were not written by the saints themselves, but added later by the "tradition." Yet the final verses in Campantar's and Cuntarar's poems seem too full of enigmatic autobiographical details, and too distinctive in style, to be attributed to others. In any case, the "tradition" views the words as the saints' own.

[82] Ñāṉacampanta Ōtuvār, Caṭṭaināṭar temple, Cīrkāḻi. Personal interview, July 1978.

[83] Personal interview, July 1978.

at the temple.[84] In contrast with the classical (Carnatic) concert, there are no purely musical high points in the *Tēvāram* concert. Just as the *Tēvāram* singer's embellishments and emphases call attention to particular nuances of religious meaning in the text, his audience responds to evocative, moving words and passages with the sort of noises of appreciation and excitement largely reserved for musically exciting moments in the Carnatic concert. The contrast is further heightened in the context of the current linguistic situation in Carnatic music in Tamilnadu, where the majority of the audience does not understand Telugu, the principal language of the Carnatic song repertoire, and therefore cannot respond to shades of meaning and poetic excellence in the lyrics.[85]

The Tamil Śaiva audience perceives the *ōtuvār* as a medium, in a certain sense, a mediator between the text and itself, rather than as a virtuoso artist. It responds to the performance, rather than to the performer. Listeners more often speak of "a moving rendering" than of "a great singer." In such a view, the *ōtuvār* is seen as a "good" performer when the audience feels that, through creative selection and foregrounding as well as through a "moving" rendering, he has revealed hidden meanings and subtle beauties in the saints' hymns that are by reputation beautiful and rich in devotional themes. Nevertheless, the fact remains that, even as my own response to Appar's "vāṉavaṉ kāṇ" will forever be associated with Ñāṉacampanta Ōtuvār's moving performance of that verse one summer morning in Cīrkāḻi, the unique interpretations of particular hymns by individual singers surely color and shape the contemporary Tamil Śaiva devotee's understanding of the hymns. It is in this sense that the *ōtuvār*, just as much as the commentator or philosopher, is an "interpreter" of the tradition. That the Tamil Śaivas deeply value this least pretentious

[84] This is certainly the case at the festival of Tamil music (in particular, Tamil hymn music) organized annually by the Tamiḻ Icaic Caṅkam. I attended the festival in December 1979–January 1980 and recorded several performances of Tamil *bhakti* hymns by *ōtuvār*s and others. The majority of the audience at the *Tēvāram* concerts were Tamil Śaiva devotees.

[85] William J. Jackson has pointed out, in his recent thesis on Tyāgarāja, that this composer's Telugu songs evoke a unique kind of religio-aesthetic response based on "glossolalia," the adoption of a tongue other than one's own for purposes of worship, aesthetic experience, etc. In Jackson's view the combination of "simple" *bhakti* lyrics and a sophisticated "foreign" language (Telugu) (associated with the court and arts) in Tyagaraja's *kṛti*s create the kind of experience that Tamil Hindus associate with religious texts in "other" languages (especially Sanskrit)—a sense of mystery, dignity, and awe, here united with the intimate and comforting lyricism of *bhakti*. William J. Jackson, "Tyāgarāja: Musician Saint of South India" (Ph.D. diss., Harvard University, 1984), p. 167. I suggest that the Tamil listener's experience of the Nāyaṉār's hymns is based on quite a different "religious" experience of language: the comforting, enveloping intimacy of one's mother tongue, quite devoid of the distancing "mystery" associated with religious texts in other tongues.

and most directly appealing of interpreters speaks for the continuing importance of the experience and expression of devotional love in Tamil Śaiva religion. The themes and values of this tradition, and its very conception of the ideal religious experience, are communicated and reaffirmed in every sensitive performance of the *Tēvāram* hymns.

CHAPTER 5

On Translating the Hymns

Poem, Stanza, Song

The *Tēvāram* hymns are among the earliest examples of the stanzaic song (*patikam*) in Tamil. When the poets call their songs *pattu* ("ten"), they are referring to the hymn as a sequence of ten four-line stanzas in a single meter. The poems of the early Caṅkam anthologies (*tokai*) vary greatly in length and, in fact, were grouped together on the basis of length as well as subject matter.[1] The shortest of these poems, all of which are in the *akaval* meter, are found in the *Aiṅkuṟunūṟu* ("Five Hundred Short Poems"; poems of 3–6 lines) and *Kuṟuntokai* ("Anthology of Short Poems"; poems of 4–8 lines) anthologies. A certain resemblance to the *patikam* format may be seen in the grouping together of some of these poems in "tens" (*pattu*) on the basis of thematic similarity; however, though some of these groups of ten contain formulaic phrases that function as a refrain, each poem is considered to be a self-sufficient entity, an autonomous piece.[2] The detached stanzaic form came into vogue in Tamil in the descriptive and didactic literature produced by late classical authors,[3] many of whom were Jain and therefore familiar with Sanskrit literature, in which the stanza of four *pāda*s or quarters ("lines") is the standard poetic form. The *veṇpā*, a short stanza which in its four-line variety is similar to the four-line stanzaic poems of Sanskrit *kāvya* poetry, became the most popular form with late classical writers of independent short poems.[4] This type of stanzaic poetry lacks the musical (*icai*) associ-

[1] The poems of the Caṅkam age, regardless of their length, are unitary in nature. Even the longest poem is considered to be no more than a single stanza and often consists of one or two sentences. Such poems are called *taṉippāṭal*, "the solitary stanza (or poem)." Zvelebil, *Tamil Literature*, 1974, p. 7.

[2] Zvelebil calls the combination of classical poems in anthologies such as the *Aiṅkuṟunūṟu* "thematic cycles." Ibid., p. 7n.

[3] From the third-fourth centuries on. E.g., the *Tirukkuṟaḷ* of Tiruvaḷḷuvar (ca. A.D. 400?) and the *Nālaṭiyār* (The Great Quatrains) (A.D. 750?), compiled by Patumaṉār. See Zvelebil, *Tamil Literature*, 1974, pp. 117–27.

[4] For a prosodic description of the *veṇpā* meter, see Hart, *Poems*, pp. 199–201.

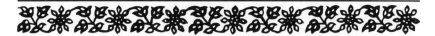

ations of the *Tēvāram* hymns.[5] The early Śaiva and Vaiṣṇava *bhakti* saints, such as Kāraikkāl Ammaiyār, were the first poets to compose longer poems by linking *veṇpā* and other stanza types.[6]

The closest analogues to the *patikam* in terms of meter and form can be found in some of the songs (*icaip pāṭṭu*) embedded in the late classical (fifth century?) epic *Cilappatikāram* (The Epic of the Anklet), written by the poet Iḷaṅkōvaṭikaḷ, who is said to have been a Cēra prince who became a Jain monk. The themes and titles of these songs—"*Āycciyar kuravai*" ("The Kuravai Song and Dance of the Herdswomen"), "*Kāṉal vari*" ("The Vari Songs of the Seashore"), "*Vēṭṭuva vari*" ("Song and Dance of the Hunters")—suggest that they have their origins in folk-song and dance forms.[7] Most of the *Cilappatikāram* songs consist of four-line stanzas that have a regular, musical beat and are linked to their neighbors by a refrain. The structural organization of these stanzaic groups is different from that of the *patikam*: the "*Kāṉal vari*," for instance, consists of a number of short "songs," each composed of two to four stanzas in a single meter, with a refrain.[8] Some of the *Cilappatikāram* stanzas have metrical patterns very similar to those of the *Tēvāram* hymns.[9]

Music and Meter

Classical Tamil prosody is based on the rhythmic combination and disposition of vocalic elements in the line (*aṭi*) of verse.[10] It can be described, in a qualified sense, as a time-oriented, rather than a stress-based or syllabic prosody. English and Sanskrit prosody are examples of the latter types. In Tamil verse, the basic metrical unit is the *acai* (lit., "movement"), which is of two types: *nēr*, simple metrical unit, a single long or

[5] Although some meters can be chanted in a singsong "tune." The *Tēvāram* saints themselves call their hymns *icait tamiḻ* (musical Tamil verse). The majority of the Caṅkam poems and the verses of the didactic anthologies belong to the category of *iyal* (literature, poetry). Of the late classical meters, the *kali* and *paripāṭal* meters are said to have musical associations. See S. Subrahmanyan, *The Commonness in the Metre of the Dravidian Languages*, Research Project Publication no. 22 (Trivandrum: Dravidian Linguistics Association, 1977), p. 305.

[6] On the Tamil Pirapantam genre (Sanskrit Prabandha), see Zvelebil, *Tamil Literature*, 1974, pp. 193–219. According to Zvelebil, Pirapantams are different from anthologies of independent stanzas by virtue of "internal cohesion and connectedness, either formal or based on unity of content," p. 193.

[7] Subrahmanyan, *Commonness in Metre*, p. 306 lists these song types found in late classical works.

[8] *Cilappatikāram* I.7; verses 2–4, 5–7, 8–10, 11–13, 14–16, 17–19, 20–22, 25–27, 28–30, 31–32, etc.

[9] These are varieties of the *kali* meter. See Chidambaranatha Chettiar, *Advanced Studies*, pp. 98–129.

[10] In my description of Tamil meter, I have followed Zvelebil, *Smile of Murugan*, app. 3, p. 275. See also Hart, *Poems*, ch. 8.

short syllable (represented by ¯); and *nirai*, compound metrical unit, made up of two short syllables, or a short followed by a long syllable (⏑⏑ or ⏑¯ , here represented by =).[11] These metrical units combine in various permutations to form the foot (*cīr*). In the classical meters, given these basic guidelines, there can be great variation in the combination of *acai*s in a line, as long as the combined syllabic length or duration of the feet remains constant: this means that, within a foot, simple and compound units (¯ and =) may be substituted for each other, which results in varying rhythmic patterns for the line. As George Hart points out, this is in contrast to the standard syllabic meters of classical Sanskrit poetry, in which "the length of the line is determined by the number of syllables it contains, not by the number of time units, or syllabic instants in it, as in Tamil."[12] Indeed, in the classical Sanskrit meters, not only is the number of syllables in each line (*pāda*, "quarter") of the stanza specified, the length of each syllable and its position in the verse are also prescribed, thus rendering the rhythmic pattern of the entire stanza constant. This last feature had important implications for the *patikam* genre.

The majority of the new meters of the *Tēvāram* are variations on the many "supplemental" meters that evolved out of the classical Tamil meters.[13] Such meters are formed by adding auxiliary members consisting of feet in particular *acai* combinations to basic metrical types. It is in *bhakti* poetry that we see these meters being used extensively and, in the case of the *Tēvāram*, almost exclusively.[14] Comparing the *Tēvāram* poems with earlier poetry, we find that the main differences between the *patikam* and earlier verse are: the adoption of the stanza with four lines of equal length as the basic unit and standard form, even within larger structural frameworks (the entire hymn); and the use of a fixed basic pattern of feet, and therefore, beat, for all four lines. Both phenomena reflect a general trend in Tamil poetry, attributable in part to the influence of Sanskrit poetry and in part to the requirements of musical verse.[15] The Nāyaṉārs modi-

[11] In both kinds of metrical units, the syllable may be followed by a consonant. See Zvelebil, *Smile of Murugan*, p. 275.

[12] Hart, *Poems*, p. 201.

[13] See Chidambaranatha Chettiar, *Advanced Studies*, chs. 11–16.

[14] Ibid., ch. 16. Veḷḷaivāraṇaṉ, *Paṉṉiru tirumuṟai varalāṟu*, pp. 428–38.

[15] As noted earlier, the stanzaic poems of the Caṅkam anthologies varied in length. In the *Cilappatikāram*, the stanzaic songs rarely exceed three or four stanzas and are placed within the larger framework of the verse narrative in the *akaval* meter. In the *bhakti* hymns, for the first time we find larger structural entities that are composed entirely of identical stanzaic units. The use of symmetrical or near-symmetrical patterns in the four lines is a gradual development that reaches its peak in the Murukaṉ hymns of the fifteenth-century poet Aruṇakirinātar. "Now a poem has, in addition to the basic prosodic properties of Tamil metres, also the *cantam* [Sanskrit *chandas*, meter] or a rigidly set pattern of rhythm based on syllabic quantity."(Zvelebil, *Tamil Literature*, 1974, p. 109). In Aruṇakiri's *Tiruppukaḻ* hymns the line itself is organized into feet that are rhythmically identical (except the last foot of the line), while the lines have an absolutely identical rhythm, with no substitutions (of two

fied the regular beat patterns of Tamil song (*icai*, music) traditions such as those exemplified in the *Cilappatikāram* and adapted classical "poetic" meters to create their new song genre. It is only appropriate that the traditional concern regarding the meters of the *Tēvāram* has not been to classify or identify them as subvarieties of "poetic" meters but to associate these metrical patterns with the specific melodic and rhythmic patterns to which the hymns are to be sung.

Meter, melody, and rhythm converge in the *kaṭṭaḷai* pattern or "rule" of each hymn.[16] The pattern of feet in a line of *Tēvāram* verse is identical with the metrical aspect of the *kaṭṭaḷai*, and has a fixed tune. In purely metrical terms, when we scan a *Tēvāram* verse we find that the feet are distributed in a regular rhythmic pattern in the four lines, which creates a measured musical beat:[17]

eṉait|tō| rū|ḻiy| aṭi|yā| rēt|tav| imai|yōr| peru|mā|ṉār|
niṉait|tut| toḻu|vār pā vam| tīrk|kum| nima|la ruṟai|kō|yil
kaṉait|ta| mē|ti| kā|ṇā| tā|yaṉ| kaim|mēṟ| kuḻa|lū ta|
aṉait|tuñ| ceṉ|ṟu| tira|ḷuñ| cā|ral| aṇ|ṇā| malai|yā|rē

Campantar I.69.6 (Poem 80)

This verse is composed of four six-foot lines of thirteen *acai*s per line; except the final foot, all the feet have two *acai*s.[18] The basic rhythmic pattern (*kaṭṭaḷai*) or "rule" of the entire hymn can be discerned by scanning the first line of this or any other verse in this *patikam*.

Alliteration, Rhyme, and Refrain

The tunes of the *Tēvāram* hymns are not the only aspect of these songs that must remain "unheard" melodies for those who read them in translation; the songs are also rich in soundplay of many kinds. The Nāyaṉārs inherited two basic types of conventions of repetition of sound from clas-

shorts for a long, or vice versa). See Zvelebil, *Smile of Murugan*, app. 2, p. 280, for an illustration of *cantam* in Tamil poetry. Campantar occasionally uses metrical forms in which the four-line standard is not observed. See my discussion of alliteration below.

16 See my discussion of *kaṭṭaḷai* in Chapter 4 above.

17 Within certain conventional limits, the combination of *nēr* and *nirai* in the *acai*s that make up a foot in the classical poems can vary greatly from line to line. In general, the classical poems employ lines of equal number of feet, but here too, variation is possible. As pointed out by the Tamil poeticians, not only the number of *acai*s but the number of "letters" (*eḻuttu*) in the *kaṭṭaḷai* line is fixed. The parallelism of the lines themselves, combined with the symmetrical or near-symmetrical patterns of feet in the four lines, creates an overall effect of regularity that distinguishes the *Tēvāram* verses from their predecessors.

18 The final foot, made up of three *acai*s, is called *veṇcīr*.

sical Tamil poetry: *mōṉai*, in which the initial sound (vowel or consonant) of a line is repeated at the beginning of another foot within the same line; and *etukai*, in which the second consonant, syllable, and sometimes a cluster of syllables of two or more lines are identical.[19] *Etukai*, or second-syllable rhyme, became a regular marker of line boundaries in the *Tēvāram* songs. In the Campantar verse quoted above, the *etukai*, *mōṉai* pattern of the four lines is as follows:

1 *eṉaittō* rūḻiy aṭiyā rēttav imaiyōr perumāṉār

2 *niṉaitt*ut toḻuvār pāvan tīrkkum nimalar uṟaikōyil

3 *kaṉaitta* mēti kāṇā tāyaṉ kaimmēṟ kuḻalūta

4 *aṉaitt*uñ ceṉṟu tiraḷuñ cāral aṇṇā malaiyārē

Eṉaitt-, *niṉaitt-*, *kaṉaitt-*, and *aṉaittu-* form the *etukai. Mōṉai* patterns of many varieties can be found in a single line of verse, as here. The alliteration between *e* and *ē* in line 1, and *ni-* and *ni-* in line 2 fulfill the requirement of *mōṉai*. In line 2, in addition to *ni- ni-*, there is initial alliteration in *toḻuvār* and *tīrkkum*; in line 3, *kaṉaitta* alliterates with *kāṇātu*, *kaimmēṟ*, and *kuḻal*; and in line 4, *ceṉṟu* and *cāral*, as well as *aṉaittuñ* and *aṇṇāmalai*, provide *mōṉai* designs. A consideration of the first two lines of Campantar I.10.1 reveals the complexity of sound patterning that can be achieved even in the shorter meters of the *Tēvāram*:

1 4 6 1 1 8 10
uṇṇāmulaiy umaiyāḷoṭu muṭaṉākiyav oruvaṉ
5 7 7 5 9 7 9 5

4 8 10 6 10
peṇṇā kiya perumāṉmalai tirumāmaṇi tikaḻa
2 5 2 7 5 7 3 7 5 7 3

Identically numbered elements above are identical in sound. In longer meters such as the *tāṇṭakam*, the alliterative patterns can be even more complex, crossing line boundaries and extending over the entire stanza; Appar's "vāṉavaṉ kāṇ" (VI.301.1; Poem 20), analyzed in Chapter 4, is a good example of alliteration in *tāṇṭakam* verse.

Besides its obvious musical quality, alliteration in the Nāyaṉārs' songs is often used to create interplay of meaning and subtle affective undercur-

[19] *Etukai* and *mōṉai* patterns are catalogued in manuals of poetics. For a detailed list, see Subrahmanyan, *Commonness in Metre*, pp. 326–35. *Etukai* and *mōṉai* are a standard feature of all kinds of literary forms in Tamil. E.g., "kaṟka kacaṭaṟak kaṟpavai kaṟṟapiṉ / niṟka ataṟkut taka" (*Tirukkuṟaḷ* 391) and the proverb "*mā*miyār uṭaittāl *maṇ*kuṭam / *maru*makaḷ uṭaittāl poṉkuṭam."

rents. The first two lines of Campantar's II.148.1 (Poem 15) provides a good illustration of this phenomenon:

1 *ma*ṟaiyāṉai *mā*cilāp puṉcaṭai *mal*kuveṉ

2 *pi*ṟaiyāṉaip *pe*ṇṇoṭā ṇākiya *pe*mmāṉai

[My heart can think of nothing
other than] the brahmin who is the Veda,
he who bears the white moon
on his pure, matted red hair,
the Lord who is both man and woman

Maṟaiyāṉai, the first word in the verse, is related by alliteration to *mācilā*, which is properly an adjective qualifying *puṉcaṭai* ("matted red hair"). The alliterative link between *ma* and *mā* resonates with connections in meaning as well: *maṟai*, "Veda" (hence *maṟaiyāṉ*: "Veda-chanter," "god who is [in] the Veda") has connotations of ritual purity and the sacred that are carried over to *mācilā* ("flawless," "pure"), thus emphasizing the identity of Śiva, the matted-hair ascetic, as the pure god of the Vedas and their ritual universe.[20] The varied, staggered repetition of words and lines in the *ōtuvār*'s *viruttam* performance further highlights and enhances such resonances of sound and meaning.

The refrain of the *Tēvāram* hymn links the hymns with the Tamil folk song and other musical genres. It may form part or all of the fourth line of the stanza. A comparison of the fourth line of verses 6, 7, and 8 of Campantar I.69 (Poem 80) gives an idea of the way in which the poets vary themes, words, and sounds in the refrain. Literal and free translations are given for each line.

4 aṉaittuñ ceṉṟu tiraḷuñ cāral *aṇṇā-malaiyārē* [text]
all going, gathering slope—Aṇṇā-malai-god (god of Aṇṇāmalai hill-shrine) [literal trans.]
"The Lord of (the hill-shrine of) Aṇṇāmalai, on whose slopes the entire herd gathers" [free trans.]

4 antip piṟaivan taṉaiyuñ cāral *aṇṇā-malaiyārē*
the evening crescent moon, coming, embraces slope-Aṇṇāmalai-god
"The Lord of Aṇṇāmalai, whose slope is embraced by the evening moon"

[20] The matted hair of Śiva actually suggests the wild aspects of this god who destroyed Dakṣa's sacrifice. The paradox of the wild, ascetic god who is also related to the Veda and ritual purity is a standard ingredient in the mythology of Śiva.

4 aṟantāṉ kāṭṭiy aruḷic ceytār *aṇṇā-malaiyārē*
the sacred Law showing, grace granted, Aṇṇā-malai-god.
"The Lord of Aṇṇāmalai, who granted grace (to the gods),
revealing the sacred Law."
Campantar I.69.6,7,8

While Appar specialized in the *kuṟuntokai* and *tāṇṭakam* meters—his skill in the latter earned him the name "*tāṇṭakavēntar*" (King of the Tāṇṭakam form)—Campantar composed seventy-two hymns in a number of prosodic forms in which auditory and visual principles of patterning are blended in a complex manner to produce poems that are essentially audiovisual conundrums or puzzles.[21] Campantar's hymns in such forms as Moḻimāṟṟu and Tāḷaccati are based on the principles of play on sound or meaning, or on the arrangement of syllables and lines within the verse. These poetic forms show the influence of the Sanskrit *kāvya* poetic tradition, in which authors of court epics composed entire cantos in the *citrakāvya* ("decorative" or "pictorial" poetry) mode, consisting of verses based on alliteration, puns, and other types of wordplay.[22] For instance, Campantar III.374 is in the Iyamakam form (Sanskrit *yamaka*), in which the same cluster of syllables is repeated in different senses in two halves of a line of verse; III.375 is a Mālaimāṟṟu couplet, in which the letters and syllables of the first line of the verse, when read backwards, are identical with those of the second line.[23] In the Cakkaramāṟṟu and Eḻukūṟṟirukkai forms, the poem has a graphic design, creating pictures of a wheel and a chariot, respectively; the chariot form is achieved by splitting the lines into seven "decks" of three to thirteen segments in a regular pattern.[24] For obvious reasons, I have omitted such poems from this anthology of translations from the *Tēvāram*. Nevertheless, it is important to be aware of them, since they reveal Campantar as a "literary" poet, a self-conscious craftsman displaying his skill in the sophisticated "Sanskritic" style of his day.

[21] Appar's Kuṟuntokai poems are found in Book V, and his Tāṇṭakam poems are in Book VI of the *Tēvāram*. Campantar's "pattern" poems are distributed in the three books of his hymns, and identified in editions of the poems.

[22] On *citrakāvya* in Sanskrit poetry, see A. K. Warder, *Indian Kāvya Literature*, vol. 3 (Delhi: Motilal Banarsidass, 1977), pp. 223–28.

[23] Campantar III.374, "tuṉṟu koṉṟai*nañ caṭaiyatē* tūyakaṇṭa*nañcaṭaiyatē*"; III.375, "yāmāmā nī yāmāmā yāḻīkāmā kāṇākā / kāṇākāmā kāḻīyā māmāyānī māmāyā."

[24] In some of these unusual forms Campantar adopts shorter or longer stanzaic patterns, e.g., the Irukkukkuṟaḷ, a short couplet, as in hymns I.90–96. K. Veḷḷaivāraṇaṉ discusses compositional forms in Campantar's hymns in detail in *Paṉṉiru tirumuṟai varalāṟu*, pp. 428–52. See Somasundaram, *Tirujñānasambandhar*, pp. 198–202, for a clear and concise description of Campantar's "pattern" hymns; Somasundaram also provides a graphic representation of the Eḻukūṟṟirukkai (Rathabandha, "Chariot") poem (Campantar I.128).

The Language of the Poems

The Tamils of today practice a form of diglossia in which a "pure" or "literary" language ("*centamiḻ*") is used in formal and written contexts, while the spoken language consists of a wide variety of dialects that diverge in various ways from the literary form. Though modern literary Tamil is recognizably continuous with the Tamil of the Caṅkam anthologies, it also shows significant differences in vocabulary and grammatical forms. The rhetorical framework and patterns of the Caṅkam poems, many of which are dramatic monologues, may convey to us some idea of the spoken language of the classical age, but that language is far removed from modern spoken Tamil. In contemporary Tamilnadu, Caṅkam literature is the province of scholars and advanced students of Tamil. The situation is somewhat different with the *Tēvāram* hymns. The language of these hymns stands somewhere between the literary language of the classical age and standard modern literary Tamil. It contains many archaic words, often makes use of the conventions, formulae, and vocabulary of Caṅkam literature, and has a recognizably "classical" tone. At the same time it is simpler in style and closer to modern literary usage, so that the general, overall sense of the hymns is directly accessible to the average Tamil reader or listener.

The diction of the poets, like their religion, is a blend of Sanskritic and Tamil elements. Words of Sanskrit origin, such as *īcaṉ* (Sanskrit *īśa*, the Lord), *mūrtti* (*mūrti*, image, form), *vētam* (Veda), *pātam* (*pāda*, foot), and *kītam*, (*gīta*, song), occur side by side with Tamil words, some of them having the same meaning, such as *iṟaivaṉ* (Lord, king), *maṟai* (Veda), *aṭi* (foot), and *pāṭṭu*, *pāṭal* (song). In some cases, even where the context is primarily brahmanical, the poets prefer to use Tamil words with largely indigenous and local cultural associations: e.g., *viṉai* for karma, *māl* for Viṣṇu, *vīṭu* for *mōkṣa* (liberation), *veṇṇīṟu* for *bhasma* (ash). Words used to denote objects, experiences, and ideas deeply rooted in Tamil literature and culture tend to be decidedly Tamil in their linguistic orientation: *aṉpu*, *kātal* (love); *virumpu-*, *mēvu-* (to desire, to love); *kuṉṟu*, *malai* (hill); *toḻu-* (to worship, serve); *kōyil* (palace, temple); *kō*, *kōmāṉ* (king, prince, lord); *kaṭal* (sea); *poḻil* (grove). In several songs the poets use proverbs and vivid colloquial expressions that are familiar to the Tamil even today: "My heart is whirled about / like yoghurt in a churn" (Appar IV.97.3; Poem 188); "[I am] like one who puts aside the oil lamp / to warm himself with a firefly" (Appar IV.5.7; Poem 239). The saints' own coinages have become slogans, popular sayings and "proverbs" today, the most famous being Appar's "We are slaves to no man" ("nāmārkkuṅ kuṭiy allōm," VI.312.1; Poem 240), and "My task is only to serve" ("eṉ kaṭaṉ paṇi ceytu kiṭappatē," V.133.9; Poem 172), and

Cuntarar's "Life is an illusion, / all things end in dust" ("vāḻvāvatu māy-amm itu maṇṇāvatu tiṇṇam," VII.78.1; Poem 69).

Following the work of Parry and Lord,[25] scholars have applied the idea of the formula and formulaic composition to many folk and oral traditions in world literature. Kailasapathy's book on Caṅkam poetry is a study of "Tamil heroic poetry" from the point of view of oral poetics.[26] Hart has pointed out that formulae and conventions can be as much a part of the technique of the "literary" as the "oral" poet, and that the poems of the classical anthologies are probably a highly stylized "literary" form modeled on earlier poems composed by bards in the oral tradition and making self-conscious use of "oral" formulae.[27] As successors of the Caṅkam poets, and as poets working with a form that is oral and musical, the *Tēvāram* saints use a large number of formulaic phrases, constructions, and themes. These range from epithets such as *piṟaicūṭi* ("he who is crowned with the crescent moon") to combinations such as *māl-kaṭal* ("the great sea") and *vampulām poḻil* ("fragrant grove"). As noted in the discussion of the refrains above, such formulaic phrases are really bases that are capable of being expanded or contracted according to the demands of meter and context. Thus "maṅkai paṅkaṉ," "the lady's spouse" or "he who shares his body with his lady," can be expanded to "vārār mulai maṅkai paṅkaṉ," "the spouse of the lady whose breasts are bound by the breastcloth," or "vāruṟu [or vārkoḷ] vaṉa mulai maṅkai paṅkaṉ", "the spouse of the lady with the beautiful breasts bound by the breastcloth," and so on. *Caṭaimuṭi*, "crown of matted hair," can be prefixed by *piṟaiyaṇi* ("adorned by the crescent moon"), or *nīrulāvu* ("where the river flows"), and so forth.

The poets are often motivated by considerations of musicality to create "easy" rhyming phrases, and to extend shorter patterns of *etukai* in their verses, by using words such as *malinta/mali*, *ulām/ulāvu/ulavu*, *uṭai/uṭaiya*, *koḷ/koṇṭa/koṇṭator*, *ār/ārnta*, *taru/tarum*, *vaḷar*, *tikaḻ*, *ilaṅka/ilaṅkum*, and *cēr*, used in the sense of "endowed with" or "possessing." The effect can be one of circumlocution laced with wordplay, as in the four lines of Campantar I.65.1:

1	mai*cēr*kaṇṭar . . .	"He whose throat is (*cēr*) dark"
2	mey*cēr* poṭiyar . . .	"He who smears (lit., 'has,' *cēr*) ashes on his body"

[25] Milman Parry, *Les Formulas et la métrique d'Homère* (Paris, 1928), and Albert B. Lord, *The Singer of Tales* (London, 1960), pioneer works advancing the theory of improvisation and formulaic composition in bardic and other oral traditions.

[26] See esp. Kailasapathy, *Tamil Heroic Poetry*, ch. 4.

[27] Hart, *Poems*, pp. 152–58. Though the *Tēvāram* authors were "lettered" men, and the hymns themselves are sophisticated literary works, as musical compositions in the Indian context, the hymns are very much in the realm of oral composition and transmission.

3 kai*cēr* vaḷaiyar . . . "(Women) who wear (*cēr*) bracelets on their wrists"
4 pai*cēr* aravalkulār . . ."(Women who have mounds of Venus like the hood-ed (*cēr*) cobra"

Sentence and Line

In addition to being an independent formal unit, the *Tēvāram* verse also tends to be grammatically independent, most often consisting of a single sentence that is completed within the boundaries of the stanza. The poets favor certain formulaic patterns in constructing these stanzaic sentences. A common pattern is the string of epithets and nouns culminating in a verb, in the *stotra* style, as in "maṟaiyāṉai mācilā . . . ," Campantar II.148.1 (Poem 15).[28] In another common motif the poets link an iconographic or mythological description of Śiva in one half of the verse with the description of a shrine, landscape, or the activities of devotees in the other half. The formula might read like this: "The abode of the Lord who is x . . . is y . . . where. . . ." In this latter type of verse, the descriptions, especially in the longer meters, can become very complex, a complexity facilitated and accentuated by features inherent in Tamil grammar and syntax, which will be discussed below.

Phrases, epithets, and clauses fit neatly into the "slot" created by the metrical line within the verse. However, there are also many poems where the Nāyaṉārs create a pattern of enjambment, in which a new idea, image, or formulaic unit begins within one line and is completed in the following line,[29] as in Campantar I.103.8 (where the beginning of a new formulaic unit is indicated by a solidus):

iṭanta*pemmā* / *ṉ*ēṉamatāyu maṉamāyum
toṭarnta*pemmāṉ* / ṟūmaticūṭi varaiyārtam
maṭantai*pemmāṉ* / vārkaḻalōccik kālaṉaik
kaṭanta*pemmāṉ* / kātalceykōyil kaḻukkuṉṟē

1 (a) The *Lord* (*pemmāṉ*) who gored (the elephant); / (b) (by the gods) who turned into the boar and the goose
2 the *Lord* who was pursued; / (c) crowned with the pure moon, the great mountain's
3 daughter's *Lord*; / (d) raising his foot bound by the hero's anklet, the god of Death (*kālaṉ*)

[28] See my discussion of the *stotra* form in Chapter 3 above.

[29] Kailasapathy suggests that this kind of syncopation of the grammatical and metrical lines is part of the Caṅkam technique of versification. *Tamil Heroic Poetry*, pp. 146, 177–78.

4 the *Lord* who conquered— / (e) The temple he loves is Kaḻuk-kuṉṟu.

In this verse, the description of Śiva's attributes and deeds precedes his name, and "*pemmāṉ*" (the Lord), the grammatical subject of each of the descriptive phrases (b), (c), and (d) is separated from the phrase and placed at the beginning of the following line. In recitation as well as in musical performance, this kind of overflowing pattern creates a sense of suspense and syncopated rhythms in the verse.

Patikam and Poem

In this study I have often treated *Tēvāram* verses as though they were independent poems. My justification for this, of course, has been the fact that they are treated as such within the Tamil Śaiva tradition. In modern usage the word *patikam* can denote either one stanza or an entire sequence of ten or eleven verses. In many *Tēvāram* hymns, in addition to the unity created by meter, an overall sense of unity may also be provided by the refrains, place names and other constants, and patterns of descriptive formulae. In other poems, each verse may stand out much more as a separate vignette, the ten verses drawing upon diverse aspects of the stock of Tamil Śaiva devotional themes. In either case, the result is a flexible structure that permits the reader and listener to treat and respond to one verse, several verses, or the entire poem, as meaningful wholes.

The Text and the Translation

In selecting hymns for translation, I had several models before me in the form of anthologies of selections compiled by scholars and teachers in the Tamil Śaiva tradition. The best-known anthologies of this type are the *Umāpaticivam tēvāra aruḷmuṟait tiraṭṭu* and the *Akattiyar tēvārat tiraṭṭu*.[30] The former was compiled by the fourteenth-century Śaiva guru Umāpati Civācāriyār; it consists of ninety-nine stanzas from the hymns of the three *Tēvāram* poets, organized under ten categories corresponding to the states and stages of the soul in its relationship with the Lord (*pati*) according to the Śaiva Siddhānta philosophy. The latter is a popular "digest" consisting of twenty-five hymns, whose compilation is attributed to Akattiyar, the legendary sage and culture-hero of the Tamils.[31] Tradition

[30] *Umāpaticivam tēvāra aruḷmuṟait tiraṭṭu*, with the commentary of Pa. Irāmanāta Piḷḷai (Madras: SISSW Publishing Society, 1961); and *Akattiyar tēvārat tiraṭṭu: Mūlamum uraiyum*, with Glossary and Commentary by Kayappākkam Catāciva Ceṭṭiyār (Madras: SISSW Publishing Society, 1976).

[31] On the Akattiyar legend, see Nilakanta Sastri, *Development of Religion*.

has it that by reading these twenty-five songs in order, a devotee may get the benefit of reading all seven books of the *Tēvāram*.[32] Yet other collections exist, designed to serve as guides for pilgrimage or remembrance of sacred places, and provide a selection of verses addressed to Śiva at each of the sacred places (*pati*) at which the Nāyaṉārs sang.[33] My own aim in putting together an anthology of selections from the *Tēvāram* hymns has been to provide those interested in Indian religion and civilization with a sourcebook of accurate, representative translations from an important text in Tamil religious history. In selecting the hymns, I have tried to represent the full range of content and style in the *Tēvāram*. I have also been guided by Tamil Śaiva taste and practice in the choice of poems: many of the best-known and most beloved verses of the saints can be found here, and the selections range from single stanzas to entire hymns. I have divided the translations into four sections that are designed to cover the major themes of the religion of the Nāyaṉārs. I have given English headings of my own for individual verses, hymns, or groups of hymns in which I see a particularly coherent or striking presentation of a theme. In the case of the few hymns that have traditional Tamil titles, I have given the Tamil title along with my English translation of the title.

In the absence to date of a complete critical edition of the *Tēvāram*, I have based my translations on the standard popular edition, the "Kaḻakam" edition, published by the South India Śaiva Siddhānta Works Publishing Society.[34] In numbering the hymns I have followed the Kaḻakam edition, which provides a continuous numbering for the corpus of each poet (e.g., Campantar 1–383), at the same time indicating the number of the Tirumuṟai book in which a particular hymn appears. Where the Kaḻakam edition provides information regarding both the *paṇ* designated for the hymn and the sacred place to which it is dedicated, I give only the latter information. Alternative names of shrines have been given

[32] Almost every important sacred text in Hinduism has been excerpted and summarized in this way. There are "Rāmāyaṇas" and "Bhāgavatas" of varying lengths, ranging from two to two hundred verses. The ultimate purpose of all such capsule versions is the same: to enable the reader to cover the entire text effectively in a short time, thus earning the merit that, as the *phalaśruti* verses specify accrues to devotees who have read the entire work.

[33] E.g., *Paṉṉiru tirumuṟaip peruntiraṭṭu*, ed. Pa. Irāmanāta Piḷḷai (Madras: SISSW Publishing Society, 1961, 1980); the series of publications on regional sites related to the *Tēvāram* (e.g., *Kāvirit teṉkarait talaṅkaḷ* ["Sites on the southern bank of the Kaveri"], 1965), published by the Madras Center of the Tarumapuram Atīṉam; and occasional publications by such organizations as the Puracait Tiruneṟik Kaḻakam (Puracaivākkam Religion Society).

[34] *Tēvāram*, vol. one, Tirumuṟai I–III, *Tiruñāṉacampantar tēvārap patikaṅkaḷ*, ed. Kayappākkam Catāciva Ceṭṭiyār (Madras: SISSW Publishing Society [Kaḻakam], 1973; originally published in 1927); and *Tēvāram*, vol. two, Tirumuṟai IV–VII, *Tirunāvukkaracar, Cuntaramūrtti tēvārap patikaṅkaḷ*, ed. Kayappākkam C. Ceṭṭiyār (Madras: SISSW Publishing Society [Kaḻakam], 1973; originally published in 1928–1929). Hereafter: *Tēvāram* Kaḻakam edition.

in parentheses. Thus, in the anthology that follows in Part Two, Campantar's verse "antamum ātiyum" (Poem 30) is indicated as:

30. Campantar I.39.1 *Vēṭkaḷam (Tiruvēṭkaḷam)*

Of the other editions of the *Tēvāram* available to me, I have regularly consulted the Tarumapuram Ātīṉam's edition, published in seven volumes with commentary and notes.[35] The Ātīṉam edition is not a critical edition, and the commentaries represent the views of individual contemporary commentators. Since there is no real tradition of earlier commentaries available to us, I have benefited greatly from the commentaries in this edition; however, I have not treated them as absolute authorities in the matter of interpretation, nor have I found the readings in this edition superior to those in the Kaḻakam edition. It is only after completing the present volume that I was able to consult the new edition of the *Tēvāram* undertaken by T. V. Gopal Iyer, directed by François Gros, under the auspices of the Institut français d'indologie in Pondicherry.[36] In general, my own evaluation of variant readings and difficult passages is in agreement with Gopal Iyer's.

In translating the hymns I have tried to stay as close to the original as possible. What this means in practical terms can be seen by comparing my translation of a *Tēvāram* stanza with the Tamil original. In the Tamil below, the square brackets indicate the limits of the clauses, which are marked by Roman numerals. Parentheses in the literal translation indicate implications or possible meanings.

I				
eṉaittō rūḻiy	aṭiyā	rēttav	imaiyōr	perumāṉār
[In every cosmic age	devotees	praising	Himalayan gods	king/lord]

II					III
niṉaittut	toḻuvār	pāvan	tīrkkum	nimalar	uṟaikōyil
[thinking (in the heart)	who worship	sin	ending	pure one]	[dwelling temple]

IV			V
kaṉaitta mēti	kāṇā	tāyaṉ	kaimmēṟ kuḻalūta
[bellowed buffalo	not seeing	herdsman]	[in hand flute-playing]

[35] *Tēvāram (Paṇmuṟai)*. Tirumuṟai I–VII. *Tiruñāṉacampantar, Tirunāvukkaracar, Cuntaramūrtti Tēvāram*, published in seven volumes with commentary by various scholars. Tarumapuram: Tarumapuram Ātīṉam, 1953–1964. Hereafter: *Tēvāram* Ātīṉam edition.

[36] The hymns of Ñāṉacampantar have been published in *Tēvāram: Hymnes Śivaïtes du pays tamoul*, vol. I, ed. Gopal Iyer, and the hymns of Appar and Cuntarar in vol. II (1985) in the same series (hereafter: *Tēvāram* Pondicherry edition). This edition, pp. lx–lxxii (in the introduction, "Towards Reading the *Tēvāram*," by F. Gros), and pp. lxxiii–xc (Iyer,

VI			VII	VIII
aṉaittuñ	ceṉṟu	tiraḷuñ	cāral	aṇṇā malaiyārē
[all together	going/ coming	gathering]	[slope(s)]	[Aṇṇāmalai (hill) shrine.]

The king of the Himalayan gods,	I
the Lord whom devotees praise	I
in every age of the universe,	I
the pure one who destroys sin	II
for those who worship him with love,	II
dwells in the shrine of Aṇṇāmalai,	III / VIII
on whose slopes	VII
the herdsman looks for a lost buffalo	IV
whose bellow he hears,	IV
and when he plays his flute	V
the whole herd gathers around.	VI

Campantar I.69.6 (Poem 80)

The interlinear translation shows that the word order of the English translation is different from that of the original. Since Tamil has what A. K. Ramanujan aptly calls a "left-branching syntax",[37] phrases such as "in-the-universe's-every-age-devotees-praising-Himalayan-gods-king" read in reverse order in English: "The king of the Himalayan gods, the Lord whom devotees praise in every age of the universe." I have had to supply the prepositions "of" and "in," which make clear in English the relationships between "king" and "Himalayan gods," and "praise" and "age." In the Tamil, it is only from the position of "*imaiyōr*" directly before "*perumāṉār*," and from the general context of the phrase, that we may infer that the two words are connected by a (possessive) case relationship. The same is true of "*ūḻi*" and "*ētta*." All the nouns are in the base or nominative form, and "ētta" (praise) is neutral in regard to the gender, number, and other particulars of the noun that is the subject of the act of praising.

In the interlinear translation I have numbered from I to VIII the phrases and clauses that make up the sentence which is the verse in the order in which they appear in the Tamil. The reordering of these units in the English version reflects the difference between Tamil and English syntax and word order. The Tamil verse is thematically and structurally divided into two halves, the first half (the first two lines) devoted to the description of Śiva and the second to a description of the environs of the hill-shrine of

"Tamil Introduction"), provides a detailed discussion of the manuscript tradition of the *Tēvāram*.

[37] Ramanujan, *Hymns*, p. xvii.

Aṇṇāmalai. In my translation I have tried to keep this thematic division intact. In the Tamil, "*aṇṇāmalaiyārē* is not only the predicate of the sentence but also the constant element of the refrain in the hymn and the last word in the verse.[38] The dramatic effect of the placement of "*aṇṇāmalaiyārē*" at the end of the verse is lost in the English, but the overall structural relationship between the image of Śiva and the image of Aṇṇāmalai in the original is retained.

In poems where keeping the continuous sentence structure of the Tamil would have resulted in awkward English, I have translated the verse in several sentences. There are also many verses composed of short sentences in the Tamil that lend themselves well to being rendered into brief English sentences. The reader should keep in mind that even in translations where I have kept the single-sentence structure of the original, the effect of my English sentence, where the relationships between words and clauses are clearly defined by means of relative pronouns and prepositions, is bound to differ from the complex coherence of the original, which stems from the "ease with which many vaguely related things can be included in the same sentence" in Tamil.[39] Neither the linear structure nor the sound and rhythmic effects of Tamil verse can be imitated in English; I have not tried to re-create these features in English, except to retain the formal device of the refrain in the translation of entire hymns. I have tried to capture in the tone of my translations the unique mix of "classical" elegance and grandeur and colloquial textures that characterizes the Tamil originals. I hope that the strategies outlined above have resulted in translations that are faithful both to the words and design of the *Tēvāram* verses and to the idiom and rhythms of modern English speech.

Even if one were to ignore the problem of the lack of a critical edition of the *Tēvāram*—and this is a continuing problem, given the situation of the text in a semi-oral and musical tradition—the lack of a classical tradition of *Tēvāram* commentary analogous to that which is available for the hymns of the Āḻvārs is a serious obstacle to any attempt at a "definitive" translation. As I have noted earlier, the language of the *Tēvāram* is midway between the language of the Caṅkam poems and "later" Tamil, and the hymns contain a large number of words of which the only attested occurrence is in a particular verse in the *Tēvāram*. The ambiguity of poetic syntax in Tamil gives rise to several possible interpretations for the same phrases. The hymns of Cuntarar are notorious for their obscurity, as will become apparent in my discussion of particular problems in

[38] According to Hart, the descriptions in many classical poems look forward to a word or phrase at the end of the poem, without which the description is incomplete. This results in a particular sort of coherence in form and meaning. Hart, *Poems*, p. 186.

[39] Ibid.

PART TWO

An Anthology of Hymns from the *Tēvāram*

SECTION I

Mūrtti: Images of the Lord

A thousand scriptures speak
of his attributes and signs,
his shrines, his paths,
his greatness—
O witless people,
that your hearts have not been won!
Appar V.204.6

The poems in this section focus on the person and nature of Śiva as the poets of the *Tēvāram* visualize them. Śiva Mahādeva, the great god of the pan-Hindu tradition, is the "Lord" of these poems, and many verses celebrate him in his cosmic dimensions. He is identified as Īśa, the "Lord" of the theistic Upaniṣads,[1] the Supreme Deity who manifests himself in and as all things in the universe. Like the awesome and life-giving Rudra-Śiva of the Vedic *Śatarudrīya* litany, Śiva of the *Tēvāram* is manifest in the wild aspects of nature, in forests and bodies of water, in healing plants, and in all forms of life. As Aṣṭamūrti (Tamil *aṭṭamūrtti*), Śiva is the five elements, the sun, the moon, and the sacrificer. He who is the energizing force in all life is also Hara, the destroyer, associated with death and the symbols of death. Above all, he is "*śiva*," "the auspicious Lord," he who can transform even the terrifying and gruesome aspects of existence into a blessing. This cosmic vision of God is tempered by the intimacy of the *bhakti* perspective of the saints, in which Śiva is portrayed as the "beloved Lord" of his devotees.

The Āgamic heritage of the religion of the Tamil poets is most clearly expressed in the iconographic descriptions of Śiva that are the hallmark of the *Tēvāram*. The Āgamas give the specifications for up to twenty-five *mūrtis* (iconographic forms) in which Śiva may be represented.[2] For each

[1] E.g., The *Īśa* and *Śvetāśvatara* Upaniṣads.

[2] See Dorai Rangaswamy, *Religion and Philosophy*, 1: 194–95, for a list of these forms.

mūrti the manuals describe in detail the attire, posture, weapons, ornaments, and accessories of Śiva as well as the representation of other figures and objects involved in the conception of the *mūrti*. For instance, Kālasaṃhāramūrti ("the Lord who destroys Kāla [Death]") is described[3] as standing with his right foot on a lotus seat, with the left raised up to kick Kāla on the chest; he displays three eyes, tusks, matted hair, four or eight arms, "the right hands in the former case carrying the trident lifted up to the ear and the hatchet or *varada* pose, the left hands being in *sūcī* pose near the navel and *vismaya* pose near the crown."[4] Kāla (Yama, Death) and the boy Mārkaṇḍeya, the two other characters involved in this myth, are also described. The textual prescriptions are followed, with minor variations, in Pallava and Cōḻa temple sculpture and bronzes. (See illus. 12.) In the *Tēvāram* descriptions, however, we encounter a poetic iconography in which selection of detail is governed not by the canons of temple sculpture but by the aesthetic of devotion. In the typical stanza the poet presents only a few details of a particular *mūrti*, a vignette rather than a full-fledged portrait.

As with most Hindu deities, the iconography of Śiva reflects the accretion and synthesis, over centuries, of multiple mythological and artistic traditions, further varied by regional differences. In the introductions to the sections on poems relating to Śiva in his volume of translation from classical Sanskrit poetry, D.H.H. Ingalls provides an excellent account of the iconography of Śiva in the Hindu tradition.[5] In a detailed study of the saint Cuntaramūrtti's visualization of Śiva, Dorai Rangaswamy compares the description of the *mūrtis* in the Āgamas and Purāṇas with Pallava temple sculpture and the descriptions in the hymns of Cuntarar.[6] My own general account here is offered with the aim of helping readers make their way through what may appear to be a bewildering array of attributes. It is also my intention, in the process, to point out details that are typical of the Tamil or South Indian traditions.

As with the Sanskrit poets, Śiva's head and hair are favorite subjects with the *Tēvāram* saints. The god's crown of flame-colored matted hair (*caṭai, caṭaimuṭi*), which indicates his persona as the great *yogi* (ascetic), is often described in minute detail.[7] In the Tamil hymns, Śiva's hair is

[3] Ibid., pp. 359–60, contains a complete description of the Kālasaṃhāramūrti.

[4] Ibid., p. 360.

[5] Ingalls, *Anthology*, sections 4, 5.

[6] Dorai Rangaswamy, *Religion and Philosophy*, 1: 179–499.

[7] It is interesting to note that, in contrast to the Sanskrit *kāvya* poets, the *Tēvāram* poets rarely describe Śiva as the meditating yogi, although Śiva's yogic persona is the basis of his form as Dakṣiṇāmūrti, the Teacher, a popular form in Tamil poetry and sculpture. For classic descriptions of Śiva as the yogi in Sanskrit poetry, see Kālidāsa, *Kumārasaṃbhava* III.44–51, and Śūdraka's benedictory stanza in the play *Mṛcchakaṭikā*.

always portrayed in motion, swaying as he dances, rides his bull, or wanders as a homeless beggar. The matted locks or braids are adorned by the crescent moon (*mati*, *piṟaimati*), the river Ganges (Gaṅgā), one or more skulls (*talai*, *veṇṭalai*), snakes (*aravu*), and flowers. Most important among the flowers and leaves that Śiva wears in his hair are the golden *koṉṟai*, the *vaṉṉi*, and the *mattam* (datura).[8] Representing Śiva's fiery anger and destructive power is the third, vertical eye in his forehead.[9] The god's earrings are often described, especially in order to suggest his androgynous form as Ardhanārīśvara, in which he shares his body with his spouse Umā (Umai) or Pārvatī, the daughter of the Himalaya mountain (*malaimakaḷ*, *malaiyāṉ makaḷ*). Thus in many *Tēvāram* hymns Śiva is pictured as wearing a man's earring, the dangling *kuḻai* or *kuṇṭalam*, on one ear, and the woman's scroll or stud (*curuḷ*, *tōṭu*) on the other.

Śiva is "the Lord with the stained throat" (*kaṟaikkaṇṭaṉ*), his throat having turned blue (*nīla-*) or black (*karu-*) upon his swallowing the poison emitted by the snake Vāsuki when the gods and demons, using the snake as their churning rope, together churned the milk ocean in search of ambrosia. Like his devotees, the Lord wears a string of *akku* (*akṣa*, *rudrākṣa*, "Śiva's eye") seeds around his neck, often entwined with a snake.

Śiva's "coral-red" (*pavaḷavaṇṇam*) or fire-hued body is covered with white ash (*nīṟu*, *pūti*, *vīpūti*) from the burning-ground (*kāṭu*, *iṭukāṭu*), where he loves to dance his midnight dance. His lower garment is a loincloth with a waistband (*kīḻuṭai*, *kīḻār kōvaṇam*), flayed elephant hide (*kariy uri*),[10] tigerskin (*pulittōl*), or a combination of these. Skulls and snakes adorn his chest, as does the sacred thread, symbol of brahminhood. In his several arms—these range from four to eight—the god holds various things: fire (*tī*, *aṉal*), a small drum (*uṭukkai*, *takkai*), a young deer or fawn (*māṉ*, *māṉmaṟi*), a battle-axe (*maḻu*), or a trident (*cūlam*, *cūlappaṭai*, *mūvilaivēl*). Certain weapons or attributes are specific to particular *mūrtis*. In their stanzaic vignettes the poets freely draw upon this repertoire in various combinations. According to the mythological tradition, Śiva acquired many of his accoutrements and attributes in the course of his conflict with the sages of Tārakavaṉam (*dārukavana*, the Pine Forest), who were angered when, as punishment for their arrogance, the god appeared

[8] Other flowers and leaves of the Tamil country mentioned in connection with Śiva in the *Tēvāram* are *kūviḷam* and *erukku*. The poets also mention the tradition of offering a collection of "eight fresh flowers" (*eṭṭunāṇmalar*) sacred to Śiva. See V. S. Agrawala, *Śiva-Mahādeva* (Varanasi, 1966), p. 27, for a discussion of the ritual of the "eight flowers" (Sanskrit *aṣṭapuṣpikā*) in connection with the Pāśupata cult.

[9] Śiva destroyed Kāma, the god of Love, with fire emitted from this forehead eye.

[10] Śiva flayed the hide of the elephant-demon Gajāsura, and danced with the hide, dripping with blood, draped around him.

before their wives as a naked beggar and seduced them.[11] The Pine Forest sages tried to use black magic against Śiva; they dispatched various hostile creatures armed with magic spells to destroy the god. But Śiva simply flayed the tiger and put its skin on as a garment; picked up the drum, fire, deer, snakes, and severed heads that were thrown at him and made them into his weapons; turned the horrible goblins and spirits that attacked him into his retinue; and began dancing on the dwarf Apasmāra (*muyalakaṉ*), demon of ignorance.

Śiva's close association with animals is reflected in his persona as Paśupati (*pacupati*), "Lord of the Beasts," a name that the Tamil Śaivas interpret as meaning "Lord of Souls" (*pacu*). Like most Hindu gods, Śiva has a *vāhana* (vehicle or mount), the white bull (*viṭai*) Nandi. Identified as Nandin or Nandikeśvara, one of the *gaṇas* ("multitudes," spirit attendants) of Śiva in Kailāsa, this bull can be found seated facing the sanctum in all temples of Śiva. The *gaṇa* host is made up of different sorts of beings: grotesque, dwarflike goblins or spirits (*pūtam*), the emaciated ghosts (*pēy*) that dance with Śiva in the burning-ground (*iṭukāṭu*) where corpses are cremated. Some of the *gaṇas* are human devotees turned into spirits.[12] The band of spirits accompanies Śiva when he rides on his bull and becomes a band of musicians when he performs his dance.

Śiva's feet are a standard item in the descriptive repertoire. Invoking them as symbols and embodiments of the Lord's grace, the poets call them "beautiful [lit., rosy] feet" (*cēvaṭi*), "golden feet" (*poṉṉaṭi*), "holy feet" (*tiruvaṭi*), flower-feet (*pūṅkaḻal*), feet that offer refuge, and feet that kicked at Death (in the myth of Mārkaṇḍeya). The feet are also described in iconographic terms as "adorned by ringing anklets" and "wearing the hero's or warrior's band (*kaḻal*)," suggesting Śiva's personae as dancer and Tamil hero.[13] The importance given to the Lord's feet must be understood in the context of the pan-Indian conception of venerating the feet of a person of higher rank as an act of deference and love. In India, one shows respect for one's superiors, elders, parents, teacher, and masters by placing one's head upon the feet of the honored one and by symbolically accepting the dust from those feet as a sign of favor or blessing. "Aṭiyār," the Tamil Śaiva term for "devotee," literally means "one who is at the feet (*aṭi*) [of the Lord]."

[11] *Kanta purāṇam*, Dakṣa Kāṇṭam, chs. 13, 14. See Dorai Rangaswamy's discussion, *Religion and Philosophy*, 1: 527–30.

[12] The Nāyaṉār Kāraikkāl Ammaiyār became one of Śiva's ghosts or demonic spirits (*pēy*). The *gaṇas* are also called *pāriṭam*, "attendants."

[13] In the classical civilization of the Tamils, heros and great warriors received the *kaḻal*, an ornamental band or ring worn midway between ankle and knee, as a prize for victory and valor. The *kaḻal* can be seen on Śiva's leg in many Cōḻa bronzes of Śiva as the Lord of the Dance.

Among the particular *mūrtis* of Śiva, Appar, Cuntarar, and Campantar favor Naṭarāja, the dancing Lord (see illus. 8), and Bhikṣāṭana, Śiva the Beggar Lord (see illus. 9), the two forms that developed in South Indian iconography and mythology in rich and unique ways. The Bhikṣāṭana form of the Lord figures in the myths of Śiva's conflict with the sages of the Pine Forest. Unlike the Naṭarāja form, the Bhikṣāṭana *mūrti* is not associated with specific shrines but forms part of the mythological and festival-related traditions of all the major Tamil shrines. The character of Śiva is perhaps best revealed in his celebrated form as Lord of the Dance. According to the pan-Hindu tradition, Śiva has many dances, most of which are vigorous and violent (*tāṇḍava*), in keeping with his function as Destroyer.[14] The Lord dances at twilight and in the night; his favorite arena is the burning-ground for the dead, but he also dances in various other places in celebration of his victory over demons.[15] Drawing from Tamil Śaiva lore, the *Tēvāram* saints add local varieties of dance (Tamil *kūttu*) to Śiva's repertoire; among these are the *paṭutam*, *pāṇi*, *koṭukoṭṭi*, and *pāṇṭaraṅkam*, some of which are described in the *Cilappatikāram* epic.[16] The poets seem to be aware of the local myths regarding Śiva's dance at Tiruvālaṅkāṭu and Tillai (Chidambaram) shrines, although they do not mention these myths in their fully developed form, in which Śiva defeats the Goddess in a dance contest.[17] Along with Kāraikkāl Ammaiyār, the *Tēvāram* poets provide us with the earliest descriptions of the celebrated dance of Śiva in the "Little Ampalam hall in Tillai (Chidambaram)" (*tillaic ciṟṟampalam*), a dance that lies at the core of Tamil Śaiva mysticism as elaborated in the Siddhānta philosophy and is represented in the Cōḻa bronzes of the Dancing Lord.[18] According to Tirumūlar's *Tirumantiram* and later texts, in this dance Śiva performs his fivefold

[14] See Ingalls, *Anthology*, section 4, and Dorai Rangaswamy, *Religion and Philosophy*, 1: 441–67.

[15] Śiva's dance as Gajāsura-saṃhāra-mūrti, cloaked in the elephant hide, is a popular theme in Pallava and Cōḻa sculpture.

[16] On the *koṭukoṭṭi* and *pāṇṭaraṅkam* dances, see Dorai Rangaswamy, *Religion and Philosophy*, 1: 394–96. The author (p. 394) suggests that *pāṇṭaraṅkam* probably means "the white dance hall, . . . the place of ashes." In association with the myth of the burning of the three cities, it may mean the place where the cities were burned to ashes. It may also simply suggest the dance in the burning-ground. Śiva, and perhaps Durgā, are described as dancing these two dances in *Cilappatikāram* VI.40–45.

[17] For a discussion of the myths of the dance contests with the Goddess, see Shulman, *Tamil Temple Myths*, pp. 211–23.

[18] Over time, an elaborate local mythology has grown around the arenas (Sanskrit *sabhā*, Tamil *capai*) of Śiva's dances in the Tamil country. The dance in Tillai is known as the *ānandatāṇḍava*; as Lord of the Golden Hall (*kaṉakacapai*, *poṉṉampalam*) in Tillai, Śiva performs it in the Citsabhā ("Hall of the Supreme Consciousness"). Five other dances are performed in halls at Maturai, Puttūr, Kuṟṟālam, Tiruvālaṅkāṭu, and Tirunelvēli. The seventh dance, the Dance of Destruction, is all-pervasive.

cosmic activity (*pañcakṛtya*) of creation, preservation, destruction, "veiling," and grace, each symbolized by a particular aspect of the icon.[19] The complex symbolism of the Tamil Naṭarāja is best summarized in the conclusion of Ananda Coomaraswamy's famous essay on the dance of Śiva: "The Essential Significance of Shiva's Dance is threefold: first, it is the image of his Rhythmic Play as the Source of all Movement within the Cosmos, which is represented by the Arch: Secondly, the Purpose of his Dance is to Release the Countless souls of men from the Snare of Illusion: Thirdly the Place of the Dance, Chidambaram, the Centre of the Universe, is within the Heart."[20]

Like the sculptors of reliefs and icons in Tamil shrines, the *Tēvāram* poets portray Śiva's myths in two modes: the iconic and the dynamic. In the former, the myth functions as a part of Śiva's persona, the focus being on creating an iconic image of the god; in the latter, the myth or narrative comes to the fore, and the Lord is portrayed as principal actor in a dramatic event. The myths of the eight Vīraṭṭāṉam shrines often receive such dynamic treatment, as do the legends of famous devotees such as Arjuna, Caṇṭīcar, and Kaṇṇappar. Four myths, used repeatedly in both iconic and narrative modes, stand out in the *Tēvāram* corpus: the burning of the three cities of the demons, the revelation of Śiva in the cosmic pillar or flame-*liṅga* to the arrogant Brahmā and Viṣṇu, Śiva's devouring of the poison emitted at the churning of the cosmic ocean, and his subjugation of the demon Rāvaṇa when the latter tried to uproot Kailāsa hill (see illus. 11).[21] Appar, Campantar, and Cuntarar impart a suggestive, poetic dimension to the understanding of these seminal myths in the Tamil Śaiva tradition, which play an important role in Tirumūlar's exposition of Tamil Śaiva mystical doctrine in his *Tirumantiram*.[22] We have already noted the distinctive manner in which Appar and Campantar use two of these myths: the former ends all his hymns with a description of the legend of Rāvaṇa, and the latter devotes the eighth and ninth verses of his hymns to the Rāvaṇa myth and the myth of the cosmic *liṅga* (illus. 10).

Two details of the *Tēvāram* image of Śiva remain to be discussed: the presence of Śiva as the *liṅga*, and his relationship with the Goddess. Since ritual worship forms such an important part of the religion of the *Tē-*

[19] See Ananda Coomaraswamy, "The Dance of Shiva," in *The Dance of Shiva: Fourteen Indian Essays*, revised edition (New York: Noonday Press, 1977), pp. 66–78, at 70–71. In this classic essay, Coomaraswamy discusses the meaning of the dance of Śiva in the Tamil context. For a more wide-ranging study of Naṭarāja, consult C. Sivaramamurti's monumental *Naṭarāja in Art, Thought and Literature* (Delhi: National Museum, 1974).

[20] Coomaraswamy, "Dance," p. 77.

[21] The *mūrti*s of Śiva associated with these myths are, respectively: Tripurāri or Tripurāntaka-mūrti, Liṅgodbhava-mūrti, Viṣāpaharaṇa-mūrti and Rāvaṇānugraha-mūrti. For brief summaries of the major myths of Śiva in the *Tēvāram*, see Appendix D below.

[22] Tirumūlar, *Tirumantiram*, Tantiram 2 (Kaḻakam edition).

vāram,[23] for all their celebration of the many *mūrtis* (lit., "embodiment," "embodied form") of the Lord, the poet-saints are also profoundly aware of the Lord as, and in, the *liṅga* (lit., "sign"), which is an aniconic image. It is to the *liṅga* that ritual worship is offered, be it in the shrine or at the home; and it is in the *liṅga* that the Lord is established (*sthāvara*, Tamil *tāparam*) and "dwells" in the *garbhagṛha* (inner sanctum) at the heart of the Śiva temple. While at one level the *liṅga* represents the phallus, the male "sign," this is not the primary significance of this image for the Tamil Śaiva community. The consciousness of the *liṅga* as the primal image of Śiva, as the image that represents the power and infinite potentiality of the divine and that is Śiva as simultaneously manifest and unmanifest (sakala-niṣkala) informs the *Tēvāram* hymns on a metaphysical plane as well as in concrete descriptions of ritual worship (cf. illus. 5 and 10).[24] As for the Goddess, we see that compared to her prominence in the later literary sources of Tamil Śaivism and later versions of Tamil temple myths (*talapurāṇam*), her role in the *Tēvāram* is a relatively subdued one.[25] Here she is most often invoked as the inseparable "consort" and companion of the Lord, the lovely and gentle feminine figure who tempers the harshness of his personality, the sensitive witness of his heroic deeds (see illus. 6).[26] At the same time, Appar, Cuntarar, and Campantar affirm the importance of the Goddess in their vision of Śiva: to them, she is none other than the gentle, feminine side of the Lord, which they invoke in nearly every hymn, calling Śiva "the Lord who shares his body with the Goddess" as Ardhanārīśvara, the symbol of perfect love, unity, equality, completeness (see illus. 7). Śiva in the *Tēvāram* is rarely portrayed as the playful householder of the Sanskrit stanzaic tradition or the later Purāṇas: the god's wife and his two children (Skanda/Murukaṉ and Gaṇeśa) are no more than shadowy figures in his personal history; nor is Śiva's band of spirits described with attention to individuality; these *gaṇas* remain "*gaṇas*," undifferentiated "crowds, multitudes."[27]

Whatever the particular focus of their description of Śiva in different verses and poems, the *Tēvāram* saints emphasize lordship, divine grace, auspiciousness, and beauty as the chief attributes of their God. The lewd

[23] See Part One, Chapter 3 above.

[24] On the symbolism of the *liṅga*, see Stella Kramrisch, *Presence of Śiva*, ch. 7; and J.W.V. Curtis, "Space Concepts" in *Experiencing Śiva*, ed. Clothey and Long, pp. 87–101.

[25] For the prominent role of the Goddess in the later *talapurāṇam* literature, consult Shulman, *Tamil Temple Myths*.

[26] The Goddess has a central role in the theology of Māṇikkavācakar. See Yocum, *Hymns to the Dancing Śiva*, ch. 5.

[27] Consult Ingalls, *Anthology*, section 5. Among the three *Tēvāram* saints, Cuntarar occasionally uses the ironic mode, making teasing remarks about Śiva's two wives (Pārvatī and the Ganges) and his comical family.

beggar, the dancer in the burning-ground, is at the same time the brahmin scholar who chants the Veda, the charismatic local hero of the Caṅkam tradition, skilled artist, and patron of the arts. As for the poets, like all of Śiva's devotees, they are, above all, connoisseurs and lovers of the supramundane beauty of the Lord.

1 The Beautiful Lord

(POEMS 1–19)

The Red One

1. Appar IV.114.1

On strong shoulders like coral hills
lie coils of matted hair
like branching sea-coral.
Around the hair a hooded snake
winds like a streak of coral.
With the snake my Father bears
the coral red eye,
and the young moon
is a white flower on his crest.

Portrait in Silver

2. Appar IV.113.1

He bears a skull
like a silver conch shell.
His twisted white sacred thread
shines like a strand of silver rope.
Matted hair crowned with the white moon
bright as beaten silver leaf,
wearing white bones,
the brahmin has smeared silver ash
on his coral skin.

The Golden Lord

3. Cuntarar VII.24.1 Maḻapāṭi

O god with the golden form,
you bind the tigerskin around your waist,

and wear the golden *koṉṟai* blossom
on gleaming red hair!
O King, great jewel, ruby in Maḻapāṭi,
O Mother, whom can I think of
but you?

Bull Rider

4. Campantar I.71.7 *Naṟaiyūrc Cittīccaram*

A heron feather and the bright datura
adorn his matted hair.
His flame-red body
is covered with white ash.
Over his girdle and loincloth
he has bound a tigerskin
encircled by lovely snakes.
Thus, with anklets ringing,
the Lord of Cittīccaram shrine
comes riding on his bull.

5. Appar VI.307.7

If you would quickly get rid of your evil karma,
say, "Kaṇṭiyūr, Kaṇṭiyūr!,"
home of the Lord who rides on his red-eyed bull,
as Daṇḍin, Guṇḍodara, and Bhṛṅgirṭi,
illustrious Nandin, Śaṅkukarṇa,
he who created the world in ancient time,
and he who measured the universe,
all sing his praise in the Pallāṇṭu hymn,
to the chorus of potbellied goblins with narrow eyes.

The Lute Player

6. Campantar I.73.8 *Kāṉūr*

The coral-red Lord
who loves to dwell in Kāṉūr of fragrant groves

4. Śiva wears the flower of the datura (*mattam*) in his hair.

5. The poet names several of Śiva's *gaṇa*s (attendant spirits) in this hymn, including the bull Nandin. Among those who sing the "*pallāṇṭu*" ("long live . . .") hymn that is traditionally addressed to kings and gods are Brahmā the creator god and Viṣṇu the Strider.

6. "Lute": *vīṇai* (Sanskrit *vīṇā*), a stringed instrument similar to the *yāḻ*. The *vīṇā* has

came to me chanting sweet Tamil poems.
He stayed,
playing the lute, singing songs
to the beat of the *muḻavam* and *montai* drums.
Now he is gone,
taking my beauty with him,
leaving me pale as the *kumiḻ* flower.

The Lord Who Is Half Woman

7. Campantar I.77.1 *Acciṟupākkam*

My master who rules over Acciṟupākkam,
displays two forms,
having taken as half of himself
the soft girl with waist small as gathered lightning.
He has flowing matted hair like a mass of gold,
in his body the color of sea-coral
mingles with the hue of fire,
and on the expanse framed by twin shoulder-hills
he wears the white sacred thread and the rich ash.

8. Appar IV.8.10

An earring of bright new gold glows on one ear;
a coiled conch shell sways on the other.
On one side he chants the melodies of the ritual Veda,
on the other, he gently smiles.
Matted hair adorned with sweet *koṉṟai* blossoms
on one half of his head,
and a woman's curls on the other, he comes.
The one is the nature of his form,
the other, of hers;
And both are the very essence
of his beauty.

survived as an important instrument in the tradition of South Indian classical (Carnatic) music. In some of his iconographic forms Śiva is portrayed as playing the *vīṇā* (*vīṇādhara*). "*Tāḷam vīṇai paṇṇi*": literally, "strumming the *vīṇā* to keep time [to his song]." The speaker in this poem is a lovelorn woman in the *akam* tradition. "*Kōlanīrmai*": excellent beauty, the quality of beauty. The *kumiḻ* is a white flower.

8. "A woman's curls": *kuḻal*, a way of dressing the hair in tubular coils.

*

9. Cuntarar VII.84 *Kāṉappēr*

1
When shall I see, to my heart's delight,
the devotees who worship his feet,
the bright young crescent moon,
the body like a white lotus that he shares
with the Goddess with soft young breasts?
When shall I see his eight arms,
the beauty of the bright, fragrant matted hair
and his throat like a shining dark cloud
in which he placed the poison
devoured at the contest of the demons and gods?
When shall I see and worship the young man
who lives in Kāṉappēr of green fields?

5
When shall I see the majesty of his bull,
the cluster of *koṉṟai* blossoms on his bright fragrant hair,
the form he lovingly shares with the Goddess
who has a slim waist and a smile white as jasmine?
When shall I see the glorious dance he performs
in the great hall of Tillai city,
the mighty axe, the fire blazing in his hand,
the sound of the cymbals
played by devotees singing his praise?
When shall I see the young man
who lives in Kāṉappēr of green fields?

10. Appar IV.80 *Kōyil (Tillai)*

2
The Lord with the holy form
rides on a mighty bull.

9, v. 1. "Goddess with soft young breasts": "*cūtaṉa meṉmulaiyāḷ*," literally, "woman with soft breasts which are also high, like the pointed, conical pieces used in gambling boardgames (*cūtu*)." v. 5. "Cymbals": "*kallavaṭam*." Judging from the descriptions in the *Tēvāram*, the *kallavaṭam* seems to be a kind of rhythm instrument with which singers and dancers accompany themselves. It is not clear whether it is a small drum or the kind of castanets that devotees of Hindu gods still use as accompaniment for singing and dancing.

10, v. 2. Appar refers to the famous brahmin community (*tillai mūvāyiravar*, the three thousand brahmins of Tillai) attached to the Tillai (Chidambaram) temple. Known as "*kōyil*" (*the* temple), Chidambaram is the great sacred center of Śiva's dance. v. 3. Ayaṉ: Brahmā. Māl: Viṣṇu.

The husband
of the lovely daughter of the mountain
wears the tigerskin.
He lives in Ciṟṟampalam in Tillai,
home of brahmins
who are a blessing for the whole world.
I, who have seen his holy feet with these eyes,
have nothing left to see.

3
Ayaṉ and Māl worship him every day
with flowers and incense and sandal paste,
for even they could not behold his form.
I, who have seen with these eyes
the cloth of silk on the ash-smeared god
in Tillai's golden Ciṟṟampalam,
have nothing left to see.

Śiva's Mysteries

11. Campantar II.140 *Tiruvāṉmiyūr*

1
You who rule the earth
as the sense within speech,
dwelling in Tiruvāṉmiyūr
where fish leap in the salt marsh
by the shore on which big waves dash
deep-sea conches and white shells,
explain the wonder of your joining
the mountain's daughter.

2
You who wear the dancer's anklet
on your beautiful feet,
dwelling in Tiruvāṉmiyūr,
where devotees, deep in meditation,

11. The entire hymn is constructed on the pattern of questions regarding Śiva's wonderful attributes. v. 1. "Sense within speech" echoes the opening verse of Kālidāsa's Sanskrit epic poem *Raghuvaṃśa*. v. 2. Here "*kaḻal*" must mean "foot" and not "warrior's band or anklet," since the *kaḻal* is usually worn above the ankle. In his androgynous form, Śiva wears the hero's *kaḻal* on one leg, and the woman's anklet (*cilampu*) on the other. v. 11. "Seeking the grace": read "*aruḷ ceyya*" instead of "*aruḷ ceyta*." Cf. *Tēvāram* Ātīṉam edition.

worship you with sandal paste and cool water
and fragrant smoke from aloe sticks,
explain the wonder of your taking for your color
the sunset's brilliant hue.

3
You who wear a tigerskin
and live in Tiruvāṉmiyūr,
where green groves flowing with honey
stand close to cool wooded marshes by the sea,
explain the wonder of your love
for dancing with fire,
cloaked in the elephant's hide.

11
Seeking the grace of the Primal Lord
who lives in Tiruvāṉmiyūr,
Ñāṉacampantaṉ of Kāḻi, who once received divine wisdom,
sang this hymn of question and answer,
for the good ascetic who shares his body with the Goddess.
Those who remember these words with pious thoughts
will rule the far world of heaven.

The Auspicious Lord

12. Campantar I.98.1 *Cirāppaḷḷi*

My heart rejoices
when I sing
of the one who has all good things
and nothing evil,
him who has an old white bull,
and Umā as half of himself,
the Lord who has the unattainable treasure,
and Cirāppaḷḷi's hill.

12. "Who has the unattainable treasure": "*ceṉṟaṭaiyāt tiruv uṭaiyāṉai*", literally, "who has the treasure which one may not obtain by seeking out or pursuing." The phrase "*ceṉṟu aṭaiyāt tiru*" (or variants such as "*ceṉṟaṭaiyāc celvam*") occurs frequently in the poems of Appar and Campantar. It describes the nature of release, the implications being that release is the ultimate treasure or wealth, that Śiva alone holds this treasure, that it cannot be won through seeking, and that it can be "attained" only through Śiva's grace.

13. Appar IV.8.1

Other than the Lord's name,
is there in this world a perfect good,
in which all blessings abide?
Just think, he is a beggar who wears a hide;
over the hide, a snake dances; he eats the food of the poor;
his temple is the burning-ground, his dish, a skull.
Seeing these blessings,
the gods themselves know his nature
and honor him in their hearts.

14. Campantar II.221.1 KŌḶAṞU TIRUPPATIKAM (A CHARM AGAINST EVIL PLANETS)

He shares his form with the Goddess
whose shoulders curve gracefully like the bamboo.
He holds the ocean's poison in his throat,
he plays the lute.
Wearing the bright moon and the Ganges
on his crown of matted hair,
he has entered my heart and abides here.
So let my star be the sun or the moon,
Mars or Mercury or Jupiter,
let it be Venus, or Saturn, or the two snakes!
All the planets and stars are good stars for us,
all bring good luck to Śiva's devotees!

The Brahmin Lord

15. Campantar II.148.1 *Kacci Ēkampam*

My heart can think of nothing
other than the brahmin who is the Veda,
he who bears the white moon
on his pure, matted red hair,
God who is both man and woman,

13. "The food of the poor": "*kavaṇaḷavuḷḷa vuṇku,*" literally, "food consisting of morsels the size of pebbles."

14. Apart from the stars and planets after which the seven days of the week (*nāḷ*) are named, the Hindus include in their list of nine "planets" (*navagraha*) Rāhu and Ketu, the ascending and descending nodes of the eclipse, portrayed as two halves of a serpent.

15. "The brahmin who is the Veda": "*maṟaiyāṉai*" can mean "he who has the Veda," a brahmin; or "he who is the Veda."

the Supreme Lord
who dwells in the beautiful shrine
of holy Ēkampam in Kacci.

16. Campantar II.147.1 *Cīrkāḻi (Kāḻi)*

They will find enduring joy,
who praise the auspicious god
who knows the four Vedas
and the six sacred sciences,
who is himself the sacred Word
recited by scholars of the scripture,
who has taken for his home
the shrine in Kāḻi's ancient walled town.

*

17. Appar IV.30.2 *Kaḻippālai*

He gave us the desire for heaven,
made us perform the rite of sacrifice.
He gave us the music of modes for singing him,
made us practice devotion as *bhaktas.*
He granted grace to Māl
who spanned the earth with a stride.
He placed an eye on his forehead.
He is the chieftain
of Kaḻippālai's seashore tract.

18. Campantar I.16.6 *Puḷamaṅkai*

He is the king,
a shower of rain for the world.
Pure gold, first being,
living in grove-encircled Puḷamaṅkai,
he is my own; he is music, he is
like the light of the morning sun.
Ālanturai is the shrine where he abides.

16. "The six sacred sciences": *aṅga*, the six disciplines related to the study of the Veda.

17. "Heaven": the world of Śiva where his devotees may join their Lord. "Modes": *paṇ*. Māl: Viṣṇu. Śiva is here called "*cērppaṉ*," a term used in the Tamil classical tradition for rulers of seashore lands.

18. Ālanturai is the name of the temple in Puḷamaṅkai.

19. Appar VI.311.10 VIṈĀVIṬAITTIRUTTĀṆṬAKAM (THE TĀṆṬAKAM POEM OF QUESTION AND ANSWER)

You'd like to say:
"Our Lord has long matted hair.
He is the one who shares himself
with the dark-eyed Goddess.
He lives in Kacci Mayāṉam,"
but the Lord is more than this.
There is no one like him,
he isn't any one person,
he doesn't live in any one place,
and you can't compare him
to anything in the world.
If it weren't for his grace,
you would have no eyes to see
his form, his color and nature,
you wouldn't be able to say:
"This is how he looks;
this is his color; this is the way he is;
this is God."

2 The Lord Is All Things

(POEMS 20–28)

20. Appar VI.301.1 *Civapuram*

See the god!
See him who is higher than the gods!
See him who is Sanskrit of the North
and southern Tamil and the four Vedas!
See him who bathes in milk and ghee,
see the Lord, see him who dances, holding fire,
in the wilderness of the burning-ground,
see him who blessed the hunter-saint!
See him who wells up as honey
in the heart-lotus of his lovers!
See him who has the unattainable treasure!
See Śiva! See him who is our treasure
here in Civapuram!

21. Appar IV.54.8 *Pukalūr*

As water, as fire, as earth, as sky,
as the glorious rays of the sun and moon,
as the lord whom the Himalayan gods supplicate,
as the deity hard to comprehend,
the Lord of holy Pukalūr,
who dances in many places,
is the highest god among the gods.

22. Campantar I.134.4 *Pa̱riyalūr Vīraṭṭam*

He who has no beginning in birth
is the brilliant god who makes
the beginning and end,
and the birth and flourishing
of those who are born.

20. "He who has the unattainable treasure": "*ce̱ṉṟaṭaiyāc celvaṉ.*" See note to Poem 12 above. The "hunter-saint": Kaṇṇappar.

22. "Fierce spirits": "*viṟar pāriṭam.*"

He is the god who lives
surrounded by fierce spirits
in the Vīraṭṭam shrine
of the splendid holy town of Pa̠riyalūr.

23. Appar VI.308 Nin̠ṟa tiruttāṇṭakam (The Tāṇṭakam Poem of the Lord Who Stands)

1
As wide earth, as fire and water,
as sacrificer and wind that blows,
as eternal moon and sun,
as ether, as the eight-formed god,
as cosmic good and evil, woman and man,
all other forms, and his own form,
and all these as himself,
as yesterday and today and tomorrow,
the god of the long red hair stands,
O wonder!

3
As rock, as hill, as forest,
as river, as streams and small canals,
as salt marshes by the sea,
as grass, as bush, as plants and herbs,
as the city, as the one who smashed the three cities,
as the word, as meaning in the word,
as the stirring of all life,
as the places where life stirs,
as grain, as the earth in which it grows,
as the water that gives it life,
the Lord who blazed up as the great flame stands,
O wonder!

24. Appar IV.48 *Āppāṭi*

1
The Lord of Āppāṭi
who wears the blooming *kon̠ṟai* in his hair,
is manifest

23. Verse 3 in particular vividly presents the concept of Śiva as immanent in all life forms, moving and still. A similar description in *Tiruvācakam* 1.26–30 has several verbal echoes ("*pullākip pūṭāki* . . ."). The images are closely associated with the imagery of Rudra as the god of plant life and the great healer in the *Śatarudrīya*.

as the seven seas, wind, all-embracing ether,
life's breath in the body,
earth and bright fire,
the light of the day,
and the cool moon
of evenings fragrant with flowers.

3
The Lord of Āppāṭi
whose spouse shares half his form,
is manifest
as the chants of the Veda,
as the meaning of the chant,
as the friend of those who sing melodious songs;
the god with the eye on his forehead
is the very love that those who love him feel.

7
The Lord of Āppāṭi
is both inside and outside,
form and no-form.
He is both the flood and the bank,
he is the broad-rayed sun.
Himself the highest mystery,
he is in all hidden thoughts.
He is thought and meaning, and embraces
all who embrace him.

25. Appar VI.243.1 TIRUVĀRŪRT TIRUTTĀṆṬAKAM (THE TĀṆṬAKAM POEM OF THE LORD IN TIRUVĀRŪR) *Tiruvārūr (Ārūr)*

The gorgeous gem, delicious honey, milk,
the sweet taste of sugar cane, clear sugar syrup,
precious gem, the sound
of flute, drum, cymbals, and lute,
great gem, coral, pure gold and pearl,
the crest jewel of Paruppatam hill,
rare gem who destroys our sin,
our Lord in Ārūr—
I was a dog, who once failed
to know and remember him.

25. "Precious gem": "*kurumaṇi*," "precious or priceless gem," can also mean "a rare teacher (guru)." "Paruppatam hill": "*paruppatam*," Sanskrit *parvata*, can signify any hill or mountain, but in the *Tēvāram* hymns it most often refers to Śrīśailam (Śrī-parvata) in the Andhra area. In this hymn Appar is speaking of his past as a Jain monk.

26. Appar VI.261.1 *Āvaṭuturai*

My treasure and good fortune, Lord sweet as honey,
golden flame of heaven, O form of blazing light,
my friend, my flesh,
heart within my flesh, soul within my heart,
wish-fulfilling tree,
my eye, dark pupil in the eye, image that dances within!
Save me from the hidden disease of karma,
bull among the gods, you who live in cool Āvaṭuturai!

The Cosmic Person

27. Appar IV.4.8 *Tiruvārūr (Ārūr)*

The god who has
a thousand feet like a thousand red lotuses,
a thousand shoulders like a thousand golden hills,
a thousand long strands of hair like a thousand suns,
and has taken for himself a thousand names,
is our Lord who lives in Ārūr.

*

28. Appar VI.229 *Karukāvūr*

1
He is my bright diamond,
good days, and auspicious stars,
and evil planets, too.
He is ambrosia untasted,
butter in milk, juice in the fruit,
melody in song.
With Umā as half his self, he is

27. This verse evokes the vision of the Lord as the Cosmic Person (Puruṣa) as described in the Vedic *Puruṣasūkta* (*Rig Veda* X.90) and the *Bhagavadgītā* (XI.9–12). It also refers back to the praise of Rudra-Śiva in the Vedic *Śatarudrīya* litany. Appar's comparison of Śiva's tawny hair with the sun, or rather, the sun's rays, echoes one of the Sanskrit epithets of the sun: "*sahasra-raśmi*," "the thousand-rayed one."

28, v. 1 This refers to the Hindu belief that the planets (*kōḷ*), days, and the "stars" (lunar asterisms, *nāḷ*) by which days are identified have evil influences on human lives. See Poem 14. "Speech on my tongue": "*nāviṟku uraiyāṭi*," literally, "speaker on my tongue, the one who makes me speak." Śiva is also the eye that the world sees. v. 7. Ātirai: The day associated with the asterism Tiruvātirai (Ātirai) in the month of Mārkaḻi in the Tamil luni-solar calendar is sacred to Śiva. See Appar's description of the Tiruvātirai festival in Tiruvārūr in Poem 98.

speech on my tongue.
My Father in Karukāvūr
is the source of all things
and the eye that beholds the world.

2
He is the seed, he the sprout and root;
True friend to his devotees, he takes the forms we desire.
Milk-white god, the refuge we seek,
he is the supreme Light.
He conceals himself from
all the gods in heaven who praise him,
yet dwells within my heart.
My Father in Karukāvūr
is the eye that reveals all things
to me, his devotee.

3
My Lord is the flower and its color,
the King who dwells as fragrance within the flower.
The Lord who shares his form
with the lady of the beautiful bracelets
is the god of all the true faiths,
and brings endless pain
to those who do not praise him.
Dwelling in my heart, he saved me from Death.
My Father in Karukāvūr
is my eye.

5
None can fully grasp
the greatness of his manifestations
as the creator of the universe,
as the god who dug into the earth.
He smashed the enemy's three citadels,
burning them with terrible fire.
He bears the trident, axe, and snake,
and rides the bull.
Absent from evil hearts,
My Father in Karukāvūr
is my eye.

7
A snake encircles his waist,
he sits under the banyan tree,

the Ātirai is his festival day.
The cosmic gods themselves honor the sacred crown
on which he bears the moon.
Destroyer of karma, he dwells in my thoughts,
and in every human heart on this wide-famed earth.
He who shares his form with Umā
drank the poison that arose from the surging sea.
My Father in Karukāvūr
is my eye.

8
He is drum and drumbeat,
the measure of all speech.
The ash-smeared god, the supreme Light,
destroyer of our sin, is our one path to release.
The Lord who kicked at terrible Death
firmly eludes evil men—
they can't see him.
My Father in Karukāvūr,
is my eye.

11
He burned the enemy's three cities
with terrible fire;
pressing down on the arrogant demon,
in an instant he crushed his ten heads,
then graciously listened to his sweet songs.
He quelled the five senses,
he felled Death with his foot,
he is the mantra that gives us release.
My Father in Karukāvūr
is my eye.

3 Naṭarāja: Lord of the Dance

(POEMS 29–36)

29. Appar IV.81.4 *Kōyil (Tillai)*

If you could see
the arch of his brow,
the budding smile
on lips red as the *kovvai* fruit,
cool matted hair,
the milk-white ash on coral skin,
and the sweet golden foot
raised up in dance,
then even human birth on this wide earth
would become a thing worth having.

30. Campantar I.39.1 *Vēṭkaḷam (Tiruvēṭkaḷam)*

When our Lord who is both end and beginning
dances to the deep sound of the *muḻavam* drum,
holding blazing fire in the hollow of his hand,
as the mountain's daughter watches,
the Gaṅgā's murmuring stream with foaming waves
flows over the cool crescent moon.
He who smears his body
with ash from the burning-ground
is our Lord who dwells
in Vēṭkaḷam's fine town.

29. A very popular verse, describing Śiva as Naṭarāja, the Cosmic Dancer. "*Paṉitta*" (dewy, full of waterdrops) refers to the cool waters of the Ganges which run through Śiva's hair; hence "cool" matted hair. "*Poṉ*" in "*poṟpātam*" ("golden foot") is a term of endearment.

30. The poet describes the effect of Śiva's vigorous dancing on the river and moon that he bears on his matted hair. The alliteration in this verse nicely evokes the sounds of the Ganges and the drum: "*cantam ilaṅku nakutalai kaṅkai*," "*mantamuḻavam iyampa*." The verse begins with the phrase "end and beginning," "*antamum ātiyum*," significantly placing Śiva's destructive function first, since it is the basis of his role as creator.

The Dance in the Burning-Ground

31. Appar IV.2.6 *Atikai Vīraṭṭāṉam*

We belong to him whose light
is the flickering firebrand in the burning-ground;
the throbbing beat of the *tuṭi* drum
and his host of eighteen kinds of spirits
surround him;
the Vedic song that few may learn,
and, on the stage, the dance
that even the learned may not know—
all these, and the broad Keṭilam river, are his.
We fear nothing; there is nothing for us to fear.

32. Campantar I.134.5 *Paṟiyalūr Vīraṭṭam*

The skullbearer who dances
in the burning-ground for the dead,
the god who dances the *paṭutam* dance
in the cremation-ground,
is the Lord of the Vīraṭṭam shrine
in Paṟiyalūr of blossoming groves
and wise scholars of the sacred Veda.

*

33. Appar IV.121.1 *Ārūr*

The Lord of Ārūr,
who wears the *akṣa* beads
along with the snake,
is the dancer who delights
in performing to the band
of attendant goblins with gaping mouths,
who play the *kokkarai* and flute,
the lute and the *koṭukoṭṭi* drum.

31, 32. In these and other descriptions of Śiva's dance in the cremation-ground, the Tamil saints effectively portray him as the god of paradox who encompasses both the Vedic ceremony and the shamanistic dance, as the auspicious god who renders even the place of death pure.

33. "*Akṣa*": Tamil *akku*; the Rudrākṣa (Rudra's eye) seeds sacred to Śiva, worn by devotees and used as rosaries.

34. Appar IV.80.1 *Kōyil (Tillai)*

If there are men who want to see anything in the world
other than the dance of Araṉ, whose feet we serve,
in Ciṟṟampalam shrine in Tillai,
where the arecca tree with broad fronds grows tall,
the streets are lined with great mansions,
and all the fields are watered
by streams full of *vāḷai* fish—
then they are but devil-devotees,
seeing worthless things with rheumy eyes.

35. Appar IV.92.9 *Aiyāṟu*

See the holy feet of Aiyāṟu's Lord,
feet that dance
in the burning-ground for rotting corpses,
making the earth heave,
as the *paraṇṭai* and the *montai* drum resound,
bands of ghosts gather around the *muḻavam* drum
and strike its curved head,
and jackals provide
the long, high wail of the flute.

36. Campantar I.46 *Atikai Vīraṭṭāṉam*

1
Surrounded by short, fat goblins,
holding fire in his hand
and wearing a garland of full-blown *koṉṟai* flowers,
the Lord dances, as bees sing the Maruḷ mode,
in Atikai Vīraṭṭāṉam on the northern bank
of Keṭilam's clear stream where *keṇṭai* fish leap.

2
He waves the fire lifted up in his hand;
the strands of flame-red hair
adorned with *koṉṟai* blossoms thick with bees
sway, as he dances

35. "Ghosts": "*pēy*." The spirits of the dead which inhabit the cremation ground, and serve as Śiva's attendants. Following the *Tēvāram* Pondicherry edition I read "*montai*" (a drum) instead of "*āntai*" (owl). "*Paraṇṭai*" is an obscure word; it seems to indicate a musical instrument. See the *Tamil Lexicon*.

36, v. 4. The heads of the *muḻavu*, a concert drum that is the ancestor of the contemporary South Indian *mṛdaṅgam* drum, were smeared with black paste to give it resonance.

with the Goddess with speech sweet as sugar cane
and soft breasts like tender coconuts or lotus buds,
in his beloved Atikai's Vīraṭṭāṉam shrine.

3
The great deadly snake at his waist
dances along
as he who is skilled in the Vedic chant,
he who performs the *paṭutam* dance
on his begging rounds
and takes many forms,
dances in the Vīraṭṭāṉam shrine in Atikai,
where the moon rests on the rooftops.

4
The Lord who destroyed the demon forts
dances, in the Vīraṭṭāṉam shrine in Atikai,
crowned with the young moon
and holding fire in his hand,
to the sound of drums smeared with black paste,
to the melodious chant of the Veda,
and the praise-songs of all the gods in heaven.

5
The Lord who holds fire
and bears the broad river on his head
dances, trailing strands of fire-red matted hair,
in the burning-ground for the dead
in the gutted, desolate outskirts
of the blessed town of Atikai,
"blessed" because all good fortune
is rooted here, and will not leave the Vīraṭṭāṉam shrine.

6
The god crowned with the bright moon
dances, playing with flickering fire
in the hollow of his hand
and singing with Umā
who is graceful as a tender vine,
in the Vīraṭṭāṉam shrine in Atikai,
place of fertile fields encircled by streams.

7
The supreme Lord,
the highest Deity,

Primal Being of the Veda,
surrounded by his band of spirits
and clad in tigerskin,
dances as Umā sings and devotees praise his feet,
in the Vīraṭṭāṉam shrine
on Keṭilam's northern bank.

8
The bowman who shot at the citadels,
he who swiftly subdued the demon,
crushing the power of the huge arms
with which he lifted the rocky hill,
and then granted him grace,
dances, wearing skulls bleached white,
with open mouths and grinning teeth,
in the Vīraṭṭāṉam shrine in Atikai.

9
The Strider and the four-headed god
could not behold the ever-growing form
of the Lord with the ash-smeared chest
and sacred thread,
who dances, holding a stinking skull,
in the Vīraṭṭāṉam shrine
in Atikai where fragrant blue waterlilies bloom.

10
Clad in *aśoka* leaves
or with no clothes at all,
bearing a beggar's water jug
and dry gourd for dish, they toil;
their doctrines are self-contradictory,
but our Lord who is joined with Umā
wears a garland of fragrant flowers,
and dances in the Vīraṭṭāṉam shrine.

11
They will be rid of karma
who consider as their life support
the Tamil garland that Ñāṉacampantaṉ from Kāḻi,
town fragrant with seaside *nāḻal* trees,
has composed on the all-embracing feet,
adorned with the hero's band,
of the Lord of Atikai Vīraṭṭāṉam,
whose clear stream is lined with banks of reeds.

4 Bhikṣāṭana: The Beggar

(POEMS 37–39)

37. Campantar I.40.1 *Vāḻkoḷiputtūr*

With ash-smeared breast,
he rides on the bull.
Followed by his band of spirits,
he wanders through towns
with sacred flags,
begging for food,
chanting the beggar's call.
Let us offer fragrant flowers
and behold the feet
of the god with the dark throat,
who lives in Vāḻkoḷiputtūr
with lovely Umā,
whose long eyes curve like swords,
as half his self.

38. Campantar II.138 *Valañcuḻi*

1
O dazzling light
praised by your devoted servants
in Valañcuḻi where bees sing,
drunk on cool fragrant honey
flowing out of blossoming flowers,
tell me why you once
wandered about as a beggar, singing songs.

37. "God with the dark throat": "*kaṟaik kaṇṭan*," literally, "he whose throat is stained dark [with the poison he drank at the churning of the ocean]." The beggar's cry: "Ladies, give me alms," is quoted in other verses in this hymn.

38, v. 2. "Large white egret": "*pāral veṇkuruku*." "Heron": "*nārai*." See B. L. Samy, *Caṅka ilakkiyattil puḷḷiṉa viḷakkam*, (Madras: SISSW Publishing Society, 1976), chs. 2, 4. v. 3. "Full-bloomed lotuses": "*kiṇṇavaṇṇamalkuṅ kiḷar tāmarai*," literally, "lotuses that flourish, blooming like cups"; "*-malkum*" is the reading in the *Tēvāram* Pondicherry edition. v. 6. Poṉṉi: the river Kaveri. The Pūcam festival is celebrated on the day of the asterism Pūcam in the month of Tai. Bathing in rivers is the focal ceremony of this festival.

2
O god bright with a budding white smile,
you who live in Valañcuḻi
where the large white egret
and the heron with open bill
look for prey among surging white waves,
tell me why you roamed the world,
carrying a dank white skull.

3
O you who smear the chalk-white ash
all over your body,
and live in Valañcuḻi
where the wild goose walks
on fine sand, colored gold from the pollen
of full-bloomed lotuses,
tell me why, though the gods themselves praised you,
you begged for alms in a white skull.

6
O treasure and light
who holds the little fawn,
living in Valañcuḻi
where you end the troubles
of those who bathe in Poṉṉi's swelling current,
fragrant with many flowers,
on the festival day of Pūcam,
tell me, why this pretense of poverty,
this begging with a disgusting white skull?

39. Appar VI.223 *Āmāttūr*

1
He came to us singing songs in varied rhythms,
and took us by force.

39. In this hymn Appar plays on the popular conception of Bhikṣāṭana, the "Beggar Lord," as a seducer of married women. He also uses the conventions of classical *akam* love poetry; the speaker in the poem is a woman who has fallen in love with the handsome beggar. The mythological context of the scene is Śiva's seduction of the wives of the Pine Forest sages. v. 1. "*Vaṇṇam*": a type of musical composition with complex rhythms, or the method of singing a composition in several tempos or with rhythmic variation. v. 9. "Axe": the "*kallalaku*," "a sharp weapon," is different from the battle-axe (*maḻu*) that Śiva carries. In some hymns it is mentioned along with the *kaṭṭaṅkam* (*khaṭvāṅga*), a weapon made of bone.

He shot the arrows of his eyes at us;
with speeches that stir up passion
he skillfully seduced us, made us sick with love.
The skullbearer god has mounted his swift bull;
wearing a skin, his body covered with white ash,
a sacred thread adorning his form,
come, see the Master as he goes riding where all can see him.
The Lord of Āmāttūr is a handsome man, indeed!

2
When he lingered at my door, wearing the white ash,
his spreading matted hair crowned with a white wreath,
singing the Kāntāram mode to the *vīṇā*'s tune,
I asked: "What is your town,
O man with the throat dark as a sapphire?"
Pretending to be in pain, he entered my house.
Then, saying, "O girl with the slim waist,
if you wish to know my town, I'll tell you—
it is Āmāttūr, where bees buzz on the cool lotus flower,"
the Lord disappeared.

3
Bearing the axe, the skullbearer came
riding on a swift bull;
making sweet speeches, he entered our homes;
he won't take alms from us, nor will he leave.
Instead, he speaks only deceptions and wiles,
as if to seduce all who look at him.
The Lord of Āmāttūr, who will neither accept
the petty alms we offer him,
nor reveal his designs,
is a handsome man, indeed!

5
The white bull he rides is in no way inferior
to rolling chariots, horses, and elephants.
The dark-throated one with the fiery red form,
the god whom the Himalayan gods praise,
owns no wealth, yet is a rich man.
The Lord of Āmāttūr, who wears a tigerskin,
and a garland of cool blossoms,
and rides surrounded by his demons,
is a handsome man indeed!

8

We agree that you ride a truly excellent white bull.
Tell me, do you come from a town called Oṟṟiyūr?
Why do you stay? Or, if you wish to go,
why have you seduced us with a glance
of your forehead-eye?
O you who always torment us thus,
we think we know your town—
Ēkampam is its name.
Surely you leave us in anger, my Lord!
Our Lord of Āmāttūr is a handsome man, indeed!

9

In plain sight of all,
the man from Kāḷatti who carries a sharp axe
mounted his swift bull, appeared at my door,
entered my house, and begged for alms.
Yet when I rose to meet him, he disappeared
without a proper farewell.
"What town do you really come from?
Is it Turutti, or Paḻaṉam, or Neyttāṉam?"
The Lord of Āmāttur, who has left me to suffer,
is a handsome man, indeed!

5 Śiva's Myths

(POEMS 40–54)

The Liṅga of Fire

40. Campantar I.100.9 *Paraṅkuṉṟam (Tirupparaṅkuṉṟam)*

Paraṅkuṉṟu is the shrine
of the Lord who shares his body
with the girl who plays with a ball,
the god who rose
as a splendid column of light,
whose greatness was beyond the grasp
even of Māl who in a single stride
once spanned this whole earth,
and the ancient god who emerged
from his bright navel,
and gave the sacred Vedas to the world.

41. Appar IV.20.10 *Tiruvārūr (Ārūr)*

Ayaṉ of the lotus flower
and the god who dismembered Iraṇiyaṉ
sought to know him;
but for all their seeking,
they could not contain in their vision
our Lord who was the great flame.
Entering the hearts of devotees
who sing and worship him,
and chant the Pallāṇṭu hymns for him,
I have sought and found
that Lord of Tiruvārūr.

40. "The girl who plays with a ball": "*pantiyalaṅkai maṅkai*"; the Goddess is portrayed as a very young girl. "Ancient god": *uravōṉ*, Brahmā, "the elder, the ancient one."

41. Ayaṉ: *aja*, "the unborn," Brahmā. Viṣṇu, in his man-lion (Narasiṃha) incarnation, dismembered the demon Iraṇiyaṉ (Hiraṇyakaśipu). Pallāṇṭu hymns: see Poem 5.

The Three Cities

42. Campantar I.11.6 *Vīḻimiḻalai*

When the gods cried, "Save us from peril,
O Lord seated under the ancient banyan tree!"
the celestial beings united to become his chariot;
Ayaṉ, the creator, yoked the Vedas as horses;
the world-mountain became the bow,
its string was the great snake.
Māl was the arrow, with wind for its feathers.
With swiftly kindled fire he shot at the citadels.
Vīḻimiḻalai is his abode.

Mārkaṇḍeya and Death

43. Appar IV.31.9 *Kaṭavūr Vīraṭṭam*

Resisting the charms
of women with eyes curved like the *cēl* fish,
Mārkaṇḍeya became Śiva's devotee,
bathing his God every day
in streams of milk, and good yoghurt and ghee,
seeking thus to put an end to the pain of ignorant life.
It was for him that the Lord
of the Vīraṭṭam shrine in Kaṭavūr
once kicked at Death.

44. Campantar I.52.3 *Neṭuṅkaḷam*

You who live in Neṭuṅkaḷaṁ,
end the karma of your servants
who bring water and flowers for your worship every day,
always singing the praise of your golden foot
with which, O pure one,
when he who faithfully served at your feet invoked you,

42. The gods invoke Śiva in his form as Dakṣiṇāmūrti, the wise teacher, who is "seated under the banyan tree."

43. "The pain of ignorant life": "*maruṭṭuyar*," the pain of an existence caused and characterized by ignorance about the nature of *pacu*, *pati*, and *pācam*. Tirukkaṭavūr, one of the eight Vīraṭṭāṉam sites, is said to be the place where Śiva rescued Mārkaṇḍeya from death (see illus. 12).

you kicked at terrible Death, crying:
"You shall not take my devotee's life!"

*

45. Appar IV.50.1 *Kuṟukkai Vīraṭṭam*

He whose foot and head
neither Māl the Strider nor Brahmā could see,
though they searched into the depths of the universe
covered with flood waters,
is our Lord of the Vīraṭṭam shrine in Kuṟukkai,
who became a rude hunter
for the sake of Arjuna,
and gave him a bow and arrow, sacred mantras,
and a chariot with fluttering flags.

Dakṣiṇāmūrti, the Teacher

46. Campantar I.132.1 *Vīḻimiḻalai*

The temple of the god
who sat under the tall banyan tree,
and graciously taught the four ancient sages
the enlightened way
by discoursing on the essence of the four true Vedas,
is Miḻalai, where parrots in groves flowing with honey,
hearing the sound of famed pundits
daily reciting the sacred texts,
explain the meaning of the chant.

Rāvaṇa and Kailāsa

47. Appar IV.39.10 *Aiyāṟu (Tiruvaiyāṟu)*

When the ignorant demon
tried to lift the great hill, he felt faint;

45. The second half of the verse refers to the *Mahābhārata* episode of Arjuna's combat with Śiva, who challenged him disguised as a hunter. "The depths of the universe / covered with flood waters": the Ātīṉam commentator takes "*nīr eṉum pilayam*" to mean "the netherworld" (*pātāla*) (cf. *Tēvāram* Ātīṉam edition). "Rude": "*tuṭiyuṭai*," rough, aggressive, insulting.

47, 48. These two verses are typical of the final verse in Appar's hymns, which he regularly dedicates to the legend of Rāvaṇa's effort to uproot Mount Kailāsa (see illus. 11). In

seeing his pain, the wise god
pressed down with his little toe, till
the demon was crushed,
and fell down on the earth;
yet when he gained wisdom,
the Lord who dwells as honey in Aiyāṟu
blessed him with his grace.

48. Appar IV.80.10 *Kōyil (Tillai)*

When the arrogant demon,
proud of the strength of his arms,
roared, and lifted the great hill
with his mountainous shoulders,
the spouse of the mountain's daughter,
the Lord of Tillai's beautiful Ampalam hall,
laughed, and bore down with his toe
to crush the demon's ten crowned heads.
I, who have seen that toe with these eyes,
have nothing left to see.

49. Campantar I.72.8 *Kuṭantaik Kārōṇam*

The Lord first bore down on the mountain
with the tip of his sweet-smelling foot,
crushing the many hill-like shoulders
and all ten heads of the proud and terrible demon.
Then, pleased to hear him sing the sacred hymn,
he granted him a bright sword.
Such is the Lord of Kārōṇam shrine
in cool Kuṭantai
upon Poṉṉi's fertile banks.

---

the *Tēvāram* hymns as a whole, and in Appar's verses in particular, Rāvaṇa appears as the paradigm for the repentant sinner who is redeemed by the infinite grace of the Lord. Appar's special fondness for the Rāvaṇa myth is perhaps explained by his feelings of guilt regarding his past as a Jain monk; the saint's sense of identification with Rāvaṇa comes across very powerfully in his hymns. The Tamil tradition has tended to treat Rāvaṇa with greater sympathy than have the other regional traditions of India; Rāvaṇa has even been featured as the "hero" of the *Rāmāyaṇa* story in recent interpretations of the epic. For a discussion of the role of the demon-devotee in Tamil myth, see Shulman, *Tamil Temple Myths*, ch. 5.

49. "Sacred hymn": "*uraiyār kītam*," the melodious Vedic (Sāman) chant. Kārōṇam: Sanskrit "Kāyarōhaṇa," one of the shrines associated with the Pāśupata sect.

50. Appar IV.19.11 *Ārūr (Tiruvārūr)*

He bore down with his precious toe, so that
the cloud-covered mountain shook,
and the shoulders of the invincible warrior,
the wicked demon, were crushed,
and red streams of blood from his wounds
bathed his frame, while the Lord himself
wore the cool powder of milk-white ash on his chest.
I saw that Lord in Ārūr.

*

51. Appar VI.310

1
He cured my disease and took me for his own,
he took Atikai Vīraṭṭāṉam for his domain.
He severed the head of Brahmā, god of the lotus seat,
and took the skull for his begging bowl.
He drained all the blood
from arrogant Vāmana's giant frame,
took up the deer in his left hand,
and the battle-axe in the right.
The skullbearer took Kāma's body with a glance,
and from Kaṇṇappaṉ he took loving service.

3
He wears a crown of matted hair,
bears the waxing moon and the winding snake
on his head.
He wears the ringing anklet

50. "Invincible": "*tuñcāppōr*," "tireless in combat."

51. This is a hymn in which the poet builds the entire hymn around the shades of meaning of a verb. The key word in this poem is "*koṇṭār*," "he took" (from *koḷ*, "to take"). Appar contrasts the things Śiva has taken from him—his disease, ignorance, himself—with the objects he has taken from others, in the context of myth. The mythological references include: the decapitation of Brahmā and the burning of Kāma, the god of Love (v. 1), Śiva's drinking of Viṣṇu's blood (v. 1) and his subsequent wandering over the universe in his form as Kaṅkāḷa, with the skeleton of Viṣṇu's doorkeeper slung over his shoulder. Verse 3 contains one of the few references in the *Tēvāram* to "*muyalakaṉ*" (*apasmārapuruṣa*, "the demon of forgetfulness or ignorance"), the dwarflike figure on whose body Śiva dances as Naṭarāja, Lord of the Dance. In the same verse, Appar refers to Śiva as Harihara, the form in which he is united with Viṣṇu (Māl). The "Cuntaraṉ" of verse 5 is probably the mythical Ālālacuntaraṉ who was said to have been born on earth as the poet-saint Cuntaramūrtti.

and the sounding hero's band on his legs,
he cast defiant *muyalakaṉ* under his foot.
In his right hand he bears the sharp battle-axe,
and holds Māl in loving embrace
in the left half of his frame.
He carries a bundle of bones on his shoulder,
and the *tuṭi* drum in his hand.
He cured my painful disease and took possession of me.

5
He pierced Andhaka with his sharp trident,
and yoked the sacred Vedas as horses to his chariot.
He took Cuntaraṉ for his fanbearer and friend,
and the burning-ground as stage for his dance.
He bent the Mandara mountain into his bow,
and took Mākāḷaṉ for his gatekeeper.
He revealed himself in the Veda and Āgama texts,
ended my days as a Jain, and took me for his own.

9
He cut off the head of the sacrifice,
and took Bhaga's eye.
He knocked off the Āditya's teeth,
and severed the head of the arrogant priest
of the rite.
He cut off powerful Agni's arm,
and the foot of mighty Yama, guardian of the sacrifice,
and he kicked at the Moon.
Thus he destroyed insolent Dakṣa's sacrifice,
striking fear into every heart.
He is the pure one who has taken me for his own.

52. Appar IV.14 TACAPURĀṆAM (THE TEN MYTHS)

1
When the Himalayan gods let go
of the snake coiled around the great hill,
and ran in fear as the poison,

"In the Veda and Āgama": "*tantiramantirattarāy*"; cf. Campantar I.61.3 ("*mantirattāṉ tantirattāṉ*") and Appar VI.268.8 (Poem 118). Verse 9 is devoted to a detailed description of Śiva's destruction of the sacrifice conducted by his arrogant father-in-law Dakṣa. In this verse, I have taken "*meccaṉ viyāttiraṉ*" as referring to the officiating priest. Appar also refers several times to his reconversion to Śaivism.

52. In this hymn Appar celebrates ten important myths in the Tamil Śaiva tradition. v. 3. "The six faiths": the six sectarian groups in the Hindu classical tradition, each taking a

darker than Tirumāl's body,
shot out in a powerful stream
and burned the sky,
they cried: "Save us, O Lord!"
The one who was moved to compassion,
and devoured the deadly poison,
to shield them from harm,
is the King of the highest gods.

2
When the roaring flood waters
rose and covered the great worlds,
a column arose on earth, that was
the Supreme Deity itself;
then Brahmā and Māl,
exclaiming, "He is incomparable!"
bowed on both sides, having found
neither head nor foot of the Great One,
the first and highest God,
who took form as Śiva—
He is our only refuge.

3
Before the creation of Time,
measured in days and eons,
the fiery god stood as the One,
then became the three gods
and took form as the six faiths.
He it was who swallowed
earth with heaven and all seven worlds,
became the dwarf,
the infant who floated on the banyan leaf,
and the high god to all these—
That Lord is our only refuge.

---

particular deity for the center of its cultic focus. Other possible interpretations: six different religious traditions; six sects within Śaivism (*akaccamayam*); the six "schools" (*darśana*) of Indian philosophy. This verse presents the Tamil Śaiva conception of creation, with Śiva playing the supreme role, as the material cause of the universe as well as its creator and animating principle. In this progression, Śiva is precosmic Being and the three cosmic gods, as well as the Supreme Deity. It is in this sense that Viṣṇu's deeds of becoming the dwarf and the infant are attributed to Śiva. See the discussion of the sixfold classifications and of creation from the Śaiva Siddhānta point of view in Sivaraman, *Śaivism*, chs. 1, 3. v. 5. Ari: Viṣṇu, Māl. v. 10: This myth of Tirumāl's worship of Śiva is often narrated in the *Tēvāram* hymns.

4
When all seven worlds, high heaven,
and earth with its long seashores and mountains,
were oppressed, the Himalayan gods
sang his praise,
lifting up their hands in prayer.
The god who dances with fire
then split open the body
of the fleeing demon Tāraka
and danced the great dance
to quench his undying fury—
His feet are our only refuge.

5
When the three citadels, unmoored,
flew about wreaking destruction
in heaven and on earth,
oppressed by their assault,
the frightened gods, led by Ari himself,
sought his protection.
Then, moved to compassion, the gracious savior
kindled his deadly arrow with fire,
shot fire from the snake that was his bowstring,
bent his mountain-bow to its fullest,
and reduced the citadels to ashes—
He is our only refuge.

6
It was the day that dark-hued, red-eyed Death
with curved white tusks and flaming hair
came looking for him:
as he performed the morning worship
with fresh flowers, Kāla came near,
and pursued with his life-grabbing noose
the boy who fled in fear.
The Lord's feet which sent that Death
to his own end
are the feet that the gods worship and praise
and place on their heads.

7
Seeing the terrible fate of the Himalayan gods,
of the frightened Lord of the Sacrifice,
of Fire and of the Moon,

who came for their share of the offering
at pious Dakṣa's great sacrifice,
Ayaṉ and Māl, themselves gripped by fear,
withdrew, begging, "Forgive our ignorance
and other faults,"
and the fire-hued Lord emerged victorious.
To see and know the feet
of that Lord, my Father, is the way.

8
When the Goddess, lady of all blessings,
ran up to him in play
and covered his eyes with her hands,
darkness engulfed all seven worlds,
and to dispel the dark, an eye
blossomed on his forehead; upon which,
the frightened young woman
uncovered the other eyes, and begged for mercy.
The three-eyed god who then graciously opened
his moon- and blazing sun-eyes
is our only refuge.

9
At Indra's command, impelled by cloud-dark Māl,
the god with five arrows
conjured up spring in the sugar-cane grove,
with cooing cuckoos and a soft breeze.
When Madana had shot his flower arrow at him,
fire blazed forth from the forehead-eye
of our fire-hued father,
burning to ashes the god's handsome form,
and terrifying the Himalayan gods—
The Lord is our only refuge.

10
When Tirumāl, missing a single flower
of the thousand lotuses needed for the rite,
offered his eye in place of the flower, much pleased,
our Father, the Lord, gave the god of the ocean
the mighty wheel of deadly power
that he had once with great effort
set spinning with his bright foot,
till it split open the demon's heart.
That Lord is our only refuge.

11
"Your swift chariot will not run on Kailāsa hill,
give up your bravado,
Don't urge me on! Don't break the sacred Law!"
Harshly chiding the charioteer who spoke thus to him,
the demon commanded: "Drive on!"
When, going faster forward,
he reached the hill and tried to lift it,
his head and shoulders cracked and gave way,
crushed by the toe of my Lord's foot,
which my heart remembers.

53. Appar IV.73 *Cēṟai*

1
After the daughter of rich Himalaya
had parted from him,
he married her again
for her many arduous penances
and gave her half of himself,
taking on a glorious new form.
He is our treasure in Cēṟai,
shrine of the good path.

2
Falling for the wiles
of wicked Jains who do not have the discrimination
to see the Truth as it is,
I took their words for true,
and wallowed in them,
till he wrenched me free, took possession of me,

53. The ninth verse of this hymn is not available. "*Cenneṟi*," in the refrain of the hymn ("*cenneṟic celvaṉār*"), is the name of the shrine at Cēṟai. The word also means "the good path," the path to release through total devotion to Śiva in the Tamil Śaiva mode. The "treasure" is, of course, release, but in the context of devotion, it is Śiva himself as the desired goal. v. 1. Appar relates the story of Śiva's marriage to Umā or Pārvatī. Dakṣa's daughter Satī, wife of Śiva, committed suicide at Dakṣa's sacrifice, embittered by her father's insulting treatment of her husband. She was reborn as Pārvatī, daughter of the mountain Himalaya, and gained Śiva for her husband after performing severe penance, involving many ascetic practices. The wedding of Śiva and Pārvatī is the subject of Kālidāsa's Sanskrit epic poem *Kumārasaṃbhava* and is a popular subject in South Indian temple sculpture and iconography. v. 2. "Wicked Jains": "*kuṇṭar*." The word "*kuṇṭar*," which the poets frequently use to describe the Jain and Buddhist monks, can mean either "scoundrels, wicked men," or "fat, degenerate men."

healed me of earthly sickness and the disease
of existence itself.
He is our treasure in Cēṟai,
shrine of the good path.

3
He willingly went to the dreadful forest
as the hunter who defeated in combat
Arjuna of the long bow, and thus favored him,
for he had stood for a long time
in single-minded penance
and worshipped his God's feet.
He is our treasure in Cēṟai,
shrine of the good path.

4
For Bhagīratha
who had performed strict penance,
firmly subduing the five senses,
he bore lightly on his red hair
the Ganges which descended with force
in many angry streams.
He is our treasure in Cēṟai,
shrine of the good path.

5
The young man who piled the sand high
and poured fresh milk on his God with love,
cut off the foot of his father who had
kicked out at the Lord.
Right then, Śiva gave to the boy
the good name
"beautiful Caṇṭīcaṉ, the 'angry one.' "
He is our treasure in Cēṟai,
shrine of the good path.

6
As terrible Bhairava of the end of Time
bearing the flashing trident
and the drum with the deafening roar,
he flayed the elephant
and laughed aloud, terrifying Umā.
He is our treasure in Cēṟai,
shrine of the good path.

7
When the Himalayan gods surrounded our Lord,
strewed flowers, praised him, and cried, "Save us!"
at once he graciously went forth,
to burn in an instant, with terrible flames,
the three solid citadels in the sky.
He is our treasure in Cēṟai,
shrine of the good path.

8
Making him who once created
this entire universe, and Māl himself, cry:
"You are our sole Lord!"
and beg for mercy, and praise him,
he showed himself
as infinite light, red fire, a column
of which they could tell
neither beginning nor end.
He is our treasure in Cēṟai,
shrine of the good path.

10
When the demon of unequaled power
tried to lift the great hill
and felt his majestic heads
and strong shoulders give way,
moved to love, he cried, "My Lord,"
and the Lord gently lifted his flower-soft foot
to show his grace.
He is our treasure in Cēṟai,
shrine of the good path.

54. Campantar I.75 *Veṅkuru (Cīrkāḻi)*

1
My Lord who kicked fierce Death,
and sent him, howling for dear life, to death,
when he fell upon the boy

54. In verse 2 Campantar refers to the origin legend of the temple in Cīrkāḻi. According to this legend, the tower of this divine temple rose above the cosmic flood that engulfed the universe. Seated in a boat made of the primal syllable "Aum" (*praṇava*), Śiva and Umā approached the *śikhara* (peak) of the temple and moored their boat there. The story accounts for the name "Tōṇiyappar" given to the Lord in Cīrkāḻi: "*tōṇi*" means "a boat." Tōṇipuram ("city of the boat") is one of the twelve names of Cīrkāḻi. v. 7. Campantar describes the burning of Kāma, when the Love-god tried to disturb the Lord's yogic medi-

who worshipped his God with flowers
every day at dawn
is Umā's lover who loves Veṅkuru's shrine
set among seaside groves
which the tide embraces every day,
bringing with it coral and conch shell;
and here he abides.

2
He shares his body with the Goddess;
he wears the moon and snake on his matted red hair;
melodiously he sings the modes, and dances
as he goes on his begging rounds;
my Lord reveals his gracious will.
He loves Veṅkuru's temple
now descended to earth,
having once risen high and touched heaven,
as it floated on the Ocean's cosmic flood
which covered earth and reached the sky;
and here he abides.

3
The formless one took form
as a rough, wild hunter.
For the Goddess' sake he first fought,
and then kindly gave Arjuna his desire.
He loves Veṅkuru
where the woods brim with honey,
flower pollen blinds the eye,
and bees sing the Nēricai mode;
and here he abides.

4
On his matted hair he wears the *koṉṟai*, *vaṉṉi*, *erukku*,
mattam, *kūviḷam*, and other flowers swarming with bees.
Riding his bull, while his goblins sound
the *koṭukoṭṭi* and *kuṭamuḻā* drums,
he tunefully sings and chants the Veda.

---

tation. Here the incident is connected to Śiva's form as Yoga-dakṣiṇāmūrti, "the Lord who is the yogi and Teacher." In verse 11 there is a play on the two meanings of the word "*vimāṉam*" (the peaked tower of a temple; the aerial cars of the gods). "High heaven": "*viyaṉulaku*," the great world of the gods. "Ñāṉacampantaṉ, to whom the Vedas were revealed": Campantar describes himself as "*naṉṉiyanūlaṉ*," "he whom the texts reached." It is reasonable to take this as a reference to the revelation of Vedic learning to him as the child prodigy.

With the Ganges' stream in his hair,
moon-crowned, Goddess Umā at his side,
he desires Veṅkuru;
and here he abides.

5
With matted hair, his body ash-smeared,
the *takkai* drum slung in a bundle on his shoulder,
he goes from house to house, begging,
and steals the women's hearts with his charm.
The tridentbearer shares his body with Umā,
whose cool eyes are long like *kayal* fish.
Seated on his bull, his band of spirits around him,
he rides to Veṅkuru,
the place that he loves;
and here he abides.

6
He loves Veṅkuru, where, at night,
waves dash against the shore, and scatter
shells and oysters on the sand,
which burst open and yield precious pearls,
driving the darkness out.
Everywhere in this town, the sky is clouded
with fragrant smoke from the holy sacrifices
of brahmins who preserve the noble Vedas;
and here he abides.

7
When the mad elephant rushed upon Umā
who is slender as a creeper,
he swiftly seized him and flayed his hide
to dispel her fear.
This is the wise teacher
who sat in the shade of the sacred banyan tree,
calmly teaching the sacred Law,
when the god with the sugar-cane bow
came there to disturb him,
and he reduced Kāma to ashes with a glance.
He loves Veṅkuru,
and here he abides.

8
This is the Lord who bore down hard with his toe
on the many heads and shoulders of the evil demon,

to crush him when he tried to lift Kailāsa hill,
and then gave him a flashing sword.
The Lord with the matted red hair
adorned with beautiful blossoms
of *kōṅkam* and *cerunti*, *koṉṟai* and *kūviḷam*,
loves the shrine of Veṅkuru
fragrant with the golden flowers of the *vēṅkai*;
and here he abides.

9
Trying to measure the form of our Lord
with the river in his hair,
Brahmā, flying into high heaven,
and Ari, digging deep in earth,
searched in vain;
but the three-eyed god
with his beautiful body smeared with ash,
even while the gods in heaven worship him,
desires to take us alone in love.
He loves Veṅkuru's shrine,
and here he abides.

10
He can't be found in the false doctrines
of the heretic Jain and Buddhist monks.
These are his gracious acts:
For the sake of the Goddess
he smashed cruel Dakṣa's sacrifice;
and he willingly chose the frightful disguise
of the hunter who goes with his foul dogs in the forest,
terrifying men with his call.
He loves Veṅkuru,
and here he abides.

11
Ñāṉacampantaṉ, to whom the Vedas were revealed,
has composed and sung
these ten good verses
on the Lord who loves Veṅkuru and abides here
out of love for its temple tower
that touches the sky.
The gods will bring celestial cars
for those who dance,
and sing this hymn in musical modes,
with love for Śiva,
and they will reign as kings in high heaven.

SECTION II

Kōyil, Ārūr: Beloved Abodes

The shrine is a center in more senses than one: it is situated at the center of the sacred landscape in a palpable manner; it is, at the same time, identified with the center or navel of the universe, the spot through which passes the *axis mundi* linking heaven, earth, and the nether regions.[1] In this section, beginning with the *Tēvāram* descriptions of the shrine as sacred center, we move to the sacred geography of the Tamil Śaivas. We have noted that this early Tamil devotional poetry is distinguished by its preoccupation with particular sacred places, with Tamil towns and landscapes. The poets' descriptions of the activities and lore associated with such sacred sites have become part of the very conception of them.

To the Nāyaṉārs, the temple or shrine (*kōyil*) is the place at which God has graciously chosen to manifest himself; it is his beloved (*ukanta*, *mēviya*, *nayanta*) abode (*iṭam*). He is happily and graciously (*iṉitu*) established (*amarntār*, *uṟaivār*) there. In concrete terms, and in keeping with its origin in the Tamil cult of the king (*kō*), the temple is a palace (*kōyil*, a king's house), a dwelling of monumental proportions.[2] The conception of the temple as palace continued to be productive in South Indian temple building for centuries after the age of the Nāyaṉārs, as is obvious from the increasingly elaborate temple complexes, some of them resembling fortified cities and housing several subshrines within a series of walls

[1] For the ideas of sacred space as the "space at the center" of the universe, and of the shrine as the sanctified image of the cosmos, see Mircea Eliade, *The Sacred and the Profane: The Nature of Religion*, translated from the French by Willard R. Trask (New York: Harper & Row, 1959), ch. 1. For center symbolism in relation to the Tamil temple, consult Shulman, *Tamil Temple Myths*, ch. 2.

[2] See my discussion of the conception of God as king in Tamil *bhakti*, in Part One, Chapter 3 above. Also refer to A. Appadurai, *Worship and Conflict under Colonial Rule: A South Indian Case*, Cambridge South Asian Studies 27 (Cambridge: Cambridge University Press, 1981), ch. 1.

(Chidambaram, Maturai, Tiruvārūr).[3] Although it is not appropriate to go into the details of the historical development of architectural style in the South Indian temple here, it is important to note the fundamental elements of the temple as it evolved in the days of the Nāyaṉārs, during which the Pallavas actively pioneered in the building of structural temples in stone (*kaṟṟaḷi*; from *kal*, stone, rock; and *taḷi*, temple), and subsequent developments in the Cōḻa and Pāṇṭiya temples, that contributed to the ideal structural image of the temples which dot the Tamil landscape today. At the core of the Śiva shrine is the small, dark cell, the sanctum, called *garbhagṛha* ("womb-house"), generally on a square plan, which houses the *liṅga* (see illus. 5). Above it rises a pyramidal superstructure crowned by a curvilinear structure of varying design. The term "*vimāna*," "that which is proportionally measured out," usually refers to this central shrine structure comprising the *garbhagṛha* and its superstructure (see illus. 13). The curvilinear structure at the top is called "*śikhara*" (mountain peak).[4] These, along with the *maṇḍapa* hall in front of the entrance, formed the basic features of the fully developed Pallava structural temple of the age of the Nāyaṉārs and after. Among the more elaborate features of the South Indian temple are the detached *maṇḍapa* (hall; Tamil *maṇṭapam*),[5] *matil* (Tamil "wall"), multiple *prākāras* (walkways, corridors), subshrines for minor deities, the *gopuras* (Tamil *kōpuram*, high-towered gateways),[6] and the separate shrine for the Goddess (originally called

[3] The four principal shrines located in the Tiruvārūr complex are: the Pūṅkōyil or Mūlaṭṭāṉam; Tyāgarāja temple; Araneṟi; and Paravai-uṇ-maṇṭaḷi. The three poets dedicated hymns to each of these temples, excepting the Tyāgarāja shrine. For a survey of the development of the Tiruvārūr temples, see Balasubrahmanyam, *Early Chola Temples*, pp. 192–97. A detailed study of the Gangaikondacholisvaram temple in the city of Gangaikondacolapuram may be found in Balasubrahmanyam, *Middle Chola Temples*, ch. 4.

[4] For a detailed discussion of the historical development and symbolism of the parts of the Hindu temple, see Stella Kramrisch's classic study, *The Hindu Temple*, 2 vols. (Calcutta: University of Calcutta, 1946; reprint, Delhi: Motilal Banarsidass, 1976). On *vimāna*, see 1: 131–34; *śikhara*: 1: 181–82. Balasubrahmanyam, *Early Chola Temples*, provides a sketch of the component parts of a *vimāna* (the tenth-century Mūvarkōyil in Koṭumpāḷūr).

[5] Great, semidetached halls became a feature of most of the important shrine complexes. Cuntarar is said to have had a vision of the sixty-two saints in the "Tēvāciriyaṉ" (Sanskrit *devāśraya*?) hall. Cēkkiḻār inaugurated the *Periya purāṇam* in the "Āyirakkāl" (Thousand-pillared) hall at the temple in Chidambaram.

[6] It is important to note that the most striking and imposing feature of South Indian temples after A.D. 1000 (the date of the Brihadīśvara temple in Tanjore) is not the central *vimāna* but the great gate towers, the *gopuras* that punctuate the walls of the enclosure. Stella Kramrisch points out that "taken as a whole, the South Indian Temple . . . in the centuries of its greatest expansion . . . is a hypaethral temple, an open air sacred enclosure, with high walls, be they as many as seven, marked in the four directions by Gopuras whose height decreases towards the centre, where the main temple is marked by its position" (Kramrisch, *Hindu Temple*, p. 203).

"Kāmakkōṭṭam").[7] In the conception and relative disposition of the various parts of the Tamil temple we see a regional reflex of the many meanings of the Hindu temple as "the body and house of God," as mountain, cave, and model of the cosmos. The cosmic symbolism is most powerfully and simply present in the basic requirement for all Tamil temples: each temple must have a body of water (a river or a tank [Sanskrit *tīrtha*, a sacred ford, a place of pilgrimage]), a specific local tree (Tamil *talavirukṣam*) and the "mountainous" body of the shrine itself, together representing the archetypal tree, rock, and water that survived the cosmic flood.[8]

Other than the *vimāna*, the *Tēvāram* poets do not often mention the architectural features of the temple. Yet they are very careful to distinguish among types of shrines and refer to particular temples by the appropriate technical terms: thus the temple at Mīyaccūr is called an "*iḷaṅkōyil*" (a temporary or newly built shrine) and the one at Kaṭantai (Peṇṇākaṭam) is called "*tūṅkāṉaimāṭam*" (an apsidal temple, with a *gajapṛṣṭha* ["elephant's back"] *vimāna*).[9] Such references indicate the variety of "temples," ranging from simple, natural shrines in remote places to elaborate brick and rock-cut structures, that the Nāyaṉārs must have come across in their travels. Such names as the Little Ampalam hall (Ciṟṟampalam) in Tillai no doubt refer back to the public worship halls of the Tamils, such as the *maṉṟu* and *potiyil* of Caṅkam times.

In several hymns the *Tēvāram* poets refer to local legends and the origin myths of the shrine that is featured in the hymn.[10] Describing the linguistic origin of place names is a common motif in the hymns. Campantar devotes an entire hymn to the folkloric etymology of the twelve names of Cīrkāḻi (Poem 104).

The Nāyaṉārs' conception of the sacred place or "place of pilgrimage" (*pati*, *kṣēttiram*) includes in its scope the larger settlement within which the shrine is situated. These sacred sites, as we have seen above, vary in size and prominence. From the poet's descriptions we gather that while some shrines which they visited were found in remote places, others were great urban centers of government, trade, and culture. Kanchipuram, Maturai (the Pallava and Pāṇṭiya capitals), and Tiruvārūr (Cōḻa cultural

[7] On the significance of a separate shrine for the Goddess, see Shulman, *Tamil Temple Myths*, pp. 221–23.

[8] Ibid., p. 47.

[9] On the special features of the Mīyaccūr and Peṇṇākaṭam temples, see Balasubrahmanyam, *Early Chola Temples*, pp. 190–91. Balasubrahmanyan points out that both shrines found at Mīyaccūr today (the apsidal, main temple and the Iḷaṅkōyil shrine) must have been extant in the time of the Nāyaṉārs since Appar's hymn in Mīyaccūr is dedicated to the Iḷaṅkōyil, while Campantar sings of the deity in the main shrine.

[10] David Shulman summarizes and analyzes the later Tamil puranic versions of these local legends in *Tamil Temple Myths*.

center), were shrine centers of the latter type. The Nāyaṉārs dedicated a large number of poems to these and other preeminent shrine centers. The growing popularity of the Tamil Śaiva cult, and the travels and hymns of the Nāyaṉārs themselves, were catalysts to the growth in the cultic and general cultural importance of shrines such as Tillai, whose names suggest connections with the wilderness.[11] To the Tamil Śaivas there is magic in the very names of Śiva's places. Campantar, Appar, and Cuntarar, and other Nāyaṉārs wrote lists or catalogues of holy places, entire hymns filled with the sonorous names of Śiva's abodes.[12] The organic nature of the association of the sacred place with the presence of Śiva is emphasized in alliterative formulae in which the name of the Lord (unique to a particular shrine) is coupled with the name of the place. Such names as "*maṟaikkāṭuṟai maṇāḷar*" (the bridegroom in Maṟaikkāṭu), "*maḻapāṭiyuḷ māṇikkam*" (the ruby in Maḻapāṭi), and "*āmāttūr aṇṇal*" (the Lord in Āmāttūr) reveal more than the Tamil sense of aesthetic delight in the sounds of the language.[13]

I noted in Part One that, out of the 274 shrines they visited or sang about, the Nāyaṉārs dedicated the largest number of hymns to shrines in the Cōḻa region (Cōḻanāṭu), the venue of their most extensive travels. In this region, Kāḻi or Cīrkāḻi, Campantar's birthplace, commands the largest number of hymns. Campantar alone sang 67 out of the 71 *patikam*s to Śiva at this site. The Cōḻa shrine center of Tiruvārūr (see illus. 13) stands next, with 37 hymns, 23 of them by Appar. By contrast, Tillai or Puliyūrc Ciṟṟampalam (Chidambaram, the "Kōyil" of later times) receives only 11 songs. Campantar also favored Vīḻimiḻalai; he composed 15 out of the 24 hymns this site receives. Tiruvaiyāṟu (Aiyāṟu) and Iṭaimarutūr follow, with 18 and 12 *patikam*s each. In the Naṭunāṭu region, Appar sang 16 out of a total of 18 songs dedicated to Atikai Vīraṭṭāṉam, the place of his conversion. Maturai, in the Pāṇṭiya kingdom, receives 11 hymns. Cuntarar alone dedicated a hymn to Añcaikkaḷam in the Cēra region, and Campantar and Cuntarar together sang three *patikam*s to the Sri Lankan shrines of Tirukkōṇamalai and Mātōṭṭam (Kēṭīccuram). Five different shrines in the Pallava center of Kanchipuram receive a total of

[11] "Tillai" is the ancient name of the shrine at Chidambaram, deriving from "*tillai*," the sacred tree of the shrine. It is said that this sacred place was once a forest of *tillai* trees.

[12] Campantar II.175, Poem 71; Cuntarar VII.47, Poem 72. Prior to these poets, the Nāyaṉār Aiyaṭikaḷ Kāṭavarkōṉ had produced the *Kṣēttirat tiruveṇpā* ("the holy Veṇpā stanzas on the sacred places"), *Tirumuṟai* XI.

[13] David Shulman (*Tamil Temple Myths*, p. 139) suggests that "the frequent alliteration of place names with the names of the local goddess" shows that the goddess is intimately connected with the soil. The alliterative connection that the saints routinely make between the names of Śiva and his abodes indicates that to them, Śiva, as much as the Goddess, is a deity of the soil, a god of the place. See my discussion of alliteration in the hymns, Part One, Chapter 5.

17 hymns, out of which Kacci Ēkampam (the Ekāmranātha shrine) gets 12. Of the remaining shrines, the sites favored by all three saints receive between 4 and 9 hymns each.[14]

The poets' descriptions of sacred places are, by and large, formulaic, emphasizing through conventional metaphors their beauty, abundance, and prosperity. Like the itinerant bards of the Caṅkam tradition, the Nāyaṉārs exalt their patron and king by praising his land and its delights. Descriptions of lush gardens and fields alternate with cityscapes in which "tall mansions touch the clouds." The larger among Śiva's sacred towns are inhabited by beautiful women and pious men who throng the streets on festival days. Centers like Campantar's native Cīrkāḻi are described as "walled cities" (*kaṉṉaṭainta matiḻ piramapuram*).[15] The description of Tillai, Vīḻimiḻalai, Marukal, and Ceṅkāṭṭaṅkuṭi attest to the antiquity of these towns as brahmin settlements (*brahmadeya*). Appar, Cuntarar, and Campantar also connect particular villages and towns with figures in Tamil Śaiva cult history: Kāḷatti (Kālahasti) is the town of the hunter-saint Kaṇṇappar; Āppāṭi and Cēyñalūr are associated with Caṇṭīcar; Tirukkaṭavūr with Mārkaṇḍeya; and Āṉaikkā with King Kōcceṅkaṇāṉ. The three saints themselves have special connections with certain towns. As already mentioned, Campantar sang 67 hymns to Śiva in Cīrkāḻi, his native town. Several of Appar's poems set in Atikai Vīraṭṭāṉam have autobiographical references, as do Cuntarar's poems to Śiva in Tiruvārūr, Oṟṟiyūr, and Veṇṇeynallūr.[16]

A large number of *Tēvāram* verses are constructed according to a formula in which one half of the verse is devoted to a description of the natural landscape of the sacred place; occasionally entire hymns are framed with this formula. In such "landscape" poems the agricultural landscape of the Kaveri Delta dominates, and the Kaveri or some local river figures as an important feature of the description. To some extent, the Nāyaṉārs attempt to correlate the five landscapes of Caṅkam poetry with shrines in appropriate settings: temples in hill towns such as Aṇṇāmalai, Kāḷatti, Kuṟṟālam, and Mutukuṉṟu (Vṛddhācalam) become occasions for the use of *kuṟiñci* (hill) landscape conventions, and seashore towns such as Irāmēccuram, Valañcuḻi, Cāykkāṭu (Pūmpukār), Cīrkāḻi, Mayilai, and Maṟaikkāṭu (Vedāraṇyam) are the arena for verses in the *neytal* (seashore) subgenre.

Appar, Cuntarar, and Campantar refer to a limited number of landscape details from the vast repertoire of the Caṅkam poems; the conven-

[14] See Appendix A for statistics on sacred places to which five or more hymns were dedicated.

[15] Campantar II.176.11.

[16] See Section IV below.

tions used also tend to be narrower in their suggestive power.[17] Through their stereotyped and diffuse allusions to flora and fauna and to classical landscape types the *Tēvāram* poets aim at creating a general atmosphere of lush natural beauty. In the typical description all is cool, green, and therefore beautiful (*taṇ-*, *pai-*, *am-*). The air is thick with the cloying fragrance of the jasmine (*mullai*) and other flowers blossoming in shady groves. Gardens overflow with honey; ripe plantains and falling coconuts muddy the rich fields full of sugar cane and rice. Riverine herons and egrets (*nārai*, *kuruku*), the peacock (*mayil*), the green parrot (*kiḷi*), and the sweet-voiced *kuyil* inhabit the gardens and woods; the streams and field canals teem with every kind of fish (*kayal*, *cēl*, *vāḷai*, *keṇṭai*). Occasionally we come across a description that has the authentic ring of actual experience, the vividness of scenes that may be encountered in the hills and fields of the Tamil countryside even today: hill tribeswomen shoot stones at parrots who come to eat the millet they are guarding; a buffalo, frightened by a falling coconut, blunders into a paddyfield. Such scenes are juxtaposed with fabulous descriptions of gems and pearls streaming from such sources as elephants, snakes, and stalks of bamboo on the hills.

Because they are the beloved abodes of Śiva, the temple, town, and landscape of the *Tēvāram* hymns become the principal arenas of devotional activity for the Tamil Śaivas. It is at these sacred centers that pilgrim-devotees gather, to see and experience the Lord in his exalted manifestations, to sing his praise, to perform his ritual worship, and to celebrate his great festivals. This community of devotees who congregate at the *pati* includes not only young men and women, Pāśupata ascetics, pious brahmins, and dancers and singers but also gods and sages, demigods and legendary figures, even the animals of the forest.[18] Drawing upon rich material from classical poetry, folklore, local legends, mythology, everyday life, and religious activity of various kinds, the poets of the *Tēvāram* provide valuable insights into the processes by which the lore of sacred places developed in the Tamil Śaiva tradition. The enduring appeal of the hymns for the Tamil Śaivas, lies, of course, in their affective dimension. One does not become a pilgrim to Śiva's abodes out of a sense of obligation, but out of an active and powerful love of these places, analogous to the love that draws the Lord himself to his abodes where "he loves to dwell."

[17] See my discussion of the difference between Caṅkam and *Tēvāram* poems, Part One, Chapter 3.

[18] See Appar IV.21 (Poem 98).

1 The Temple

(POEMS 55–68)

55. Appar VI.309.5

The unholy town where no temple stands,
the town where men do not wear the holy ash,
the town which does not resound with sacred song,
the town which is not resplendent with many shrines,
the town where the white conch is not reverently blown,
the town where festive canopies and white flags are not seen,
the town where devotees do not gather flowers for the worship rite,
that town is no town, it is a mere wilderness.

56. Cuntarar VII.41.3 *Kaccūr Ālakkōyil*

You have many temples.
Honoring them, singing their praise,
I have been cured of confusion and karma,
O master of the path that the gods do not know!
O Lord, you sat under the spreading banyan tree
and taught the sacred Law
at the beautiful temple, the auspicious temple,
the Ālakkōyil temple
in the northern part of cool Pūṅkaccūr town!

57. Appar VI.247.1 *Tiruvārūr*

Was it the day you rose as the One
praised by the universe
or the day the one form became three?
Was it the day you angrily quelled Death,
or the day you burned Love to ashes with a glance?
Was it the day you created heaven and earth

56. Ālakkōyil may be a reference to the origin of this and other shrines that are similarly named, as small shrines established under a banyan (*āl-*) tree. Śiva is the "master of the path that the gods do not know" ("*vāṉōr aṟiyāneṟiyāṉ*"). He alone can show the path of release to his devotees, and they alone can receive his grace. "Confusion": "*māl*"; the effect of karma.

or the day you took the young deer
and shared your self with the beautiful Goddess?
Was it before or after these deeds
that you took Tiruvārūr for your shrine?

58. Campantar I.4.11 *Pukali (Cīrkāḻi)*

They will be kings on heaven and earth,
who can sing this melodious hymn
which Ñāṉacampantaṉ, renowned scholar of the four Vedas
and poet of good learning,
has composed in praise of the blessed Lord
who lives with the gentle Goddess in Pukali,
exclaiming at the wonder of the Lord's desire
to dwell in its celestial temple.

59. Appar V.125 *Mīyaccūr Iḷaṅkōyil*

1
There are man-made temples
and natural shrines,
and temples of many other kinds;
but see, here is a fine temple
for Araṉ with the cool, matted red hair,
who vanquished Death—
the new shrine at Mīyaccūr.

5
How glorious is the new shrine
at holy Mīyaccūr
for the red-hued Lord
who dances holding all-devouring fire,
frightening the fierce snakes that adorn him!

6
To this day, he will not leave
the new shrine at Mīyaccūr
where, along with the Goddess
who wears a glittering girdle,
he lives, wearing the crescent moon
and garlands of flowers

59. Iḷaṅkōyil: A newly built temple or a *bālālaya*, a shrine to which the central image in a temple is moved while the temple is being renovated; a "temporary" abode.

entwined with the cool golden *koṉṟai*
on his red hair.

The Lord's Journeys

60. Appar IV.19.5 *Tiruvārūr*

The Lord who wanders through many a fair town,
decked out in lovely white bones,
riding his white bull,
finds such delight
in the ancient city of Tiruvārūr
fragrant with sweet blue lilies,
that he still dwells in the temple here,
and will not leave.

61. Appar VI.239.10 Tiruvārūr

In Nallūr he danced for a long time,
in Paḻaiyāṟu, mounted his white bull.
He wandered begging in many towns,
sojourned in Cēṟṟūr for the whole world to see,
then hid in the shrine at Talaiyālaṅkāṭu.
He dwelt with delight in Peruvēḷūr's temple,
halted in Paṭṭīccuram for the night,
entered Maṇaṟkāl,
revealed himself in Cāttaṅkuṭi's shrine,
and swiftly reached Tiruvārūr,
where he stayed.

62. Appar VI.216 PUKKA TIRUTTĀṆṬAKAM (THE TĀṆṬAKAM POEM OF THE LORD'S ARRIVAL) *Kōyil (Tillai)*

1
He lives in Marukal and Mayilāppūr,
where the evening moon shines on wide streets;
He who lives in Koṭumuṭi in Koṅku,

60. Appar refers to "*pūṅkōyil*," the central shrine in the Tiruvārūr temple complex.

61. Śiva's journey can be traced along a cluster of shrines in Tanjore district.

62. "Puliyūr" or "Perumpaṟṟap puliyūr" is yet another name for Tillai. Note the alliteration in "Marukal, Mayilāppūr," "Koṭumuṭi, Koṅku, Kuṟṟālam, etc." v. 2. "Our unfailing wealth": "*poyyāp poruḷ*," release through Śiva.

in Kuṟṟālam and in Kuṭamūkku,
went to Koḷḷamputūr. The homeless wanderer
stopped at Tarumapuram and Takkaḷūr for many days.
Then, smeared with shining white ash
and surrounded by his band of spirits,
he reached the Little Ampalam in Puliyūr,
and there he stayed.

2
Our man of Naṉipaḷḷi, who wears the snake at his waist,
rode to Nallūr, where he stopped for a while.
He halted in Pācūr for half a day, and went
to Paritiniyamam for twelve days.
He spent seven days in Miḻalai on the river,
ever filled with Vedic chant
and the smoke of sacrifice.
Our worldly pleasure, our unfailing wealth,
then reached the Little Ampalam in Puliyūr,
and there he stayed.

63. Appar VI.272 *Valampuram*

1
See the Lord with the holy forehead-eye
and the fierce snake around his arm,
the Lord surrounded by all the gods,
even the god dark as a sapphire, who once
measured the universe, and the god of the Vedas!
See how once, as I followed him,
worshipping and singing with other sweet-voiced women,
he went to Valampuram
with broad highways and fertile fields,
and stayed there.

3
The dear Lord who revealed
his own fiery form on one side
and the form of Ari on the other,
seemed to enter the shrine
of Tāṉtōṉṟi in Ākkūr, and yet,
when I, a woman of evil karma, followed him,

63. The speaker in this poem is a woman in love with Śiva. Appar refers to the myth of the fiery *liṅga* in verse 1, and Śiva's form as Harihara (Ari–Hari; Araṉ–Hara), Viṣṇu-Śiva, in verse 3.

he had vanished without a trace.
My Lord who wears the sacred thread
and the hide on his beautiful ash-smeared frame,
the chanter of the Veda, spoke lies,
and going to Valampuram,
he stayed there.

7
He came to me dancing, dressed in silk,
his coral body smeared with cool sandal paste,
his tender feet hurting from the dance.
I said: "What town are you from, my Lord?"
And then I wanted to die,
for he stared wildly at me and made lying speeches
as he walked in circles away from me,
as if he were going to another town,
till he reached Valampuram,
and there he stayed.

8
He said, "My town is Paḻaṉam,
home of many devotees,
it is the ancient sacred town of Paḻaṉam,
and it is Pācūr as well.
Going to good Naṉipaḷḷi tonight,
I will reach Naḷḷāṟu tomorrow."
He named no single town as his own.
Then the handsome ash-smeared Lord
walked with a carefree stride,
till he reached Valampuram
with fine streets and rich fields,
and there he stayed.

Sing the Shrine!

64. Campantar I.8 *Āvūrp Pacupatiyīccaram*

1
Sing the town where his lovers worship him,
saying, "God of blessings, ash-smeared Lord of the hosts,
he dwells in the hearts of his devotees,
he wears the moon as a wreath on his head,"

64, v. 2. "The beggar": deriving *attiyar* from "*atti*," Sanskrit *arthin*, "suppliant."

the town of sweet-smelling groves
and broad highways with palaces whose roofs touch the sky,
and the ceaseless sound of hymns set to musical modes—
O tongue, sing the shrine of Pacupatiyīccaram in Āvūr!

2
Sing the town where the Lord dwells with the Goddess,
as his servants praise him,
crying, "He gives us release! Age does not touch him!
Dweller in Kaṉṟāppūr, three-eyed god,
the beggar who smashed Dakṣa's sacrifice!"
Sing the town where the gardens flow with pure honey
from blossom clusters swarming with bees,
and the temple resounds with devotional songs—
O tongue, sing the shrine of Pacupatiyīccaram in Āvūr!

*

65. Campantar I.80.7 *Kōyil (Tillai)*

They are the leaders of the world,
who bow their head to the Little Ampalam shrine
of the Lord whom the world praises
as the destroyer of the citadels with his bow,
as the god who is crowned with the rippling stream,
and loves the mountain's daughter
who shares his form.

66. Appar V.161 *Kacci Ēkampam*

1
Rejoice, O heart, though you see
nothing but the fruit of past deeds!
End your misery!
Wander as a devotee
of Ēkampam's Lord with matted red hair
adorned by flowers swarming with bees!

6
Banish darkness! Go worship with joined palms
Ēkampam in Kacci,

66. Kacci Ēkampam: The temple of Ēkampaṉ or Ekāmranātha (colloquial Tamil "Ēkāmparēcuvarar") in Kanchipuram (Kacci). v. 6. "Darkness": "*iruḷ*" is *āṇavamalam*, the primordial impurity that clings to the soul and prevents it from knowing its true nature. "Those who have renounced the world": "*paṟṟilār*," "those who have renounced everything (except Śiva), true devotees." Siva himself is "*arumporuḷ*," "the treasure that is rare, hard to attain, invaluable."

abode of the Lord with curly red hair,
the rare treasure who gives the blessings
of wealth, and good family, and liberating grace
to those who have renounced the world.

67. Appar V.157 *Nallam*

1
When Yama's men come to seize your life,
O helpless ones, what can your kinsmen do?
Praise the feet of Nallam's Lord who rules us!
Your misery will end.

2
I'll tell you of a way to end
the pain of a life wasted in useless talk—
go to Nallam, home of the naked god,
fire-red one who smashed Dakṣa's sacrifice.

3
Sinners, in vain do you lust after
women with long braids, and become their slaves!
To reach Śiva, go to the Araneṟi shrine
in holy Nallam, city of our Lord.

4
This body dear to you
is worthless the moment life departs.
Go to Nallam, sacred abode of Umā's lord.
That is our only good.

5
Before the tongue falters, and the body trembles,
Sing Nallam, home of the Lord who rides on the white bull.
Worship the Lord, keep company with his servants
and shun the others.

9
Before your time on earth is spent,
worship and sing as you can,
Nallam, home of the king of brahmins who chant the Veda,
Lord of Māl and Brahmā of the lotus seat.

67, v. 10. The poet puns on the name "Nallam," deriving it from "*nalla*," "good." "*Nalla nallam*," "Nallam, the place of blessing."

10
The good life is theirs, whose tongues can chant
the good name of Nallam, sacred abode of the Lord
who swiftly destroyed the strength of the demon
whose shoulders are like hills.

68. Campantar I.59 *Tūṅkāṉaimāṭam*

1
You who seek a place to perform penance
to end the chain of existence,
which is nothing but birth and death and insidious disease,
become servants at the shade of our Lord's feet,
worship Tūṅkāṉaimāṭam temple in Kaṭantai
surrounded by trenches and walls,
where the sweet sound of Vedic chant
rises in every house!

5
The shifting illusions of this life
are transient, perishing with death.
If you want to put an end to your confusion
and reach the highest world,
worship Kaṭantai's Tūṅkāṉaimāṭam temple,
place of healing,
where devotees ceaselessly worship the Lord's feet
with his glorious names.

6
Before your senses are dulled and your hearing fails,
before cataracts dim the eye,
before grey hair and wrinkles appear,
before the advent of old age,
worship Kaṭantai's Tūṅkāṉaimāṭam temple
with its ancient river,
abode of the Lord who shines like gold,
and has the river in his matted red hair.

10
The penance which will end the wretchedness of existence

68. Kaṭantai is also known as Peṇṇākaṭam. Tūṅkāṉaimāṭam: The type of temple that has a *gajapṛṣṭha vimāna*, a tower shaped like an elephant's back. See Dorai Rangaswamy, *Religion and Philosophy*, 1: 9. v. 10. "Jains who pluck out their hair." Campantar refers to the Jain monks' practice of denuding the scalp by plucking the hairs out in handfuls. See Poem 80, v. 10.

which is nothing but consuming hunger and disease,
is to reject the lying nonsense
spoken by the Jains who pluck out their hair
and the Buddhist monks who wear the ochre robe,
and to worship the abode
of the Lord and his lovely Goddess,
Kaṭantai's Tūṅkāṉaimāṭam temple
which will destroy your sin.

2 The Lord's Dear Town

(POEMS 69–73)

69. Cuntarar VII.78 *Kētāram*

1
Life is an illusion,
all things end in dust.
The sea of birth is a waste,
the body is a trap made of hunger and disease.
Do good deeds without delay,
say "holy Kētāram,"
place of him whose immense form
sent Viṣṇu with the long eyes
and Brahmā of the lotus seat
searching above and below!

6
Are not the Lord's temples sacred
as places of pilgrimage?
Go bathe in cool Kurukṣetra,
plunge in the Godāvari and Kumari,
reach enlightenment in the holy hills,
both north and south,
say "Kētāram," sacred place
where the parrot feasts
on the glossy plantain fruit!

70. Campantar I.45.12 *Ālaṅkāṭu (Tiruvālaṅkāṭu)*

Those who know these verses
which Ñāṉacampantaṉ of Caṇpai town,

69, v. 1. "*Paṟi*": "a trap, the body." The word is used in the sense of "the body" in verse 2 of this hymn. v. 6. Kurukṣetra: the renowned battlefield of the *Mahābhārata* epic, situated in North India; a place of pilgrimage. The Godavari flows through central India. On the mythical river Kumari, see Shulman, *Tamil Temple Myths*, p. 54. "Holy hills": "*cīparppatam*" (Sanskrit Śrīparvata), Śrīśailam, South Indian counterpart of Kailāsa. In *Cuntaramūrtti Tēvāram*, the commentator A. Cōmacuntaram Ceṭṭiyār takes "taḷicālaikaḷ tavamāvatu tammaip peṟil aṉṟē" to mean "temples and holy places will yield the fruit of penance only if the worshipper has taken refuge in Śiva."

70. Alaṅkāṭu: "Forest of banyan trees." Banyan trees put out hanging roots that eventually grow into trees, which form a colony; they also live to a great age.

where the streets are fragrant with sandal paste,
has sung through the Lord's grace,
in praise of our god
in lovely, cool Paḻaiyaṉūr Ālaṅkāṭu,
will turn every place they visit
into a place of pilgrimage.

71. Campantar II.175 TIRUVŪRKKŌVAI (THE ANTHOLOGY OF SACRED PLACES)

1
Ārūr, Tillai's Little Ampalam, Vallam, Nallam,
North Kacci, Acciṟupākkam,
good Kūrūr, Kuṭavāyil, Kuṭantai, Veṇṇi,
sea-girt Kaḻippālai, south Kōṭi,
rich Nīrūr, fertile Niṉṟiyūr and Kuṉṟiyūr,
Kurukāvaiyūr, Nāraiyūr, ancient
Kāṉappērūr, and good Neyttāṉam with fine, large fields—
babble these names of the moon-crested god's great abodes!

2
Aṇṇāmalai and Īṅkōy hill, Mutukuṉṟu
on the Muttāṟu and Koṭuṅkuṉṟu,
precious Kaḻukkuṉṟu, Kailāsa and Kōṇam,
Kaṟkuṭi, Kāḷatti and Vāṭpōkki,
love Paraṅkuṉṟam and Paruppatam, hills of the Lord

71. In this "anthology" (*kōvai*) Campantar gives a topographical classification of the shrines of Śiva in the Tamil region. There is much rhyming in verse 1; verse 2 is devoted to the hill shrines of Tamilnadu and other regions. Verse 3 of this hymn lists the different types of places and place names connected with Śiva's shrines:

3
Eight places called "*aṭṭāṉam*,"
all the abodes of the handsome Lord, called "*kā*,"
eight more called "*tuṟai*," nine "*kāṭu-*,"
three "*kuḷam-*," five "*kaḷam-*," four "*pāṭi-*," and
three "*pāḻi-*"—these are the beloved abodes
of the spouse of the mountain's daughter with the fragrant hair.
Love these, and the good Lord's town of Pācūr,
for your greatest sins to be dissolved!

"*Aṭṭāṉam*": "the places of the eight heroic deeds," e.g., Atikai Viraṭṭāṉam. "*Kāṭu*" and "*kā*": "forest," e.g., Ālaṅkāṭu, Āṉaikkā. "*Tuṟai*": "harbor, resting place," e.g., Āvaṭuturai. "*Kuḷam*": "reservoir, tank." "*Kaḷam*": "field," e.g., Netunkaḷam. "*Pāṭi*": "settlement," e.g., Āppāṭi. "*Pāḻi*": "site of a Jain temple or settlement," e.g., Arataipperumpāḻi. v. 4. Temples that have the suffix "*-paḷḷi*" probably refer to sites that formerly accommodated Jain monasteries or ancient shrines built as burial mounds for heroes and kings ("*paḷḷippaṭaik kōyil*"). See N. Venkataramanayya, *An Essay on the Origin of South Indian Temple* (Madras: Methodist Publishing House, 1930), p. 2, and Nilakanta Sastri, *Development of Religion*, pp. 98–99.

who shares his form with the Goddess
whose speech is sweet as music.
Meditate day and night on these,
and you will cross the ocean of suffering!

4
Aṟappaḷḷi, Akattiyāṉpaḷḷi, Kāṭṭuppaḷḷi,
dwellings of the ash-smeared god who bears the river,
Ciṟappaḷḷi, Cirāppaḷḷi, Cempoṉpaḷḷi, holy Naṉipaḷḷi,
fine Makēntirappaḷḷi, town of the birthless one,
Iṭaippaḷḷi, beloved abode of the river-haired Lord,
and the "*paḷḷi*" where he gave the wheel
to Māl who worshipped him—
simple heart! Meditate on these!

72. Cuntarar VII.47 Ūrttokai (The List of Sacred Towns)

1
Ocean in Kāṭṭūr, Kaṭampūr's Hill, Lord of Kāṉappēr!
Sprout in Kōṭṭūr, Aḻuntūr's King, Bull in Koḻunal,
Lord of Paṉaṅkāṭṭūr, you whom the world praises in song,
God who rides on the bull, make me sing of you without fail!

2
Lord in Kurakkuttaḷi in the *pālai* tract of Koṅku,
O young man, Kuṟṟālam's god!
sky-wanderer, Chief of the gods, bridegroom in Vāymūr,
O handsome Lord adorned with the conch earring,
you who dance at night,
holding aloft blazing fire in the burning-ground,
end your devotees' fears!

4
Father in Ārūr, Aiyāṟu's ambrosia, King in Aḷappūr,
Lord of Karukāvūr, whose pastures border on cloud-kissed groves,
dweller in Pērūr, Lord in Paṭṭi, giver of the birthless state,
King of Pācūr, you are sung by the whole world!

73. Cuntarar VII.47.10

They belong to Śiva's world,
who sing in ecstasy this garland of Tamil verses

72. Alliteration and rhyme seem to be the governing principles in Cuntarar's selection of towns in this "*tokai*" (list).

that the devotee Ūraṉ—
son of Caṭaiyaṉ, and father of the girl Ciṅkaṭi
with long dark eyes curved like the young mango,
and speech sweet as honey—
has sung in contemplation of the many sacred places
ruled by the Father who wears the elephant hide.

3 Sacred Landscapes

(POEMS 74–84)

On the Banks of the Kaveri

74. Campantar II.246 *Mānturai*

1
Let us praise the tender feet
worshipped by the gods,
the feet of our Lord who dwells in Mānturai
on the northern bank of the Kaveri
which flows like a stream of gold,
bearing the blossoms of the golden *vēṅkai*,
ñālal, *cerunti*, and *cenpakam*,
ivory and sandalwood, and the flowers
of the *kuruntu*, *curapunnai*, and *mātavi*.

2
We know nothing other than
the spouse of the Goddess with the flowing hair
and the brow curved like a sword,
the god who burned with his fiery eye
Kāma of the five arrows, son of basil-adorned Māl,
and dwells in Mānturai
on the northern bank of the Kaveri
whose stream carries
the sweet *viḷā* and *cāti* fruit
along with gems from the bamboo.

3
We know no act higher than the worship
of our flawless gem whom the gods celebrate,

74. With his description of the golden flowers that float in the Kaveri's current (v. 1), Campantar offers a visual justification for "Ponni" ("the golden river"), the affectionate term by which the Tamils have traditionally referred to this river, on account of the agricultural and commercial riches it has brought them. "*Turai*," in the names of settlements such as "Mānturai," signifies a beach or riverbed. The *"mā"* here refers to the mango tree. v. 2. "Basil-adorned Māl": "*tuḷavamāl.*" Viṣṇu/Krishna wears the leaves of the sacred basil in his hair.

the god who begs for alms in a dead man's skull,
our Lord who dwells in Mānturai
on the northern bank of the Kaveri,
whose stream bears clusters of fruit
of the *pūkam* and *kūntal* palm
from the hills where the trees
are thick with honeycombs.

75. Campantar I.5 *Kīlait tiruk kāṭṭuppaḷḷi*

2
They will put an end to pain,
who become pious men
versed in the sacred texts,
and servants of the Lord who binds
the snake around his waist,
and dwells in Kāṭṭuppaḷḷi
where the Kaveri crashes upon her banks,
laden with flowers and pearls
and fine gems and gold.

5
Let us sing the feet of the tridentbearer,
the Lord who dances with ringing anklets,
and loves his abode
where his loving devotees praise him,
Kāṭṭuppaḷḷi on the Kaveri
who rushes down in many gurgling streams,
washing sandal- and aloe wood
with soft sounds onto her banks.

6
They will put an end to pain,
who become the servants
of the Lord who binds the winding snake
around his waist,
dances to the sweet music of the hollow flute and *yāḻ*,
and loves Kāṭṭuppaḷḷi
where women with long, flowing hair toss aside as weeds
the full-bloomed blue and red lily
and lotus growing in paddyfields.

75. Kīḻait tiruk kāṭṭuppaḷḷi: Lower Kāṭṭuppaḷḷi.

7
Our Lord with the blackened throat
and body white with ash
loves Kāṭṭuppaḷḷi
where strong peasants transplanting rice
find relief for aching wrists
in breaking hard lumps of cane sugar.
The devotees who worship his feet
with flowers, and water, and love,
will end their karma and serve the Lord.

76. Campantar I.130 *Tiruvaiyāṟu*

1
Tiruvaiyāṟu is the place
where the female ape, in fright,
leaps up on a branch to look for rainclouds,
taking for thunder the roll of drums
when women dance, going around the shrine
where the Lord dwells who delivers us from fear
when the five senses wander out of their cages,
and cease to function,
the phlegm rises, the reason fails,
and we are afraid.

2
The temple of the Lord who binds
the great, hooded cobra around his waist,
and, riding on his bull
along with the mountain's daughter,
goes begging with the cry:
"Give me alms, O women of sweet speech!"
is Tiruvaiyāṟu
where whorled conches from the ocean's stormy waves,
borne by the Kaveri's tide
and tossed on her banks at night,
yield bright pearls.

76, v. 3. "The red-legged little egret": "*ceṅkāl veṇkuruku.*" Samy, *Caṅka ilakkiyattil puḷḷiṉa viḷakkam*, pp. 44–45, points out that, among the many species of birds called *kuruku* in Caṅkam literature and the *Tēvāram*, the one described as "*pacuṅkāl veṇkuruku*" (the *veṇkuruku* with the yellow-green legs) can only refer to the little egret (*ciṟu veḷḷāṅkuruku*). He also notes that Campantar's description of this bird as having "red legs" tallies with the fact that the legs of the little egret turn a reddish color during the nesting season.

3
The temple of the god who carries a dead man's bones,
the Lord of Kailāsa hill and Kāṉappēr,
the trident holder,
bull rider who shares his body with the Goddess,
is Tiruvaiyāṟu
where the red-legged little egret
ruffles its feathers with its sharp bill
to shake them dry of the water's cold
and looks for prey in the fresh waters
of a grove flowing with honey.

7
The temple of the mountain's lord,
the bowman who shot the great arrow
which shattered the three fortresses
that oppressed great heaven,
is Tiruvaiyāṟu,
where the cuckoo sings on every hill,
and the lush sugar cane slumbers in fields
caressed by a soft breeze that bears the scent
of flowers full of rich honey.

8
The temple of the Lord
who first crushed the ten heads
and mighty shoulders of the demon-king
when he dared to lift Kailāsa hill,
and then blessed him,
is Tiruvaiyāṟu,
where the young buffalo runs,
scared by a coconut falling from a shady young palm,
and blunders into a bed of waterlilies,
scattering the ripe grain in a paddyfield.

10
Reject the words of those worthless, wily rogues,
the scantily clad, wicked Jains
and the Buddhist monks!
O devotees, love him, become his men!
The temple in which
our eight-armed, three-eyed Lord sweetly dwells
is Tiruvaiyāṟu,

where the Poṉṉi's blossom-filled stream
brings fine gems.

Our Man of the Hills

77. Campantar I.10 *Aṇṇāmalai*

1
Karma will vanish without a trace
for those who worship Aṇṇāmalai
where waterfalls descend with the muffled roar of drums,
hill where the Lord who is half woman,
the one who united with Umā whose breast no child has sucked,
shines resplendent as a great sacred gem.

2
Karma will end
for those who meditate on the feet,
adorned by beautiful anklets,
of the Lord in Aṇṇāmalai
in whose woods wild bulls mate with cows,
when the mango branch,
let go by a male ape who's plucked its honey-sweet fruit,
touches the dark raincloud,
and small drops strike the mountain's rocky cliffs.

78. Campantar I.43 *Kaṟkuṭi*

3
The Śaiva who wears the datura flower
and the cool moon with sparkling stars
on his crown, on which the broad river flows,
is the chieftain of Kaṟkuṭi's great hill
where broad-chested hunters burn dark aloe wood
to clear the land,
raising sweet-smelling smoke.

77, v. 1. The phrase "whose breast no child has sucked" (*uṇṇāmulai*) has become a standard epithet for the Goddess Umā. "*Tirumāmaṇi tikaḻa*" ("shining like a great sacred gem") has been interpreted variously as referring to the landscape (gems on the mountain), the Goddess, and Śiva.

78. Compare verse 8 with *Kuṟuntokai* 74, translated in Ramanujan, *The Interior Landscape*, p. 47.

8
Our friend who gently bore down with a toe
to crush under the Great Hill
the tough heads of Rāvaṇa who tried to insult the Lord
with a show of brute strength,
is the chieftain of Kaṟkuṭi's great hill,
where the leafy bamboo,
bent and let go by the elephant,
springs back with such force
as to pierce the dark clouds.

79. Campantar I.12 *Mutukuṉṟu*

1
Let us go to Mutukuṉṟu,
where the Muttāṟu's stream brings offerings
of flowers, cool sandalwood,
aloe, and bright saffron for the Lord.
Let us go to the abode of the fire-hued god
with the crown of long matted hair,
the one who devoured the poison that rose from the sea
when the gods churned it with the mountain-churn.

2
Let us go to high Mutukuṉṟu,
in whose mountain caves
the fierce lion with blazing eyes
and cruel curved claws
roars when he hears the thundercloud.
Let us go to the place
where the Śaiva who meditated in the spacious shade
of the great banyan tree sweetly dwells
with the slender Goddess.

79. Mutukuṉṟu: Sanskrit "Vṛddhācala" ("ancient mountain"). In verse 3 Campantar uses the technical terms "*pacupācavētaṉai*" and "*viḷaiyātator paricil*" to describe the bondage of the soul with reference to the three *malas* (impurities). I have followed P. S. Somasundaram's excellent interpretation of these lines, in which he suggests that *pacuvētaṉai* and *pācavētaṉai* refer to the primordial impurities that afflict the soul, while the *mala* of *māyā*, the embodied condition, is a *luminous* binder (*oṇṭaḷai*) because it is a part of, and offers the possibility of, the Lord's grace. See Somasundaram, *Tirujñāṉasambandhar*, pp. 117–19. Verse 10 is replete with associations with the *kuṟiñci* or "hill" landscape of classical Tamil poetry: Murukaṉ, god of the *kuṟiñci* landscape, and the Kuṟiñci musical mode, which is appropriate to this landscape.

3
Let us go to lofty Mutukuṉṟu,
on whose slopes the crescent moon sails
with the brilliant, thousand-rayed sun.
Let us go to the abode of our Lord
whose grace alone can destroy
the primordial impurities that afflict the soul,
along with the luminous chain that binds us.

10
Let us go to Mutukuṉṟu,
where maidens with flowers in their dark hair
sing the praise of Murukaṉ
in the sacred Kuṟiñci mode.
Let us go to the place of the bull-bannered Lord,
the mountain's son-in-law,
Araṉ whom the Jains and Buddhists do not know.

80. Campantar I.69 *Aṇṇāmalai*

1
The Lord whom the gods praise,
and devotees worship with flowers,
the god who blessed the demons
on the day he burned the three citadels,
is the Lord of Aṇṇāmalai,
on whose slopes
herds of wild cows run about,
terrified by the thunderclap.

2
The Lord of the gods
who wears on his crest the moon emerging from clouds,

80. Aṇṇāmalai, modern Tiruvaṇṇāmalai, is a popular pilgrimage center today. It is celebrated as the site of Śiva's manifestation as the fiery cosmic *liṅga*. Hunters' women still build tree platforms (v. 2), from which they watch the ripening millet and chase parrots and other marauding birds with cries of "Āyō!" and stones shot from slings. v. 3 Here Campantar refers to the myth of the fiery *liṅga*. "Carnal sins," "*ūṉattiraḷ*," can also mean simply "the body." Following V. A. Devasenapathy, P. S. Somasundaram accepts the reading "*ūṉattiruḷ*": "the darkness that afflicts the soul," *āṇava-mala*. See Somasundaram, *Tirujñānasambandhar*, pp. 118–19. In verses 5 and 9 the poet alludes to gems and pearls of fabulous origin (bamboos, various animals) gathered by the hill tribes. v. 8. It is not clear whether the reference to the Lord revealing the Law (*aṟam*, dharma) to the gods is a reference to a particular myth, such as the one of his discourse to the sages under the banyan tree, or simply an elaboration of the Rāvaṇa myth. In verse 10 Campantar refers to several practices of the Jain monks that the Śaivas found offensive.

and bears the ocean's poison in his throat
for the good of the world,
is the Lord of Aṇṇāmalai,
where parrots, sweet of speech,
perch with mocking cries of "Āyō!"
on the tree platforms
built by hunters' women
who speak foul words.

3
The Lord who stood as a blaze of knowledge
and unfailingly ends the carnal sins of his devotees,
is the Lord of Aṇṇāmalai,
whose slopes become the nightly refuge
for elephant herds, and bears,
and the wild boar and deer.

4
The Lord of the gods,
the spouse of Umā who has a slender waist,
the bull rider with long matted hair,
the destroyer of the enemies' cities,
is the Lord of Aṇṇāmalai
on whose slopes
the huge elephant in rut falls wearily asleep,
having searched in vain for its lost mate.

5
The Lord of the gods,
the spouse of beautiful Umā,
he who once bent his bow of war
to set fire to the three cities,
is the Lord of Aṇṇāmalai,
on whose slopes
waterfalls bring large pearls and gems
gathered in forest tracts
by gypsy hunters with long bows.

6
The king of the Himalayan gods,
the Lord whom devotees praise
in every age of the universe,
the pure one who destroys sin
for those who worship him with love,
dwells in the shrine of Aṇṇāmalai,

on whose slopes
the herdsman looks for a lost buffalo
whose bellow he hears,
and when he plays his flute
the whole herd gathers around.

7
The Highest Lord who destroys
for his devotees who meditate on him,
the bondage of past karma
as well as the fruit of future deeds,
lives in the shrine of Aṇṇāmalai,
on whose ancient rocky slopes
echoing with the beat of drums
the evening moon rests.

8
The Lord of Aṇṇāmalai
revealed the sacred Law to the gods
when they begged him to display his power,
and when the demon dared to lift the hill
in an arrogant show of strength,
crushed his chest,
yet blessed him with his grace.

9
The Lord of the gods,
whom Tirumāl and Brahmā could not find,
so that they might end their long search,
is the Lord of Aṇṇāmalai,
on whose slopes
bands of gypsy women wander,
hawking piles of pearls
gathered from tall old bamboos.

10
Do not listen to the words of the mad Jain monks
who carry mats, and pluck their hair,
and eat their food standing.
Love and worship the spouse
of Umā of the full breasts,
the Lord who dwells in the shrine of Aṇṇāmalai,
whose slopes shelter packs of lions.

11
They will attain an enduring life
honored by the gods,
who learn and know these ten poetic verses
which Ñāṉacampantaṉ of Kāḻi, praised by good men,
has composed on the Lord of Aṇṇāmalai,
on whose slopes
serpents creep at night.

81. Campantar I.99 *Kuṟṟālam*

1
O fellow devotees!
Kuṟṟālam, on the tall slopes
of whose fragrant hill
striped bees make music
in woods full of *vēṅkai* trees,
is the fair town beloved of our Lord
who wears the blooming *koṉṟai* wreath,
and likes to bathe in sweet milk and ghee!

4
O fellow devotees!
Kuṟṟālam, whose slopes abound
in ripe mango fruit, clusters of plantain
and the honeyed fruit of the jack,
is the fair town beloved of our naked Lord
who wears the snake and tortoise shell
along with the *akṣa* beads,
and dances holding fire.

5
O little devotees!
Kuṟṟālam, on the slopes of whose hill

81. This hymn, and the following one (on Kāḷatti), are particularly rich in references to the flora and fauna considered to be typical of the hill landscape in the Tamil region. Kuṟṟālam continues to be a popular hill resort and palce of pilgrimage, famous for its waterfall. The hill landscape of Kuṟṟālam has been immortalized in the eighteenth-century poem *Kuṟṟālak kuṟavañci*, written in the Kuṟavañci genre, in which the life of the Kuṟavar hill tribes forms an important theme. v. 1. "Make music": "*yāḻcey*," literally, "make the music of the *yāḻ*." v. 4. The jackfruit tree (*kuṟumpalā*) is the sacred tree at the shrine in Kuṟṟālam. v. 6. "*Kaimmā*": literally, "the beast with the trunk," qualifying "*vēḻam*," "elephant." v. 7. Blue lilies: "*nīlaneytal*," two kinds of dark waterlilies, the Blue Nelumbo and the Nymphaea Stellata.

the monkey with her young one
feasts on clusters of sweet plantain fruit
is the fair town beloved of the Lord
who bears the pointed trident
and the bow that he bent
toward the three cities.

6
O elders!
Kuṟṟālam, on whose slopes
gypsy women with eyes dark as the blue lily
shoot gems, trying to drive away
parrots who eat the ripe millet
from their fields,
is the fair town beloved of my Master,
the Lord who cloaked himself
in the flayed hide of the great elephant.

7
O devotees!
Kuṟṟālam, in whose spacious groves
rich in cool ponds full of blue lilies
the peacock dances with his mate,
is the fair town of our trident bearer,
the god who quelled Death
with his foot.

10
O devotees!
Kuṟṟālam, on whose great cool slopes
mating bees on the *kuruntam* trees
sing the Cevvaḻi mode,
is the fair town beloved of the Lord
whose gracious nature transcends the slander
of the Buddhists who eat seated
and the Jains who eat standing.

82. Campantar III.327 *Kāḷatti*

1
If you ask,
"What hill does he love?"

82. Kāḷatti or Kālahasti is celebrated as the site of the heroic sacrifice of the hunter-saint Kaṇṇappar, referred to in verse 4 of this hymn. v. 3. "Sent forth": "*vakuttu*," which

The answer is: Śiva who showed his grace
by transforming into ambrosia
the poison spewed by the great ocean
to torment the gods and demons
loves Kāḷatti's hill,
where hunters' women
shoot gold and gems from strong slings
to chase boars and deer and parrots
who come to eat the grain they guard.

2
If you ask,
"What hill does he love?"
The answer is: Śaṅkara of the moon-crowned matted hair,
the god who skillfully burned in an instant
with his ancient fiery bow
the three castles of the demons,
loves Kāḷatti's hill,
where darkness is banished
by sparks rising from bamboos brushing
against each other,
and rays of light streaming from
shining gems rooted up by stout boars.

3
If you ask,
"What hill does he love?"
The answer is: Śiva who sent forth
Kālī who came swiftly at his command
to kill Dāruka who was drunk with power,
loves Kāḷatti's hill,
where black apes gather in packs
to feast on the many kinds of sweet fruit
they have plucked,
and frolic boisterously upon the rocks.

---

can mean both "created" and "appointed (for a purpose)." This verse refers to the myth of Kālī and Dāruka, not Tāraka (*tārakaṉ*) as the *Tēvāram* Kaḻakam edition has it. v. 6. In agreement with the *Tēvāram* Pondicherry edition I read "*par akam*" ("in the world") instead of "*pāratam*" (the *Mahābhārata*). The "golden mountain" in verse 7 is Mount Meru, situtated at the center of the Hindu univese. v. 9. "Manifest Śiva": "*cakalacivaṉ*" (*sakala-śiva*), "Śiva revealed in form"; the two other aspects of Śiva are unmanifest (*niṣkala*), and manifest-unmanifest (*sakala-niṣkala*), as in the *liṅga*. See Narayana Ayyar, *Origin and Early History of Śaivism*, p. 359. Koccaivayam (v. 11) is one of the twelve names of Cīrkāḻi.

4
If you ask,
"What is his hill?"
The answer is: The moon-crowned Lord,
dancer in the burning-ground,
bull rider who shares his body
with Umā whose shoulders are as graceful as the bamboo,
belongs to Kāḷatti's hill,
where the hunter who worshipped the Lord,
bathing him in water from his mouth,
plucked out his own flower-eye
with a cruel arrow,
and thus joined the Lord's feet.

5
If you ask,
"What hill does he love?"
The answer is: Śiva who killed,
to the beast's thundrous trumpeting,
the elephant who attacked him,
like a dark cloud looming over a hill,
terrifying Lady Umā,
loves Kāḷatti's hill
rich in bubbling waterfalls and streams,
and bamboos that shed sparkling pearls.

6
If you ask,
"What hill does he love?"
The answer is: Araṉ who took
the turbulent Ganges in his matted hair,
moved by the sincere penance
of Bhagīratha of worldwide fame,
loves Kāḷatti's hill
where grey smoke rising from dark aloe wood
which gypsies kindle and burn
in wide trenches in the fields
spreads over the sky.

7
If you ask,
"What hill is his abode?"
The answer is: He who devised for Māl
the strategy of piercing with the wheel

the demon Jalandhara of invincible might,
dwells on Kāḷatti's hill,
which shines in the dark like the golden mountain,
lit by rays from great bright gems
emitted by winding snakes.

8
If you ask
"What glorious hill does he love?"
The answer is: Śiva who blessed
Rāvaṇa of the fire-red curls
by bearing down with one lovely toe
upon the great mountain,
breaking the demon's strength,
loves Kāḷatti's hill,
where elephants, striped tigers, and lions
flee in terror when they hear
hunters bearing great bows
coming over the tall slopes.

9
If you ask,
"What hill does he love?"
The answer is: The manifest Śiva
who would not reveal his form
to the two who opposed him,
thinking, "We will quickly measure him
from head to foot!"
loves Kāḷatti's hill
where the *vēṅkai*'s golden blossoms
grace the wedding rites
in which young men of the highland tracts
marry women lovely as peacocks.

10
If you ask,
"What hill does he love?"
The answer is: Śiva who concealed his great nature
from the monks who shroud themselves in robes
and those who eat standing,
loves Kāḷatti's hill
where the cow-elephant eats
the sprouts of cool sandal trees

in the dense woods that cover that hill,
and frolics with her young.

11
The highest world is within easy reach
for those who can sing in good Tamil modes
these words that Ñāṉacampantaṉ of worldwide fame,
good lord of Koccaivayam, noble town
rising tall with palaces and towers,
has sung on Kāḷatti's hill,
beloved of Śiva
who dances in the burning-ground.

The Earth's Wild Places

83. Cuntarar VII.32 *Kōṭikkuḻakar*

1
Why do you live alone
on the seashore battered by fierce winds?
My sin is great,
that I must see you thus.
Handsome Lord at Kōṭikkuḻakar,
who keeps you company here?

2
Is it because you once
devoured the ocean's poison
that you now favor Paravai, the sea?
Handsome Youth at Kōṭikkuḻakar,

83. Kōṭikkuḻakar: The temple at Kōṭikkarai (modern Point Calimere on the southern part of the peninsula), where the deity is also known as Kōṭikkuḻakar (*kōṭi*: tip, edge, end, here denoting the tip of the land; *kuḻakar*: a handsome youth). The shrine Cuntarar visited must have been situated near a forest close to the seashore. The word "*paravai*" in verse 2 refers to the sea, but there is also a possible reference to Cuntarar's wife, Paravai, who was a temple dancer in Tiruvārūr. v. 5. The "Lady of the Forest" (Kāṭukiḻāḷ) is an ancient Tamil goddess. The cobra's hood (v. 6) is a conventional standard of comparison in Tamil poetry for a woman's mound of Venus (*aravēr alkul*). The poet plays on the meanings of "*oṟṟi*" (mortgaged object) and "*ār*" (who? stranger) in his fanciful etymologies for the names of the two towns Oṟṟiyūr and Ārūr in verse 8. This hymn and the one that follows evoke the "*pālai*" or "wasteland" landscape of classical Tamil poetry; in *pālai* poems the hero, seeking wealth, travels alone through wild landscapes. Being situated on the seashore, Kōṭikkuḻakar could have provided the setting for a seashore (*neytal*) landscape poem; the isolation of the temple and the mood of the place suggest the *pālai* instead. For typical vignettes of the seashore landscape, see Poem 54, dedicated to Veṅkuru (Cīrkāḻi).

bordered by lush groves,
why do you live alone here, my Lord?

3
O supreme Lord who lives south of joyful Maṟaikkāṭu
where many devotees sing your praise,
Handsome Youth at Kōṭikkuḻakar,
where flowering groves abound,
why do you live alone, my Lord?

4
This is a great wilderness
resounding with the hoot of the owl,
which terrifies the beautiful Goddess;
cruel wicked hunters live here.
Handsome Lord at Kōṭikkuḻakar,
Why have you made for yourself
a temple in this place?

5
You who share your body
with your spouse with long, kohl-darkened eyes,
Lady Ganges lives in the same frame.
Tell me why you have taken
yet another companion,
the Lady of the Forest,
with bracelets on her wrists,
to live with you
in the temple of Kōṭikkuḻakar
with blossoming groves?

6
Sharing your form with the Goddess
whose mound of Venus is like a cobra,
you dwell south of Maṟaikkāṭu
fragrant with *maravam* trees.
Handsome Youth of Kōṭikkuḻakar
full of *kuravam* groves,
my Lord, you live alone
with darkness for your friend.

7
Dear ambrosia who dances
with the sounding warrior's ring,
to the music of drum and flute,

Handsome Youth of Kōṭikkuḻakar
bordered by flourishing groves,
O God, why do you live alone, my Lord?

8
Did you find Oṟṟiyūr a mortgaged town?
Did you leave Ārūr,
thinking it a stranger's place?
O Handsome Youth crowned with the young moon,
my Lord of Kōṭikkuḻakar,
Why do you live alone?

9
Though Viṣṇu the Strider
and the god with the four heads
could not measure your form,
you wander as a homeless beggar.
Is this the reason, O Lord,
that you have made your temple
on the shore where wild hunters live?

10
Those who know these ten verses
composed by the poet of Ārūr
in praise of the handsome young Lord
of Kōṭikkuḻakar, the shrine at land's end,
south of Maṟaikkāṭu and many other towns on earth,
will surely abide in Śiva's glorious world.

84. Cuntarar VII.49 *Murukaṉpūṇṭi*

1
Why do you live with the slim girl
in the great town of Murukaṉpūṇṭi,

84. According to the hagiographical tradition, this hymn refers to an incident in Cuntarar's life: while he was returning to Tiruvārūr bearing gold and gifts given him by the Cēra king, his friend and patron, the poet and his entourage were robbed by highwaymen in the forest near Murukaṉpūṇṭi in the hill country. When Cuntarar appealed to Śiva, the Lord appeared, drove the hunters away, and restored the goods to his devotee. v. 1. "Vaṭukar" refers to people from the areas where Telugu and Kannada are spoken today. "Wealth": literally, "clothes" (*kūṟai*). The idea is that these robbers will strip the innocent traveler of all his possessions. In verse 3 Campantar refers to the repugnance with which caste Hindus view the slaying of cattle. v. 7. Uttiram festival: the festival of Uttiram (Uttaram), held in the month of Paṅkuṉi, an important festival in the temple calendar. For a Caṅkam "pālai" poem with similar images, see Kuṟuntokai 274, translated by Ramanujan, *The Interior Landscape*, p. 81.

home of strong, wild hunters,
Vaṭukar tribesmen with curved bows and foul words,
who waylay men, who jump on travelers with fierce yells,
stab them, and rob them of their wealth?

2
Why do you live, with no one to guard you,
in the great town of Murukaṉpūṇṭi
fragrant with jasmine dust,
home of hunters who threaten travelers
with their bows,
stone them, beat them up, and rob them
of their goods?

3
O my Lord, having become a beggar
to expiate for your sin,
why do you live in the great town of Murukaṉpūṇṭi
where many tribes live like apes,
home of sinners who kill and eat cattle,
fearless of blame,
men who rob and murder innocent souls every day?

7
Wearing the white loincloth,
with ash-smeared body, you chant the Veda,
delighting in the Uttiram festival
at wave-washed Oṟṟiyūr's shrine.
O my Lord, to fulfil what purpose,
guarded by whom, and why, do you live
in the great town of Murukaṉpūṇṭi,
home of marauding highwaymen?

4 Celebrations

(POEMS 85–99)

Rites

85. Appar V.129.1 *Iṭaimarutūr*

Wherever I hear
the sound of drums, the music of hymns,
the Vedas chanted,
there my heart remembers
God our Master,
the Lord who dwells in Iṭaimarutu.

86. Appar IV.31.4 *Kaṭavūr Vīraṭṭam*

Kaṭavūr Vīraṭṭam's Lord
is like sweet sugar cane
to those who become the madman's devotees,
who rise at dawn to bathe, to gather fresh flowers,
and lovingly offer them in worship,
lighting lamps and burning incense for the rite.

87. Campantar III.333.1 *Caṇpai (Cīrkāḻi)*

The beloved abode of the handsome Lord
and the fair Goddess with the beautiful hair
is Caṇpai town,
where the Himalayan gods
come down to praise him,
singing, "O Lord who dwells in our hearts,"
and perform the evening rite,
worshipping with incense and lamps.

88. Campantar III.284 *Kāṉappēr*

1
Devotees have no refuge
other than the feet of the Lord

of Kāṉappēr with groves full of fragrant flowers,
where the bull elephant with his mates
bathes at dawn and gathers flowers with his trunk
to worship the Lord in the sacred rite.

6
My heart worships as a temple
the hearts of blameless devotees who love Kāṉappēr,
home of the god crowned with the white moon,
who spread out his matted hair
to bear the flood
that descended on him.

7
If you desire a cure
for every disease that afflicts imperfect flesh,
take the flower of knowledge
and seek Kāṉappēr
where the wild bull elephant worships
while his mate sweeps the temple yard clean
with her trunk.

*

89. Campantar I.64.1 *Pūvaṇam*

Holy Pūvaṇam of the south,
resplendent with rich tribute
paid by the Cēra, Cōḻa, and Pāṇṭiya,
crowned kings of the realm,
is the abode of the Lord
who shares his body with the Goddess,
and wears the crescent moon
along with the sounding river, the dancing snake,
and beautiful flowers on his matted hair.

90. Campantar I.82.1 *Vīḻimiḻalai*

The temple of the Lord
who took the great golden mountain for his bow
and, fitting the string with the arrow of fire,
destroyed the three flying citadels,
is Vīḻimiḻalai, whose citizens welcome
his good devotees who come from everywhere.

91. Appar V.133.1 *Kaṭampūr*

The abode of the Lord with the long, bright, matted hair,
on which the cool waxing moon
nestles with the winding snake,
is the temple in Kaṭampūr
which resounds day and night
with sacred song and the beat of the *kiṉṉaram* drum.

92. Appar IV.20.3 Tiruvārūr

O Father, you dwell in Tiruvārūr, whose streets
are resplendent with officers of the divine command,
celestial nymphs with precious necklaces,
initiated devotees who worship you by right,
Virati ascetics with matted hair,
brahmins and Śaivas,
Pāśupatas and men of the Kāpālika sect!

Festivals

93. Appar V.128.1 *Iṭaimarutūr*

Let us go on Pūcam day
to bathe at Iṭaimarutu, our Lord's abode,
where crowds of devotees,
having renounced all earthly desires,
seek his feet with fresh, fragrant flowers.

94. Campantar II.192.5 *Iṭaimarutūr*

You took for your shrine
the good temple at Iṭaimarutu

92. Appar's description indicates that Tiruvārūr was a great and active Śaiva center in his day. The Viratis (members of the Mahāvrata cult), Pāśupatas, and Kāpālikas were followers of early Śaiva cults and sects with extreme practices in dress and ritual. "[Those] who worship you by right": "*urimaiyiṟ ṟoḻuvār.*" This could refer to priests, temple dancers and singers, and others employed in ritual service at the temple, as well as to initiated members of the cult, who have earned the right to perform the *pūjā* ritual for the *liṅga* (*civapūcai*). "Officers of the divine command": "*aruḷip pāṭiyar*" appears to be a technical designation for those in charge of carrying out royal commands in connection with the temple and its activities. See the commentary in the *Tēvāram* Ātīṉam edition.

93, 94. Iṭaimarutūr, or Tiruviṭaimarutūr, was an important Śaiva center in the days of the poet-saints. Here, as in other shrines throughout the Tamil region, devotees celebrate the Pūcam festival with bathing in rivers in the month of Tai (January-February). In the Mayi-

where, for the blessing of the world,
scholars praise you with the Vedic chant,
and great seers and gods gather to bathe
on the day of the Pūcam festival
in the month of Tai.

95. Campantar I.71.5 *Naṟaiyūrc Cittīccaram*

The Lord of Cittīccaram shrine in Naṟaiyūr,
who has the river in his hair,
the poison stain on his throat,
and the Veda on his tongue,
goes resplendent in ceremonial dress,
as his devotees and perfected sages
sing and dance his widespread fame,
and the sound of festival drums
beaten on the streets where the temple-car is pulled
spreads on every side.

96. Appar IV.50.2 *Kuṟukkai Vīraṭṭam*

For seven holy days before
the festival of Aṭṭami, the Eighth Day,
the Lord of Kuṟukkai Vīraṭṭam
goes in procession in his dancing form,
as Ayaṉ and Māl and all the gods
bow to him and praise him,
calling him their Lord.

97. Campantar I.12.7 *Mutukuṉṟam*

Let us go to Mutukuṉṟam's temple,
abode of the brahmin who rides the bull,
the fire-hued god with the moon on his hair,
before whom, on festival days,

---

lāppūr festival hymn (Poem 99) Campantar speaks of the tradition of devout women offering feasts to Śiva's devotees at the Pūcam festival.

95, 96, 97. These verses present vignettes of Tamil temple festivals in the age of the Nāyaṉmār. Many of the traditions described here continue to be followed in South Indian temple festivals: the image of Śiva in his various personae—as bull rider, dancer, beggar—is processed through a prescribed route around the shrine, sometimes carried in a palanquin or platform, sometimes pulled in a great temple-car (*tēr*); drums and women's folk and classical dances continue to play an important part in the festivities. In Poem 96, "the Eighth Day" refers to the Aṭṭami festival (from Sanskrit *aṣṭamī*, the eighth day of the lunar fortnight), devoted to Śiva's *gaṇa* attendants.

women dance in the hall of the dance
to the sound of song and drum.

98. Appar IV.21 TIRUVĀTIRAIT TIRUPPATIKAM (THE HYMN FOR TIRUVĀTIRAI DAY) *Tiruvārūr*

1
He goes on his begging rounds
amid the glitter of a pearl canopy
and gem-encrusted golden fans.
Devoted men and women follow him,
along with Virati ascetics in bizarre garb,
garlanded with white skulls.
Such is the splendor of Ātirai day
in Ārūr, our Father's town!

2
Folk from far and near,
good men and rogues, and
those who pray every day for an end to disease—
our Lord of Ārūr is kinsman
to all those who cry,
"O my jewel, golden one, dear husband! My son!"
Such is the splendor of Ātirai day
in Ārūr town!

3
On every street, white flags flutter,
canopies studded with great bright gems
glitter, festooned with strands
of priceless coral and pearl.
Such is the splendor of Ātirai day
of the Primal Lord in Ārūr!

4
Gathered together, his servants sing him;
now they praise his virtues,
now quarrel amongst themselves,

98. The Tiruvātirai festival, commemorating Śiva's association with the lunar asterism Ātirai in the month of Mārkaḻi (December-January), is considered by Tamils to be the most important celebration of Śiva, along with the Night of Śiva (Mahāśivarātri). Appar's detailed description of this festival may easily be applied (with a few exceptions) to Tiruvātirai as it is celebrated in the temple at Chidambaram (Tillai) and other major centers today. v. 5. "Cymbals": "*kallavaṭam*," hand-cymbals or castanets? See note to Poem 9.

babbling like madmen,
while the gods come every day to bow to him.
Such is the splendor of Ātirai day
in Ārūr, town of the Lord who is half woman!

5
As the blare of the moon-white conch,
the *paṟai* drum's beat,
and the jingle of the cymbals of dancing devotees,
spread everywhere, peacocks,
thinking that the rains have come,
dance in delight.
Such is the splendor of Ātirai day
in Ārūr town!

6
They sob and tremble,
they stare and shout.
They frighten others, forget themselves,
and go wild. Dashing their heads,
they cry, "My Lord, God! Elder kinsman! O Father!"
Such is the splendor of Ātirai day
in Ārūr, town of the Lord!

7
Women with coral-red lips
and those who meditate on the dear one's feet,
young men and women
engaged in the play of love,
Indra and all the gods and the perfected seers
praise him.
Such is the splendor of Ātirai day
in the sole Lord's Ārūr town!

8
The ascetic god goes in procession,
led by the immortal gods
whose heads are bowed to him,
while lovely celestial women
with shoulders graceful as the bamboo
follow behind, and ash-smeared devotees
surround him, singing his praise.
Such is the splendor of Ātirai day
of the Lord in Ārūr!

9
"The days that pass without worshipping you
are miserable," cry some devotees.
Others say, "Happy are the days
on which we praise you."
"Let us follow you! Show us grace!"
cry yet others.
Such is the splendor of Ātirai day
of the Lover of Ārūr!

10
It is glorious with unceasing
singing and dancing about the Lord's glory,
as devotees worship and sing the praise
of the god who stood revealed
in the cosmic flood that engulfed the earth.
Such is the splendor of Ārūr, which place
every town in the world praises in song.

99. Campantar II.183 *Mayilāppūr (Mylapore)*

1
Pūmpāvai, O beautiful girl!
Would you go without having seen the feasts

99. In this hymn Campantar lists the major festivals of the year at the Śiva shrine, in order of their occurrence, according to the Tamil calendar. From verse 2 through verse 7 the Tamil months are listed in order: Aippaci, Kārttikai, Mārkaḻi, Tai, Māci, Paṅkuṉi. The Kapālīccaram shrine in Mayilai (modern Mylapore) is located in the heart of the old brahmin quarter of the port city of Madras. Situated as it is in a great urban cultural center, this shrine of Śiva Kapālīśvara ("the Lord who bears the skull") is a well-known and prestigious temple. Most of the festivals described in Campantar's festival calendar for Mayilai are celebrated on a grand scale at the Kapālīśvara temple. The images of the sixty-three Nāyaṉārs are processed on the temple streets of Mylapore at the Festival of the Sixty-three in Cittirai (April). Paṅkuṉi Uttiram is celebrated in all Śiva shrines in the Tamil region. Appar's Tiruvātirai hymn testifies to the importance of the Tiruvātirai festival in Mārkaḻi, associated with the asterism Ātirai. The Great Purification (v. 10) is the Peruñcānti festival.

An interesting story provides the context for this hymn. When Campantar was visiting the temple in Mayilai, he was told the sad history of the maiden Pūmpāvai, daughter of a wealthy and pious merchant named Civanēcaṉ. Civanēcaṉ had such great admiration for the boy-saint Campantar that he had brought up Pūmpāvai with the intention of giving her in marriage to the Nāyaṉār. However, the maiden died from a snakebite. The father was inconsolable, and the entire community mourned the death of the girl. They stored Pūmpāvai's ashes and bones in an urn, and awaited a visit from Campantar. At the request of the people of Mayilai, the saint approached the urn, sang this hymn in which he reproached the girl for having left the world without having seen the glorious festivals celebrated at Kapālīccaram shrine. At the end of the hymn, Pūmpāvai stood up, restored to life; the people of Mayilai rejoiced. When Civanēcaṉ offered his daughter in marriage to Campantar,

in which our Lord who loves the temple
in beautiful Mayilai,
whose beach is lined with fragrant *puṉṉai* trees,
the Lord who dwells in Kapālīccaram shrine,
feeds his many devotees who love him?

2
Pūmpāvai, O beautiful girl!
Would you go without having seen the feast
enjoyed by holy men
at Aippaci's Ōṇam festival
held at the Kapālīccaram shrine
of our Lord whose sacred ash is our blessing,
in great Mayilai,
town of beautiful young women
with sparkling, kohl-darkened eyes?

3
Pūmpāvai, O beautiful girl!
Would you go without having seen,
on the rich streets of great Mayilai,
town of beautiful young women with bracelets,
and town of our Lord in Kapālīccaram temple,
the flawless celebration of the ancient Kārttikai feast
at which young girls
with sandal paste on their breasts
light many lamps?

4
Pūmpāvai, O beautiful girl!
Would you go without having seen
the Ātirai festival day
in great Mayilai town with wave-washed shores,
in whose settlements live strong heroes
who win battles with their sharp spears,
town of our Lord who dwells in Kapālīccaram shrine
surrounded by dark woods?

the saint gently declined, saying that since he had given life to Pūmpāvai, he could only be a father to her. In the poem's refrain, "O beautiful girl, would you go" ("*pōtiyō pūmpāvāy*"), "*pūmpāvai*" (lit., "beautiful girl") is usually taken as a reference to the maiden Pūmpāvai. v. 8. "The furious demon": I read "*taṉṉā varakkaṉ*," "the demon who acted without delay," "the impatient, angry one." The *Tēvāram* Pondicherry edition suggests the reading "*taṇ ār*": "endowed with grace"?—qualifying Śiva?

5

Pūmpāvai, O beautiful girl!
Would you go without having seen
the Taippūcam festival
celebrated by women who feed guests
with good boiled rice and ghee,
in the great town of Mayilai,
home of many beautiful women
with sparkling kohl-darkened eyes,
town of our Lord with the sacred ash,
who dwells in the Kapālīccaram shrine?

6

Pūmpāvai, O beautiful girl!
Would you go without having seen,
in Mayilai,
fringed with coconut palms with broad fronds,
and town of our Lord who dwells in Kapālīccaram shrine,
the festival of bathing in the sea
in the month of Māci,
at which women dance, singing the praise
of the feet of the Lord
who rides the mighty bull?

7

Pūmpāvai, O beautiful girl!
Would you go without having seen,
on the streets of great Mayilai,
always busy with festive crowds,
the festival of Paṅkuṉi Uttiram
with its great sound of celebration,
at which beautiful women
sing and distribute alms,
at the Lord's Kapālīccaram shrine,
center of many festivals?

8

Pūmpāvai, O beautiful girl!
Would you go without having seen
to your heart's content
the festival of the Eighth Day,
in honor of Śiva's eighteen *gaṇa*s,
resounding with melodious hymns,
in glorious Mayilai, at the Kapālīccaram shrine

of the Lord who blessed the furious demon
by crushing his arms?

9
Pūmpāvai, O beautiful girl!
Would you go without having seen
the ceremony of the golden swing
held for him who dwells in Kapālīccaram shrine,
where devotees praise the feet of the Lord
whom the four-headed god on the lotus seat
and Nārāyaṇa himself
could not fully comprehend?

10
Pūmpāvai, O beautiful girl!
Would you go without having seen,
at the Lord's Kapālīccaram temple
surrounded by green groves,
the festival of the Great Purification
slandered by the naked Jains
and the base Buddhists in voluminous robes?

11
They will attain release,
who know these ten fine verses of praise,
composed by Ñāṉacampantaṉ in pure Tamil,
as a song for Pūmpāvai, the beautiful girl
with the sweet, flower-adorned hair,
in praise of the Lord who dwells
in Kapālīccaram shrine
set among fragrant groves.

5 Brahmin Ways

(POEMS 100–103)

100. Campantar I.81.1 *Kāḻi (Cīrkāḻi)*

The stone-walled town of Kāḻi
is the sacred abode
of the Lord who destroyed the citadels with his bow,
so that virtuous brahmins,
tenders of the sacred fire,
benevolent chanters of the four Vedas,
praised his shining golden feet.

101. Campantar I.132.9 *Vīḻimiḻalai*

The temple where the Lord dwells,
whose beginning and end
Brahmā of the lotus seat and Māl,
becoming the wild goose and boar, could not find,
and who revealed himself when they praised him,
is Miḻalai, town of brahmins who arrange the grass altar
according to the Vedic rite,
and offer *samidh* sticks and butter
in the sacrificial fire
for the welfare of the world.

102. Campantar I.80.1 *Kōyil (Tillai)*

Sin will not take hold
of those who seize the feet
of the Master who wears the young white moon
on his hair and loves to dwell

101, 102. The hymns dedicated to Tillai are full of references to brahmins and brahmin culture, which confirms the antiquity of the brahmin settlement in that place; further confirmation is provided by the references in the hymns of Cuntarar and others to the "brahmins of Tillai" (*tillaivāḻ antaṇar*). The hymns to Vīḻimiḻalai and Iṭaimarutūr, two other brahmin settlements provided for by Pallava and Cōḻa rulers, also emphasize brahmin connections. *Samidh* sticks (Poem 101) are the fuel twigs or sticks used in the Vedic fire ritual. In Poem 102, "cosmic evil": "*kali*," planetary evil, the age of strife in the cycle of cosmic time.

in the Little Ampalam in Tillai,
home of men who have conquered cosmic evil
through sacred learning
and the tending of the sacred fire.

103. Campantar I.6 *Marukal and Ceṅkāṭṭaṅkuṭi*

1
Young man who lives in Marukal
where the moon caresses the highways,
and brahmins who chant the sacred Veda and Aṅga texts
praise your feet every day,
tell me,
why do you love Kaṇapatiyīccaram
where you perform your midnight dance,
bearing fire,
in splendid Ceṅkāṭṭaṅkuṭi
where the streams are full of red *kayal* fish?

3
Young man who lives in Marukal,
on whose wide streets smoke rises high
from red fires tended by brahmins
who wear the deerskin and sacred thread,
tell me,
why do you love to dance,
with the bright hero's band ringing on your leg,
at Kaṇapatiyīccaram in beautiful Ceṅkāṭṭaṅkuṭi,
lush with gardens and cool fields full of *cēl* fish?

5
Young man who lives in Marukal
where the flags on tall palaces touch the sky,
and drumbeats and festive sounds never cease,
as brahmins chant the sacred texts,
tell me,
why do you love to dance in the burning-ground
at the Kaṇapatiyīccaram shrine in beautiful Ceṅkāṭṭaṅkuṭi
with groves full of *cēṭakam* flowers?

103. The occasion for this hymn was Campantar's visit to the two villages of Marukal and Ceṅkāṭṭaṅkuṭi. The Pallava minister and Nāyaṉār Ciṟuttoṇṭar built the Kaṇapatiyīccaram shrine in Ceṅkāṭṭaṅkuṭi; according to the *Periya purāṇam*, it was at the minister's invitation that Campantar visited the Kaṇapatiyīccaram temple.

9
Young man who lives in Marukal,
town of brahmins who chant the Vedas
to praise you whose beginning and end
four-headed Brahmā and Viṣṇu of the serpent-couch
could not know,
tell me,
why do you love Kaṇapatiyīccaram shrine
fragrant with smoke from burnt incense and aloe
in beautiful Ceṅkāṭṭaṅkuṭi
praised by singers of good Tamil hymns?

10
Lover of the mountain's daughter in Marukal
where virtuous souls worship, shielding themselves
from wretched Jain monks who live on a diet
of bitter fruit and dried ginger served on the *marutu* leaf,
tell me,
why do you love to dance at night,
clothed in the mottled hide,
at Kaṇapatiyīccaram shrine in pure Ceṅkāṭṭaṅkuṭi?

6 Talapurāṇam: Local Legends

(POEMS 104–126)

104. Campantar I.63 PALPEYARP PATTU (THE TEN ON THE MANY NAMES [OF CĪRKĀḺI]) *Piramapuram (Cīrkāḻi)*

1
O Lord of Piramapuram, "Brahmā's town,"
where Brahmā of the lotus seat, the Grandfather,
four-headed god who chants the Veda
with faultless tongue, praised and worshipped you,
O you who bear the bright axe and carry
a skull for begging bowl,
you take not alms alone
from women with striped bracelets,
but their beauty as well.

2
O Lord of Vēṇupuram, "Bamboo Forest,"
where the majestic sound of drums
arises and spreads over the land
once ruled by Indra according to the sacred Law!
Wearing the moon on your matted hair with the river,
you go begging at the houses
of women of sweet speech
and long eyes curved like *kayal* fish,
and you steal their sleep.

105. Campantar II.184 *Veṇkāṭu (Tiruveṇkāṭu)*

7
The three-eyed god of Veṇkāṭu's temple
and its good Mukkuḷam pond

104. In this hymn, Campantar alludes to the legends associated with eleven of the twelve names of Cīrkāḻi: Piramapuram, Vēṇupuram, Pukali, Veṅkuru, Tōṇipuram, Pūntarāy, Cirapuram, Puṟavam, Caṇpai, Kāḻi, and Koccaivayam. Kaḻumalam, the twelfth name, occurs in verse 12 of the hymn. v. 2. The comparison of a woman's eyes with *kayal* or other fish is common in Tamil literature. The shape of the eye is supposed to resemble that of a fish; the Goddess in Maturai is "Mīṉākṣī," "the Fish-eyed Goddess." In this verse I have taken the reading "*peyalār caṭai*" ("matted hair with the river") against the *Tēvāram* Pondicherry edition's reading ("*piyalārcaṭai*": "hair that lies on the nape of the neck"?).

105, 106. Veṇkāṭu and Vīḻimiḻalai are among the many shrines associated with the legend

which washes karma away,
blessed the elephant Airāvata
who worshipped him here.
The Lord who wears the *akṣa* beads at his waist
is the one who gave Viṣṇu his wheel
and destroyed the demon Jalandhara.

9
We do not consider them to be feeling human souls,
whose hearts do not melt at the thought
of the Lord of exalted Veṇkāṭu,
place of the white elephant's penance,
the god whose shining majesty could not be grasped
by the one whose seat is the sweet lotus
and the god who lies on the sea
though they rose and plunged high and low.

106. Campantar I.132.8 *Vīḻimiḻalai (Tiruvīḻimiḻalai)*

The temple of the pure Lord
who crushed with his toe
the demon's crowned heads and shoulders
when he tried to lift Kailāsa hill,
trusting in his mighty arms and legs,
is Miḻalai, whose tall temple tower arose
when Māl, desiring the wheel
that destroyed proud Jalandhara's frame,
devoutly worshipped the Lord in this place.

The Flood

107. Campantar I.53.4 *Mutukuṉṟam*

Mutukuṉṟu, home of our Lord who blesses
those who sing his praise

of Śiva's gift of the wheel (*cakra*) to Viṣṇu, who thereafter adopted it as one of his four attributes. According to the Śaivas, Viṣṇu could kill the demon Jalandhara only after he had worshipped Śiva at one of his shrines and obtained the wheel from him. Legend connects the name Veṇkāṭu (Sanskrit Śvetāraṇya, "White Forest") with the devotion of the white elephant Airāvata, the mount of Indra, king of gods; it is said that Śiva released Airāvata from a sage's curse after the elephant had worshipped him at Veṇkāṭu. The Mukkuḷam reservoir in Veṇkāṭu is famed for its miraculous powers; it is the aspiration of Śaiva pilgrims to bathe in this "sacred water" (*tīrtha*). The lives of the Śaiva Siddhānta philosopher Meykaṇṭār and Paṭṭiṉattār, author of hymns in the eleventh *Tirumuṟai*, are associated with the shrine and the reservoir.

107, 108. Mutukuṉṟam ("Ancient Mountain," Sanskrit Vṛddhācala, contemporary

is the shrine that rose above the flood,
when the cold ancient sea
had overrun the entire earth,
destroyed the abode of the gods,
and covered the land, leaving visible
only four-headed Brahmā and his world.

108. Campantar I.131.9 *Mutukuṉṟam*

The hill of the god whose great form
Brahmā of the lotus seat and Māl of the basil garland
could not fathom
when they rose and plunged in space
as eagle and boar in search of him,
is Mutukuṉṟam which rose high above
the ceaselessly roaring ocean
which surged up to cover the good earth.

109. Campantar III.376 *Kaḻumalam (Cīrkāḻi)*

3
Say that the abode
of the Śaiva who wears the *koṉṟai* wreath,
along with the river and the flowers in his hair,
the god whose feet are praised by his good devotees,
is Kaḻumalam, great as the only shrine
that floated on the roaring flood that covered
every sacred place and the whole earth.

9
If you ask, "What is the abode
of the deity who became a column of fire,
praised by the god of the lovely lotus
and the one who lifted the great mountain?"
Name good and beautiful Kaḻumalam,
the only shrine that floated
on the ocean lined with dark cliffs

Tamil Vṛddhācalam) is one of the many Tamil shrines whose origin is linked with its survival of a cosmic flood at the end of a cycle of cosmic time. The shrine survives because, as David Shulman points out, it is "the idealized, ordered microcosm at the center of the universe" (Shulman, *Tamil Temple Myths*, p. 75). The origin myth of the Tamil temple is thus a cosmogonic myth.

109. See note to Poem 54 for a brief discussion of the origin legend of the Cīrkāḻi temple.
v. 9. In his incarnation as Krishna, Viṣṇu lifted up the mountain Govardhana and used it as an umbrella to protect his cowherd friends from torrential rain.

when the roaring cosmic flood spread over the universe,
destroying all life.

The King Who Built Many Temples

110. Cuntarar VII.98 *Naṉṉilam*

10
Umā's Lord who crushed the demon with his toe,
so that he lay groaning, like a dark hill
under Mount Kailāsa, and then blessed him,
is our Lord who loves the great temple in Naṉṉilam
built by a king, glorious ruler of the Cōḻas,
Lord of the lands watered by the pure stream
of the turbulent Kaveri.

11
They will enter the highest world,
who know these ten verses
sung by the poet of Tiruvārūr,
Caṭaiyaṉ's son and father of beautiful Ciṅki,
on the Lord who loves
the great and beloved temple of Naṉṉilam
built by King Kōcceṅkaṇāṉ
whose war elephants have long, curved tusks.

*

111. Campantar III.335.6 *Māṇikuḻi*

Māṇikuḻi, where the Keṭilam's stream,
fragrant with sandal, dark aloe, and fine blossoms,
flows into the fields,

110. The temple at Naṉṉilam is one of the seventy temples that, the Vaiṣṇava saint Tirumaṅkai Āḻvār tells us (*Periya tirumoḻi* 6.6.8), were built by the early Cōḻa king Kōcceṅkaṇ or Kōcceṅkaṇāṉ. All three poets of the *Tēvāram* celebrate this king for his temple-building activity and speak of the legend of Kōcceṅkaṇ being the reincarnation of a devout spider who lived in Āṉaikkā (see poems 266, 267, and 268). Campantar identifies the *māṭakkōyil* (raised temple) shrines at Vaikal-māṭakkōyil and Ampar (Campantar III.276 and 277) as temples built by Ceṅkaṇāṉ. The Cōḻa king is revered as one of the sixty-three Nāyaṉārs. v. 11. Ciṅki: Ciṅkaṭi, one of the two adopted daughters of Cuntarar.

111, 112. Kaṭavūr or Tirukkaṭavūr Vīraṭṭam is the site connected with Śiva's triumphant rescue of the boy Mārkaṇḍeya from Death. Māṇikuḻi may have acquired its own local association with the Mārkaṇḍeya legend through the process of folk etymology: the term "*māṇi*" means "a brahmin boy" or "student." In the refrain of 113, Campantar refers to the town by the name "Utavimāṇikuḻi."

is the place of the Lord with the throat dark as a sapphire,
who kicked to death Death himself
when he came to seize
the life of the young boy
as he worshipped his God with fresh flowers.

112. Appar IV.108.1 *Kaṭavūr Vīraṭṭam*

The Supreme Lord who lives in Kaṭavūr
is the one whose foot felled with a kick
Death himself,
dark-bodied god with terrible curved tusks,
fire-red hair and coiled tongue,
who had come for the boy Mārkaṇḍeya
as he worshipped his God
to put an end to the sorrow of ignorant life.

113. Appar IV.48.4 *Āppāṭi*

Our god in Āppāṭi
is the Master who granted
grace to Caṇṭi
when the devotee cut off the foot
that his father raised
to kick the *liṅga* he had fashioned,
to worship with love the king of the celestial gods,
the Primal Being, our Lord.

114. Campantar I.48.7 *Cēyñalūr*

O you who dwell in Cēyñalūr's fine temple
how wonderful
that you crowned with your own garland of flowers
and gave sainthood
to the boy who passionately cut off the foot
that his father,

113, 114. Here, again, is a case of a Śaiva legend acquiring local associations with two villages. Cēyñalūr is said to be the native village of Caṇṭīcar; Āppāṭi ("village of cowstalls") is often cited as the location of Caṇṭīcar's defiance of his father. In Poem 113, "devotee": "*pātaṅ koṇṭavaṉ*," literally, "he who has seized the [Lord's] feet." "*Liṅga*": "*tāparam*" (Sanskrit "*sthāvara*"), the stationary aniconic image of Śiva. The *Tēvāram* Ātīṉam edition reads "*taṇṭiyār*" for "*caṇṭiyār*" (Caṇṭīcar). Caṇṭīcar is also known by the name Taṇṭīcaṉ ("the one with the stick"); according to some versions of the Caṇṭīcar story, the boy struck his father with a shepherd's staff, which immediately turned into an axe. In Poem 114, "Garland of flowers": Śiva's garland or wreath of *koṉṟai* flowers.

angry with the child for offering milk to his God,
had raised to kick at his worship!

Rāmāyaṇa Sites

115. Campantar II.179.2 *Puḷḷirukkuvēḷūr*

The abode of the brahmin
who toils as a wandering beggar, bearing
the Goddess in half his frame,
and the other woman on his matted hair,
is Puḷḷirukkuvēḷūr,
place of the truthful one who flew up
to overpower the liar, Rāvaṇa,
and died fighting with him.

116. Campantar III.268.2 *Irāmēccuram (Rāma's temple to Śiva)*

They will be rid of karma,
who have loving thoughts
for Irāmēccuram, temple built by the hero
to atone for the sin
of severing with his bow
the ten great flower-crowned heads
of southern Laṅkā's king who stole his queen.

115, 116. These verses allude to place legends connected with characters in the epic *Rāmāyaṇa*. "The truthful one" of 115 is Jaṭāyu, the great vulture who attacked the demon Rāvaṇa when the latter was speeding away in his flying chariot with Rāma's wife Sītā. At the end of a long battle, Jaṭāyu was mortally wounded, but he lived to tell Rāma about his encounter with the demon. The entire hymn II.179 is devoted to praise of Jaṭāyu and his brother Sampāti, extolling the devout penance with which they propitiated Śiva at Puḷḷirukkuvēḷūr; in this verse Campantar expounds on the folk etymology of the name of this town, in which the word "*puḷ*" ("bird") is supposed to refer to the renowned bird-heroes of the *Rāmāyaṇa*. Puḷḷirukkuvēḷūr, also known as Vēḷūr or Vaittīśvaran Kōyil, is connected with the Tarumapuram Ātīṉam, an important center of Tamil Śaiva religious authority. Poem 116 again refers to the abduction of Sītā by Rāvaṇa. The origin legend of the shrine at Irāmēccuram ("Rāma's temple to Śiva") narrated here and in 117 is an ancient one. Though the demon Rāvaṇa deserved to be killed, Rāma incurred sin by killing him, since Rāvaṇa was also a learned brahmin and a pious devotee of Śiva. Situated on a narrow strip of land in the part of the South Indian peninsula facing northern Sri Lanka, Irāmēccuram (Rameswaram) is one of the four major Hindu pilgrimage sites representing the sacred geographical boundaries of India in the cardinal directions.

117. Appar IV.61 *Irāmēccuram*

1
With deep love, think every day
of holy Irāmēccuram,
abode of the brilliant god,
temple built with devotion
and consecrated with ritual offerings
of fragrant flowers by pious Māl
when he had killed the sinful demons.

3
Though I ceaselessly have on my tongue
the holy name of Irāmēccuram,
temple built on the causeway by Māl
when he had bridged the ocean with great rocks,
and achieved his goal,
swayed by five who dwell in my flesh,
I whirl about with an impure mind.

4
O heart, if you seek a good end, go worship
at holy Irāmēccuram, be saved
at the temple built with love
by beautiful Māl with the mighty discus
when he had killed the evil demons
with shoulders like hills.

6
Simple heart, go to my red-haired Father
in holy Irāmēccuram,
temple built by Māl
when he had defeated in battle and annihilated
the demons who had fought with him,
arrogant in their might.

10
They will abide with the Lord,
who can see with their eyes
the temple in holy Irāmēccuram,

117. "Māl" here refers to Viṣṇu in his incarnation as Rāma. In verse 3 Appar mentions the bridge of rocks that Rāma, aided by his army of monkeys, built across the ocean, linking the Indian peninsula with Sri Lanka. Following the Śaiva Purāṇas, which speak of Rāma's erection of a temple on the causeway, I have taken "*tiṭal*" (lit., "island") as referring to the causeway itself. v. 10. "Red-eyed (ceṅkaṇ) is an epithet frequently used to describe Māl (Viṣṇu).

made by red-eyed Māl, when he had killed
the cruel, heartless demons
who engaged in deadly battle with the god,
ignorant of the pious life.

*

118. Appar VI.268.8 *Puḷḷirukkuvēḷūr (Vaittīśvaraṉ Kōyil)*

The Lord whom the gods
praise with a thousand names,
the one who gives the unattainable treasure
to his faithful devotees,
he who is all mantras and tantras and healing potions,
and through his grace cures our incurable disease,
the warrior who took up his mighty bow
to burn the three cities,
the Lord in Puḷḷirukkuvēḷūr—
I, who have failed to sing his praise,
have wasted my life!

119. Appar IV.65.9 *Cāykkāṭu*

It was Cāykkāṭu's Lord
who gave Viṣṇu his wheel
when he worshipped him reverently
with a thousand fragrant flowers,
and, lacking a single blossom,
offered his own lotus eye
in its place.

118. The village of Puḷḷirukkuvēḷūr, near Māyavaram, is today famous as "Vaittīśvaraṉ Kōyil," "Temple of the Lord who is our Physician." People come to the temple here from all over Tamilnadu in the belief that Śiva Vaittīśvaraṉ will cure even incurable diseases. Appar's verse celebrates the Lord as the healer in Puḷḷirukkuvēḷūr. In the vision of the saints, Śiva cures the "incurable disease" ("*tīrā nōy*") of existence itself. Though the collocation "mantras and tantras" usually denote the Vedic and Āgamic texts, in this hymn, along with "*maruntu*" ("medicine," "healing draught"), they can be taken to connote other strategies used for curing disease in the Tamil region: the mantras and tantric rites employed by healers and priests of local goddesses and gods in curing illness of various kinds. "The unattainable treasure": "*eṉṟum vārāta celvam*," release.

119, 120. The motif of the "lesser" gods (in the Śaiva view), especially Viṣṇu and Indra, becoming devout worshippers of Śiva figures in the place legends of many Tamil shrines. In these stories, Śiva tests the devotion of the worshipper by making one of the thousand lotuses required for the rite disappear; the devotee offers his own eye in place of the flower; Śiva rewards him with his grace and grants him whatever he desires. In Poem 120, "you took his eye": "*kaṇ cūlvippatē*," literally, "you made him dig out his eye."

120. Appar IV.100.4 *Kacci Ēkampam*

O great Kāñci's Lord
who wears the crescent moon on long matted hair!
O god with the poison-stained throat!
To subdue Māl's pride you took
his eye in place of the missing flower
when he worshipped you every day
with single-minded devotion,
offering a garland of a thousand lotuses.

The Goddess in Kanchipuram

121. Cuntarar VII.61.10 *Kacci Ēkampam*

When the Goddess Umā herself
honored the Lord with worship,
when she who loved him and treasured him in her heart
began the sacred rite,
seeing her devotion, he caused the river to flood,
frightening her, so that she ran and embraced him—
and then he revealed himself.
Surely it is to see
Kampaṉ the Trickster, our Lord,
that I am endowed with eyes!

The Devout Rat of Maṟaikkāṭu

122. Appar IV.49.8 *Kuṟukkai Vīraṭṭam*

When the grey rat in rich Maṟaikkāṭu,
pushing with his snout,

121. The ancient legend of the union between Śiva and Umā-Pārvatī at Kanchipuram and its connection with the name of the Ēkampam shrine or the "Ekāmranātha" temple, forms the theme of the whole of VII.61. Verse 10, translated here, paints a dramatic picture of the principal "event" in the myth. In one of the many local versions of her penance for obtaining Śiva as her husband, the maiden Umā performed the ritual worship of a sand-*liṅga* on the banks of the river Kampā (linked with the name "Ēkampam"). Pleased, yet desirous of testing the strength of the Goddess's love, Śiva caused the river to flood, threatening to sweep the *liṅga* away. The frightened Umā at once embraced the *liṅga*, shielding it with her breasts. Śiva, Ēkampaṉ, or Kampaṉ ("the Lord of the Pillar"; related to Vedic "Skambha"?) emerged from the *liṅga*, and God and the Goddess were united. "Kaḷḷak Kampaṉ" ("Kampaṉ the Trickster") is one of the three forms of the Lord in the Ēkampam shrine.

122. This is one of the many local legends in which the "lower" animals are rewarded by

coaxed the flame to keep
the lamp in the shrine burning bright,
the Lord of Kuṟukkai Vīraṭṭam gave him
sole dominion over earth and sky
and the far world of heaven.

Toṇṭaimāṉ and the Jasmine Creeper

123. VII.69.10 *Vaṭatirumullaivāyil*

O God who once bound with a *mullai* creeper
the elephant of King Toṇṭaimāṉ of matchless fame,
and then revealed yourself, granting him
everlasting bliss,
Lord of holy Mullaivāyil, ever praised by good men,
god who rides on the white bull, object of every art,
free me from suffering,
O Lord of Souls, Supreme light!

Brahmā Worships Śiva

124. Appar IV.49.1 *Kuṟukkai Vīraṭṭam*

The Lord of the Vīraṭṭam shrine in Kuṟukkai
where bees hum, flitting from flower to flower,
enlightened the chanter of the Veda,
Brahmā, who worshipped his feet
at the time of the first creation.
Showing himself as a blaze of light, the Lord
stands beyond words.

Śiva for extraordinary acts of devotion. Though the song is dedicated to Śiva at Kuṟukkai, the incident relates to Maṟaikkāṭu.

123. Here Cuntarar gives us the tradition surrounding the origin of the shrine at Mullaivāyil ("Place of the Jasmine Creeper") in Toṇṭaināṭu. When a Toṇṭaimāṉ chief was out hunting, a jasmine (*mullai*) creeper wound itself around the legs of his elephant. When the king tried to cut the creeper away with his sword, the sword struck a *liṅga* of Śiva hidden under the *mullai* vine. The *liṅga* began to bleed, and the king was distressed. His fear was allayed by Śiva, who revealed himself and told him to build a temple on that spot. "Everlasting bliss": "*ellaiyil iṉpam*," "bliss that has no bounds in space and time," "release."

124. Kuṟukkai Vīraṭṭam is the site where Śiva cut off one of the heads of Brahmā.

Indra's Curse

125. Campantar I.101.7 *Kaṇṇārkōyil*

They say that "Kaṇṇārkōyil," "Temple of the eyes,"
where young girls gather to worship every day,
is the shrine where the Lord dispelled
the sage's curse that Indra had once earned
and graciously gave him
a thousand eyes.

The Woman of Paḻaiyaṉūr

126. Campantar I.45.1 *Paḻaiyaṉūr Ālaṅkāṭu*

Our Lord in Paḻaiyaṉūr Ālaṅkāṭu,
home of men who feared for their honor
when they heard of the woman
who took her lover's life by foul means,
is the god who comes to me in my dreams
and makes me praise him.
He is the one who enters my heart
to awaken his remembrance
when I have been unaware.

125. Local tradition connects the shrine of Kaṇṇārkōyil with the legend of Indra and Ahalyā narrated in the *Rāmāyaṇa*. When the sage Gautama found out that Indra had committed adultery with his wife Ahalyā he cursed the king of gods, saying that he would thenceforth bear a thousand vaginas on his body as a reminder of his crime. When Indra worshipped Śiva at Kaṇṇārkōyil, the god helped Indra by changing the thousand vaginas into eyes (*kaṇ*).

126. This verse provides evidence for the antiquity of the story of Nīli, the goddess/demoness, and her many associations with the shrine at Ālaṅkāṭu. In its simplest form, the legend focuses on the injustice done to a woman who was murdered by her husband, her revenge on her husband in a subsequent birth, and the voluntary suicide of the Vellala community of Paḻaiyaṉūr upon realizing their responsibility for these deaths. See Shulman, *Tamil Temple Myths*, pp. 195–97. The Tamil Śaiva tradition associates Paḻaiyaṉūr Ālaṅkāṭu with another demoness/woman/saint, the early Nāyaṉār Kāraikkāl Ammaiyār, as also with Śiva's dance contest with the goddess Kālī.

SECTION III

Aṭiyār: The Ways of Love

The emotional core of Tamil Śaiva *bhakti*—the relationship of love between Śiva and his devotees, and the many ways in which this love is felt and expressed—forms the major theme of the poems presented in this section. We begin with hymns in which the saints focus on Śiva as the beloved Lord, invoking him in emotionally charged images and metaphors. In such verses, the Lord is the saint's master, bridegroom, friend, father, mother, and kinsman; he is all the things that the poet-devotee loves and treasures in the world. Pan-Indian images mingle with characteristically Tamil ones. To the Nāyaṉārs, as to devotional poets all over India, the Lord is a flame, a blaze of light.[1] Appar calls Śiva his "eye" (*kaṇ*), and all three poets speak of the Lord being sweeter than sugar cane (*karumpu*) or honey (*tēṉ*), these being popular metaphors for the beloved in Tamil culture.

The poets devote entire hymns to the virtues and transformative powers of the Lord's emblems. Chanting "namaccivāya," the *pañcākṣara* mantra or the five sacred syllables in which Śiva's name is invoked, and contact with the sacred ash are extolled as sure paths to the Lord's grace. Appar wishes to be branded with the trident and the bull, Śiva's insignia. The greatest affective value is attached to the Lord's feet, supreme symbol of his power and grace; these beautiful, flower-soft feet are the devotee's ultimate refuge, and his highest aim is to rest in their "cool shade."[2]

In the world view common to the major religious traditions of India, *karma* (action, deed; Tamil *viṉai*) implies fruit or result that must be "suf-

[1] Śiva's association with fire and light symbolism takes many forms in the Tamil tradition. The god's manifestation as the fiery cosmic *liṅga* is located in the shrine of Aṇṇāmalai; here Śiva dwells in his elemental form of fire. The most important festival at this shrine is the festival of lights (Tamil *tīpam*, Sanskrit *dīpa*) in the month of Kārttikai. In his *Tiruvaruṭpā*, the nineteenth-century mystical poet Irāmaliṅka Aṭikaḷ further developed the theology of Śiva as light. See Zvelebil, *Smile of Murugan*, p. 113.

[2] See the comment above on the symbolism of feet in Indian civilization in the introduction to Section II of Part Two.

fered" by the doer in embodied form. Out of the network of deeds done by each soul in relation to it and others, a chain of embodiments or births results. One who wishes to attain release (*mokṣa*, Tamil *vīṭu*) from this chain of karma must make determined efforts along well-defined "paths" to achieve this goal. The Śaiva Siddhānta and other theistic philosophical systems developed complex doctrines regarding the nature of souls, karmic bondage, and final release, and the relationship between these and God. The *Tēvāram* saints do not often use terms such as *pacu*, *pācam*, and *malam*, which are commonplace in the works of Tirumūlar and Māṇikkavācakar and in post-*Tēvāram* Tamil Śaiva devotional literature in general. At the same time, it is clear that the Tamil Śaiva idea of the process of karma (for which the saints use the Tamil *viṉai*) and bondage through primordial impurities (*malam*) that afflict the soul (pacu) is central to the poets' religion.[3] Appar, Campantar, and Cuntarar are deeply concerned about the sorrow of existence and the binding nature of karma, and they see devotion to Śiva as the basis for all "paths" to release from bondage. Their conception of release is typical of the salvific vision of the *bhakti* as opposed to the non-*bhakti* traditions in Hinduism. The *Tēvāram* hymns (and the signature verses in particular) abound in popular pictures of the rewards of turning toward Śiva; here we are told that through unfailing and total devotion the devotee will attain a variety of "states," ranging from earthly sovereignty to the privilege of dwelling in the world (Sanskrit *loka*; Tamil *ulaku*) of the gods or heaven (*vāṉulaku*), or Śiva's world.[4] Such pictures are certainly intrinsic to the saints' view of the process of "release." Nevertheless, it is clear that to Appar, Campantar, and Cuntarar, the very act of reaching (*cēr-*) Śiva's feet is both the means and the ultimate end. In that act of taking refuge (*caraṇ aṭai-*) devotees are "released"; they have crossed the ocean of sorrows (*tuyar*, *iṭar*), for the Lord, through his grace (*aruḷ*), puts an end to karma (*viṉai tīr-*).

The verses in which the Nāyaṉārs speak directly of their states of mind in relation to the Lord have much in common with the poetry of mystical love in many religious traditions. The *Tēvāram* poets sing of the many stances and moods of the *bhakta*, which range from the mood of unre-

[3] See Sivaraman, *Śaivism*, for a detailed study of the Śaiva Siddhānta view of karma, bondage, and liberation. P. S. Somasundaram discusses in detail the theology and philosophy of Campantar in *Tirujñāṉasambandhar*, esp. ch. 3, 4.

[4] The concept of souls "dwelling," in accordance with their merit, for limited periods of time in a hierarchy of "worlds" (*loka*)—such as the worlds of the gods and the ancestors—is found in the early Upaniṣads. The Śaiva and Vaiṣṇava sects in South India have their own versions of such worlds derived from pan-Indian and local folklore mixed with the ideas developed in the "classical" texts. At the top of the hierarchy, roughly analogous to "highest heaven," are Kailāsa and Vaikuṇṭha, the celestial "abodes," respectively, of Śiva and Viṣṇu. Also included in this popular mythology of karma and reward is the notion of the hells (*naraka*) supervised by Yama or Dharmarāja, god of Death and retribution.

quited love and the powerful longing for union with the beloved, to absolute faith and joy in the certainty of grace. Such introspective passages are rare in Campantar's poetry; Appar gives subtle and powerful expression to the emotional aspect of Tamil Śaiva religion; and Cuntarar's poems exhibit the most dramatic swings of mood. Taken as a body, the work of each poet reveals a distinctive persona and a personal religion. Thus we see that Appar often speaks in a mood of self-abasement, presumably because of his sense of guilt over his past as a Jain monk. In sharp contrast to Appar, Cuntarar, who claims that he was forcibly possessed by Śiva and blessed with the name of the "Rude Devotee," is indeed rude, in every sense of the term—he mocks and reproaches Śiva, and goes from expressions of abject slavery to familiar entreaty to high-handed demands. Poems referring to specific incidents in the lives of the saints have been placed in Section IV, but a number of selections representative of each poet's unique religious sensibility are included in this section. It should be noted that these poems have not been arranged to reflect a "spiritual biography" in chronological order. Anyone familiar with mystical poetry will recognize here the universal patterns of the spirit's alternation between pain and grace in its stormy relationship with God.

The variety of rhetorical frameworks employed in the *Tēvāram* makes for variations in the tone of the hymns. The hymns that are directly addressed to Śiva and those that provide a description in the third person are in the tradition of *stotra* praise-poems, while the communal aspect of Tamil Śaiva *bhakti* is clearly brought out in those poems in which the saints address their words to their fellow devotees. No audience is specified for many poems cast in the first person, but there are also verses in which the poet—or the "I" of the poem—addresses his own heart (*maṉam*, *neñcu*) and emphasizes the introspective nature of the verse. Any or all of these formats may be found in a given hymn. There are also a few poems in which the speaker in the poem is the lovelorn heroine of the *akam* tradition. Poems of this type are particularly interesting, for both the rhetorical effect created by the assumption of a persona and the fact that images and metaphors drawn from explicitly erotic love are rare in the *Tēvāram*.

The strong strain of asceticism in Tamil Śaiva religion—fully developed in the Siddhānta philosophy and the *cittar* cult—is represented in hymns in which the body and the senses are portrayed as obstacles to the devotee in his or her efforts to realize the Lord's grace. Images of revulsion for the body, and for decay and death, dominate some poems. In others the saints use the theme of the imminence of death (Yama and his men) and the tortures of Yama's hells as a compelling reason for focusing one's senses and thoughts on Śiva. Such poems are counterbalanced by hymns in which—in keeping with the *bhakti* emphasis on the use of the senses in the apprehension of the divine—the senses and the body are seen as indispensable instruments for acts of devotion.

Although the poetry of the inner life unambiguously conveys the essence of the Nāyaṉārs' devotion, no picture of Tamil Śaiva *bhakti* is complete without a sampling of hymns in which the saints define and describe the external modes of devotion and the attitudes upon which these are based.[5] The three saints lovingly invoke the details of ritual worship. Devotees and others prepare themselves for worship; they gather flowers and bathe the *liṅga* with the "five gifts of the cow" (*āṉaintu*), light lamps at the shrine, and make offerings of incense, unguents, chant, and song. In such descriptions the poets are careful to emphasize the criterion of true *bhakti*: that worship alone is true that expresses genuine devotional emotion; hence the subgenre of hymns in which the true Tamil Śaiva devotee is distinguished from these who masquerade as devotees. It is also for true devotion in the ritual idiom that saints such as Kaṇṇappar and Caṇṭīcar are repeatedly celebrated in the *Tēvāram*. Seen in this context, it is clear that the often-quoted verse "Why bathe in the Ganges?" ("kaṅkaiy āṭileṉ") (Poem 207) is not a rejection of ritual acts but an affirmation of the requirement that all acts of worship arise out of true love for God. In the final group of poems in this section, the poets extol the act of singing as the quintessential expression of love of the Lord.

[5] See my discussion of ritual and love in Tamil Śaiva *bhakti* in Part One, Chapter 3.

1. Cuntarar, Appar, and Campantar. Cōḻa bronze; Pangal temple.

2. Campantar with the cup of divine wisdom. Cōḻa bronze; Nallambal temple.

3. Appar, cradling his hoe in his arms. Cōḻa bronze; Tirucchengodu temple.

4. Cuntarar and his wife, Paravai Nācciyār. Cōḻa bronze; Nallūr temple.

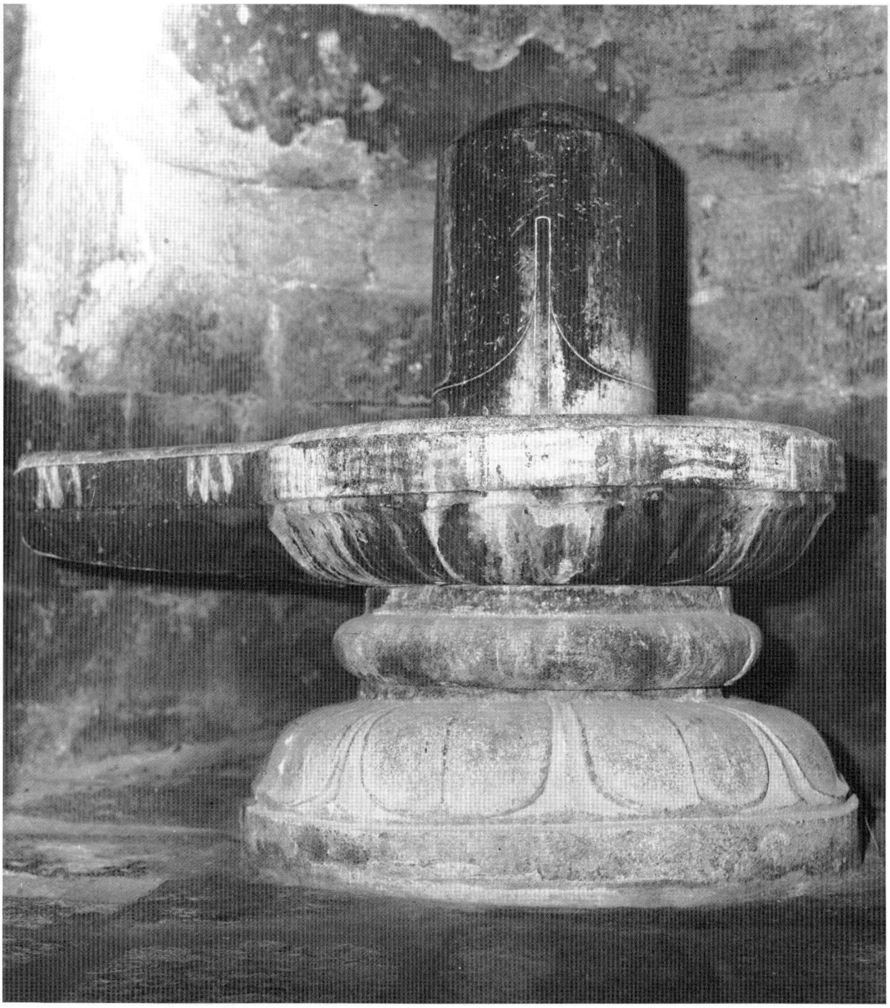

5. Śiva: *Liṅga*. Stone, in sanctum; Nārttamalai.

6. Śiva with the Goddess. Cōḻa bronze; Tiruvēḷvikkuṭi temple.

7. Śiva as Ardhanārīśvara, the Lord who is half woman. Cōḻa bronze; Tiruveṇkāṭu temple.

8. Śiva Naṭarāja, Lord of the Dance. Cōḻa wall relief; Gangaikondacolapuram.

9. Śiva Bhikṣāṭana, the Lord as beggar. Cōḻa bronze; Tiruvaiyāṟu temple.

10. Śiva manifesting himself in the cosmic *liṅga*. Cōḻa wall relief; Punjai temple.

11. Rāvaṇa tries to lift Kailāsa and is crushed by Śiva; Rāvaṇānugraha-mūrti. Cōḻa wall relief; Tirunelvēli temple.

12. Śiva saves the boy Mārkaṇḍeya from Death in the central panel; Kāla-saṃhāra-mūrti. On the left is Death coming with his noose; on the right is the boy embracing the *liṅga*. Cōḻa wall relief; Thanjavur, Brihadīśvara temple.

13. The central shrine structure (*vimāna*) in the main temple at Tiruvārūr. North façade.

14. Ñāṉacampanta Ōtuvār in the courtyard of Cīrkāḻi temple.

15. Verses from the *Tēvāram* (Appar IV.196) inscribed on the wall of Tiruvāṉmiyūr temple, to which hymn IV.196 is dedicated.

1 The Lord Is Sweet

(POEMS 127–143)

127. Appar IV.113.6

He dwells in heaven and in the great Veda;
he lives on sea-girt earth and in Tirumāl's heart.
He is in the sweet tunes of love
and in the hearts of his lovers.
My Lord who has the poison stain on his throat
is in the eye, heart, and head
of this old dog, his slave.

128. Appar V.204.1

The *vīṇā*'s pure sound, the light of the evening moon,
a gentle breeze, springtime sun,
a pool humming with bees—like these is the shade
at my Lord, my Father's feet.

129. Appar V.135.1 *Iṉṉampar*

I hold none dearer to me
than myself; yet within my self
there is one dear to me—
Iṉṉampar's Lord
who is the breath of life,
which enters and leaves me,
and abides within.

130. Appar IV.70.4 *Naṉipaḷḷi*

As song in the mode,
juice in the fruit,
sight in the eye,
elixir for the heart's desire,

127. In the expression "this old dog, his slave" ("*paḻanāyaṭiyēṉ*"), Appar combines *paḻavaṭiyār*, a term used for servants who by hereditary right serve the master in a family and *nāyaṭiyēṉ*, "I, a dog, my master's humble servant."

thought in the mind,
as all the seven worlds,
the Lord of Naṉipaḷḷi
ends the karma
of all who seek him.

131. Appar V.177.2 *Kuraṅkāṭuturai*

My pearl, my precious gem,
glittering branch of coral, bright flame—
when I call him, "My Father
who lives in Kuraṅkāṭuturai
with blossoming groves,"
my tongue tastes
an incredible sweetness.

132. Appar V.131.2 *Veṇṇiyūr*

When I think of the skullbearer
who wears a wreath of flowers in his hair,
the Lord with the white moon who likes to live
in Veṇṇi's ancient city,
a flood of ambrosia
wells up in my tongue.

133. Appar V.128 *Iṭaimarutūr*

6
My heart melts with love
for the handsome god
who bears the river in his hair,
Iṭaimarutu's Lord who rides on the bull,
the youth who ends the karma
of those who sing his praise.

10
Sweeter than sweet fruit, raw cane sugar,
lovely women with fresh flowers in their hair,
sweeter than sole dominion over vast lands,
is Iṭaimarutu's Lord
to those who reach him.

134. Appar V.207 MAṞAKKIṞPAṈĒ YEṈṈUN TIRUK KUṞUNTOKAI (THE KUṞUNTOKAI POEM ENTITLED "HOW SHOULD I FORGET HIM?")

5
Honey, milk, moon, and sun,
youth crowned with the celestial white moon,
wisdom incarnate as the fire
that consumed the god of spring—
How should I forget him?

6
Sugar, sweet syrup of sugar cane,
bright one, brilliant as a lightning flash,
golden one, my Lord who glitters
like a hill of gems—
How should I forget him?

7
Sugar cane, lump of sweet sugar candy,
bee in the fragrant flower,
light that dwells in the light of every flame,
our Lord who loves flower buds gathered at dawn—
How should I forget him?

Metaphors

135. Appar IV.76

2
Plow the field with true faith.
Sow the seed of love, water it with patience,
and pull out falsehood's weeds.
Look into yourself,
build a fence with virtue.
Stand rooted in the right path—
Harvest the state of Śiva!

134, v. 5. "The god of spring" (*vēṉilāṉ*), Kāma, god of Love, who was burned by fire from Śiva's third eye.

135, v. 2. "Patience": "*poṟai*," also tolerance, nonviolence. "Look into yourself": "tammaiyum / tammaiyuḷ nōkkik kaṇṭu"; "know the true nature of the self through yogic meditation." v. 4. Here Appar speaks of the ritual of *pūjā* to the *liṅga* as the Āgamic equivalent of the Vedic sacrifice. For the idea of the body as the "mobile temple" (*naṭāmāṭak kōyil*), see Tirumūlar, *Tirumantiram* 1821 (Kaḻakam edition).

4
The body is the temple,
the loving heart is the devotee.
Truthfulness will do for ritual purity,
the jewel of the mind is the adorned *liṅga*.
With love as milk and ghee
generously mixed with water,
with hymns as oblation,
let us offer worship
as sacrifice to the Lord.

136. Appar V.204.10

Like fire in kindling wood,
like rich ghee in milk,
he dwells hidden within you.
Plant your love as churning stick,
churn hard with the rope of feeling.
The Lord will come forth,
bright as a great gem.

*

137. Appar V.135.4 *Iṉṉampar*

Iṉṉampar's Lord
moves my mind to focus
on him who makes love flow
from his servants
who call out with joy
like peacocks
at the sight of rain.

138. Campantar II.142.4 *Aiyāṟu (Tiruvaiyāṟu)*

Aiyāṟu's Lord is the kind god
who delights in listening
when women with melodious voices,

138. *Vaṇṇam* is a genre of melodic composition with complex rhythmic dimensions. "Hymns": "*vāymoḻi*"; literally, "word-of-mouth." Originally signifying the Veda, the sacred Word, the term is used to denote sacred hymns in the names of such works as the *Tiruvāymoḻi*, a collection of hymns by the Tamil Vaiṣṇava saint Nammāḻvār. See Ramanujan, *Hymns*, pp. x–xi. I have taken the word "*vali*" to mean "power, glory." The hypothetical reading "*vari*," signifying "*varippāṭal*," yet another type of song, would make better sense in this context.

coral-red lips, countless virtues,
and eyes sharper than spears,
sing his glory
in *vaṇṇam* songs and hymns of praise.

Remembrance

139. Campantar III.279.1 *Karukkuṭi*

See my Lord
who dances with blazing fire
in Karukkuṭi, place worshipped
by the entire earth with the sounding sea,
the pure one who haunts me
day and night, in sleep and in waking,
and in bright remembrance of him!

140. Appar IV.57.1 *Āvaṭuturai*

Youth who shines as a ruby,
as a cluster of emeralds!
Being who enters my heart,
stirring memory!
Come to me in my sleep,
be my friend,
give me refuge in your grace,
O dweller in Āvaṭuturai!

Our Kinsman

141. Appar VI.309.1

You are my father and mother, you are my Lord.
You are loving uncle and aunt to me.
You are lovely women and rich treasure,
my only family, friends, and home.
You give me the pleasures of this world
and the other, and save me in the end.
O sole friend who moves my heart to leave this world,
O my gold and precious gems and pearls!
You are my God, my treasure who rides the bull!

142. Appar IV.95.1 *Pātirippuliyūr*

The Lord who graciously made himself three
to create the universe
has chosen to dwell within my heart
as the mother who gave me birth,
as my own father, as those born with me.
The beloved of the Himalayan gods
lives in holy Pātirippuliyūr
as unseen friend to all of us,
his loving devotees.

*

143. Appar IV.15 PĀVANĀCAT TIRUPPATIKAM (THE SACRED HYMN THAT DESTROYS SIN)

1
The ancient holy shrine that the bondless reach,
the coral rooted in Pācūr,
our glowing fruit in the Little Ampalam,
the sacred form that none may touch,
Veṟṟiyūr's spreading flame, king of gods,
our supreme Lord in wave-washed Oṟṟiyūr,
I have placed him within my heart.

2
The Lord who is the Goddess in Āṉaikkā,
our Father who dwells in Ārūr,
the lump of sugar candy in Kāṉappēr town,
sugar cane that sprouts in Kāṉūr,
Vāymūr's rare conch whom the gods of heaven praise,
the wild elephant of great Kailāsa,
I shall not forget the moon, the flame.

3
The sun who wears the cool moon as a wreath,
the cure for the world-illusion,

143. Much of the affective impact of this hymn is related to the bonds of alliteration and assonance established between Śiva's epithets and the names of his abodes: e.g., in verse 1, line 1: "paṟṟaṟṟāṟ cēr paḻampatiyaip pācūr nilāya pavaḷattai." v. 1. "The ancient holy shrine": "*paḻam pati.*" C.K.S. Mutaliyār notes that this is a traditional name given to the shrine at Puṉavāyil (Mutaliyār, *Periya purāṇam* commentary). v. 2. "The Goddess in Āñaikkā": "*āṉaikkāvil aṇaṅkiṉai.*" According to the local legend of the temple at Āṉaikkā, in this place Śiva revealed himself in the form of the Goddess as Śakti (power) to Brahmā, the creator. "Rare conch": *valampuri*, a kind of conch that spirals towards the right; it is considered to be a valuable object.

the King in the ancient town of Atikai,
the Lord who lives in Aiyāṟu,
fate and fame, the light
that the gods desire and seek,
the treasure, the young shoot of wisdom—
when I think of him, my heart is filled with joy.

4
Our pearl in Puṟampayam, gold in Pukalūr,
world-illumining sun in Uṟaiyūr and
Cirāppaḷḷi's high hill,
eye for those who can see in Kaḻukkuṉṟu
of roaring cataracts—
I have reached the royal lion
of Atikai Vīraṭṭāṉam's holy shrine.

5
Great gem in Kōlakkā, poison-eater who dwells
in Kuṭamūkku, sweet honey in Ālaṅkāṭu,
rare flower that crowns immortal heads,
ripe fruit soaked in milk, pure gold in Parāytturai,
the tridentbearer, incomparable god,
I have worshipped him to my heart's content.

6
The ruby who dwells in Marukal, flower garland
in Valañcuḻi, wish-giving tree in Karukāvūr,
bright flame hard to behold, the birthless one
in Peruvēḷūr, our beloved Lord in holy Vāñciyam
who never leaves his lovers,
I have placed him in my heart.

7
The handsome royal lion, gorgeous bull in Irāmēccuram,
our dancer on Kuṟṟālam's hill,
who embraces the breast
of the Goddess with the beautifully dressed hair,
eternal bridegroom who lives in
Neṭuṅkaḷam of shady groves,
flame-hued Father,
I have encircled him in love's embrace.

8
Crescent moon that rises in the evening,
the bridegroom who lives in Maṟaikkāṭu,

sweet juice of sugar cane, my gracious Lord in Aṇṇāmalai,
Faultless one who appears as the light
in Turutti, city of gardens,
the Lord of the celestial gods,
I have devoured him in desire.

9
Our light in Cōṟṟutturai, pure gem in Turutti,
King of Paḻaṉam on the river, our rare gem in Ālavāy,
sliver of moon in Neyttāṉam,
with broad ash-smeared shoulders,
mighty ocean, proud bull,
I have worshipped him to my heart's content.

10
Pure one in Puttūr, fighting bull in Pūvaṇam,
sprouting seed in Miḻalai, brahmin in Vēḷvikkuṭi,
he who burned the enemy's three cities,
ancient one who lives in Potiyil,
healing draught in Māttūr,
I have placed him within my heart.

11
Their sin will be destroyed,
who bathe him in a flood of loving thought,
and offer the garland of song at his feet,
saying, "My Father, my Lord and Master!"
to the firstborn one, rider on the strong white bull,
the god who is the color of the sunset sky,
and quelled the demon's might.

2 The Lord's Emblems

(POEMS 144–153)

Hail Śiva!

144. Campantar III.307 NAMACCIVĀYAT TIRUPPATIKAM (THE HOLY HYMN OF "HAIL ŚIVA!")

1
It guides to the good path
all those who melt with love
and flow with tears as they chant it.
It is the essence of the four Vedas.
Chant our Lord's name; say, "Hail Śiva!"

2
When true devotees say it,
it is like honey from fragrant flowers.
It is the crown jewel of pure gold
for the whole world.
Chant our Lord's name; say, "Hail Śiva!"

3
Thinking of him,
great love welling up in their heart,
if they finger the *akṣa* beads,
it will bring them the glory of the gods.
Chant our naked Lord's name; say "Hail Śiva!"

144–146. "Namaccivāya": Tamil for the Sanskrit chant "namaḥ śivāya," the refrain of the Vedic *Śatarudrīya stotra*. In Poem 145, verse 1 is believed to be a reference to an actual event in Appar's life. The Jains, angry with Appar for reconverting to Śaivism, bound him to a heavy rock, and cast him into the ocean. To their amazement, upon the saint's chanting "Hail Śiva!" the rock floated up in the water, and Appar emerged unhurt. See Poem 241. Verse 2 is modeled after a verse genre in classical Sanskrit poetry in which the device of parallel definition of diverse objects is employed. In Poem 146, "Pañcākkaram": Sanskrit *pañcākṣara*, the five syllables of the "namaḥ śivāya" *mantra*.

4
Yama's henchmen themselves will fear
those who chant it
with sweet sincerity.
Chant the name of the three-eyed god
dear to his pious devotees; say, "Hail Śiva!"

5
Evil will fall away
from those who say it,
even from murderers and wicked men.
Chant the good Lord's name; say, "Hail Śiva!"

145. Appar IV.11 NAMACCIVĀYAT TIRUPPATIKAM (THE HOLY HYMN OF "HAIL ŚIVA!")

1
When I sincerely worship the sweet golden feet
of the radiant immortal,
the brahmin who is the essence of the Veda,
even if I were to be bound to a rock
and cast into the sea,
the chant of "Hail Śiva!"
would save me!

2
The full-bloomed lotus
is the ornament of flowers;
to provide for Aran̲'s bathing rite
is the ornament of the cow;
impartial rule
is the ornament of kings;
the chant of "Hail Śiva!"
is the ornament of the tongue.

146. Campantar III.280.1 PAÑCĀKKARAP PATIKAM (THE HYMN OF THE FIVE SACRED SYLLABLES)

Remember every day with an aching heart,
remember in sleep and in waking,
the five syllables
that kicked out and terrified
Death himself, come to take away
the innocent boy who praised the Lord's feet.

147. Appar V.174 *Māṟpēṟu*

1
The Lord of Māṟpēṟu and the Goddess
dwell with delight in the hearts
of even the most ignorant of his devotees
who chant with feeling
the five holy syllables of his name.

2
Have no fear, O heart!
Meditate on Araṉ's names every day.
If you wish to be rid of karma, just say:
"O Lord who swallowed the great bitter poison!"
And Māṟpēṟu's Lord
will reveal himself as buried treasure.

3
O rogues who quote the Lawbooks!
Of what use are your caste and clan?
Just bow to Māṟpēṟu's Lord as your sole refuge—
In an instant, his grace will be yours.

4
I'll say it again,
listen, you wretched people!
Chant the five sacred syllables,
the fruit of great penance,
and you will gain the Lord who abides in Māṟpēṟu
as the cure for your stubborn disease.

5
I'll proclaim this aloud,
O people of the earth!
If you praise the bull rider's feet,
the Lord of Māṟpēṟu will conquer Death,
and rule you as flawless gold,
answer to all your prayers!

6
Even if you have lost the great wealth
you had earned,

147, v. 3. "Clan": "*kōttiram*" (*gotra*). Brahmins trace their lineage through *gotras* ("families") of Vedic seers. Campantar belonged to the Kavuṇiya (Sanskrit "Kauṇḍinya") *gotra*. "Caste": "*kulam*," "family." v. 4. "I'll say it again": "*iruntu colluvaṉ*," literally, "I will declare emphatically."

even if Death the Ender's call is near,
if you just cry, "Save me,
O great dancer in the burning-ground!"
Māṟpēṟu's Lord
will end your pain.

7
If you wail, "O Araṉ, My Lord,"
you will be saved.
If you just think of his rosy feet,
Māṟpēṟu's Lord who protects the universe
will make you rule the world.

10
If you exclaim,
"Māṟpēṟu, in whose woods monkeys leap,
is the place of him who bore down
to crush from head to foot
the demon who tried to lift the hill!"
Endless bliss is yours.

148. Cuntarar VII.48 *Pāṇṭikkoṭumuṭi*

1
Renouncing all my ties, I think
only of your holy feet.
Thinking of them, I have achieved
the purpose of my birth.
O good sage of Pāṇṭikkoṭumuṭi shrine
in fine Kaṟaiyūr praised by the wise,
even if I should forget you, my tongue
would still say: "Hail Śiva!"

2
Friend, the days when I ignored
those who praise your feet,
the days on which I myself have failed you,
I think of these as evil days.
O dancer in Pāṇṭikkoṭumuṭi worshipped by the Kaveri
with the garland of her circling stream!
Even if I should forget you, my tongue
would still say, "Hail Śiva!"

3
I will think of the day on which
I should forget you

as the day of my death,
the day when the senses fail,
the day life leaves the body,
the day when I shall be carried away on the bier.
O poet in glorious Pāṇṭikkoṭumuṭi
washed by the Kaveri's cool, swelling tide,
Even if I should forget you, my tongue
would still say, "Hail Śiva!"

The Lord's Trident, Ash, and Bull

149. Appar IV.110 *Tūṅkāṉaimāṭam*

1
O bright flame
of cloud-covered Tūṅkāṉaimāṭam in Kaṭantai,
I ask a boon of your golden feet!
If you would save the soul of this ardent devotee,
banish dark Death, place
your trident's bright seal on me!

2
O beloved of your devotees,
if you fail to take pity on me, and cure my disease,
thinking, "What does my little servant seek?"
the blame will be yours.
So, blessed Lord of Tūṅkāṉaimāṭam
in Kaṭantai of lotus pools, cover me
with ash from your holy feet!

10
O my true God
who lives in Tūṅkāṉaimāṭam
in Kaṭantai of dark groves that touch the moon!
With a single toe you suppressed
the demon who tried to take Kailāsa
because it hindered the course of his chariot wheels.
When will you take me,
having placed on me
the emblem of your bull white as the snowy peak?

149, v. 2. "Disease": "*arumpiṇinōy*," literally, "wasting disease," probably refers both to karma and to the physical ailment from which Appar suffered before his reconversion to Śaivism. The Lord's emblems are invoked as signs of his grace.

Śiva's Feet

150. Appar IV.97.1 *Cattimuṟṟam*

Before Death the king
destroys me with swift strength,
brand me with the print of your flower-feet!
If you fail,
O Śiva-sprout who dwells in holy Cattimuṟṟam,
you who bear the crackling fire in your hand,
deadly karma will surely engulf me!

151. Appar IV.82 *Kaḻumalam*

4
The Lord of Kaḻumalam's feet possess us—
feet that dance in the ancient modes
as his goblins sing, striking up their *paṟai* drums
that resound all over the world,
and pious men listen to the Vedic chant
and the discourse on the sacred texts.

7
O heart, think
of the Lord of Souls
who can destroy powerful binding karma
as soon as your thoughts turn to Kaḻumalam!
Surpassing those who believe
that their bonds will be severed only when they join Śiva,
worship the feet that possess us forever!

152. Appar IV.95 *Pātirippuliyūr*

2
Always think of them as your support, O heart!
Though the surging ocean surround
and cover the whole earth,
I see a refuge for us,
the dear feet of our friend, Umā's lover,
holy Pātirippuliyūr's Lord,
who wears the streak of the young moon
as a wreath on his hair.

151, v. 7. "Lord of Souls": "*pacupati*," also "Lord of Beasts." "Powerful binding karma": "*pantittirunta valviṉai*," karmic bonds of the past. The root "*āḷ-*" is used in the sense of "to rule" as well as "to possess."

152, v. 9. "Twin lights": "*irucuṭar*," the sun and the moon.

9

Though earth crash into the nether world,
the rising ocean cover all,
though the seven worlds
lose their bearing in space
and the twin lights fall,
do not fear, O heart!
We have found for ourselves a support,
the feet of the Lord of holy Pātirippuliyūr,
the bright god with the forehead eye.

153. Appar IV.81.10 *Kōyil (Tillai)*

The foot raised to kill the Moon
at Dakṣa's sacrifice,
the foot which sent Death to his death,
the foot which Nārāyaṇa and Brahmā
sought in vain to see,
the foot raised in dance
in Tillai's Little Ampalam hall—
that is the foot which possesses us!

3 Pain and Grace

(POEMS 154–180)

Despair

154. Appar IV.79 KUṞAINTA TIRUNĒRICAI (THE SACRED NĒRICAI POEM OF DESPAIR)

1
Why was I born,
I who cared only for my pride,
I who was caught in women's snares,
I who failed to think of my dear kinsman,
my ambrosia, the world's beginning and end,
my Lord whose form bright as the sunset sky
lay buried within my heart?

4
Once, a slave of past karma,
I failed to remember my Lord.
Now, having gone mad,
I babble like a fool.
I cannot hold in my heart
the god who is all the goodness
that dwells in me.
Why was I born?

155. Appar IV.113.10

How can the likes of me ever behold you,
when even those who are like you
could not grasp your greatness with their vision
when they tried to challenge you,
O brahmin with a shining crown of thick matted hair
that glitters like gold,

154. "Kuṟainta" in the title of this hymn suggests a range of emotions from complaint to despair.

155. "Those who are like you": "*niṉṉaiy oppār*" connotes the gods Brahmā and Viṣṇu, who tried to behold Śiva in his full glory as the column of flame.

mingles with the hue of fire,
surpasses the color of the sunset,
and shines like a flash of lightning?

*

156. Appar IV.113

4
You have never let me think of you.
If ever I remember you,
at once you make me forget
and turn to other things.
Tell me, is there anyone like me,
ever unaware, yet ever dear to you?
Long life to you, O Lord!

9
If my red-hued Lord
with the blessed name "Śiva"
were to bless me with his grace and possess me,
then, if I wander for many days
crying, "O Bhava!"
he will reveal himself to me, saying,
"This man has been calling out to me
for a long time!"

157. Cuntarar VII.51 *Tiruvārūr*

1
I know the nature of the disease
that afflicts me, makes me a sinner,
makes me stop loving and serving the Lord;
I hasten to worship him.
How long must I, a fool,
be parted from my Lord,
the one whom karma cannot bind,
great gem, my diamond,
my God in Ārūr?

2
How can I bear to be parted from my dear ambrosia
with the dark throat and the long matted hair,

157, v. 1. "The one whom karma cannot bind": with the *Tēvāram* Pondicherry edition, I read "*muttaṉai*" ("the one who is eternally free"), instead of "*muttiṉai*" ("the pearl").

great Śiva who burned to ashes
with his holy red eye
the Love-god who assaulted him
with his five arrows—
my God in Ārūr?

3
How can I,
fool born into this miserable body
destined for death,
bear to die,
parted from my Father who devoured the poison
to calm the distress of the suppliant gods
who were burned by the venom that arose
from the vast ocean rich in shells—
my God in Ārūr?

158. Appar IV.20.1 *Tiruvārūr (Ārūr)*

To see you was my only thought.
You entered my heart,
and I seized your dancing feet.
You cannot leave me now,
O Father in Tiruvārūr
where flags fluttering on great mansions
touch the young moon in the sky!

159. Appar V.171.1 *Kōḷili*

I failed to think of you in the past.
I have yet to praise your feet.
Still,
O King of holy Kōḷili
where there are many paddy fields,
do not forget me!

160. Appar IV.75

1
What is my sin that I, his servant,
have passed my life

160, v. 4. In this verse Appar describes the process by which the self (*uyir*) is illumined in and by the luminous knowledge of Śiva (*ñāṉat tī*: "fire of knowledge"). Right cognition or knowledge (*maṭam paṭum uṇarvu*), which can be achieved only through Śiva's grace (*aruḷ*), is only the first step toward the supreme knowledge, which is the mystical state of *civa-*

without seeing the worship of Kaṇṭaṉ, my Lord,
without seeing him bathed with the pure water of the Kaveri,
to the sound of the Vedic chant,
without seeing him adorned with saffron paste,
and garlands of flowers?

4
In the body's house
make a lamp of the heart.
Pour right cognition as butter,
shape the wick that is the self,
light it with the fire
of the supreme knowledge of the Lord.
The vision of the anklet-adorned feet of the Lord,
the father of the youth who sits under the *kaṭampu* tree,
will then be yours.

6
I love him who dwells in the hearts of his lovers,
whose great self is love itself.
Desiring to see him, I melt;
melting, I waste away.
How shall my heart,
ant trapped on a two-headed firebrand,
join my Father, the great Lord?

7
Like carrion crows
alighting on a carcass,
evil deeds from the past swarm upon me, delude me,
silence my words of praise for you.
O Lord of the universe,
give me right knowledge, so that I may shed
this putrid, loathsome form, oozing with pus,
this wound ridden with foul disease!

ñāṉam ("knowledge of Śiva"), the condition to which the Tamil Śaiva aspires. The conception of the yogic vision of Śiva as the luminous presence within the self is developed in detail in the great texts of the Śaiva Siddhānta, especially in the works of Uyyavantatēvar (*Tirukkaḷiṟṟuppāṭiyār*), Aruṇanti (*Civañāṉapōtam*), and Umāpati Civam (*Tiruvaruṭpayaṉ*). The earliest exposition of the idea can be found in Tirumūlar's *Tirumantiram*. See Dhavamony, *Love of God*. "The youth who sits under the *kaṭampu* tree" is the Tamil hill-god Murukaṉ, identified with Skanda-Kārttikeya, one of the two sons of Śiva and Pārvatī. This verse has a famous parallel in the verse "aṉpē takaḷiyāka" by the early Āḻvār Pūtam in the Vaiṣṇava *Nālāyirat tivviyap pirapantam*. v. 6. "Ant trapped on a two-headed firebrand" ("irutalai miṉṉukiṉṟa koḷḷi mēl eṟumpu") is a proverbial expression in Tamil for a person caught in an inescapable situation or dilemma.

Supplication

161. Campantar III.303.1 *Tiruvārūr*

The one who is the end
and beginning of the universe,
the brahmin who wears the white ash,
my father in Tiruvārūr
who has entered my heart—
When will he take me?

162. Appar IV.95.6 *Pātirippuliyūr*

Lying in the womb, I thought
only of your feet.
Committing it to memory,
I recited your name.
Through your grace, I chanted
"Hail Śiva,"
and wore the sacred ash
as the sign of my blessing.
O Araṉ of Pātirippuliyūr,
give me your own state of Śiva!

163. Appar IV.100.6 *Kacci Ēkampam*

From the day I entered the womb
my heart longed for the vision of your feet.
I am weary from a life of suffering and pain.
Lord of Tiruvoṟṟiyūr, holy Ālavāy's god,
Lord in Tiruvārūr,
seeing that I have given up everything but you,
O Ēkampaṉ of Kacci,
won't you take pity on me?

*

164. Cuntarar VII.15 *Nāṭṭiyattāṉkuṭi*

1
I won't be afraid of the snake that is your belt,
won't mock your dance in the burning-ground.

161. "[My father] . . . / who has entered my heart": "*cintaiyē pukuntāṉ.*" "*Cintai*": literally, "meditation, contemplation."

162. "The state [condition] of Śiva": "*civakati,*" the supreme state.

164, v. 3. "*Mañcēr*": "lovely," or "resting on clouds." "Fearlessly" is probably an allu-

You may not care for me, yet I'll call you my Lord.
Even if I'll never be born again, I'll never forget you.
Though you won't look at me, I will still see you,
though you won't love me, I'll still love you in my heart,
and never stop singing the praise of your feet,
O King of Nāṭṭiyattāṉkuṭi!

2
Lord with the divine form, explain the wonder
of your dwelling in the heart of a base man like me,
who loves the dance you perform at night
in the burning-ground, with a beautiful snake for your belt.
Gem who rids us of our gathered karma,
ruby-colored Lord,
I won't love anyone but you,
O King of Nāṭṭiyattāṉkuṭi!

3
When I can fearlessly serve you,
what more could I want?
O supreme Lord who shares your form
with the mountain's daughter with tender feet,
ruby-colored gem with the lovely white moon
on your red hair,
you who hold the poison in your throat
and carry a white skull,
O King of Nāṭṭiyattāṉkuṭi!

4
I do not lack learning, yet although I am your slave,
I learned nothing about your greatness.
I am no wayward soul, yet I can't understand the ways
of those who follow your way.
I cannot sing your golden feet
and hope to be saved by my songs.
I am a good man to no one but yourself,
O King of Nāṭṭiyattāṉkuṭi!

---

sion to Śiva's horrific acts and attributes, such as the snake and the dance on the burning-ground. v. 6. "Pāccil in the West" is the town of Pāccilāccirамам on the river Koḷḷiṭam (Coleroon). In the final verse, Cuntarar refers to Kōṭpuli, one of the sixty-three Nāyaṉārs. Kōṭpuli of Nāṭṭiyattāṉkuṭi was a devout Śaiva and a general in the Cōḷa army. This Nāyaṉār's claim to sainthood stems from the incident in which he put to the sword his own kinsmen and friends for having consumed, during a famine, the grain he had dedicated to the temple for feeding Śaiva devotees. Cuntarar describes Kōṭpuli as a *koṭiṟaṉ*, "one who is like pincers or jaws." Kōṭpuli is said to have given to the saint his two daughters, Ciṅkaṭi and Vaṉappakai, whom Cuntarar brought up as his own daughters.

5
I won't love those who do not love
the husband of the mountain's daughter
with flower-scented hair.
Though you won't be attached to me, I'll cling to you.
Always serving those who serve your feet,
I will sing of you alone.
Since I love you, seeking to know you
through devotion and song.
I cannot forget you,
O King of Nāṭṭiyattāṉkuṭi!

6
Since it is in my karma and nature to suffer,
I won't blame you for all I have suffered,
O cool raincloud who dwells in Pāccil in the West,
King who kicked Death!
Lord who is half woman,
brahmin who loves to bathe
in offerings of milk, yoghurt, and ghee,
though you'll go away from me,
I'll keep walking toward your feet,
O King of Nāṭṭiyattāṉkuṭi!

7
O handsome Lord, you who wear the five-hooded snake
with the crescent moon on your hair!
Chief of the immortal gods!
With all my heart I have fixed my aim upon my goal.
Wanting to be saved, I have reached your feet.
Though you won't love me, I will love you still,
for did I not once become your slave
so that I might melt with love for you,
O King of Nāṭṭiyattāṉkuṭi?

8
I can't be proud, valuing this human life—
when I think of it, my eyes fill with tears.
I will not slander your habit of begging for food,
nor mock you for riding a bull.
Though I might rise in the world,
I'll never stop worshipping you.
I can't bear the thought of future births,
so I won't press and entreat anyone but you,
O King of Nāṭṭiyattāṉkuṭi!

9
Yes, the Jains and Buddhists, no better than demons,
may get their way, with their lies and deception,
and I may have to see all the wealth they've piled up
with their cheating. But listen, O god who rides the bull,
who is so dear to me: you are the one I really know.
I see those who worship you, serve you,
and then I worship you as well
and put a stop to all my karma.
Listen, O King of Nāṭṭiyattāṉkuṭi
where there are crabs playing
in fields surrounded by green groves!

10
Even if you have no wish to sing, O devotees,
sing him and sever the bonds of sin!
Sing this hymn composed by the poet of Tiruvārūr,
father of Ciṅkati with the long hair adorned with flowers,
poet who never forgets the King of Nāṭṭiyattāṉkuṭi,
famous old town in the Cōḻa land,
home of Kōṭpuli, terrible as the jaws of death,
who defeated enemy kings in combat.

165. Cuntarar VII.24 *Maḻapāṭi*

2
Wearing the loincloth and waistband,
my body smeared with sacred ash,
I have taken refuge at your feet.
Take me, my Lord!
Lover of the Goddess with eyes curved like swords,
ruby in Maḻapāṭi, friend,
tell me, whom can I think of but you?

3
My father and mother
can't be of the slightest help to me.
Caught in the chain of birth and death,
I am worn down by the world-illusion.
Ruby in Maḻapāṭi
surrounded by great dark flowering groves,
O Father, tell me,
whom can I think of but you?

165. I have taken the *Tēvāram* Pondicherry edition reading "*kēḷā*" ("O friend") instead of the *Tēvāram* Kaḻakam edition reading "*āḷāy*," "possessed by you," "as your servant."

166. Appar IV.23 *Kōyil/Tillai*

1
I can't sing like a true devotee,
O God, great yogi!
How can I worship you?
Do not spurn me, Perfect Being, Primal Lord,
Father who dances in Tillai's Ampalam hall!
I, your servant,
have come to see your dance.

6
Seeing your dance, I will praise you.
Singing and dancing, I will hail you, crying,
"O Lord, First among the Three!"
You who put an end to the misery
of those who sing your praise,
O Dancer in Tillai's Little Ampalam,
even I have come to see your dance.

8
What shall I do, O god with the dark throat,
if my mind is confused,
and daily slips from the highest path?
I, your servant, have come
to see all your dances
in the Little Ampalam in Tillai
where the Vedas flourish in full glory.

9
Having failed to purify my heart,
and to make me meditate on you as I should,
have you not deceived me, O Lord of the immortals?
And yet, handsome one, you dance,
as your soft-spoken lady watches,
in the little hall in Tillai,
town of cloud-kissed groves!

10
Māl who ate earth as a child
and Ayaṉ who has the lotus seat,

166. In verse 10 Appar refers to a myth of Viṣṇu in his incarnation as Krishna. When the women of the cowherd village complained to Yaśodā, saying that the child Krishna had eaten dirt, Yaśodā asked him to open his mouth; inside his mouth she saw the entire universe. "Abiding wealth" ("*tiṇṇuṇṭa tiru*") suggests release as well as worldly wealth.

in vain desired to see
your holy form that pervaded space.
Yet, O Supreme Lord,
you dance to the music of modes
in the little hall of Tillai,
home of our abiding wealth!

167. Cuntarar VII.5 *Ōṇakāntaṉṟaḷi*

1
Those who worship you every day
with yoghurt and milk and ghee
don't get a penny for their devotion!
You who live in Ōṇakāntaṉṟaḷi,
won't you show me a way to release
as I wallow in this deep pit,
dancing to the tune of the five senses,
and won't be saved
unless I worship your holy feet?

2
The goddess Gaṅgā, whose waves flow
over your moon-crowned matted hair,
is a silent woman; Gaṇapati has a potbelly,
spear-bearing Kumaraṉ is a mere boy.
As for the Goddess,
she is no strict mistress.

167. This hymn is typical of Cuntarar's direct, immediate voice and his penchant for mixing the sublime with the mundane. In every verse Cuntarar criticizes Śiva's poverty and his odd habits, the poverty and suffering of his devotees, his unresponsiveness to them in their need. v. 2. "She is no strict mistress": "*kōṟṟaṭṭiyāḷāḷ*," "she who can't rule with a stick" can also be taken to mean "all she knows is how to play the *yāḻ*." Gaṇapati: The elephant-faced god, son of Śiva. Kumaraṉ: "The youth" (Sanskrit *kumāra*), another name of Murukaṉ. v. 6. The Kāmakkōṭṭam ("Abode of Kāma") is the shrine in which the Goddess, as Kāmākṣī ("She with the eyes of Desire"), is separately established in Kanchipuram (Kacci). According to local legends, the Goddess established the Kāmakkōṭṭam shrine in Kanchi in order to practice charity according to the sacred Law; hence the irony in Śiva's beggarly way of life. Separate Kāmakkōṭṭam shrines for Goddess-consorts became popular in Cōḻa times; Cuntarar's reference affirms the antiquity of the Kanchi shrine. Since "*ār*" (v. 9) can mean both "fine/precious," and "who?/someone," Cuntarar punningly speaks of Ārūr as "nobody's town." "No place to call your own": "*oṟṟiy ūrēl ummataṉṟu*" is a pun on the name of the town of Oṟṟiyūr, literally "you do not even have a mortgaged village." The poet mocks Śiva for having "raised up" his wife, implying that he is under her control. The goddess Umā, referred to in verse 2, creates other problems, being too softhearted to help Śiva rule his devotees with the necessary firmness. In verse 10 the poet describes Śiva as the Androgyne.

You who live in Ōṇakāntaṉṟaḷi, tell me,
how can we serve a master with such a family?

3
Lord who lives in Ōṇakāntaṉṟaḷi,
you won't be reasonable,
won't take pity on the devotees
who see you as their sole support,
who love and worship your feet
even when you give them nothing in return.
What should we do in times of need,
in poverty and misfortune—
pawn you so that we can eat?

4
I have praised you, saying all I can say,
but I can't get anything out of you.
Ōṇakāntaṉṟaḷi's Lord, tell me,
how will you rule us
when you won't give up this wretched life
of wandering all day
with a toothless skull for a begging bowl?

5
You don't grant grace to your devotees
who dance, and sing songs to the proper beat,
who weep and melt with love for you,
and gather to worship you in every way.
Though I am weary, wandering about, looking for you,
you never think of me.
You won't run away from me, yet you won't give me a hand,
Ōṇakāntaṉṟaḷi's Lord!

6
Lord who lives in Ōṇakāntaṉṟaḷi,
why do you go begging for alms
in the ancient city of Kacci with its dark woods,
when your Goddess who has long, dark hair
and eyes curved like swords,
the mountain's daughter who wears
the *koṉṟai* garland brimming with honey
on her high breasts,
abides here in the Kāmakkōṭṭam shrine
for the salvation of the world?

7
I fritter my life away in lies,
I'm neither a temple servant nor your devotee.
You have not possessed me with your truth,
nor given me hope for the future state.
Even if I were your servant,
you would ask nothing of me, give nothing,
say nothing to me!
Yet are you not my Master from former lives,
O Lord who lives in Ōṇakāntaṉṟaḷi?

8
I hear that Death has come with his noose
to take me away,
yet I can't put strength into my heart,
can't worship your feet and be saved!
I can't join you, since I burn in this pit
of lust and envy, anger, pride and greed,
of every vice in the book, Ōṇakāntaṉṟaḷi's Lord!

9
What can your devotees who serve your holy feet
with the sacred rites get for their love?
Your necklace is a snake, you live in
Ārūr, a town that belongs to nobody;
Oṟṟiyūr is a mortgaged city,
you have no place to call your own.
You have raised the goddess Gaṅgā up on your head,
you've made her your wife!
Your home is the burning-ground,
and your robe, the flayed hide,
O Lord who lives in Ōṇakāntaṉṟaḷi!

10
Sin will be annihilated
for those who can sing
this sequence of ten Tamil verses
in which Ārūraṉ has described Ōṇakāntaṉṟaḷi's Lord
who has the poet for his bondservant,
the bull rider who is manifest as the primal syllable "Aum,"
and binds the colorful sari with a silken scarf
over his loincloth.

The Refuge

168. Appar IV.114.10

Though the mountains should shrivel,
slowly scorched by the sun,
though the dark ocean dry up,
and the rains fail
for a long time,
yet do not fear, O heart,
that famine would grip the land,
for we have a refuge
on this wide earth,
a high golden hill
with three unwinking eyes!

169. Appar IV.113.8

What though the sky fall,
what though the earth quake,
what though the mountains slip and slide,
what though the cold sea be drained
and the great lights fall?
What matter all this
to the noble souls who serve
the one God who stands unblemished,
having devoured the ocean's poison?

The Humble Poet

170. Appar VI.305.1 *Eṟumpiyūr*

I don't know pure Tamil for song,
I can't make poems.
I knew nothing of science, and the modes of music,
of all the arts that are his own self,
and of his greatness.
He revealed his power and his way

168, 169. Śiva is compared to the golden cosmic mountain (Meru). "Great lights": the sun and the moon. Compare Poem 152.

170. Appar's disavowal of learning and competence as a poet is more typical of the *bhakti* poet's attitude toward his art than the pride in achievement expressed by Campantar in his coda verses. See Ramanujan, *Speaking of Śiva*, pp. 37–42.

to me, an ignorant man.
Like a loving mother and father,
he followed me, a refugee,
and took me for his own.
Thus have I been blessed,
to have sought and attained
my ruby on lovely Eṟumpiyūr's hill,
the golden flame.

The Lord's Grace

171. Cuntarar VII.14 *Pāccilācciramam*

1
The peerless Lord gave me
a head, heart, and thoughts
to serve him alone.
Yet I would be boasting if I were to say
that I was a true servant to him.
Alas, if I lose the madman's love,
do I have no Master
other than the supreme Lord who lives in Pāccilācciramam,
girded with the hooded serpent and loincloth?

2
I don't call you "father" or "mother,"
"O Lord," is good enough for me.
Yet Lord, you won't consider me one of your creatures,
won't show me even a little of your grace.
Alas, if he waits too long to bless his devotees,
do I have no Master
other than the Lord who lives
in Pāccilācciramam where wild geese swim in the lakes?

6
I am afraid of evil karma,
so I won't go the way

171. The refrain of this hymn ("*ivaralātillaiyō piräṉār*": "Do I have no Master other than him") can be taken as a rhetorical question. The mood of this poem combines despair with cynicism. v. 11. "Seven births" or "seven times seven births" is a popular expression for the notion of karmic effect resulting in rebirth. Tradition connects this reference to servanthood stretching over several births with the legend of Cuntarar's conversion in Tiruveṇṇeynallūr (see Section IV below).

of men who practice false ascetic vows.
My Lord knows that I know
nothing but the penance
of service at his feet.
Alas, do I have no Master
other than Pācciläcciramam's Lord who bears the trident,
though he wears nothing but the white ash?

9
Melting in a stream of love,
run to join him, O heart,
perform his loving service every day!
Pāccil's Lord saves those who call him their Lord
before the end of their days,
even without love in their hearts.
Do I have no Master other than him,
if, in spite of all my pleas,
he won't forgive my sins
and reward me for my love?

10
When I meditate on him with devotion,
when I envision his form
as he appears dressed in rags,
covered with powdery white ash,
my heart remembers
only the Lord with the throat like a sapphire,
the tongue speaks of him alone.
If he has embraced and possessed me,
but won't let me serve him,
do I have no Master
other than the Lord in Pācciläcciramam
who wears the hooded snake?

11
Not only in this birth, but in all
seven births have I been servant
to you, and to all your servants, too.
I belong to you by birthright, my heart melts for you,
show me your bright feet soft as flowers!
Alas, do I have no Master
other than my Lord in Pācciläcciramam,
who blesses those who have earned coveted fame,
if his petty ways toward me
belie the great promises he made?

12
I have never reproached my Lord,
never condemned him.
I am known as one who always sings
hymns in my Lord's praise.
Alas, do I have no Master other than him,
if he takes offense
at the words of the poet Ārūraṉ
of Nāvalūr of fertile fields,
who worships the feet of Pāccilācciramam's Lord,
sings him with his tongue,
and long remembers him in his heart?

172. Appar V.133.9 *Kaṭampūr*

The Lord of the holy *karakkōyil* temple
in South Kaṭampūr,
the spouse of the Goddess,
mother of our Kaṭampaṉ—
his task is to save
even this lowly servant.
My task is only to serve.

173. Appar IV.103.5 *Ārūr (Tiruvārūr)*

You destroyed the god who held the sugar cane bow
and gave happiness to the boy who wielded the axe
as his weapon.
Seeing these,
O Lord who lives in pretty Ārūr
surrounded by cool, blossoming groves,
how should I know your heart's pleasure,
and what should I ask of you?

174. Campantar II.176.6 *Piramapuram (Cīrkāḻi)*

Wherever his devotees are born,
into whatever form or birth,
to bless them with his grace
in that very form

172. Kaṭampaṉ: Murukaṉ. *Karakkōyil*: An apsidal temple.
173. "The god who held the sugar-cane bow": Kāma. "The boy who wielded the axe": Caṇṭīcar.
174. "In that very form": "*iṅkēy eṉṟu*," "in that very condition," "in the particular circumstances of their lives."

is the nature of Śaṅkara,
my bull-riding Lord
with body bright as the white conch,
who lives in Piramapuram, cool with
groves of fragrant flowers.

175. Appar V.161.11 *Kacci Ēkampam*

Our Lord is the one
who bore down with his toe
when Rāvaṇa, Laṅkā's king,
lifted his hill.
And he is the one
who gave the demon the good course
when he cried in distress:
"Save me, O Ēkampaṉ of Kacci!"

176. Cuntarar VII.21 *Kacci Mēṟṟaḷi*

1
O everlasting light burning bright,
I thought only of you.
You came to me,
and have never left me since.
Focus of all my thoughts,
Lord who dwells in the holy Western shrine,
Father, I will sing
no one but you.

6
I thought only of your feet.
At once you entered this carnal frame.
O my bright flame,
honey, sweet ambrosia,
King who dwells in the holy Western shrine,
I will joyfully sing
no one but you.

177. Cuntarar VII.23.2 *Kaḻippālai*

You who abide in Kaḻippālai,
wherever I, your servant,

175. "Good course": "*nalaṅkoḷ celavu*," "good life"; "the course that leads to one's welfare," "the path to release."

176. Kacci Mēṟṟaḷi: "The Western shrine in Kacci." The Mēṟṟaḷi is one of the many Śiva shrines in Kanchipuram, city of temples.

think of you, you join me there
and grant me grace.
You are Gaṅgā's Lord
who severs my karmic bonds,
and takes me right here!

178. Cuntarar VII.58 *Kaḻumalam (Cīrkāḻi)*

1
My Master who chose me,
saved me from birth and death, and gave me grace,
the gem who exalted the mountain's daughter
by placing her in half his frame,
my Lord who bears the flowing river in his hair,
he who has mingled with my stranger's heart
like water with red-hot iron,
the god with the eight forms, our King who wears
the white conch earring on one ear,
I have seen him in the fair town of Kaḻumalam
which once floated on the ocean's flood.

2
I won't look for another friend
in this birth or the next.
Once I grieved, then received the gift
of lasting remembrance of him.
I have given up my family and friends,
I worship the bright flame as my only friend,
my God who gave me the teaching,
guiding me in their proper course
through the paths of knowledge and release,
ways that the gods themselves cannot know.
I, his servant, have beheld him
in the fair town of Kaḻumalam.

3
The father of Cēntaṉ in holy Tiṉainakar,
pure gold that cuts through the chain of karma,
the golden one—
I know none other than him:

178. Cuntarar refers to the Cīrkāḻi flood myth in verse 1. Cēntaṉ (v. 3): Murukaṉ. Ūraṉ (v. 10): Ārūraṉ, citizen of Ārūr, or Nāvalūraṉ, poet from Nāvalūr. The *kuḻai*, mentioned in verses 1, 4, and 5, is a man's earring. v. 1. *veṇkuḻai*: "white earring"; v. 5. "*kuṇṭalaṅkuḻai*": *kuṇṭalam* is another term for a man's earring. In his androgynous form, Śiva wears the *kuḻai* on one ear, and the *tōṭu*, a woman's earring, on the other.

I have received this knowledge,
as my means to release.
Once, having seen in my dream
the one who is the old man and the child,
I lost my vision, and awoke in despair.
I have now seen the god with the dancing feet
in the fair seaside town of Kaḻumalam.

4
I have won over my Lord
who wears the *koṉṟai* which blooms in the rains;
I have won a heart that will never forget him.
Once a sinner, I have now been raised
to the birthless state—who is so fortunate as I?
I behold my Lord with the dark throat and the gold earring,
I sing of him, and will unite with him;
I have seen him in the fair town of Kaḻumalam
with the groves of tall sugar cane and plantain trees.

5
Raving, "O god with the golden earring on one ear,
youth with the deadly battle-axe,
Lord who wears the *koṉṟai* blossom swarming with bees,"
I worshipped him with the proper sacred rite.
Uniting my roving thoughts of the past
in the one thought of him,
I wandered in Paśupati's sacred abodes
for a long time, till
I found him in the fair town of Kaḻumalam,
where every day the tide sweeps over
the beautiful shore covered with the screwpine.

6
Thinking of the enormous evil karma I must endure,
I grieved,
then received the gift of lasting remembrance of my Lord.
Loving him, my heart thrilled,
I prayed to him, worshipping him with the proper rite.
My bud, my blossom, ambrosia, my honey,
my Master, my God, the sugar cane
that will uproot the tree of my birth,
I have seen him in the fair town of Kaḻumalam,
full of lush paddyfields.

10
Sorrow and suffering will never touch
those devotees who worship the Lord with flowers,
and with these ten verses that the poet Ūraṉ,
Caṭaiyaṉ's loving son,
having seen the holy feet of the Lord
in the fair town of Kaḻumalam,
has sung on those feet
that true devotees alone may know,
who shed tears, thinking only of the Lord
with the crown of matted hair
adorned by the *koṉṟai* and *kūviḷam* flowers.

179. Appar IV.103.10 *Tiruvārūr*

Sound the conch at dawn!
Light fragrant incense!
I am possessed
by the lotus feet of the Lord
who once bore down with his toe
to crush, till the crimson blood flowed,
the demon who tried to lift the beautiful hill
with his twenty shoulders.

180. Cuntarar VII.90 *Kōyil (Tillai)*

1
Rejoice, O heart, we have attained our Lord
of Puliyūr's Little Ampalam,
who dances with foot raised, holding the drum, blazing fire,
and the black snake in his swaying hands,
the Lord who will save you not only
when you serve the dancing god,
but all your life,
even when Dharma's men grind you in the mill.

180. The refrain of this poem evokes a vision of hell that is part of South Indian popular religion and folklore. Yama or Yamadharmarāja, god of Death, fits punishments to evil deeds in the hell of his realm (Yamaloka [Tamil *namaṉulaku*]); among the tortures to be dreaded is being cast into (oil-)mills to be slowly ground. The phrase "*taṭuttāṭkoḷvāṉ*" (translated as "he who will save you/us") in the refrain in verses 1, 5, 9, and 10 literally means: "he who intervenes, leads one away from harmful ways, and possesses one." The expression is associated with Cuntarar's own conversion in Veṇṇeynallūr, which Śiva effected in a truly dramatic manner. See Section IV below. In verse 4 Cuntarar expresses his loyalty to the Pallava king.

4
Rejoice, for we have attained our Lord
of noble Puliyūr's Little Ampalam,
who severs the bonds with which
dark Death's henchmen have bound us,
the god who gives us his precious world,
and tortures kings who fail to pay tribute
to the Pallava, rightful ruler of the earth.

5
Rejoice, for we have attained our Master, our Lord
of Puliyūr's Little Ampalam,
the god who wears the black buckskin,
and has the white moon for a wreath on his hair,
him who violently kicked aside
Death with the thundrous roar,
and gave immortality to the boy,
him who shall save us
when Dharma's men grind us in the mill!

9
Rejoice, O heart, for we have attained our Lord
of glorious Puliyūr's Little Ampalam,
who will save us when King Dharma's henchmen
grind us in the mill,
the god who has condemned to ignorance
the stupid Jains and the stinking Buddhist monks—
always serve him well!

10
Rejoice, for we have attained,
in Puliyūr's Little Ampalam,
the spouse of Umā, the Goddess whose mound of Venus
is like the hood of the winding cobra,
Lord with the bright-eyed bull,
god who dwells in many sacred places,
and will save us when Dharma's men
grind us in the mill,
the poet Ārūraṉ's Master in Tiruvārūr, and Lord
of Pērūr in western Koṅku land on the lovely Kañci's banks.

4 The Lord, My Lover

(POEMS 181–185)

181. Appar VI.239.7 *Ārūr (Tiruvārūr)*

Once she heard his name,
then learned of his lovely form.
Then she heard of his excellent town,
and fell madly in love with him.
That same day she left her mother and father
and the proper ways of the world,
lost herself,
lost her good name.
This woman has joined the feet
of the Lord, her lover.

182. Campantar I.60 *Tōṇipuram (Cīrkāḻi)*

1
King bee
who hums melodious tunes,
drinking honey from lotuses
in lovely rippling pools
in the company of your mate!
Out of compassion for me,
won't you tell my state

181. In this poem Appar describes the progression of the devotee's love for Śiva in terms of the progression of the love of a heroine for the hero in the classical *akam* love poems. "Form," "*mūrtti*," is also the technical term for the iconographic forms of Śiva. "Lovely," "*vaṇṇam*," connotes both color and natural beauty. "Lost herself": "*taṉṉai maṟantāḷ*," "became completely absorbed with her lover, forgot herself." "*Talaivaṉ*," which I have translated as "the Lord, her lover," can mean "the lover/hero" of Caṅkam love poetry as well as "chieftain" or "master."

182. The motif of lovers employing birds, animals, and even insentient objects as messengers of love is an ancient one in Indian literature, appearing in the *Rāmāyaṇa*, the story of Nala and Damayantī, and elsewhere. The classic of the *dūta* ("messenger") genre in Sanskrit poetry is Kālidāsa's *Meghadūta* (Cloud-messenger). The messenger theme also appears in Tamil *akam* poetry, and was successfully adopted by Tamil *bhakti* poets such as Campantar, Māṇikkavācakar, and Nammāḻvār. v. 1. The *pāṇṭaraṅkam* is one of Śiva's dances in the burning-ground.

to the Lord of the bright crescent moon,
who wears a garland of bones on his chest,
the *pāṇṭaraṅkam* dancer
who lives in holy Tōṇipuram?

10
Simple parrot
imprisoned in your cage,
come here, I will give you
milk and honey to drink,
as much as you wish,
if you will speak for me just once
the sweet name
of the Lord who wears the bright young moon,
king of Tōṇipuram by the sea,
where the beach is strewn
with clustered coral and pearls!

183. Campantar I.1 *Piramapuram (Cīrkāḻi)*

1
He wears a woman's earring on one ear;
riding on his bull,
crowned with the pure white crescent moon,
his body smeared with ash from the burning-ground,
he is the thief who stole my heart.
He is the Lord who lives in fine Piramapuram,
where he once blessed with his grace
Brahmā of the lotus seat
who worshipped him.

3
He bears the white crescent moon
on long, matted red hair
on which the river flows.

183. The Tamil Śaivas regard the first hymn of the *Tēvāram* corpus as the first hymn that the child Campantar composed, inspired by divine wisdom. Verse 1 of this hymn is also included and discussed in Section IV of the anthology, in the context of the life of Campantar (see Poem 221). As noted in Part One, the hero in Tamil *akam* poetry is often called a "thief" (*kaḷvaṉ*); the refrain in Campantar's poem is "eṉṉ uḷḷaṅ kavar kaḷvaṉ." Local legends (*talapurāṇam*) of the Cīrkāḻi temple are alluded to in verses 1 and 5: "Piramapuram" is so called because Brahmā (Tamil "Piramaṉ") worshipped Śiva at this shrine; the *vimāna* of this temple survived the cosmic flood. The reference to the bracelets slipping from the heroine's wrist (v. 3) suggests that she is wasting away in her lovelorn state.

He who makes the noisy white shell bracelets
slip from my thin wrist,
is the thief who stole my heart.
He is the Lord who lives in Piramapuram,
famed as the firstborn city in this wide world.

5
They praise him, calling him the Lord who is half woman,
Lord with the matted hair, god who rides the bull.
He is the thief who stole my heart.
He is the Lord who lives in Piramapuram,
famed as the shrine which once floated
on the dark ocean's cosmic flood.

184. Appar IV.6 *Kaḻippālai*

1
Her pretty coral lips murmur,
"He is the savior of the gods."
She says, "On his strong, coral-red shoulders
he wears the white ash."
The girl with the coral girdle says,
"He is beyond the infinite."
Did she see the chieftain
of Kaḻippālai's rich coral fields?

2
She says, "On his matted red hair he wears
the *koṉṟai* swarming with bees."
She says, "He also has the full-bloomed fragrant flower
of the white *erukku*."
She says, "He wears a silken upper cloth, too."
Did she see the chieftain
of Kaḻippālai's seashore tracts
overgrown with the water thorn?

184. This poem is clearly modeled after *akam* landscape poems. In it the devotee is depicted as the lovelorn heroine of Caṅkam poetry, longing for her lover who is the ruler (*cērppaṉ*) of seashore (*neytal*) tracts in Kaḻippālai. The voice in the poem is that of the nurse or foster mother (*cevilit tāy*) who is in charge of the heroine. The foster mother describes the strange delusions her daughter seems to be having; she suspects that the girl has been "possessed" by the "chieftain of Kaḻippālai." v. 1. "Savior of the gods" ("*vāṉavarkkut tāṉavaṉ*") is an allusion to the myth of Śiva's drinking of the poison. v. 2. "Water thorn": "*kaṇṭu*," *kaṇṭakam*, *nīrmuḷḷi*.

3
She says, "The young crescent moon
rests on my Lord's head."
She says, "The brilliant color of saffron
is his color."
She says, "His throat is dark,
like the spear-sharp eyes of his Goddess."
Did she see the chieftain of Kal̲ippālai
of the surging waves?

185. Campantar II.154 *Marukal*

1
"O god with matted hair!" she cries.
"You are my sole refuge!" she cries.
"Bull rider!" she cries, and faints in awe.
O Lord of Marukal
where the blue lily blooms in field waters,
is it fair
to make this woman waste from love's disease?

2
"Object of my thoughts!" she cries.
"Śiva!" she cries.
"Primal Being!" she cries.
"First among the gods!" she cries.
O our father who dwells in Marukal
where the blue lily blooms in clusters,
is it right
to afflict this woman with longing?

3
God who wears the sounding hero's band,
the flame-tongued snake

185. The speaker in this poem is the heroine's (devotee's) girlfriend, one of the personae in *akam* love poems. The girlfriend pleads with the hero (God) to take pity on her friend (the devotee). The hagiographers suggest that Campantar sang this hymn with reference to a woman in Marukal, who was mourning her lover's death by snakebite. At the end of the hymn, Śiva revived the young man, and the lovers were united. v. 8. Note the fine irony in this verse. v. 10. "Wandering packs of Buddhists," "*alarcākkiyar*" could also mean "fat Buddhists." "Ruined": "*nir̲ai nīkkin̲aiyē*," literally, "you took away the chastity of." v. 11. "Supreme Wisdom": "*vayañān̲am*," literally, "the knowledge that can be attained when one is 'completely given over to the Lord.' "

and moon-adorned matted hair!
You who delight in Marukal
rich in great scholars of the Veda!
You have taken her noisy bracelets
and with them, her well-being.

7
She never fails to cry upon waking,
"Long live my Lord's feet!"
She thinks of you day and night.
You who bear the axe and the sword,
she worships you, Lord of Marukal,
why torment her?

8
Lord of the strong-walled city of Marukal,
when Laṅkā's king lifted the mountain,
you bore down with your toe,
making him helpless.
You have made this woman,
frail as a flower garland,
the object of slander.

9
Lord of Marukal
where your immortal devotees live,
god who became a ball of fire,
so that the two could not fathom
your flaming hair and feet,
you have made this fine young woman
faint with suffering.

10
The ignorant Jains
and the wandering packs of Buddhists
go about committing crimes.
O Lord of Marukal, you who hold
the fawn in your hand,
you have utterly ruined
the young woman with thick coiled hair.

11
The fame of those who know the song
that Ñāṉacampantaṉ, the poet,

transformed by supreme wisdom,
and meditating on his god's feet,
has composed on the Lord of Marukal town,
home of men who possess
the knowledge of the Lord's grace,
will spread over heaven and earth.

5 Five Who Dwell Within

(POEMS 186–193)

186. Appar IV.46 *Oṟṟiyūr (Tiruvoṟṟiyūr)*

1
In vain I pampered the body's cage,
nurturing evil in my heart.
Like a spoon without a handle,
I can't dip into the ambrosia I seek.
As I think desperate thoughts,
like a frog caught in the snake's mouth,
protect and save me,
O King of Oṟṟiyūr!

2
When I board the boat of the mind
and strike out with the oars of my wit,
when I load my cargo of anger,
and row into the deep sea,
when, dashing against the rock of lust,
the boat capsizes,
then, as my reason fails,
give me the consciousness
that will make me think of you,
O King of Oṟṟiyūr!

187. Campantar I.50.7 *Valivalam*

You are my mother and my father.
O Śaṅkara, I want to love you forever.
The heart is willing,
but the five enemies who dwell
in this burdensome body

186, v. 1. This contains proverbial expressions: "kāmpilā mūḻai pōla" (like a spoon without a handle), and "pāmpiṉ vāyt tērai pōla" (like a frog caught in the snake's mouth).

187. "Burdensome," for "*āyam āya*," "that which is an obligation, a liability" (here brought about by past karma). "*Oṉṟal oṭṭār*" can mean both "they will not allow [me] to unite [with you]" and "they are hostile toward me."

won't let me join you.
I fear there is nothing left for me
but the illusion that is the world.

188. Appar IV.97.3 *Cattimuṟṟam*

As five who have entered
this frame full of holes
destroy the refuge I have found in you,
my heart is whirled about
like yoghurt in a churn.
Give me relief, O Father,
see, I have come to you for refuge,
perfected sage among the gods,
Śiva-sprout who dwells in holy Cattimuṟṟam!

189. Appar IV.69.1 *Kōvalūr Vīraṭṭam*

I am mere offal, a base dog,
filthy rogue who clings
to this foul body full of holes,
unaware of my true refuge.
What shall I,
a blind man who can't see the light,
grasp for support?
What shall I do,
O Lord of Kōvalūr Vīraṭṭam's shrine?

190. Campantar II.215 *Ārūr (Tiruvārūr)*

1
There are fools who fail to think of Śiva's feet
even when the breath is failing,
the mouth dries up, and the tongue will not stir,
even when they are dying men sustained by fluids alone.
Like them, you have disgraced yourself, O heart!
Yet do not be afraid,
faint from the world's illusion,
for you will be saved
if you worship Ārūr,

188, 189. The body is traditionally described as "the structure with nine orifices." Yoghurt (Poem 188) is churned using a churning stick (*mattu*) bound with ropes, to yield butter and buttermilk.

190, v. 1. This contains a graphic description of a man on his deathbed.

home of our Lord with the blue throat
who loves to ride on the leaping bull.

2
My father is gone, gone is my mother;
I, too, must die.
Death with his terrible spear
waits to carry me away.
How much longer do you wish to live, poor heart?
Yet do not be afraid,
faint from the world's illusion,
for you will yet be saved
if you worship
cool and beautiful Ārūr.

191. Appar IV.52 *Ārūr (Tiruvārūr)*

1
When I consider this vile human life,
wasted in filling up the stomach
which is like the bottomless pit of the sea,
I cry out in pain.
Five fools dwell inside me,
driving me to despair—
I, your servant, cannot live with these,
O Lord of the Mūlaṭṭam shrine in Ārūr!

2
There is nothing to hold together
this worm-infested frame
covered with skin, with nine leaky holes.
Five rogues sit within,
and torment me.
Utterly ruined, I cannot live with them any more,
O Lord of the Mūlaṭṭam shrine in Ārūr!

192. Appar IV.54 *Pukalūr*

5
Lusting after women with scented hair,
I have failed to meditate daily

191, v. 1. Mūlaṭṭam: The "Mūlaṭṭāṉam" or principal shrine in the great temple complex in Tiruvārūr. "*Muṭuku-*": "to drive, hasten, press."
192, v. 7. Pārtha: Arjuna.

on the feet of the Lord
who dwells in Kaṭavūr's Vīraṭṭam shrine
which rings with joyful song;
my unworthy heart reels.
Lord of holy Pukalūr,
What shall I do?

7
I have failed to subdue the five senses,
there is no trace of learning in me.
I don't have the good fortune
of being your servant,
nor am I pure by speaking truth,
Supreme Lord who blessed Pārtha with your grace,
O holy place of pilgrimage
for those who praise you,
Lord of Tiruppukalūr resplendent with pools!

9
I have lighted a lamp
inside my body, and pushed the wick up,
to make it burn bright.
Grasping a means to release,
I try to rise,
but the five whom you have placed within me
to bar the way,
have proved stronger by far.
Lord of holy Pukalūr,
what shall I do?

193. Appar IV.103.1 *Ārūr (Tiruvārūr)*

O devotees who pass your time
in useless talk of worldly things
and in the care of this despicable frame,
in multiplying your karma,
in fattening the belly,
in getting entangled in family affairs!
Be saved! Smear the sacred ash
on yourselves,
become faithful devotees at the shade
of the feet of the Lord who dwells
in Ārūr of lotus ponds!

6 Acts of Devotion

(POEMS 194–212)

194. Appar IV.81.5 *Kōyil (Tillai)*

Treasure our human birth as a blessing,
O dear devotees of him who blessed Arjuna
with the Pāśupata shaft!
Have we not been born to serve him,
to be possessed
by the dancer of Tillai's Ampalam hall,
who once set the three citadels
aflame with his arrow?

Worship the Lord!

195. Campantar II.176 *Piramapuram (Cīrkāḻi)*

3
I beg you, good heart,
if you seek release,
think only of my Lord's holy feet.
Mouth, always sing the good fame
of the sweet ambrosia
of Piramapuram where wild geese live.
Eyes, always look upon
the Lord alone,
that he might show you his grace.

4
O mind, offer fresh flowers
only to the majestic holy feet
of the King who helps us overcome
the fear of death.
Tongue, keeping daily the good ritual path,
speak the praise
of the fire-hued god who lives
in Piramapuram of groves full of honey.

196. Campantar II.177.3 *Cāykkāṭu*

Good heart,
think of the Lord every day.
Who knows the course
of life and death?
If for my Lord of Cāykkāṭu alone
will my head daily bear flowers,
my ear hear his great name,
and tongue praise him in song,
good karma will surely be mine.

197. Appar IV.9 TIRUVAṄKAMĀLAI (THE HOLY GARLAND OF THE ORGANS OF SENSE)

7
Hands, join in worship,
strew fragrant flowers
on the Lord who binds
the hooded snake around his waist!
Hands, join in worship!

8
Of what use is the body
that never walked around
the temple of Śiva,
offering him flowers in the worship rite?
Of what use is this body?

198. Appar IV.20 *Ārūr (Tiruvārūr)*

6
O Father, you dwell in Tiruvārūr,
abounding in sacred waters
in which the whole world joyfully gathers
to bathe,
knowing: "To worship the Lord's feet with love
is to get rid of karma,"
and where women eager for water-play
swim and dive, and splash about,
and wash their hair.

10
Ayan̲ of the lotus flower seat
and the slayer of Iraṇiyan̲
sought in vain to see the King of Tiruvārūr
in his flaming form.
I sought and found him
when I entered the hearts of his devotees
who worship and praise him,
and sing his ritual hymns.

Invoke the Lord!

199. Campantar I.86.7 *Nallūr*

The men who never leave Nallūr,
who lift up their hands in worship,
crying, "Possess me!"
those whose hearts rest in the shade
of the feet of our Lord
whom the Himalayan gods praise as their king,
will no longer be perplexed.

200. Campantar I.89.3 *Erukkattampuliyūr*

Karma cannot touch
those who can cry, "Lord of the gods!
God, bull rider, madman who is
man, woman, and in-between,
moon-crowned god,
our King who lives in Erukkatampuliyūr's
shrine, which we revere!"

Dance, Weep, Sing!

201. Campantar I.35.3 *Vīḻimiḻalai*

The devotees who know
how to weep,
to dance and sing and rise, and again
fall at the father's feet,

to worship Vīḻimiḻalai—
they are worthy servants of the Lord.

202. Cuntarar VII.22.3 *Paḻamaṇṇippaṭikkarai*

Dance, lovers of Śiva,
become devotees of the Lord, crown yourselves
with dust from his feet!
Give up worldly life, end your suffering,
O devotees, gather together,
go straight to Paḻamaṇṇippaṭikkarai,
and sing of the place!

203. Appar V.135.8 *Iṉṉampar*

Our Lord of Iṉṉampar keeps account
of those who worship him
with flowers and praise,
and weep for love of him,
and cry out in their love,
as well as
those who waste their days
unaware of him.

204. Appar V.177.8 *Kuraṅkāṭutuṟai*

O devotees who have joined our group
out of love,
dance, weep, worship him,
sing his feet,
gather at Kuraṅkāṭutuṟai,
place of our Lord!

Pilgrims and Servants

205. Appar V.162 *Kacci Ēkampam*

3
Let us hasten to make a proper pilgrimage,
to offer worship at Ēkampam
in Kacci of flowering groves,
abode of the Lord with the dark throat,
the eight-armed, three-eyed god,

chanter of the Veda,
first among the gods.

6
If you do not wish the unfortunate fate
of the Buddhists, and those of the Jain faith,
praise with feeling Ēkampam in Kacci,
place of the Lord
whose beautiful feet are worshipped
with flowers.

7
Before old age and disease overcome us,
let us be saved, seeking as refuge
Ēkampam with fragrant groves,
saving shrine of our God
who is the Lord of the splendid immortals.

206. Appar V.209 ILIṄKAPURĀṆAK KUṞUNTOKAI (THE KUṞUNTOKAI POEM OF THE MANIFESTATION IN THE LIṄGA)

1
They did not seek and enter his abodes,
or joyfully pluck flowers for his worship.
The two tried to see the beautiful flame-hued Lord
in their pride.

2
They did not attain wisdom,
bathing him in flower-scented water,
or walk around his shrine,
wearing the sacred dot on the forehead.
The two sought to follow the blazing Lord of the Universe
in his flight.

3
They did not sweep and wash his temple yards clean,
they did not carry baskets of flowers for the rites.
The two sought to find the form

206. In this hymn Appar uses the myth of the humbling of Viṣṇu and Brahmā to suggest that true devotion alone will help one obtain the vision and experience of the Lord. v. 3. "Protector": "*kāppuk koḷḷi*," "guardian." *Kāppu* (protection) can also denote the hero's band or anklet. In the Tamil Śaiva tradition, *kāppu* often specifically refers to the sacred ash (as the devotee's protection). v. 7. Appar refers to the practice of ascetics of certain Śaiva sects—such as the Pāśupatas—of carrying the axe, the skull, and other attributes of Śiva.

of the skullbearing Lord, our protector,
in pursuit.

4
They did not meditate on him,
bathing him in milk and ghee,
they did not praise him without falsehood and deceit.
The two tried to behold the fiery-hued Lord
in his true form.

5
They did not weave garlands with *erukku* buds,
they did not proudly wear the loincloth.
In sheer arrogance,
the two tried to approach very near, and behold
the Lord with the matted hair.

6
They did not climb trees to gather flowers for him,
or meditate on him,
They did not bear water for his bathing rite.
The two tried to see the wise Lord's blazing form
in its full glory.

7
They did not carry the axe or skull bowl,
they did not prostrate themselves at his feet.
The two toiled hard to reach and to see
the scholar-Lord's lovely feet.

8
They did not shine, wearing the sacred ash,
they did not weave garlands of fragrant flowers.
The two tried to find the limits of my father's,
flame-colored bull rider's, form.

9
They did not pluck and weave the petals
of the newly blossomed blue lotus
for adorning his feet.
The two tried to measure the Lord who burned
Kāma, thief of love.

10
They did not wear the *rudrākṣa* beads,
or carry the skull as begging bowl,

they did not resoundingly blow the conch at his worship rite.
The two tried to pursue and behold the flame-colored Lord
whose form is the universe.

11
The Lord with the flowing matted red hair and holy form,
whom the red-eyed god and Brahmā
pursued everywhere and could not find,
revealed himself in the *liṅga*,
saying, "I am here."

207. Appar V.213 PĀVANĀCAK KUṞUNTOKAI (THE KUṞUNTOKAI POEM THAT DESTROYS SIN)

1
You who wish to be freed from the grip
of sin and blame,
love the feet of the god
who loves to bathe in the five gifts of the cow,
think joyfully of them—
our savior will join you in grace.

2
Why bathe in the Ganges or the Kaveri,
why make a pilgrimage to Kumari's cool, fragrant beach,
why bathe in the ocean's swelling waves?
All this is in vain, if you do not think:
"The Lord is everywhere."

3
Why become a scholar or study the Law,
why give away money and food in charity,
why learn to add and multiply?
All this is in vain, if you do not say,
"He is dear to me."

4
Why chant the Veda? Why perform sacrifices?
Why study the Lawbooks every day,
why know the six Vedāṅga texts?
All this is in vain,
if you do not love the Lord.

207, v. 2. In this verse "*kumari*" could be a reference to the river Kumari. See note to Poem 69.

5
Why rise at dawn and bathe?
Why practice each rite according to the rules?
Why perform sacrifices at great altars of fire?
All this is in vain if you do not say,
"He is my friend."

6
Why roam in forest and town?
Why practice extreme penance?
Why give up meat, why stare into space?
The Lord's blessing is yours only if you say,
"He is wise."

7
Why wear strange costumes and roam in packs?
Why wander and suffer, torturing the flesh?
No fruit is yours until you sing
the Dancer who dances in the Ampalam hall.

8
Why keep fasts, why starve?
Why climb hilltops to sit in penance?
Why make pilgrimages to bathe in holy rivers?
All this is in vain if you do not say:
"He is the eternal Lord."

9
Even if you bathe at a thousand sacred places,
if you have no love for Aran̲,
you are nothing but a fool
who tries to contain a flowing stream
in a leaky pot.

10
Why torment yourself with all kinds of pious vows?
There is no help for you
if you will not cling
to the foot with the ringing hero's anklet
which crushed the frame
of the demon who lifted the hill.

208. Appar V.204.9

The Lord with the golden hair
who dwells in the hearts

of those who melt in loving thoughts of him,
laughs at the flowers and water
that false men offer at the worship rite,
mocking them.

The Devotees of the Lord

209. Campantar II.242.2 *Valañcuḻi*

My powerful evil karma has been destroyed,
now that I keep joyful company
with devotees who faithfully serve
the Lord who lives in Valañcuḻi,
sharing his form with the Goddess
who wears flowers in her hair,
our God who saved the suppliant gods
by devouring the poison spewed by the wide sea.

210. Campantar II.150.3 *Veṇṇiyūr*

They are blameless, who praise
the ripe fruit,
the sage who joins and takes over
those who are ripe with love for him,
the one Lord of the three worlds,
the good God whom good folk worship
in Veṇṇi, where he sweetly abides.

211. Appar VI.309.10 TAṈIT TIRUTTĀṆṬAKAM (THE DETACHED SACRED TĀṆṬAKAM POEM)

Were they to offer me both treasures
of Kubera's world,
and give me earth and heaven itself to rule,
the wealth of decaying mortals
would be as nothing to me,
when those who gave
were not single-minded devotees

209. "Has been destroyed": "viṇṭoḻintaṉa," literally, "has burst, split, exploded."

211. "Great Lord": "*mātēvar*," Śiva as Mahādeva. Appar speaks of "*caṅkaniti*" and "*patumaniti*," the two principal treasures of Kubera, god of wealth. Sanskrit *śaṅkha* (conch) and *padma* (lotus) are code words for extremely high figures (ten million crore and hundred billions, by one reckoning).

of our great Lord.
But the leper with rotting limbs,
the outcaste, even the foul *pulaiyaṉ*
who skins and eats cows,
even these men, if they are servants
of him who shelters the Ganges in his long hair,
I worship them,
they are gods to me.

212. Campantar II.177.1 *Cāykkāṭu*

They will never be reborn,
but will enter the highest state;
they won't lose heart on earth,
they won't suffer from hunger,
nor endure the pain of disease.
Those who know and learn to know the Lord
have no use for heaven,
for they belong to the feet
of our Lord in Cāykkāṭu in Pukār
whose long highways are lined with palaces.

7 Singing of Śiva

(POEMS 213–220)

213. Appar IV.103.3 *Ārūr (Tiruvārūr)*

Flowers make ornaments,
and so does gold;
yet if our Lord who sweetly abides in Ārūr
were to desire an ornament for himself,
simple heart, let us honor him
with the ornament of Tamil song!

214. Campantar III.329.1 *Vaikāvūr*

The home of the Lord who delights in the songs
of the lowliest of his devotees,
though stammered out in sobs,
though lacking rhyme and meter
and quite out of tune, is Vaikā,
where coconuts full of sweet water
knock down clusters of *kamuku* fruit,
which crush to pulp
ripe plantains fallen in the paddyfields.

215. Campantar II.242.1 *Valañcuḻi*

Great is the merit you have earned, my heart!
That you worship him with words,
saying praises and singing songs of love
for the chieftain of Valañcuḻi by the eternal Kaveri
whose stream is full of pearls,
is surely the fruit
of good deeds once done
on this dark sea-girt earth.

216. Appar IV.77.3

Devotees who wash the floor at the Lord's temples
will gain ten times more merit

214. "Rhyme and meter": "*kavikōḷ*" literally, "the properties of verse."
216. "The ineffable knowledge of the true faith": "colliṉ meyññeṟi ñāṉam."

than those who sweep them clean.
For those who weave fresh flower garlands for his worship,
pure heaven itself is the reward.
The ineffable knowledge of the true faith
will be theirs, who light lamps at his shrines.
And singing hymns for the Lord
is the sure path to his boundless grace.

Kaṭaikkāppu: The Fruit of Devotion

217. Campantar II.242.11 *Valañcuḻi*

Karma will not afflict them,
nor will they suffer in this birth or the next,
if they love to listen
to men who sing, having learned well
the words and music of this garland of Tamil verse
composed by Ñāṉacampantaṉ,
brahmin prince from fertile Kāḻi,
in praise of the cure for the cycle of birth,
the god who lives in Valañcuḻi
with the Goddess as half his self.

218. Campantar I.129.11 *Kaḻumalam*

Those who know as the sole guide for their tongue
these ten verses
that noble Ñāṉacampantaṉ, friend of the good,
has composed with great affection
on the feet of God who lives in Kaḻumalam's shrine
which men of learning worship and praise,
will win the Goddess of wealth
and rule the whole earth,
and be on their way
to the three-eyed Lord's feet.

219. Cuntarar VII.43.11 *Mutukuṉṟam*

Let great philosophers and wise men,
let the most venerable sages,

219. "Kissed by the . . . Muttāṟu": "*mutti muttāṟu.*" The commentator for the *Tēvāram* Ātīṉam edition takes "*mutti*" to mean "release" (Sanskrit *mukti*), reading : "the Muttāṟu that brings release."

end their misery by praising
the Lord of Mutukuṉṟu's hill
kissed by the circling Muttāṟu river,
in these words of the Lord's slave Ūraṉ—
a madman's babble.

220. Campantar II.150.4 *Veṇṇiyūr*

What shall I say
of those who do not sing
of the Primal Lord,
the sole God and savior of the three worlds,
the Lord who joins and takes over
those who love him dearly,
my Father who lives in beautiful Veṇṇi?
Poor devils!

220. "*Eṉ ceyvār*": literally, "what can they do?" "Joins": "*kalantu.*" "Takes over": "*ārttāṉai,*" from *ār-*, in the sense of "mingle, pervade, bind."

SECTION IV

Mūvar Mutalikaḷ: The First Three Saints

There is no creed nobler than Śaivism;
there is no God greater than our Śiva.
The four saints composed the beautiful sacred hymns
of the *Tēvāram* and *Tiruvācakam*,
imbued with the true meaning of the four Vedas,
for our liberation—
Their holy feet are our life support!
—Caiva Ellappa Nāvalar, *Aruṇaik kalampakam*

Of the exemplary and eventful lives of the first three saints, so well known in the Tamil Śaiva tradition after the age of the Nāyaṉārs, we catch only a few glimpses in the *Tēvāram*. Yet these glimpses have the value of illuminating for us the saints' own perspective on certain incidents in their lives that have fired the popular imagination. This section is devoted to poems containing such autobiographical and historical material. The selections are arranged in four subsections, the first three dealing with the lives of Campantar, Appar, and Cuntarar, and the fourth containing verses and hymns in which the three poets refer to other Tamil saints and devotees. Prefatory notes are attached to the first three groups of poems to help place the historical material in the context of the narrative of the saint's life as given in the *Periya purāṇam* and oral tradition. The anthology concludes with Cuntarar's celebrated *Tirut toṇṭat tokai* (The List of the Holy Devotees).

1 Campantar: The Blessed Child

(POEMS 221–233)

The Milk of Wisdom

In the closing verses of his hymns, Campantar identifies himself as a Kavuṇiyaṉ (a brahmin of the Kauṇḍinya *gotra*) from Cīrkāḻi. The saint's father and mother are identified in the *Periya purāṇam* as Civapātavirutayar and Pakavatiyār. "Tōṭutaiya ceviyaṉ," the opening hymn of the *Tēvāram* (I.1; Poem 221, see also Poem 183) is traditionally associated with Campantar's initiation into poetry and the saintly life. The three-year-old child followed Civapātavirutayar to the temple; leaving Campantar on the steps leading to the tank or reservoir (*kuḷam*) in the temple, the father went down to bathe. Crying "O Father, O Mother!" ("*ammaiyē appā*"), the child turned toward the *vimāna* of the temple. Suddenly, Śiva and the Goddess, riding on the bull, appeared before him. Śiva told the Goddess Umā to feed Campantar with milk from her own breast in a golden cup. This was the "milk of wisdom" (*ñāṉappāl*), and upon drinking it the child became "Ñāṉacampantar" ("He who is related to God through divine knowledge") and "Āḷuṭaiya Piḷḷaiyār" ("the Lord's Child"); Campantar had been blessed with the gift of sacred poetry (see illus. 2). Upon returning from his bath, the father saw milk trickling from the child's mouth. Enraged, thinking that someone had fed his child, thus breaking caste taboos against interdining, Civapātavirutayar said to Campantar: "Tell me at once, who fed you? This food might be polluting!" In reply, the child pointed to the temple and spontaneously sang hymn I.1: "He wears a woman's earring in one ear . . ." The father and all who had gathered there witnessed and celebrated the Campantar's divine vision and gift. "The milk of wisdom" incident is commemorated annually at the Cīrkāḻi temple. Although there is no reference in I.1 to the events narrated in the *Periya purāṇam*, in III.282.2 (Poem 222) Campantar does speak of "divine food in a golden cup," an angry father, and divine grace.

221. Campantar I.1.1 *Piramapuram (Cīrkāḻi)*

He wears a woman's earring on one ear;
riding on his bull,

crowned with the pure white crescent moon,
his body smeared with ash from the burning-ground,
he is the thief who stole my heart.
He is the Lord who lives in fine Piramapuram,
where he once blessed with his grace
Brahmā of the lotus seat
who worshipped him.

222. Campantar III.282.2 *Kaḻumalam (Cīrkāḻi)*

When I was rebuked by my angry father,
who rejected as a harmful thing
the sweet dish of wisdom
served in a flowerlike golden cup,
the great Lord possessed me.
He is the noble god who wears
the golden earring on one ear,
and he dwells with the innocent girl
in the rich city of Kaḻumalam.

On the Road

Like Appar, Campantar set out on an extended pilgrimage, in the course of which he received several gifts from Śiva, including a pearl palanquin and golden cymbals. In addition to winning gold coins from Śiva to aid his father and other devotees, the saint performed miracles of healing the sick and reviving the dead: he cured his Śaiva companions of a shivering fever or ague, cured a woman of epilepsy in Pāccilācciramam (hymn I.44) and brought to life the bones of Pūmpāvai in Mayilāppūr (Poem 99). Two such miraculous incidents are said to form the background of poems 223 and 224. According to the hagiographers, when Appar and Campantar were halting in Vīḻimiḻalai with their entourage, the land was afflicted by famine. Śiva of Vīḻimiḻalai came to the aid of his devotees, granting a gold coin every day to each of the saints. Appar and Campantar were able to feed friends with this money. However, the coins Campantar received were "*kaṟaikoḷ kācu*": old, soiled coins, which were out of circulation. Campantar soon discovered that, unlike Appar's entourage, his friends had to wait a long time for their food, because he had to exchange his coin at a discount (*vāci, vaṭṭam*) every day, while Appar's coin was discount-free. Disheartened at the Lord's discrimination, the saint sang

222. There is a pun in the expression "*pōtaiyār*": "like a flower"; "full of knowledge or wisdom (*bodha*)." "The innocent girl," "*pētai*," is the Goddess.

Poem 223, asking Śiva to make his own coin discount-free. The second story concerns the miracle of the temple door at Maṟaikkāṭu. Campantar and Appar traveled together to several great shrines, including the temple in Maṟaikkāṭu (Vedāraṇyam), so named because of the tradition that the Vedas themselves once worshipped Śiva in that place. Upon arriving at the shrine, the two saints and the devotees who accompanied them found that the door of the temple always remained closed, presumably out of deference to the ancient presence of the divine Vedas at Maṟaikkāṭu. At Campantar's request, Appar sang a hymn (Poem 242), asking Śiva to open the door so that his devotees might obtain the vision (*darśana*) for which they had come. At the end of the visit, Appar turned to Campantar and asked him to cause the "Sacred Closure" (*tirukkāppu*) of the door with a hymn. Hymn II.173 (Poem 224), Campantar's response, achieved the miracle.

223. Campantar I.92 *Vīḻimiḻalai*

1
Give us gold coins,
make them discount-free!
Let there be no blame,
O Miḻalai's blameless Lord!

2
O God, you rule
Miḻalai, town of brahmins!
Restore your tainted coin
to its proper worth!

224. Campantar II.173.1 *Maṟaikkāṭu*

O young man, you who live in Maṟaikkāṭu
surrounded by sweet groves,
place where the four Vedas sing your praise
and bow to you—I beg you,
quickly favor me with your grace!
Give me a sign! Kindly shut your temple door!

Victory in Ālavāy

"The brightest chapter in Sambandar's life is his expedition to Madurai and his reestablishment of Śaivism in the Pantiya capital and the reconversion of Kunpandiyan" (Suddhananda Bharati, *The Grand Epic of Śaivism*, p. 141).

The Pāṇṭiya queen Maṅkaiyarkkaraci and the minister Kulaccirai were devout Śaivas. Grieved at the excesses of the Jain monks in the Pāṇṭiya (Pandya) kingdom, and the king's support of the Jains, the queen invited Campantar to come to Ālavāy (Maturai), the Pāṇṭiya capital, and drive out the Jains. The monks attempted to set fire to the Nāyaṉār's house. Campantar sang: "Make the flame, kindled by the Jains to burn me, turn toward the Pandyan king," and the king was suddenly afflicted by a burning fever. The king's Jain physicians could not help him. In desperation, he agreed to submit to the miraculous healing power of the child-saint and promised to reconvert to Śaivism if Campantar were to succeed in his effort. The Nāyaṉār cured the king with the application of sacred ash to the chanting of his hymn "mantiramāvatu nīṟu."

When the angry Jains challenged Campantar to compete with them in religious debate, the saint was undaunted, and he reassured Queen Maṅkaiyarkkaraci regarding his capability. Campantar had to face the Jain challenge in many ways. The monks first tested the power of the saint's hymns by casting the hymns into fire (*aṉalvātam*) and then into water (*puṉalvātam*); in both cases the palm-leaf manuscripts emerged unscathed. In Poem 231 Campantar refers to this incident. Though there is no clear allusion to physical deformity in hymn III.312.1, the verb *ōṅkuka* ("rise tall, prosper," in "*vēntaṉum ōṅkuka*" ("may the king rise in fame [lit., 'rise tall']!") is interpreted as a reference to yet another miracle, in which Campantar transformed the "hunchback" Pāṇṭiya king (Kūṉpāṇṭiyaṉ) into "Niṉṟacīr Neṭumāṟaṉ" ("King Māṟaṉ who stood tall"). There is no evidence in Campantar's hymns to support the popular stories, recorded in the biographical poems of Nampi Āṇṭār Nampi, the *Periya purāṇam*, and *Tiruviḷaiyāṭaṟ purāṇam*, of Campantar's Jain opponents being impaled on stakes as punishment for their persecution of the saint. Nevertheless, the fact that the saint reserves the tenth verse in his hymns for invective directed toward the Jains speaks for the importance of the Jain controversy in Campantar's life.

225. Campantar III.378 *Ālavāy (Maturai)*

1
This is Ālavāy,
where the Lord of the host of spirits, flame-red god,
dwells with the goddess Aṅkayaṟkaṇṇi,
and gives us the Vedas and every kind of wealth.

225, v. 1. Aṅkayaṟkaṇṇi: the goddess Mīnākṣī, "Goddess who has cool eyes shaped like the *kayal* fish." v. 3. The queen is portrayed as engaging in playing ball, one of the favorite sports of young women and girls. v. 4. "The river": *aṇaṅku*, a celestial damsel; here, the river Ganges. "Honors": "appreciates virtues" (*kuṇaṅ koṭu*). The "strands of pearls" on the queen's breast (v. 7) is a fine local touch. The Pandyan (Pāṇṭiya) kingdom was famous for its pearl fisheries, and the Pandyan monarchs always wore pearls.

This is Ālavāy,
where he is sung and worshipped every day
by Maṅkaiyarkkaraci, lotus-lady,
Pandyan queen and princess of the Cōḻa clan,
virtuous woman with striped bracelets on her arms.

2
This is Ālavāy,
abode of the god who rides on the white bull,
chief of the immortals,
Śiva who fully reveals himself
to those who have utterly renounced worldly life,
This is Ālavāy,
where he is praised with loving devotion
by Kulacciṟai, the king's minister
who wears the white ash,
and willingly falls at the feet of Śiva's devotees.

3
This is Ālavāy, renowned shrine
of the Lord with the matted hair
adorned by beautiful pearls, the snake, and the river,
the flowers of the *mattam*, cool *erukkam*, and *vaṉṉi*,
and the evening moon.
This is Ālavāy,
where he is worshipped by the Pandyan queen
with coral-red lips and eyes like the carp,
who always wears Śiva's sacred ash
and plays with a ball.

4
This is Ālavāy shrine,
abode of the Lord whose matted hair is adorned
by the fragrant *koṉṟai*, the moon, and the cruel snake,
the river, and the garland of *vaṉṉi* and pretty *kūviḷam*.
This is the rich temple with tall towers,
place of worship for Kulacciṟai,
who honors and serves Śiva's devotees,
whether they come alone or in pilgrim bands.

5
This is Ālavāy,
abode of Umā's lover, the Lord who bears
the bright axe and the blazing trident,
along with the noose and goad and the fawn.

This is the shrine
where he is sweetly praised and worshipped every day
by the Pandyan queen,
majestic beauty, like a wild goose on a red lotus,
well-adorned lady with the lovely brow
and mound of Venus like a cobra's hood.

6
This is Ālavāy,
place of the Lord who bears the trident and the deer,
black-throated god whose cloak is the elephant hide,
of him who has the rippling river in his matted hair.
This is the shrine
where he is praised by pious Kulacciṟai
as all that is good and evil,
the Master and the homeless one,
the householder who has no family of his own.

7
This is Ālavāy,
where our Father dwells with Umā,
like a clear crystal hill
joined with a brilliant emerald.
This is the shrine
where he is worshipped with proper rites
by the devout Pandyan queen,
on whose breast graced by strands of pearls,
the sacred ash mingles with sandal paste.

8
This is Ālavāy, abode
of the matted-haired Lord
who won as his devotee the arrogant Rāvaṇa,
having crushed his twenty strong arms.
This is the shrine where Kulacciṟai worships,
who honors all who virtuously chant
the five sacred syllables that are the ornament of the tongue,
and wear the pious emblems
of the loincloth and sacred ash.

9
This is Ālavāy,
abode of Umā's Lord who rose in space
so that the two gods, flying up and down,
could not measure him.

This is the shrine
where the Pandyan queen with voice sweet as *paṇ* music,
daughter of the golden-crowned Cōḻa king
who is sovereign lord of the whole earth,
worships Śiva with the proper rites.

10
This is Ālavāy,
abode of the Lord of the Universe,
who is beyond the deluded doctrines
of the base Buddhist monks.
This is the shrine
where devout Kulacciṟai worships every day,
delighting in the praise heaped on the Lord's glory
by devotees who come from everywhere.

11
They will reign in bliss,
praised by the Himalayan gods,
who can sweetly sing these Tamil verses
of Ñāṉacampantaṉ of stone-walled Kāḻi,
praising in Ālavāy the holy feet of Ālavāy's Lord,
adorned by the adoration
of virtuous Kulacciṟai and the Pandyan queen.

226. Campantar III.309 *Ālavāy (Maturai)*

1
Save me,
O Red Lord who lives in holy Ālavāy!
Make the flame
kindled by the false Jains to burn me,
slowly consume the Pandyan king instead.

3
Save me,
O Cokkaṉ of Ālavāy
who destroyed Dakṣa's sacrifice!
Make the flame
kindled by the crooked Jains to burn me,
turn toward the Pandyan king instead.

226, v. 3. Cokkaṉ: "the Seductive Lord" (Cokkanātar), Tamil counterpart of Sundareśvara ("the Beautiful Lord"), the name of Śiva in the Maturai temple.

11
They will own the blameless treasure,
who can recite the ten verses Ñāṉacampantaṉ sang
to direct the flame toward the Pandyan king,
pleasing the world
by the grace of the Father,
the Primal Being in Ālavāy.

227. Campantar II.202 TIRUNĪṞṞUP PATIKAM (THE HYMN OF THE SACRED ASH) *Ālavāy*

1
The sacred ash is our mantra,
the ash covers the bodies of the gods;
the sacred ash is all beautiful things,
the ash is all that is praised.
The sacred ash is the tantra text,
the ash is the core of our faith.
The sacred ash belongs to the Lord of Ālavāy,
spouse of Umā of the red lips.

11
They are pious men,
who can sing the ten verses
which Ñāṉacampantaṉ, prince of Pukali,
sang in praise of the sacred ash
of Ālavāy's Lord who rides on the mighty, warlike bull,
to cure the southern king of his burning disease.

228. Campantar III.297 *Ālavāy*

1
Doe-eyed lady, great Pandyan queen, listen!
Do not fear for my safety, thinking me a child, barely weaned.

227, v. 1. "The tantra text": the Āgama. As in Poem 118 ("mantiramun tantiramum maruntum āki"), in this context mantra and tantra also refer to the magical formulae and rites used by folk healers. The implication is that the ash is the most powerful mantra of all, and it is indeed used as a healing agent. "Faith": *camayam*, "religion." v. 2. "Southern king": "*teṉṉaṉ*," a title of the Pandyan king.

228, v. 1. "Elephant": Āṉaimalai, a hill near Maturai, a stronghold of the Jains in Campantar's time. v. 2. Prakrit: *pākatam*; the various Middle Indo-Aryan dialects used by the Jains. The Śaivas looked down upon the Jains for using these "corrupt" languages in their religious writings and discourse. The contempt for Jain names (v. 4) expresses a similar prejudice.

With Araṉ of Ālavāy by my side,
I will easily defeat those scoundrels
who practice many torturous rites,
living on Elephant and other hills!

2
With Araṉ of Ālavāy by my side,
I will easily defeat those filthy Jain monks
who wander like elephants in rut,
and eat their food standing, embarrassing pious men,
and mutilate the good Sanskrit of the Āgama and mantra texts,
loudly declaiming in the corrupt Prakrit tongue.

4
With Araṉ of Ālavāy by my side,
I will easily defeat
those blind fools with names like
Candusena, Indusena, Dharmasena,
dark Kandusena, and Kanakasena,
who roam about like apes, and know
neither good Tamil nor the Sanskrit language.

11
There is no misery
for those who can chant these ten verses
well composed by the Tamil poet Ñāṉacampantaṉ,
prince of glorious Pukali,
in the court of the Pandyan king
with the glittering crown, proclaiming,
"Since Cokkaṉ of holy Ālavāy dwells within me,
I will easily defeat those Jain rogues!"

229. Campantar III.305 *Ālavāy*

1
Three-eyed god
who flayed the wild elephant
and put on the hide,
is it your gracious will
that I should defeat in debate
the Jain rogues who offer no sacrifice?

229, v. 11. "Dishonor": "*paḻi*," blame; the dishonor of being souls bound by karma.

4
Primal Lord, O god in holy Ālavāy,
for the sake of justice,
will you favor me with your grace,
so that I may defeat in debate
the evil Jains
who do not study the sacred texts?

5
O world-renowned god,
you who live in holy Ālavāy
crowded with devotees who worship you,
tell me, will you favor me with your grace,
so that I may steadily defeat in debate
the Jain monks who eat out of their hands?

10
Axe-bearing youth in holy Ālavāy
with softly murmuring streams,
will you favor me with your grace,
so that I may destroy the destructive Jains
who gather beached fish from salt marshes by the sea?

11
If you want to put an end to dishonor
say the words of true Ñāṉacampantaṉ
who cries, in rhythmic Tamil verse,
"O god of holy Ālavāy which rings with Tamil song!"
to blot out the stain of the wicked Jains.

230. Campantar III.366 *Ālavāy*

1
God who shares his body with the Goddess,
Primal Being who dwells in southern Ālavāy,
may your glory reign supreme in the world!
Is it your gracious will,
that I should defeat in debate, and destroy,
the indecent Jain monks
who slander the Vedic sacrifice?

230, v. 3. Unlike the Buddhist monks who shaved their heads, the Jain ascetics plucked out the hair in handfuls. v. 11. "Emaciated": "*vāṭalmēṉi*," "with bodies emaciated from starvation." "Kūṭal" or "Nāṉmāṭakkūṭal" is another name for the city of Maturai.

3
Lord who holds the fawn and the axe,
Primal Being who dwells in southern Ālavāy!
May your glory reign supreme in the world!
Is it your gracious will,
that I should annihilate in debate
those great sinners
who neglect the Vedic rite and wear mats as robes,
the base men who pluck the hair from their heads?

11
They are blessed, who can sing this hymn
composed by Campantaṉ of Kāḻi, city of great towers,
to torture the emaciated Jains,
when he had left the court
of Kūṭal Ālavāy's king.

231. Campantar III.345 *Naḷḷāṟu*

1
Cast into the bright flames
the holy name of Naḷḷāṟu's Lord
whose body is cool and gleaming
from embracing the beautiful, cool, lustrous breasts
of the mountain's daughter,
woman who glows with the loveliness
of a young sprout!
It will emerge unharmed—
This is the truth!

11
They will become pure souls free of sorrow,
who know these ten true verses
that Ñāṉacampantaṉ, of Kaḻumalam town—
where the Lord who is our good recourse dwells,
embracing the beautiful breasts
of the young woman with the slender waist—
recited in the court of the king
when his verses were cast into the flames.

231, v. 11. "True verses": "*coṟṟeri*" can mean either "the truth in words," or "a sequence of verses." "Our good recourse": "*naṟṟiṟam*," "the good path or course (to release)."

232. Campantar III.312.1 TIRUPPĀCURAM (THE HYMN OF BLESSING)

Long live brahmins!
May the gods and cows flourish!
May cool rain fall!
May the king rise in fame!
May evil things perish!
May Śiva's name prevail!
May the whole world be freed from suffering!

Divine Marriage

Campantar's union with Śiva was effected in as miraculous a manner as the rest of his dealings with his Lord. In spite of Campantar's reluctance, the parents arranged a marriage for the sixteen-year-old saint with the daughter of Nampāṇṭār Nampi, a friend of Civapātavirutayar. The wedding ceremony commenced with great pomp in the town of Nallūrp Perumaṇam, where thousands of devotees of Śiva and Campantar had gathered for the event. As soon as the ceremony was completed, Campantar sang his final hymn (Poem 233) in which he begged the Lord to unite with him and thus liberate him from all earthly ties, including marriage. At these words, a great blaze of light enveloped the saint and his wife. At Campantar's command the entire assembly entered this flame and thus joined the saint in his final beatific union with his God. Campantar's "divine wedding" is commemorated annually at the temple in Nallūrp Perumaṇam.

233. Campantar III.383.1 *Nallūrp Perumaṇam*

Not for me is the wedding rite
in which the bride mounts the stone.

232. The first verse of this hymn of blessing (*pācuram*) contains a formulaic benediction, in which the poet blesses brahmins, cows, and the king, and prays for rain. According to the traditional legend, when the Jains cast the manuscript that contained their heretical doctrine ("*atti nātti*," "[God] is and is not") into the Vaikai River, it floated away. By contrast, this hymn, which Campantar composed on the spot and cast into the river, floated against the current and survived the ordeal. Cēkkiḻār gives a detailed exposition of the meaning of all the verses in this *patikam* in *Periya purāṇam* 2720 ff. (edition with the commentary of C.K.S. Mutaliyār).

233. Nallūrp Perumaṇam, now known as Āchāḻpuram, is the venue of the annual celebration of Campantar's wedding and union with Śiva in the month of Vaikāci. The ceremony in which the bride places one foot on the grinding stone and swears fidelity to her husband (*ammi mitittal*) is an ancient rite that continues to form part of Tamil weddings.

I have sung many hymns
in many towns, from Kaḻumalam on.
Have they not yielded their truth,
O god who is crowned
with the fragrant flowers of my words,
O Master who dwells in Nallūrp Perumaṇam,
home of your devotees?

2 Appar: The Reformed Monk

(POEMS 234–245)

Affliction and Reform

Tirunāvukkaracar (Appar; see illus. 3) was born Maruṇīkkiyār in Tiruvāmūr, near the holy shrine of Tiruvatikai (Atikai) Vīraṭṭāṉam, to the Vellala Pukaḻaṉār and his wife Mātiṉiyār. Maruṇīkkiyār's sister Tilakavatiyār (Tilakavati) was betrothed to Kalippakai, one of the sixty-three Nāyaṉārs. When Kalippakai died in battle, Tilakavati devoted her life to Śaiva piety, while Maruṇīkkiyār, in search of a fulfilling personal religion, turned to Jainism. He became a respected Jain monk in the Digambara sect, took the name Tarumacēṉar (Dharmasena), and soon became head of the Jain monastery in Tiruppātirippuliyūr. Tarumacēṉar began to suffer from acute colitis; though he tried many remedies, he could find no cure for the intense pain that racked his stomach. Meanwhile, Tilakavati prayed to Śiva, Lord of Atikai, to cure her brother and to bring him back to the true faith. Impelled by her devotion and Śiva's grace, Tarumacēṉar returned to Tiruvāmūr, where Tilakavati gave him the healing sacred ash (*tirunīṟu*) and the five-syllable mantra "namaccivāya." She then took him to the temple at Atikai, where Tarumacēṉar burst into song, composing the hymn "*kūṟṟāyiṉavāṟu*" (IV.1; Poem 234). Upon singing the second verse, the monk was miraculously cured, and at the end of the hymn the Lord's voice was heard declaring: "I name you Tirunāvukkaracar (Sanskrit, Vāgīśa), King of Speech!" Nāvukkaracar, later called "Appar" ("father") by Campantar, dwelt for a long time in Atikai Vīraṭṭāṉam, devoting himself to Śaiva worship and piety.

The other hymns in this group are typical of the songs in which Appar repents his life as a Jain and celebrates his transformation.

234. Appar IV.1 *Atikai Vīraṭṭāṉam*

1
You won't cure my deadly disease.
I do not know what evil deeds I have done.

234. The commentators do not agree on the interpretation of verse 5 of this hymn. According to M. S. Māṇikkavācaka Mutaliyār (*Tēvāram* Ātīṉam edition), the guardian who

O bull rider, I cling to your feet
day and night,
yet you won't reveal yourself,
but make my belly and bowels twist with pain.
I can't bear this any longer,
O Lord who dwells in Atikai's
Keṭila Vīraṭṭāṉam shrine!

2
I made my heart your abode,
I always think of you.
Yet I am tortured by pain beyond imagining.
Why won't you cure this poisonous disease
that twists my guts,
and deliver me from fear,
O Lord who dwells in Atikai's
Keṭila Vīraṭṭāṉam shrine?

4
Once you were angry with me,
afflicted me with disease
as punishment for my ignorance.
Now that I am your own true servant,
won't you free me from this burning pain?
Tell me, is it not the duty of the Master
to end the karma of those who seek refuge,
O Lord who dwells in Atikai's
Keṭila Vīraṭṭāṉam shrine,
home of women who have
the graceful gait of the wild goose?

5
I spurned the good protection
of those who cared for me, turning instead
to the man who stood on the shore.
Since he has pushed me into deep water,
telling me to find my own way,

"cared" for Appar is his sister Tilakavatiyār, and the man or men on the shore ("*karai niṉṟavar*") represent(s) the Jains who converted Appar to their religion. C.K.S. Mutaliyār (commentary on *Periya purāṇam* 1335) suggests that the guardian and the man on the shore are one and the same person. In verse 7, it is best to take "*uyarntēṉ maṉaivāḻkkai*" as meaning "I renounced [transcended] worldly life [with none but you for my master]"; this is in keeping with the tradition that Appar was a Jain monk before his conversion. The alternative is to take the phrase as meaning, "I took pride in worldly life . . . because I had no master to guide me."

I have found no safe haven,
can't swim ashore.
I have never heard of such a thing,
and my bowels writhe in pain,
O Lord who dwells
in the Keṭila Vīraṭṭāṉam shrine
in Atikai with the sounding river!

6
I have never failed to worship you
with flowers and incense and water,
never failed to sing you in melodious Tamil songs.
In joy and in sorrow I have remembered you,
your name has never left my tongue!
O Lord who wanders begging for alms
in a dead man's skull,
cure me of the deadly disease
that consumes my flesh—
I suffer, O Lord who dwells in Atikai's
Keṭila Vīraṭṭāṉam shrine!

7
I rose above worldly life, above household and riches,
but had no master to guide me.
You have possessed me now, I have become your good servant.
Yet you will not cure
the painful disease that afflicts me.
I am terrified, I faint, as my bowels
are twisted and ravaged by pain,
O Lord who dwells in Atikai's
Keṭila Vīraṭṭāṉam shrine!

9
O god with a body that glitters like gold,
Lord with the matted red hair
and slender crescent moon!
You won't put an end to my troubles,
to my anguish, and my disease.
If this is how you reward your devotees,
how will men like me ever know you?
Your love is my only hope,
O Lord who dwells in Atikai's
Keṭila Vīraṭṭāṉam shrine!

10
You cloak yourself in the elephant's flayed hide,
and dance on the burning-ground.
Don't you remember granting grace to the haughty demon
after you had crushed him under the high hill?
I faint, I writhe in pain, I fall, I rise—
banish my pain,
O Lord who dwells
in the Keṭila Vīraṭṭāṉam shrine
in Atikai with the sounding river!

235. Appar IV.39 *Tiruvaiyāṟu*

1
O god who pierced the delusion
that afflicted me
when I joined the Jains
and became a wicked monk!
O bright flame, celestial being
who stands as the pure path,
bull among the immortals,
honey who dwells in Tiruvaiyāṟu!
I wander as your servant,
worshipping and singing your feet.

2
Calling it a great penance, everyday I carried
the peacock-feather fan under my arm;
a fool, I was whirled about
like the great bar of a loom;
but now that I rejoice in the company
of my honey who dwells in Tiruvaiyāṟu
praised and adored by Vāli,
my heart swells in beauty.

235. In this hymn Appar criticizes some of the practices of the Jain monks: the "yellowing teeth" of verse 4 are attributed to the monks' practice of not brushing their teeth. In verse 2 Appar refers to the local tradition that Vāli, the monkey-king who was killed by Rāma in the *Rāmāyaṇa*, worshipped Śiva at Tiruvaiyāṟu. v. 5. "False vows": C.K.S. Mutaliyār (*Periya purāṇam* commentary) takes "*vaṭukkaḷ*" to mean "men of bad character," instead of "heresies" or "false practices." Māṇikkavācaka Mutaliyār (*Tēvāram* Ātīṉam edition) interprets "pallurai" in verse 7 as referring to the Jain doctrine of relative pluralism (*anekānta-vāda*), which gives rise to the Jain style of relativistic argument (*syādvāda*), in which propositions are shown to be valid only when they can assert the simultaneous truth of seemingly contradictory ideas.

3
O mind who made me cling
to the Jains who carry mats around,
considering it a great penance—
what shall I do with you?
O heart who cleaves to my honey
who dwells in Tiruvaiyāṟu with its lotus pond,
I love you!

4
I don't know how to get rid
of the heart that loved
the weak and filthy Jains
with their yellowing teeth.
Those who know
how to worship with fragrant offerings
my honey who dwells in holy Aiyāṟu
which the whole world praises
will put a stop to karma.

5
Fool heart, why did you
torture yourself with false vows,
thinking it a great penance
to smear the body with bitter powders?
Go to the honey who dwells in Tiruvaiyāṟu
where the *vāḷai* fish leap in pools,
and meditate on him—
That is the true ascetic vow.

7
When I think of the long years spent
in following the contradictory teachings of the Jains,
I feel faint.
When I think day and night
of the honey who dwells in holy Aiyāṟu,
town of jasmine groves,
I am filled with sweet delight.

236. Appar IV.102 *Ārūr (Tiruvārūr Mūlaṭṭāṉam)*

1
Pursued by packs of Jain monks, powerful rogues,
will I ever have the good fortune

236. The "Lord-who-dwells-in-the-anthill" in verse 2 is Vaṉmīkanātar, the name by

of becoming the devotee
of devotees who come weeping for love,
to the holy Mūlaṭṭāṉam shrine
of him of the beautiful feet adorned by ringing anklets,
Śiva of the shining matted hair,
who lives in Ārūr, town of cool rippling streams?

2
Will I who committed many crimes,
taking for truth the doctrines of those wandering monks,
the naked Jains who fast by night,
ever have the good fortune
of becoming the devotee
of devotees who serve
Tiruvārūr's Lord-who-dwells-in-the-anthill,
who once became a hunter
and defeated Arjuna in combat
with his bow?

3
Pursued by wicked monks
who eat in barbaric ways,
will I ever have the good fortune
of becoming the devotee
of devotees who serve the feet
of the Lord who destroyed the citadels
with his fiery bow of war,
of him who rides the mighty, red-eyed bull,
the deity of Tiruvārūr's holy Mūlaṭṭāṉam shrine,
who holds the unattainable treasure?

4
Will I, who have left the heartless,
filthy, shaven-headed monks,
and seek to expiate my sins
by thinking of Īśa alone,
ever have the good fortune
of becoming the devotee
of the lordly devotees who contemplate the Lord,
and perform the worship rite for the shining deity
of Ārūr's holy Mūlaṭṭāṉam shrine?

---

which the central *liṅga* in the Mūlaṭṭāṉam shrine is known. The name derives from the origin legend of the Tiruvārūr shrine. v. 5. "Devotees of great austerity": "*poruntum tava-muṭai-*" devotees who are very pious and have the accumulated merit of penance (*tapas*).

5
Will I, who have left the ways
of the naked Jains who eat in silence,
I who repent, and reflect on him,
and call out, "O Hara!"
ever have the good fortune
of becoming the devotee
of devotees of great austerity,
who serve the Lord of the holy Mūlaṭṭāṉam shrine
in Ārūr with great, majestic walls?

237. Appar IV.100.1 *Kacci Ēkampam*

You gave me learning;
with my learned doctrines,
you made me join the Jains,
made them try to kill me.
When illness struck, you cured me,
freed me from the monks,
and graciously united with me
to awaken me to the truth.
So—if I fail in your service,
you will lash me with a tamarind switch,
and kindly punish me,
O Kacci Ēkampam's Lord!

238. Appar V.177.6 *Teṉ Kuraṅkāṭuturai*

Once he made me run about
with the naked Jains,
then made me sing sweet songs
for his golden feet.
Kuraṅkāṭuturai's Lord
saved me from karma,
and joined me with his true devotees.

Metaphors for Fruitless Labor

239. Appar IV.5 *Tiruvārūr*

1
I thought I could be saved
without worshipping the feet

239, v. 1. Jain monk's swing: "*uṟi*," refers to the swinglike chairs in which Jain monks

of the god who covers his body with white ash.
I wandered, carried about in a Jain monk's swing,
lost my good heart,
failed to worship with joined palms
the Lord who dwells in Ārūr
where peacocks dance to the cuckoo's song
in gardens full of flowers
waiting to be gathered.
I was a thief who steals sour fruit,
leaving the ripe ones on the tree.

2
He made me a frame of bones,
filled it out with skin and flesh,
and gave me form.
Ārūr's Lord put an end to my karma,
gave me lasting joy,
and made my heart a temple,
in which he abides with love.
Thus he blessed me,
making me his own loving servant.
I, who did not deserve to dwell in his presence,
was one who let go of the hare
to run after a crow.

3
Once I multiplied sin,
following the words of scoundrel monks.
The Lord of Ārūr melted my heart,
casting out the falsehood I had in me.
He drew me close and showed me sickness,
then cured my disease and became my master.
I, who did not deserve to dwell in his presence,
was one who rejected the good Law
to buy evil instead.

4
As a wicked, shaven monk I roamed,
unabashed at the laughter
of women with full breasts.
He made even me an object of his love;
the Lord of Ārūr bathed me in milk,

---

were carried about. Various Tamil proverbs form the refrain in this hymn. Some, like the proverb about milking a barren cow (v. 6), continue to be popular.

showed me his feet,
and, as his servants sang sacred songs of praise,
blessed me with his pure smile.
I, who once failed to know him,
was one who sets out to shape a doll
out of drops of dew.

5
I was a deadly snake, dancing to the tunes
of evil men.
Filthy, foul-mouthed, I wandered aimlessly,
begging for food, eating with both hands,
truly a wretch!
The Lord of Ārūr united his golden form with mine,
considering me one of his creatures.
I, who failed to let him
abide within my self,
was a fool who gets punished
for the clever man's misdeeds.

6
As a Jain monk I wandered,
head shaven, studying worldly texts.
To me he taught the incomparable doctrine,
entered my heart,
and there revealed the Truth.
I, who never thought of the Lord of Ārūr
who is dear ambrosia to his servants
whenever they think of him,
was one who grows weary,
milking a barren cow in a dark room.

7
Not knowing the true path,
shaven-headed and red-eyed,
eating out of my hands,
I wandered through long streets of towns,
unashamed at the laughter of all who saw me,
till he gave me discrimination.
I, who did not have the good fortune
of drinking with my lips
the honey that wells up in Ārūr,
the Lord who brought me to my wits,
was witless indeed,

like one who puts aside the oil lamp
to warm himself with a firefly.

8
A shaven monk, I stood by the words
of the base, ignorant Jains.
I was a hypocrite, running away
and bolting the door
at the sight of lotus-eyed young women.
A miserable sinner
who did not know the Lord of Ārūr
who saved my soul and possessed me,
I was one who starves to death,
begging for food in a deserted town.

9
He destroyed the three citadels
of the evil demons, the enemy,
smashing them with a single arrow;
he felled Kāma and Kāla with his eye and foot.
I, who did not belong
to our dear Lord in Ārūr
who is untouched by desire, anger, and pride,
was one who takes pride
in wasting his time
while the path to release awaits him.

10
He crushed the shoulders and feet
and the ten heads
of the mighty demon who fiercely challenged him;
he cut off one of the heads
of the god with the lovely lotus seat.
I, who failed to love
our dear Lord in Ārūr,
the god whose throat is dark
from swallowing the deadly poison,
was as one who wastes away,
gnawing on a bar of iron
while sugar cane lies at hand.

Confrontation in Kanchi

The Śaiva hagiographers speak of several incidents in which the Jains used their influence on the Pallava king in Kanchipuram to take revenge on Appar for his desertion. Poem 240, in which Appar rejects the glory, authority, and command of the king, was the saint's reply (*maṟumāṟṟam*) to the minister who presented him with a summons from the Pallava court. In spite of his defiance, Appar was taken to Kanchi and subjected to a number of tortures: he was incarcerated in a lime kiln for a week, given poison, thrown in the path of a raging elephant, and then bound to a heavy rock and cast into the sea. The saint emerged unscathed from all these ordeals. The king's (Mahendravarman's?) faith in Śaivism was restored; he reconverted to Śaivism and built a temple for Śiva near Atikai. Of the many miraculous incidents mentioned above, Appar refers to one alone, that of the rock (Poem 241).

240. Appar VI.312 MAṞUMĀṞṞAT TIRUT TĀṆṬAKAM (THE TĀṆṬAKAM POEM OF THE REPLY)

1
We are slaves to no man,
nor do we fear death.
Hell holds no torments for us,
we know no deceit.
We rejoice, we are strangers to disease,
we bow to none.
Joy alone is ours, not sorrow,
for we belong forever
to Śaṅkara, who is the supreme Lord,
our King who wears the white conch earring on one ear,
and we have reached
his beautiful, flower-fresh feet.

2
The wide world is our home;
generous householders in every town
give us food.

240. The opening lines of this hymn: "nāmārkkuṅ kuṭiy allōm namaṉaiy añcōm" ("We are slaves to no man, nor do we fear death") not only have become the Tamil Śaiva credo but are seen as the manifesto of the Tamil spirit in general. Though many of the references are specific to Appar's life, the use of the first person plural gives the ideas in this hymn a more general application to the Śaiva community. In the first three verses, there are echoes of "yātum mūrē yāvaruṅ kēḷir," the famous classical poem (*Puṟanāṉūṟu* 192) of Kaṇiyaṉ Pūṅkuṉṟaṉ; there are also interesting contrasts between the two poems. See Hart, *Poets of the Tamil Anthologies*, p. 180. "*Piṇi*," translated as "disease" in verse 1, can also mean "bondage." v. 4. "Śaiva devotees": "*uruttira palkaṇattiṉōrkaḷ*" refers to the many Śaiva sects familiar to Appar. v. 6. "Rose-apple land": "*nāvalan tīvu*" (Sanskrit *jambudvīpa*), the name for the "continent" of India in Hindu cosmology. v. 9. "bonds": "*pācam*." v. 10. The tradition provides varying lists of the "eight attributes" (*eṇkuṇam*) of the Lord as the supreme being; these include infinite bliss, grace, and power. See the commentary of Aruṇaivaṭivēl Mutaliyār on Appar VI.230.4, *Tēvāram* Ātīṉam edition, vol. 6, p. 125.

Public halls are our only shelter; we sleep
in Goddess Earth's loving embrace—
all this is true.
The Lord of the warlike bull has taken us.
We lack nothing, our trials are over now.
Why need we listen to the words
of men who parade themselves in silk and gold?
We are innocent men.

3
We do not consort with women;
we rise before dawn to bathe
and chant Mahādeva's name,
our sole ornament is the sacred ash.
Tears, welling from our eyes like monsoon rains,
proclaim the melting of our stony hearts.
Why need we obey the commands
of kings who ride on elephants?
We are free from bonds.

4
Śaiva devotees are our only kin,
we wear nothing but the waistband and the loincloth.
Even our enemies cannot harm us;
all evil is turned into good for us,
and we will never be born again.
Our tongues chant "Hail Śiva!"
good name of the Lord
with the sweet, golden *koṉṟai* wreath.
We are devotees of the Lord
whose blazing forehead eye
reduced crocodile-bannered Kāma to ashes.

5
We will yield to no man;
none on earth can equal us.
We do not follow small gods,
we belong to Lord Śiva's holy feet alone.
Surely we lack nothing!
Deadly disease has fled, leaving us untouched.
We live on the merit
of having taken refuge
in the good Lord who is crowned
with a garland of skulls.

6
They alone may rule us,
whose tongues chant the name
of Śiva with the holy coral-red form,
the Lord whom the thirty-three gods
and all beings praise
as the first among the three,
the eight-formed deity.
Even if the king of this entire rose-apple land
were to command us,
we need not obey—
we are not criminals or thieves.

7
Our sole duty is joyfully to sing
the glory of him who manifests himself
as the moving and the still,
as earth, water, fire, wind, and sky,
as the small and the great,
as hard to reach, yet easily attained
by his lovers,
as the highest reality, immeasurably great,
as infinite Sadāśiva, as you and me.
Why should we parrot the words of devils?
We are blameless men.

8
Every day we meditate only on the Lord,
ruler of all the worlds,
king of the Himalayan gods,
him who blazed up as fire,
god who bears the white ash on his red body,
good lover of the mountain's beautiful daughter.
We have long renounced the doctrines
that the Jains, who eat standing,
had taught us.
Who are you to us?
And who is your king?

9
The Lord with the matted hair
and the conch earring on one ear,
with his body adorned by the ash and the snake,
bull rider clad in the tigerskin

and the silver-spotted skin of the deer—
He is the King who rules us, you see!
We are not servants of the king who commands
you and all his troops—
We are free from all bonds!

10
We have the good fortune of singing our Lord
to our hearts' content,
of repulsing the shameless Jain monks.
The king of immortals,
the Lord who graciously rules us,
Śiva, the god of gods who rose as the flame
which Ayan̲ and Māl could not know,
dwells in my heart.
If Death himself were to declare
his dominion over us and command us to serve him,
we would refuse,
for the Lord's eight attributes are ours.

241. Appar V.186.7 *Nīlakkuṭi*

When the Jain rogues bound me to a rock,
and swiftly cast me into the sea—
it was surely because I chanted with my tongue
the good name of Aran̲
of Nīlakkuṭi, where the paddy grows tall in the fields,
that I was saved!

From Atikai to Pukalūr

Appar spent his long life traveling to his Lord's shrines. Of particular interest to us here are some of Appar's hymns dedicated to shrines that tradition associates with turning points in the saint's spiritual life. In Tūṅkān̲aimāṭam, he asked Śiva to brand him with the emblems of the trident and the bull (Poem 149). The request was granted. From Tūṅkān̲aimāṭam, the saint went to Chidambaram and nearby temples. At Cīrkāḻi, Appar met Campantar; it was here that the child lovingly addressed the elder saint as his "father" (*appar*).

241. In this verse "*nīr*" ("water") is traditionally interpreted as referring to the sea. "Was saved": "*uyntēn̲*" signifies release.

Cēkkiḻār records Nallūr, Tiṅkaḷūr, and Tiruvārūr as the next landmarks in Appar's pilgrimage. Appar's request in Tiruvāvaṭuturai (poem 150), that Śiva should brand him with his lotus feet, was granted in Nallūr. In Tiṅkaḷūr, the saint brought back to life Tirunāvukkaracu, the son of his fervent devotee Appūti Nāyaṉār; it is worth noting that Appūti had named his son after Appar. Tiruvārūr is the setting for Appar's best-known hymns, including what appears to be a firsthand account of the Tiruvātirai festival (Poem 98).

In Poem 242, Appar refers to the door in the temple at Maṟaikkāṭu. In the Vāymūr hymn (Poem 243), he speaks of his travels with Campantar, of the miracle of the gold coin at Vīḻimiḻalai, and of the miracle of the temple door at Maṟaikkāṭu (see poems 223 and 224).

In his old age Appar was seized with the longing to visit Mount Kailāsa, the Himalayan abode of Śiva. The elderly saint's journey and ascent were fraught with physical hardship; though overcome with weariness, he persisted in his effort. Śiva appeared to him in a vision and in an instant transported him to the southern shrine of Tiruvaiyāṟu where, he assured Appar, the saint would see his Lord as he appeared in Kailāsa. Appar was plunged into the reservoir in Tiruvaiyāṟu temple, rose with his wounds healed, and beheld that temple transformed into Kailāsa.

The famous hymn IV.3 (Poem 244), dedicated to Tiruvaiyāṟu, records an extraordinary experience, a mystical vision in which Appar saw the whole world as Śiva in union with the Goddess or female principle, and felt the presence of the Lord's feet in everything around him. The text of the final selection relating to Appar's life (Poem 245) is taken from the hymn considered to be his last. After singing it, the saint finally "reached Śiva's feet" in Pukalūr.

242. Appar V.124 *Maṟaikkāṭu*

1

Spouse of Umā of speech sweet as music!
Lord of Maṟaikkāṭu, worshipped by the world!
Favor me with your unfailing grace!
Open the door,
let me see you with my eyes!

7

O God who wears the white ash,
infinite Lord, god of lovely Maṟaikkāṭu!

242. In the Vāymūr hymn (IV.164.8, Poem 243) Appar explicitly says: "My song opened the temple doors." v. 7. "God": "*vikirtar*." The term literally means "a person whose behavior is changing and inexplicable," "enigmatic person," but is used to refer to the deity.

Kindly open this great door,
so that your devotees may worship you!

11
O my Lord who quelled the demon with one toe,
have you no pity?
Lord of Maṟaikkāṭu with fragrant *puṉṉai* groves!
Quickly open this door!

243. Appar V.164 *Vāymūr*

1
Once he sought me out,
came to me, and gave me his sign.
The dear Lord of Vāymūr of palm groves
now asks me come to him there.
O wonder!

2
As I lay thinking of the bridegroom
in renowned Maṟaikkāṭu,
he revealed himself to me as Vāymūr's Lord,
then vanished, bidding me come to him there.
O wonder!

3
"I have found you,
O refuge for homeless wanderers!" I said.
"Fear not! I came to fetch you," said he.
"I am saved," I cried joyfully,
and arose, and hastened here.
It seems my Lord of Vāymūr
has played a trick on me.

4
I saw him with these eyes,
and did not see him leave.
Never leaving his side,
I ran along with him.
Yet Vāymūr's Lord has vanished on the road,
leaving me caught in the web

243, v. 7. Appar seems to be referring to the incident of Campantar and the "old coins" (*paḻaṅkācu*) in Vīḻimiḻalai.

of his wily tricks.
O wonder!

5
"My Lord is the only light,"
I thought, and rejoiced.
Yet the Lord of Vāymūr
who once appeared to me as wisdom incarnate,
now hides himself like a thief!

7
As though he would relieve the misery
of the devotee whose reward for singing him
was an old coin,
the Lord ran after me,
asking me to come to holy Vāymūr.
Now he hides himself.
O wonder!

8
My song opened the temple doors;
the poet who commanded them shut,
with more powerful, purer Tamil song than mine,
also waits here.
How can this madman of Vāymūr,
with the moon-crowned red hair,
hide himself?

9
When I begged to become his true devotee,
the Pure Lord who blesses even false men like me
when we think of him,
appeared before me, and said:
"Follow me to Vāymūr,"
then vanished into the golden temple by the stream.
What false vision is this?

10
With one holy, unapproachable foot
he crushed the demon to save him.
When I pray,
"May I coax forth the flame
in the lamp of holy Vāymūr!"
look—it shines for me!

244. Appar IV.3 *Tiruvaiyāṟu*

1
Singing of the Lord who wears the lovely moon
as a wreath on his hair,
and the mountain's daughter with him,
I followed those who go to his temple
carrying flowers and water for worship.
When I reached Aiyāṟu, unwearied,
I saw an elephant come with his beloved mate,
I saw the Lord's holy feet,
I saw what I had never seen before.

2
Singing of the Lord who wears the crescent moon
as a wreath on his hair,
and with him the silk-clad Goddess,
I danced around the shrine, crying:
"Hail! Hail to him!"
When I reached Aiyāṟu,
where Viṣṇu of the wheel worshipped,
I saw a cock and hen joyfully mating,
I saw his holy feet,
I saw what I had never seen before.

3
Singing of the Lord who wears the bright crescent moon
as a wreath on his hair,
and with him his Goddess adorned with jewels,
I came, smiling for joy, dancing to complex rhythms.
When I reached Aiyāṟu, where the foaming stream
eats into its banks,
I saw the banded cuckoo
come dancing with its mate,
I saw his holy feet,
I saw what I had never seen before.

10
Singing of the Lord who wears the crescent moon
as a wreath on his hair,
and with him the Goddess with speech sweet as honey,
I came, crying, "Where will my Lord
reveal his grace to me?"
When I reached Aiyāṟu,
where young women dance, I saw

a green parrot flying with its mate,
I saw his holy feet,
I saw what I had never seen before.

245. Appar VI.313.1 *Pukalūr*

What shall I think of,
other than my Lord's holy feet?
Other than his feet that I
worship with joined palms,
I have no support;
there is nothing else I wish to see!
You made nine doors for my frame.
When the time comes for them to close,
I will lose the power to feel you.
Therefore, blessed Lord,
I only wish to reach your feet,
O good Lord who dwells in Pūmpukalūr!

245. "I have no support": "*kaṇṇilēṉ*" can also mean "I have no means for seeing [other than Śiva]." "Uṇara māṭṭēṉ": "I won't be able to sense/realize/cognize you."

3 Cuntarar: The Lord's Comrade

(POEMS 246–258)

In the relatively short span of a hundred hymns, Nampi Ārūrar or Cuntaramūrtti provides us with more particulars about his life and times than either of his fellow saints. Like Campantar, Cuntarar mentions details of his personal and public life in his signature verses. From these, and from traditional accounts, we learn that Cuntarar was born in Tirunāvalūr to the Śaiva brahmin (Āticaivar) Caṭaiyaṉār and his wife Icaiñāṉiyār. He grew up in luxury as the adopted son of Naraciṅka Muṉaiyaraiyar, a Pallava feudatory prince. The poet calls himself "Ārūraṉ," and speaks of himself as the father of the girls Ciṅkaṭi and Vaṉappakai, who were given to him by his admirer Kōṭpuli Nāyaṉār. Cēkkiḻār informs us that this saint was named "Ārūrar" or "Nampi Ārūrar" after Śiva in Tiruvārūr. The name "Cuntaramūrtti," "the handsome lord," is probably connected both to the popular image of the saint as a handsome youth with expensive tastes and to the legend of Cuntarar's being the incarnation of an attendant of Śiva in Kailāsa called Ālālacuntarar. Cuntarar spent the major portion of his life in Tiruvārūr.

Cuntarar's "autobiographical" hymns can be broadly grouped under four themes: his conversion at Veṇṇeynallūr; his "Tiruvārūr" period, during which he first married the dancer Paravai, and then Caṅkili in Tiruvoṟṟiyūr, and his blindness and recovery of sight; his negotiations with Śiva for wealth and wordly goods; his final ascent to Kailāsa.

Enslavement at Veṇṇeynallūr

In several hymns Cuntarar speaks of his "conversion" experience at the Aruṭṭuṟai temple in Veṇṇeynallūr, the incident that is said to have been the context of his first hymn, "pittā piṟaicūṭī" ("O madman with the moon-crowned hair!" VII.1, Poem 246). Campantar's life ended in a divine "wedding"; Cuntarar's saintly career began with an interrupted wedding ceremony. "Taṭuttāṭkoṇṭa purāṇam," the title of the biography of Cuntarar in Cēkkiḻār's *Periya purāṇam*, refers to this incident, in which Śiva first stopped (obstructed, *taṭuttu*) the wedding, and then took Cuntarar as his servant (*āṭkoḷ-*). When the young man from Nāvalūr (Tirunāvalūr) was about to marry a woman chosen for him by his parents at

Puttūr, an old man pushed his way through the crowd and rudely demanded that the ceremony be stopped. As the astonished public gathered around him, the old man declared that Cuntarar was the bonded slave of himself and his forefathers, and that the youth would now have to work for his master. Undaunted by the indignant protests of Cuntarar and the guests, the old man produced a palm-leaf manuscript that contained a deed of sale confirming his claim. Calling him a "madman" (*pittaṉ*), Cuntarar tore up the deed, whereupon the man produced another document that he declared to be the original deed, and led Nampi Ārūrar to the council of elders at nearby Veṇṇeynallūr. The elders pronounced the deed to be in order; while the assembly looked on, the "madman of Veṇṇeynallūr" vanished into the Aruṭṭuṟai ("Shrine of Grace") temple in that town. Transformed by his mystical encounter, Cuntarar acknowledged his everlasting bondage to the Lord and cried to Śiva: "How shall I praise you?" The Lord of Veṇṇeynallūr named Cuntarar his "Rude (or Aggressive) Devotee" (*vaṉṟoṇṭaṉ*) and commanded him to sing his God as the "*pittaṉ*" (madman). Inspired, Cuntarar began his first hymn with the words "*pittā piṟaicūṭī.*"

246. Cuntarar VII.1.1 *(Tiru-) Veṇṇeynallūr*

O madman with the moon-crowned hair,
God of grace, O Lord,
how can I forget you?
You dwell forever in my heart.
In Aruṭṭuṟai, shrine of grace,
in Veṇṇeynallūr on Peṇṇai's southern bank,
you took me for your own—
how can I deny you now?

247. Cuntarar VII.62.5 *Kōlakkā*

Once in Veṇṇeynallūr
he displayed to the whole world
the contract of bondage,
and cried: "Be my slave!"
Bright cluster of pearls,
my one path to release, Lord of the gods,
the bowman who smashed the lofty, strong citadels
with his mountain bow—
I have seen him in Kōlakkā
with his soft girl.

248. Cuntarar VII.17 *(Tiru-) Nāvalūr*

1
Our holy town of Nāvalūr is the home
of the poet who possessed me
in Veṇṇeynallūr,
the god who set fire to the enemy's three cities
with a single, swift arrow,
while Viṣṇu, Brahmā, and the king of gods
obeyed his command.

2
Our holy town of Nāvalūr is the home
of the good Lord who once graciously
took me for his own,
who gave as reward
for my angry, threatening words in the assembly hall,
the name and life of the "Rude Devotee,"
who showered me with riches,
giving gold in return for abuse!

7
Our holy town of Nāvalūr is the home
of the god of the bamboo grove
who became my father and my mother,
freed me from birth and death,
and joined me forever to his golden feet,
the Lord, my lover, who took me for his own
in Veṇṇeynallūr.

11
The bonds of karma will be severed
for those who love, learn,
and listen to the Tamil hymn
composed by the scholar and rude devotee
Ārūraṉ, praising lovely Nāvalūr
as the Lord's town, our town,
the town where Naraciṅka Muṉaiyaraiyaṉ
lovingly serves the Lord.

248, v. 1. "Poet": "*nāvalar*," orator. v. 2. In his hymns, Cuntarar frequently refers to gold given by the Lord. v. 7. "The god of the bamboo grove": "Vēyavaṉār" may be a reference to the local legend concerning Śiva's concealment in a forest of bamboos. It may also simply mean: "the hunter," as suggested by the use of the epithet "*vēyāṭiyār*" (hunter) in verse 8 of this hymn, which has not been included here.

Paravai, Caṅkili, and Blindness

According to the Tamil Śaiva tradition, Cuntarar's double marriage to Paravai and Caṅkili was literally "made in heaven." The saint and his two wives had been servants of Śiva in Kailāsa, and were born on earth to be united in marriage and serve Śiva as human devotees. Cuntarar's hymns give us some idea of the complexity of his earthly life with two women, as well as of his love and concern for each.

Cuntarar settled down in the great temple center of Tiruvārūr, where he met and married the lovely temple dancer Paravai (see illus. 4). Together they lived a life of service to Śiva's temple and his pilgrim-devotees. On a visit to Tiruvoṟṟiyūr Cuntarar met and fell in love with the pious Vellala maiden Caṅkili, whose avocation was to weave floral garlands at the local shrine. The poet wished to marry her and asked Śiva to help him approach the girl. The Lord agreed to do so, but in reality he wanted to test Cuntarar's devotion and integrity. He first appeared before Caṅkili in a dream, and spoke on Cuntarar's behalf; the girl agreed to marry Cuntarar, but only on the condition that he would promise never to leave her and Tiruvoṟṟiyūr. When Śiva told Cuntarar about Caṅkili's demand, the pilgrim-poet felt that such a promise would be difficult to keep. He requested Śiva to leave the *liṅga* at the temple and take temporary residence under the *makiḻ* tree in the courtyard, leaving him free to take a nonbinding oath in the sanctum. The Lord agreed to Cuntarar's proposal, but went to Caṅkili and suggested that she insist that Cuntarar should take his oath, not in the shrine, but under the *makiḻ* tree. The saint was trapped, and took the oath under the tree. Marriage and a happy life with Caṅkili in Tiruvoṟṟiyūr followed. However, with the coming of spring, powerful memories of Tiruvārūr—of the Spring festival (*vacantōṟcavam*) in Tiruvārūr, the Lord of Tiruvārūr, and the dance and presence of his beloved wife Paravai at the shrine—stirred in Cuntarar. Unable to resist the call of Tiruvārūr, Cuntarar left Caṅkili and Tiruvoṟṟiyūr, and was struck blind on his way to Tiruvārūr.

Cuntarar speaks of his suffering in many hymns. He considers his blindness to be a punishment from Śiva for abandoning Caṅkili, yet he does not think that so harsh a punishment is deserved. He alternately pleads with and reproaches his Lord, and reports that the Lord ultimately forgave him and cured him of his affliction. In the traditional account, Śiva responded to the saint's plea in stages, at various shrines where he visited and sang hymns on his way to Tiruvārūr: at Veṇpākkam Śiva gave him a walking stick; at Kanchipuram, restored vision to one eye; and in Tiruvārūr, completely restored sight. Finally, Śiva himself interceded—as a *tūtaṉ*, a go-between—on behalf of his devotee in order to effect a reconciliation between the poet and Paravai in Tiruvārūr. Cuntarar's familiar, teasing relationship with his Lord has earned him the name "tampirāṉ tōḻar" ("the Lord's Comrade").

249. Cuntarar VII.51 *Ārūr (Tiruvārūr)*

9
How can I live far away
from my God in Ārūr?
How can I bear to be parted
from him whose glory was sweetly sung
by two before me,
the Lord with the forehead eye,
the fruit of all learning,
the god whom I love with all my heart?

10
I am an ignorant wretch,
parted from my God in Ārūr,
from him who is the seven notes of music,
the fruit of my song, my sweet ambrosia,
the dear friend who aided me in my many crimes,
and graciously blessed me
with Paravai, my woman with the lovely bright eyes.

250. Cuntarar VII.54 *Oṟṟiyūr (Tiruvoṟṟiyūr)*

1
Burdened with a foul body, I take refuge
in your holy feet—
If this is what I deserve, remember, O Lord!
Men will take milk from the cow

249, v. 9. "Two before me": Campantar and Appar. The commentator Aruṇaivaṭivēl Mutaliyār (*Tēvāram* Ātīṉam edition, vol. 7) takes "*muṉṉiruvar*" to mean Brahmā and Viṣṇu, in the context of the myth of Śiva as the flaming pillar. v. 10. "Lovely bright eyes": "*māḻai oṇ kaṇ*" can also mean "eyes curved like the mango."

250. In verse 2 Cuntarar refers to his blindness as the Lord's punishment for breaking his oath to Caṅkili. v. 4. The meaning of the first two lines is quite obscure. "If . . . it is fair": "*kaṇakkuvaḻakkākil*," "if it is legitimate." Cuntarar's reference to Śiva as the "three-eyed god" in verses 4 and 9 is pregnant with irony. v. 9. "Evil planet": "makattiṟ pukkatōr caṉi": "Saturn who has entered the house of Makam." In the South Indian astrological tradition, Saturn (Caṉi) is considered to be the "evil" planet; its entrance into the lunar mansion that converges with the karmic pattern of an individual is bound to bring bad luck. v. 10. "Sacred texts": the Vedāṅga texts.

even if it is mixed with dung.
Sinner though I am, I would never sin
against your holy feet.
Even when I slip and fall, I utter
nothing but your holy name.
You who dwell in Oṟṟiyūr, answer me,
tell me a cure for blindness!

2
Born a miserable wretch, I became yours.
What shall I tell you?
Tell me, what shall I do
for the sake of my darling Caṅkili,
O god with the eight glorious forms?
Sinner though I am, I would never sin
against your holy feet.
You who dwell in Oṟṟiyūr,
with all my faults, I am still your slave,
I accept all you have done to me!

4
Your devotees are not related to you
by birth or by marriage.
Yet what does it matter?
When they praise you, you reveal yourself to them,
you never speak harsh words to them.
O god with the three eyes, you who dwell in Oṟṟiyūr,
if you think it is fair to take away my sight,
give me at least a stick for support!

9
O son, my gem, O bridegroom,
you have become my evil planet as well!
I can't bear it when my women refuse to listen to me,
calling me a blind wretch!
How can I live without eyesight,
O three-eyed Lord, chanter of the Veda?
Is this fair, O god who dwells in Oṟṟiyūr
washed by the cool, swelling waves of the sea?

10
Those who know these ten verses
that Ūraṉ, the Rude Devotee,
chanter of the four Vedas and sacred texts

praised by the world,
very pious young man,
has sung on the dear one
who dwells at the shrine in wave-washed Oṟṟiyūr,
will surely reach the highest state.

251. Cuntarar VII.69 *Mullaivāyil*

1
Taking your glorious feet
for my blessing and lasting wealth and treasure,
I wander, committing crimes,
insulting other men, true to you alone,
O Lord of holy Mullaivāyil of fragrant groves!
Since I am your singing devotee,
free me from suffering,
O Lord of Souls, Supreme Light!

3
O brahmin worshipped by the gods,
you once flayed the elephant's hide,
frightening the Goddess.
O Lord of holy Mullaivāyil of *ceṇpakam* groves,
King of the gods!
You who dwell in great Oṟṟiyūr, town of cool groves,
god who blinded me to please Caṅkili,
free me, your devotee, from suffering,
O Lord of Souls, Supreme Light!

6
Who is so fortunate as I, bountiful Lord?
Knowing that you accept
even my deceptions and offenses as good deeds,
I have committed many sins.
O Lord of holy Mullaivāyil
who burned the three flying citadels
of the arrogant demons,
I, your devotee, have severed all my ties;

251. "*Pācupatā*," in the refrain of this hymn, literally means "O follower of the Pāśupata cult!" Here it refers to Śiva as Paśupati, "Lord of Beasts," and "Lord of Souls (*pacu*)." v. 7. The elaborate description of the charms of women in this verse might have been inspired by Cuntarar's meditations on his love for two women, a love that resulted in his present state of affliction.

free me from suffering,
O Lord of Souls, Supreme Light!

7
O treasure in holy Mullaivāyil with lush groves,
town that ceaselessly resounds with the fine dances
of dancing girls with long carplike eyes
and breasts adorned with jewels,
women lovely as peacocks, with coral lips,
bright smile, and long, dark hair!
Day and night I serve you with devotion;
free me from suffering,
O Lord of Souls, Supreme Light!

8
O Master! O Śambhu who once in Veṇṇeynallūr
took me for your slave, though I'm no better than a dog!
O Lord praised by the gods,
god who held the ocean's poison in his throat!
Bright gold that I, wandering seeker, found
in holy Mullaivāyil, city of golden palaces,
free me, your devotee, from suffering,
O Lord of Souls, Supreme Light!

252. Cuntarar VII.89 *Veṇpākkam*

1
When I cried, "Thinking, 'My Lord forgives
his devotees' faults,'
I sinned. Heedless of blame, you have blinded me.
O god with the golden earring on one pendulous ear,
are you in the temple now?"
The Lord who bears the fawn replied from within:
"I am here; now go your way!"

2
I make neither the beginning nor end of my acts;
the Lord is my sole refuge.
Yet, without thinking,

252, v. 1. "Pendulous ear": "*vaṭikātu*." The weight of the earring has elongated the ear-lobe. This detail is also found in the iconography of Śiva and the Goddess. v. 9. Cuntarar's account of the oath taken under the *makiḻ* tree must surely have been the inspiration for the tale of elaborate trickery that the later tradition has spun out of this incident in the saint's life. "Are you there"—i.e., in the Veṇkōyil shrine.

"This one has sought shelter in me; he is my servant,"
the bull rider, my Master who has the poisonous snakes,
white ash, and tiger-skin robe, replied:
"I am here; now go your way!"

3
When I cried, "I cannot tell good deeds from bad;
your holy feet are my sole refuge.
Though I, your base devotee, should err,
should you not forgive?
O god with the hooded cobra, are you there?"
He who could take pity on me
and save me with his grace replied:
"I am here; now you go your way!"

6
When I cried to the Lord with the flaming *konṟai* blossoms
on red hair crowned with the Ganges and the cool moon,
God who burned Kāma with his powerful forehead eye,
"O Lord who blinded me, are you there?"
the husband of the Goddess with the bright forehead
merely replied:
"I am here; now you go your way!"

9
When I cried, "O Lord with the golden *konṟai*,
When I asked you to leave the temple
and abide under the *makiḻ* tree,
you tricked me, and made me take the oath of fidelity
under that very tree.
Are you there, my Lord?"
As if he had just seen his worst enemy,
he replied:
"I am here; now you go your way!"

10
When I cried, "O Lord of the entire universe!
You who graciously gave me Caṅkili, lovely as a doe,
and blessed me with all the fruits of that gift,
Are you there, inside the Veṇkōyil shrine?"
The Lord gave me a stick for support,
and said:
"I am here; now you go your way!"

253. Cuntarar VII.95 *Tiruvārūr*

1
In everlasting bondage to you, I became your slave,
spurning all other masters.
With smouldering fire inside me,
pale of face, possessed by you,
when I tell you of my pain,
you say nothing.
May you live long, my Lord!

2
Sell me, if you wish, for I am not a helpless pawn,
but one who willingly became your slave.
Though I have committed no offense,
you have made me a blind wretch.
Why did you take away my sight, O Lord?
Now you alone must bear the blame.
Though you won't give me back my eyes,
May you live long, my Lord!

3
You who dwell in Ārūr, to whose groves
aṉṟil birds flock every day!
What do you care if your servant,
who tirelessly sings your praise,
clinging to you like a calf at the cow's flowing teats,
loses his sight, runs into hills,
falls into a pit?
May you live long, my Lord!

5
Is this Tiruvārūr, where the gardens swarm
with coral-red beetles?
Is this the reward you give your servants, O Lord?
What do you care if your devotee
who sings you in rhythmic hymns

253. "May you live long," "*Vāḻntu pōtīrē*," the refrain in this hymn has a tone of bitter sarcasm, driving home the depth of Cuntarar's resentment and despondency. v. 3. *Aṉṟil* birds symbolize fidelity in love. v. 5. "*Centaṉ pavaḷam*": "coral-red beetles," after the commentary in the *Tēvāram* Ātīṉam edition. v. 6. "White storks": Samy, *Caṅka ilakkiyattil puḷḷiṉa viḷakkam*, p. 36, identifies the "*ceṅkāl nārai*" of early Tamil literature as the white stork. v. 11. In Pallava sculpture, the Goddess, especially in her form as Durgā, is often depicted with a cloth band across her breasts. The Mūlaṭṭāṉam is the central shrine at the Tiruvārūr temple.

loses his sight and comes to you in complaint?
May you live long, my Lord!

6
O Lord whose matted red hair is adorned
by a garland of golden *koṉṟai* from the pastoral lands,
you who dwell in Tiruvārūr, where white storks gather,
with legs red as millet stalks!
What do you care if your servant wastes away,
afflicted by poverty and blindness,
and grieves in his heart?
May you live long, my Lord!

7
You who dwell in Ārūr,
where birds flock together in the groves,
my Master, is this the reward you give your servants?
If the best you can do is to give me a transient birth,
and a body, and a heart that will never forget you,
and then rob me of my sight,
may you live long, my Lord!

11
O three-eyed Lord who manifests himself in many forms,
Lord with eight arms and the poison-darkened throat,
you who dwell in the central shrine of Tiruvārūr temple,
with your spouse who wears a band across her breasts!
As the whole world watched,
you took away your devotee Ārūraṉ's sight.
Now you alone must bear the blame.
May you live long, my Lord!

254. Cuntarar VII.92.8 *Pukkoḷiyūr Avināci*

I worship no god other than you.
I am blind,
but if you would give me vision,
it is you that I want to see,
Lord who wears a snake as his waistband,
and lives in Pukkoḷiyūr Avināci,
O god with the stained throat,
you who can make the blind see!

"Gold, and Silk, and a Flashing Sword"

Remarkable among the *Tēvāram* hymns are those of Cuntarar's *patikam*s in which he asks Śiva to provide him not only with spiritual succor but with material goods and luxuries. In the Kōḷili hymn (VII.20, Poem 225) the poet asks the Lord to send him "men to carry the grain" that he had received in Kuṇṭaiyūr; in the hymn dedicated to Nākaikkārōṇam (VII.46, Poem 256) he asks for such things as gold, silk, good rice with ghee, a fine horse, and a flashing sword—hardly the attributes of a saint! In such poems, Cuntarar makes it clear that he needs these objects in order to provide for his wives and family. According to tradition, the saint's requests were motivated by the philanthropy he practiced with Paravai in Tiruvārūr; he and this magnanimous lady reputedly fed and cared for the hundreds of devotees who came to witness the Lord's festivals at the shrine in Tiruvārūr. In addition to grain, Śiva blessed the pious couple with gold and other goods. On one occasion the Lord's bounty came in the form of a shower of gold coins, on another, in the form of bricks turned into bars of gold. Besides confirming the traditional image of Cuntaramūrtti ("the handsome lord") as a prince and sensualist—he appears in iconography dressed in fine clothes, wearing a crown and garland of flowers, and carrying a sword—the saint's hymns tell us that Cuntarar thought of Śiva as his great patron-king, an idea explicitly articulated in Poem 257.

255. Cuntarar VII.20 *Kōḷili*

1

Thinking of you all the time,
I worship you every day.
In Kuṇṭaiyūr I got some grain
to keep from starvation
my woman with eyes curved like swords.
I have no servants, my Lord in Kōḷili,
send me men to carry the grain!

3

You have a woman as half your self;
the Lady Gaṅgā lives on your spreading matted hair;
you know well the problems
of supporting two good women.
In Kuṇṭaiyūr surrounded by beautiful groves

I got some grain.
Primal Lord, God of miracles,
send me men to carry the grain!

4
What can I say? Have you ever been blamed
for sharing your body with Umā
whose lips are red like the ripe *toṇṭai* fruit?
In Kuṇṭaiyūr, full of lush gardens,
I got some grain.
Help me in my need!
Send me men to carry the grain!

6
You who share your self with the Goddess,
with Umā who wears the *kuravam* blossom in her hair!
Surely you know that Paravai is faint from hunger!
In Kuṇṭaiyūr,
town of gardens where the *kuravam* blooms,
I got some grain.
O Lord whose girdle is a snake,
send me men to carry the grain!

7
Lord, I think only of you,
I always sing of you alone.
You who share your body
with the Goddess with the sweet-smelling hair,
my Lord in holy Kōḷili
with palaces of pure gold,
for love of me,
send me men to carry the grain!

8
Our Primal Lord who crushed the demon's
many arms and heads!
Fair Paravai, whose mound of Venus
is like the cobra's spreading hood,
is faint from hunger.
In Kuṇṭaiyūr, where monkeys leap in the woods,
I got some grain.
Take pity on me,
send me men to carry the grain!

10
They will be rid of misery, and will reign
in the heavenly world of the gods,
who know these ten verses
that the poet of holy Nāvalūr,
town praised by pious men,
has sung to the Lord
of Kōḷili rich in fertile groves,
asking him for men to carry his grain.

256. Cuntarar VII.46 *Nākaikkārōṇam*

1
You wander begging for alms
in many towns, singing hymns, teasing women,
practicing your tricks.
You roam about, wearing dead men's bones,
riding your bull.
You who conceal your wealth,
won't you take pity on me some day?
Give me strands of pearls, necklaces of diamonds
and gems to wear,
give me musk and sandal paste and sweet perfumes,
O Lord who lives in Nākaikkārōṇam by the sea!

4
You who roam the streets riding on your bull,
dishevelled hair streaming, playing on the beautiful *vīṇā*,
you have useless servants.
Handsome moon-crowned god, it is fitting
that you dance in the company of hideous ghosts.
Is it also proper, is it as a form of penance,
that you seduce innocent young women
with long, coiled hair?
Tell me, when will you give me bars of gold
to end all my trials,
O Lord who lives in Nākaikkārōṇam by the sea?

256, v. 7. Cuntarar cites the legend of Śiva's gift of gold coins to Appar and Campantar in Vīḻimiḻalai as a precedent that justifies his own request. v. 8. "The heaps of gold" probably refers to the gold in the temple treasury in Tiruvārūr, out of which Cuntarar demands a third. v. 11. "Addressing as his close friend": "*aṇmayattāl*," "intimately, with the freedom arising from intimate friendship."

5
Handsome Lord, you have made me your own slave,
I go about serving you.
Yet you wander as you please, insulting people, picking fights,
doing repulsive deeds, boasting of worse.
Give me sweet perfumes, fine clothes,
and jewels from your store,
O god who, in the ancient miracle,
rose as the cosmic flame hard to behold
even for the gods who searched for you,
O Lord who lives in Nākaikkārōṇam by the sea!

7
He came to you boasting of his strength,
and lifted the hill where you sat,
absorbed in a lover's quarrel,
with your sweet-voiced Goddess
who wears a silk cloth on her wide, bright mound of Venus,
You crushed the glorious king of Laṅkā,
then, hearing him sing your praise in hymns,
gave him a chariot and sword.
Once in Vīḻimiḻalai, home of many brahmins,
you gave gold coins every day,
so that your loving devotees might not starve.
Even thus bless me today,
O Lord who lives in Nākaikkārōṇam by the sea!

8
Once you took me, promising me a livelihood;
now you say nothing to me,
you won't do anything for me.
O Lord with the mighty trident, though you are very rich,
you won't give anything to me, your old devotee.
I want just one
of the three bright heaps of gold
you showered in lovely Ārūr—
If you won't give it to me,
I won't let you take another step.
So give me a horse to ride, swift as the wind,
O Lord of Nākaikkārōṇam by the sea!

10
Lord who holds the fawn,
you took me of your own free will,

and promised me great wealth.
You plied me with lies, and went off to Kīḻvēḷūr's shrine!
Is this fair? If you cared for me,
would you cheat me like this?
I want a blazing golden sword, gold flowers,
and silk sash,
and curry and fine rice with ghee to eat
three times a day,
O Lord who lives in Nākaikkārōṇam by the sea!

11
O Lord who is the only support
for sweet-voiced Caṅkili and Paravai, and myself,
to whom else can we turn?
Help me in my need, for I am your true devotee.
Give me strands of lustrous pearls,
shining silk and flowers,
fine musk and sandal paste!
They will rule in the world of the gods,
who know these fine Tamil verses
composed by Ārūraṉ, the poet from rich Nāvalūr,
addressing as his close friend
the Lord of Nākaikkārōṇam by the sea!

257. Cuntarar VII.34 *Pukalūr*

1
Do not sing the praise of false men
who give nothing to the suppliant,
though he flatters, and grovels,
and speaks only sweet words!
Poets! Sing our Father in Pukalūr,
who gives us food and shelter in this life.
Praise him and end your trials,
and you will surely be rulers of Śiva's world
when you reach the other shore!

257, v. 2. Bhīma and Arjuna are two of the five Pāṇḍava brothers, heroes of the epic *Mahābhārata*. Bhīma is an exemplar of physical strength, Arjuna, of skill in arms. Pāri is one of the seven great legendary "*vaḷḷal*" (patrons and donors) who supported poets in the Caṅkam age. In the *Puṟanāṉūṟu*, a Caṅkam anthology, there are several poems dedicated to Pāri as the most generous of patrons. See Hart, *Poets of the Tamil Anthologies*, pp. 162–69. Pāri continues to be the proverbial exemplar of generosity in Tamil country. v. 8. "Grain": "*eḷ*," literally, "sesame seed."

2
Though you call the weakling "Bhīma,"
"Mighty Arjuna, matchless archer!"
though you exalt the miser
with the title of great Pāri,
they won't give you a penny.
Poets! Sing our auspicious Lord
with ash-smeared body in Pukalūr,
and you will surely be rulers
of the highest heavens of the gods!

3
Though you praise them, saying
"Master of many lands, O scholar!
O generous host to your kinsmen and friends!"
they will give you nothing.
Poets! Sing our Lord in cool Pukalūr
rich in plowed fields where birds sing,
and you will surely reign in glory
over the world of the gods!

4
Though you flatter the weak old man
with grey hair and trembling limbs,
saying, "O youth with strong shoulders like hills!"
you will get nothing from him.
Poets! Sing Pukalūr of the blessed Lord
who rides on the tall white bull,
and you will surely reign as kings
in the world of the gods!

5
Though you praise the wicked man,
the great rogue, the sinner, the crooked one,
the criminal, and call him a good man,
he won't give you a thing.
Poets! Sing Pukalūr of the blessed one
with matted red hair that shines like gold,
and you will surely be rid of the sorrows of life,
and attain release!

8
Though you flatter the miser
who hoards his wealth down to the last grain,

and won't give even to the poorest of the poor,
though you hail him as your kinsman, your noble patron,
you will get nothing from him.
Poets! Sing fine Pukalūr,
where birds flock together,
and you will surely escape
being mired in sin!

11
Those who know these ten verses
that the poet Ūraṉ,
from Nāvalūr of groves fragrant with flowers,
father of Vaṉappakai, Caṭaiyaṉ's son,
the Rude Devotee,
has sung of the dear Lord
who dwells in southern Pukalūr
where fresh lilies bloom in the fields
will surely reach our righteous Lord's feet.

Ascent to Kailāsa

As with Campantar's hymns, we find few identifiable references in Cuntarar's hymns to the many miracles which he is said to have performed: saving a boy from a crocodile (in Pukkoḷiyūr Avināci); quelling the floodtide of the Kaveri (in Tiruvaiyāṟu); overcoming highwaymen in a remote forest (near Tirumurukaṉpūṇṭi). Nor are Cuntarar's adventures with the Cēra king Cēramāṉ Perumāḷ Nāyaṉār (Kaḻaṟiṟṟaṟivār), himself a poet-saint of the Tamil Śaiva canon, recorded in the seventh book of the *Tēvāram*. However, since Cuntarar dedicates a number of hymns to shrines in the Pāṇṭiya and Cēra regions—two hymns in the latter group are dedicated to the shrine in Añcaikkaḷam, the ancient Cēra capital at Karūr or Vañci—it is quite likely that the legends of the saint's celebrated friendship with the Cēra monarch and his travels in the Cēra land are based on historical fact. Cuntarar's last hymn (VII.100, Poem 258) is concerned with the poet's bodily ascent to Kailāsa, Śiva's Himalayan abode, mounted on a white elephant sent by Śiva. According to the traditional narrative, the Cēra king accompanied the poet on horseback. With this striking visionary poem, the final hymn of the *Tēvāram* corpus, we end our brief account of the life of "the Lord's Comrade."

258. Cuntarar VII.100 *Tirunoṭittāṉmalai*

1
Knowing him as my maker,
I made many hymns for his golden feet.
O wonder, that the Highest God in Noṭittāṉmalai
cared for me, though I am no better than a dog,
that he separated my soul from flesh,
and gave me a glorious elephant
on which to rise to heaven,
welcomed by all the gods!

2
Was it to end his enmity with elephants
since the day he flayed the elephant-demon's hide,
that, as I controlled the vital breaths
and remained in steady contemplation
of the Shining One,
the Highest God in Noṭittāṉmalai
blessed me with an elephant
which the great gods of heaven
themselves worshipped and made me mount?

3
I don't know any sacred chants;
delighting in the householder's life,

258. "Noṭittāṉmalai," "Hill of him who crushed [the demon]," is said to be one of the Tamil names of Mount Kailāsa. v. 1. "Separated my soul from flesh": some commentators interpret "*ūṉuyir vēṟu ceytāṉ*" as meaning "made the soul reach transcendence in the flesh" (*jīvanmukti*). v. 2. Cuntarar describes the yogic technique by which the devotee sees Śiva within himself. v. 5. The white color of the elephant signifies excellence and celestial origin. Indra, king of gods, rides on the white elephant Airāvata. v. 7, 10. The sea-god is Varuṇa. The "Father in Añcai" is "Añcaiyappar," Śiva in the temple at Añcaikkaḷam in Cēra country, the shrine connected with Vañci or Karūr, the capital of the Cēras. Cuntarar's reference to Añcaikkaḷam and the ocean make it clear that he composed this hymn in remembrance of his visit to the Cēra coastal shrine. These references may also have inspired the local tradition that Cēramāṉ and Cuntarar traveled to Kailāsa by sea. Among the paintings depicting the life of Cuntarar at the eleventh-century Cōḻa temple of Brihadīśvara in Tanjore, the scene of the ascent shows Cuntarar and Ceramāṉ on their mounts, riding the waves. Cēkkiḻār suggests that this tradition is inaccurate; he makes the two saints ascend to Kailāsa through a path in the sky. It is probably best to take the simplest reading of Cuntarar's words, namely, that he wished the ocean's waves to carry his reverent thoughts to the Lord in the seaside shrine of Añcaikkaḷam. v. 8. I have taken "*varamalivāṇaṉ*" to mean "the god who gives all blessings or boons," i.e., Śiva. The commentator to the *Tēvāram* Ātīṉam edition suggests that Vāṇaṉ is one of Śiva's *gaṇas*. In the general mythological tradition, *vāṇaṉ* (Bāṇāsura) is a son of the demon Bali.

I was a servant who always adorned himself
and committed many crimes.
O heart, how could I deserve this gift
from the Highest God in Noṭittāṉmalai,
this lovely elephant
which journeys through the sky?

4
O heart who took delight in worldly life,
as I wallowed in the deep pit
of powerful karma caused by the love of women,
the Highest God in Noṭittāṉmalai
led me out,
gave me an elephant I did not deserve,
made all the immortals
surround me in celebration!

5
Today I have seen the miracle
of your devoted servant,
who was born on earth and sang your praise,
reaching the Golden World.
The Highest God in Noṭittāṉmalai
displayed my body
on the white elephant
for the gods themselves to worship.

6
When I lived a false life,
not knowing the way to yoke the senses
and worship him with flowers,
the Highest God in Noṭittāṉmalai
entered my heart, gave me immortality,
and bestowed upon me, though I did not deserve it,
an angry elephant
before the gods of heaven themselves!

7
As I rode up the hill, seated on the elephant
whose steps shook the earth and sky,
the king of the sea himself worshipped me with flowers.
The Highest God in Noṭittāṉmalai
has saved me from destruction.

8
As heaven resounded with Hara's name,
with the chants of the Veda and Āgama,
and the hymns of the learned brahmins,
the Highest God in Noṭittāṉmalai
showed me the path,
the Lord who gives all blessings
gave me a splendid elephant to ride.

9
My Lord gave me a fine rutting elephant to ride,
and made Indra, Māl, Brahmā, and all the gods
give me ceremonial welcome,
and when sages of great ascetic power asked:
"Who is this man?"
the Highest God in Noṭittāṉmalai replied,
"This is Ūraṉ, my friend."

10
O Lord of the ocean, carry to the Father in Añcai
these ten verses
that Ūraṉ of Nāvalūr town
where the sweet sugar cane grows,
has joyfully composed
in sweet, melodious Tamil,
in praise of golden Noṭittāṉmalai,
which rises above the flood
in every age of the world.

4 The Servants of the Lord

(POEMS 259–270)

The lives of the first three saints are closely linked with the lives and acts of other Nāyaṉārs. Few among the sixty-three saints named in Cuntarar's "List of the Holy Devotees" (*Tirut toṇṭat tokai*) are actually mentioned in the rest of the *Tēvāram*. Yet wherever such reference is made, whether in passing or in detail, it serves to illuminate in an authentic, concrete manner the sense of community that informs the poet-saints' *bhakti*.

In addition to several Pallava kings and princes, the *Tirut toṇṭat tokai* contains the names of monarchs of the Pāṇṭiya, Cōḻa, and Cēra kingdoms. Cuntarar describes many of the saints as "warlike" or "victorious"; the very names of some Nāyaṉārs betray their identity as warriors, generals, or petty chieftains (Ēṉātinātar, Muṉaiyaṭuvār, Viṟaṉmiṇṭar). The culture and milieu of the warriors and princes predominate, but the list of the "Servants of the Lord" is also representative of a broad cross-section of the population, including kings and commoners, men and women, a community consisting of local figures. These Tamil personages are identified individually and in some detail, whereas the sages and devotees of puranic legend, and of distant times and places, are relegated to shadowy descriptions such as "*appālum aṭiccārntār*" ("all who seek the Lord's feet everywhere"). It is fitting that the *Tirut toṇṭat tokai* became the core of what is perhaps the crowning achievement of Tamil Śaiva literature, Cēkkiḻār's "Great Epic," which gives us a vivid sense of the people, places, and values that continue to inspire Tamil Śaiva religion to this day.

Campantar and Appar

259. Cuntarar VII.62.8 *Kōlakkā*

The Lord who was moved by
the sweet, melodious Tamil hymns

259, 260. It is clear from the references in these verses that the traditions surrounding the lives of Campantar and Appar had crystallized to a great extent by Cuntarar's time.

that Ñāṉacampantaṉ sang to him every day,
and gave him the cymbals,
while the whole world looked on,
the Lord who is the focus of my thoughts,
the Dancer who dances to his demons' songs,
the god who lives in Kōḷili's great temple,
praised by his eight hosts—
I have seen him in Kōlakkā.

260. Cuntarar VII.88.8 *Vīḻimiḻalai*

You wandered about in the wide world,
begging for food in every town.
Wishing to hear good Tamil hymns
as you dwelt in holy Miḻalai,
home of scholars of the four Vedas,
every day you gave a gold coin to your devotee.
O Lord of the rich, cool town of Vīḻi,
favor me also with such grace!

261. Cuntarar VII.67.5 *Valivalam*

Reaching Valivalam, I saw
him who loves the hymns in which I repeat
all that melodious Ñāṉacampantaṉ
and Nāvukkaracar, King of Speech,
have sung of him in their good Tamil songs.
I saw the Lord whom all the great gods revere,
the god who, knowing me as his ignorant devotee,
melted my stony heart, showed me his holy feet,
and severed every link in my chain of births.

262. Cuntarar VII.78.10 *Kētāram*

They will dwell in the highest world,
who can sing the sweet Tamil hymn
composed on our Lord's holy town of Kētāram
by Ūraṉ, lowly devotee,
and humble servant of Nāvukkaracaṉ, King of Speech,
the Tamil poet Ñāṉacampantaṉ,
and all the devotees of Śiva.

Naminanti

263. Appar IV.103 *Tiruvārūr*

2
The jewel among devotees, the humble servant
of Ārūr's Lord who wears the sweet lotus garland,
Nampinanti who led the celebration in Ārūr
of the Uttiram festival in Paṅkuṉi,
renowned in many towns,
made the oil lamps burn on water
at Tiruvārūr's shrine—
surely the whole world knows this miracle!

4
Our ambrosia in Tiruvārūr is served
not only by lordly ascetics who, like their Lord,
wear the winding snake at the waist,
and the shining moon on the head;
he has the best servant of all
in Nanti, whose glory rests
on his humble service at the feet
of every ash-smeared devotee
who came to Tiruvārūr's shrine.

6
Though men of great wealth flock to this shrine,
with flags and canopies,
fans and torches, drum and conch,
though Ārūr is the abode
of the flawless Lord himself,
yet if Nanti were to leave the town,
dark night would descend
upon the ash-smeared devotees of the Lord.

Pukaḻttuṇai

264. Cuntarar VII.9.6 *Aricirkaraip Puttūr*

The brahmin, your temple servant,
daily carried water from the Aricil

263. The Nāyaṉār Nampinanti is also known as "Naminanti" and "Nanti."
264. Cuntarar's detailed account of the exemplary devotion of Pukaḻttuṇai Nāyaṉār of

for your bathing rite.
Once, faint with hunger,
he let the water jar fall on your crown
and stood trembling.
Your gracious reward to good Pukaḻttuṇai
was the daily wage of a gold coin,
O pure one in Puttūr rich in groves!

Amarnīti

265. Appar IV.98.7 *Nallūr*

This wide world will surely tell the tale
of the merchant in Nallūr of blooming lotus ponds—
how the Lord came to him,
commanded him to guard his loincloth with the waistband,
played a trick on him,
then graciously possessed the man
and his long-eyed wife.

Kōcceṅkaṇāṉ and Caṇṭīcar

266. Appar IV.65 *Cāykkāṭu*

3
When the blameless spider encircled the Lord,
and made a canopy with thread from his mouth

Puttūr tallies in most respects with Cēkkiḻār's. The saint's hunger was due to a famine that ravaged the land. In the *Periya purāṇam* version, Pukaḻttuṇai dropped the pot on the *liṅga*, having been overcome by sleep. Śiva appeared to him in a dream, and blessed him with the daily wage that would help him continue his service to the Lord in times of great hardship. "*Akattaṭimai*" refers to temple service.

265. This is the story of Amarnīti Nāyaṉār, whom Cēkkiḻār also identifies as a merchant in Nallūr. A great Śaiva philanthropist, Amarnīti gave food and clothing to Śaiva devotees. One day Śiva came to him in the guise of a *brahmacārin* (a student of sacred learning), and left his loincloth for safekeeping with the merchant while he took his bath. Upon his return the "*brahmacārin*" found that his loincloth had mysteriously disappeared. Thereupon he demanded that Amarnīti replace it with objects equal in weight. To his surprise Amarnīti found that not all his possessions could equal one loincloth in weight. Only when the saint, along with his wife and child, ascended the scales, could the weight be made up. It was then revealed that the devout merchant and his family had become the "possessions" of none other than the Lord.

266, v. 3. In this account of the spider legend, Appar mentions the rose-apple (*nāval*) tree, which is the sacred tree of the shrine at Āṉaikkā. For the details of the legend of the spider's

for the deity who dwelt in the scant shade
of a rose-apple tree that stood exposed on open ground,
the Lord who loves to dwell in Cāykkāṭu
made him a crowned king
and gave him the earth to rule.

6
When good Caṇṭi cut off with a sharp axe
his father's foot when he obstructed the son's worship,
with mantra chants, and garlands of *koṉṟai* flowers,
with the ritual bathing of his God with milk and ghee,
the Lord who loves to dwell in Cāykkāṭu
gave him the *koṉṟai* garland
from his own cool matted hair.

Many Saints

267. Appar IV.49 *Kuṟukkai Vīraṭṭāṉam*

3
Caṇṭi sat bathing with fresh milk
the *liṅga* of sand that he had established
under the spreading green *ātti* tree;

---

rebirth as Kōcceṅkaṇāṉ, see poem 267. v. 6. Śiva's gift of the *koṉṟai* wreath or garland to Caṇṭīcar has been immortalized in a sculptured relief at the temple in Gangaikondacholapuram.

267. In verse 4 Appar speaks of the popular legend of the spider (*cilanti*) of Āṉaikkā being reborn as King Kōcceṅkaṇāṉ. According to the local tradition in Āṉaikkā (Tiruvāṉaikkā), the *liṅga* at this sacred place stood under a *nāval* (rose-apple, Sanskrit *jambū*) tree. A spider who lived on the tree felt compassion for the Lord who had to face the harsh elements. With great devotion he wove a canopy with his body's thread to shelter the image of God. Pleased, Śiva rewarded him with rebirth as the devout Cōḻa king and Nāyaṉār. v. 6. As the name "Cākkiyaṉār" indicates, this Nāyaṉār was a Buddhist who converted to Śaivism. Born in Caṅkamaṅkai, he came to Kāñci, a center of Buddhism in South India. It is said that the sight of the image of Śiva so moved Cākkiyaṉ that he began the practice of throwing stones at the image as a devotional offering. The strange but sincere devotion of this "heretic" was rewarded with Śiva's world and sainthood. In verse 7 Appar provides a graphic description of the famous deed of Kaṇṇappar, the hunter-saint of Kāḷatti. It is interesting to note that, in this hymn, with the exception of the story of Caṇṭīcar, Appar does not specify the *liṅga* as the object of worship. In verse 9 the poet refers to the Nāyaṉār Kaṇampullar, whose chosen vocation was that of lighting lamps at the temple in Tillai. A poor man, Kaṇampullar cut grass and sold it in exchange for oil to light the lamps. One day, when no one would buy his grass (*kaṇampul*), he tried to light the lamps with the grass; when this failed, he bent over the lamps, burning his own hair as fuel, whereupon Śiva appeared and rewarded him with his grace. Śiva's "holy attributes" are the eight divine qualities (*eṇkuṇam*), including power and grace. See Appar VI.312.10 (Poem 240).

when his father tried to destroy the rite with a kick,
the boy struck out at his foot
with a great, deadly axe.
The Lord of the Vīraṭṭāṉam shrine in Kuṟukkai
rewarded him with a dish of fine ambrosial food.

4
Upon the death of the spider of Āṉaikkā
who had made a sacred canopy for his god,
the Lord of the Vīraṭṭāṉam shrine in Kuṟukkai
gave him rebirth as King Kōcceṅkaṇāṉ,
in the race of the Cōḻas of Cōṇāṭu
where the Kaveri flows, mingling with many streams.

6
The Lord of the Vīraṭṭāṉam shrine in Kuṟukkai
gave to Cākkiyaṉār, who lived on rice gruel,
and threw stones at Śiva,
the kingship of heaven and ambrosial food.
This Lord loves the Kolli mode,
and dances a beautiful dance at night,
holding fire in his hand.

7
The hunter approached,
bearing bow and arrow, a guard's weapons,
the offering of meat in his hand;
holding his leather sandals, he bathed his God
with ritual water from his pure mouth.
When God's fiery eyes began streaming red blood,
and he plucked out his own eyes to stop the wounds,
the Lord of the Vīraṭṭāṉam shrine in Kuṟukkai
at once held him back.

9
The Primal Lord, who contains Umā, the Goddess,
in half his frame,
is the healing draught who ends the trials
of those who worship him.
The Lord of the Vīraṭṭāṉam shrine in Kuṟukkai
bestowed his grace on Kaṇampullar,
who followed the precious, good path to release,

and he is the one who always gives his holy attributes
to his loving devotees.

268. Cuntarar VII.65 *Ni<u>n</u><u>r</u>iyūr*

1
I heard that you once gave
wealth, and generosity, and powerful sovereignty
to the spider who served you with his offering,
turning him into King Ceṅkaṇā<u>n</u>.
So I have come to your flower feet,
O Lord of holy Ni<u>n</u><u>r</u>iyūr of the South,
where the surging Po<u>n</u><u>n</u>i brings many gems
that gangs of little boys gather in play,
and pile up on every street and porch and yard!

2
I know that you have favored
Taṇṭi who attained immortality,
receiving beautiful clothes and rich ornaments,
ambrosial food, and a garland to wear,
Nāvi<u>n</u>ukkaraiya<u>n</u>, King of Speech, who composed
seven times seven hundred sweet songs,
and Kaṇṇappar the hunter-saint.
Seeking the love and sweet grace these men have won,
I, too, have come to you,
O Lord of Southern Ni<u>n</u><u>r</u>iyūr
where parrots discourse in chaste, grammatical Tamil!

268, v. 2. In this verse, "Taṇṭi" refers to Caṇṭīcar, who received the *ko<u>n</u><u>r</u>ai* garland and ambrosial food from Śiva; this name is derived from *daṇḍa* (a stick), referring to the shepherd's staff, which turned into an axe when Caṇṭīcar attacked his father. Caṇṭīcar has a separate shrine in Tamil Śiva temples and receives special ritual honors of clothing, ornaments, and garlands. Cuntarar may be referring to the ritual as well as the mythic context. The "Taṇṭi" ("the one with the stick") of the sixty-three Nāya<u>n</u>mār is quite distinct from Caṇṭīcar. According to the hagiographers, the blind man Taṇṭi set to work to extend the temple tank at Tiruvārūr on the side where it was cramped by Jain monastic buildings. When the Jains protested, Taṇṭi claimed that if his cause were just, he would gain eyesight, and his opponents would be blinded. The king, who came to judge the dispute, witnessed Taṇṭi's triumph; the blinded Jains left Tiruvārūr. Nāvi<u>n</u>ukkaraiya<u>n</u>: a version of "Nāvukkaraca<u>n</u>." Cuntarar's claim that Appar composed "seven times seven hundred" songs (elsewhere he makes it a mere seven hundred) reflects the fondness of the Tamil Śaivas for crediting their saints with extraordinary feats. "Chaste, grammatical Tamil": "*tiṇaikoḷ centamiḻ*," literally, "the pure classical language with its grammatical categories and poetic genres." "*Tiṇai*" can mean a number of things, including classes of nouns and the landscape complexes and genres (*akam*, *pu<u>r</u>am*) of classical Tamil poetry.

269. Cuntarar VII.55 *Puṉkūr*

2
When the rains failed,
and the peasants implored you, crying,
"Save us! Give us water for our fields,
and we will give you much land!"—
you spread over the sky as a shining white cloud,
pouring torrential rain,
then yourself dammed the flood,
and took twelve more *vēli*s of land.
Seeing your act of grace,
I have come to your holy feet,
you who live in holy Puṉkūr of fertile groves!

3
When you had cured the terrible disease
of Ēyarkōṉ, owner of twelve fertile *vēli*s of land,
you turned to Caṇṭi,
who had bathed with fresh cow's milk
Śiva in an image of soft white sand,
and then cut off the foot of his father
who kicked at his God.
You gave him the flowers from your hair.
Seeing this act of grace, Lord of the demons,
I have reached your golden feet,
you who live in holy Puṉkūr of fertile groves!

4
You accept as favors
even the faults of your devotees,
men like Ñāṉacampantaṉ, skilled Tamil poet,
the King of Speech and Nāḷaippōvāṉ,
the skillful gambler, virtuous Cākkiyaṉ, the spider-king,
Kaṇṇappaṉ and Kaṇampullaṉ.
Knowing your nature to be thus,
I have come to your feet with the sounding hero's ring,
you who live in holy Puṉkūr,
where golden lotuses bloom in the pools!

269, vv. 2, 3. "*Vēli*": a measure of land. Cuntarar's hymn is the earliest reference to the saint Ēyarkōṉ Kalikkāma Nāyaṉār in connection with the obscure local legend of Śiva causing rain and receiving land from the peasants. Ēyarkōṉ is better known through the *Periya purāṇam* account in which he appears as a contemporary and erstwhile enemy of Cuntarar. This chief of the Ēyars (Haihayas?) had sworn enmity with Cuntarar because the latter had had the audacity to use Śiva as his messenger (*tūtaṉ*) in his negotiations with Paravai in

270. Cuntarar VII.39 TIRUT TOṆṬAT TOKAI (THE LIST OF THE HOLY DEVOTEES)

1
Of all who serve the brahmins of Tillai,
I am the servant.
Of Nīlakaṇṭaṉ, the blessed potter,
I am the servant.
Of Iyaṟpakai who gave without limit,
I am the servant.
Of the servants of Māṟaṉ of Iḷaiyāṉkuṭi,
I am the servant.
Of Meypporuḷ of invincible might,
I am the servant.
Of Viṟaṉmiṇṭaṉ from Kuṉṟai of spacious groves,
I am the servant.
Of Amarnīti with the soft jasmine garland,
I am the servant.
I am the poet Ārūraṉ, slave of my Father in Ārūr.

Tiruvārūr. Śiva appeared to Kalikkāmar and told him that he must approach Cuntarar for a cure for the stomach pain (*piṇi* in v. 3) that afflicted him. Saying that he would die rather than meet his enemy, Kalikkāmar ran a sword through himself. Taking responsibility for this calamity, Cuntarar tried to commit suicide. Śiva intervened, revived Kalikkāmar, and caused a reconciliation between the two saints. v. 4. "The skillful gambler": "*kaṟṟa cūtaṉ*," refers to Mūrkka Nāyaṉār, who provided for Śiva's devotees with money earned from gambling (*cūtu*, *cūtāṭṭam*). "Nāḷaippōvāṉ," "He-would-go-[to the Lord]-the-very-next-day" is the untouchable (*pulaiyaṉ*) saint Nantaṉār, who defied caste laws and merged with his Lord in the temple at Tillai. Nantaṉār is one of the most popular figures in contemporary Tamil devotional lore.

270. The refrain: "Of the servants of . . . , I am the servant": "*aṭiyārkkum aṭiyēṉ*." Further details about the Nāyaṉārs listed in the *Tirut toṇṭat tokai* may be found in the excellent, detailed comparative study of the accounts of Cuntarar, Nampi Āṇṭār Nampi, and Cēkkiḻār in Dorai Rangaswamy, *Religion and Philosophy*, vol. 2. v. 1. "*Tillaivāḻ antaṇar*": The (Three Thousand) Brahmins settled in Tillai. v. 2. Kalayaṉ: Kuṅkiliyakkalayar, who sold his wife's wedding necklace in order to provide incense (*kuṅkiliyam*) for the temple ritual. "Tāyaṉ of the complete scythe" is the Nāyaṉār Vāṭṭāyar or Arivāṭṭāyar, so called because he tried to cut off his own head with a scythe (*arivāḷ*) when he accidentally dropped the food offerings he was carrying for his special worship of Śiva. v. 3. The pilgrim who would "go . . . the very next day," "Nāḷaippōvār," is Nantaṉār. "*Cemmaiyē*": "straightaway," hence "the *very* next day." v. 4. Pēy: The female saint Kāraikkāl Ammaiyār. Kulacciṟai: The pious minister of the Pandyan king. v. 5 Some commentators take "*nāṭṭamiku taṇṭi*" to mean "the devout Taṇṭi." The translation "Taṇṭi who received vision [*nāṭṭam*, 'eye,' 'sight']," is more in keeping with the legend in which Śiva restores the blind Nāyaṉār's sight. See Poem 268. Tirumūlaṉ: Tirumūlar, author of the *Tirumantiram*. v. 6. Kaḻaṟiṟṟaṟivār: Cēramāṉ Perumāḷ Nāyaṉār, author of the *Poṉvaṇṇattantāti* and other works in the eleventh Tirumuṟai. v. 7. The commentators take "*poyyaṭimaiy illāta pulavar*" ("poets who shun crooked patrons") to mean Tamil poets of the Caṅkam age. Aiyaṭikaḷ Kāṭavarkōṉ: an early Pallava ruler, au-

2
Of Prince Eṟipattaṉ with the sharp spear,
I am the servant.
Of the servants of Lord Ēṉāti,
I am the servant.
Of Lord Kaṇṇappaṉ, famed for his knowledge,
I am the servant.
Of the servants of Kalayaṉ of Kaṭavūr,
I am the servant.
Of generous Māṉakkañcāṟaṉ with shoulders like hills,
and the servants of Tāyaṉ of the complete scythe,
I am the servant.
Of Āṉāyaṉ of Maṅkai on the turbulent river,
I am the servant.
I am the poet Ārūraṉ, slave of my Father in Ārūr.

3
Of Mūrtti who reigned over the world
through the three emblems of sovereignty,
I am the servant.
Of Murukaṉ and Uruttira Pacupati,
I am the servant.
Of the holy pilgrim who would "go to the Lord
the very next day,"
I am the servant.
Of the servants of holy Kuṟipputtoṇṭaṉ,
I am the servant.
Of great Caṇṭi, devotee of the Lord who gives us release,
the young man who worshipped the *liṅga*
and cut off with an axe the foot of his own father
when he angrily disrupted the child's sincere worship
of the Lord's holy image,

---

thor of the *Kṣēttirat tiru veṇpā.* v. 8. "Upright" ("Niṉṟacīr") Neṭumāṟaṉ is identified as the Pandyan king of Maturai who was brought back to Śaivism by Campantar. v. 9. Kōṭpuli of Nāṭṭiyattāṉkuṭi, father of Ciṅkaṭi and Vaṉappakai. v. 10. This verse lists categories of saintly persons, rather than individual Nāyaṉārs. The categories themselves are open to several interpretations, ranging from the very general to the technically specific. "Every man who meditates on Śiva" ("*cittattaic civaṉpālē vaippār*") is taken to signify yogis or *cittar*s; "*paramaṉaiyē pāṭuvār*" ("those who sing only of the Lord") could indicate poet-saints such as Cuntarar himself or those (such as the *ōtuvār*s) employed as singers of hymns in the temples. "Men who thrice daily [at the three daily rituals of worship] touch the Lord's holy image" refers to temple priests; the ash-smeared sages (*muṉivar*) are probably legendary sages who figure in puranic narratives. "*Appālum aṭiccārntār*" ("all who seek the Lord's feet everywhere") suggests devotees from distant places and far-off times. v. 11. "The noble queen" is Maṅkaiyarkkaraci, the Pandyan queen celebrated by Campantar.

I am the servant.
I am the poet Ārūraṉ, slave of my Father in Ārūr.

4
Of blessed Nāvukkaracaṉ, "Lord of Speech,"
who took for his glory
nothing other than the good Lord's name
in which all blessings abide,
I am the servant.
Of the servants of the noble lord Kulacciṟai,
I am the servant.
Of Perumiḻalaik kuṟumpaṉ and the revered Pēy,
I am the servant.
Of the servants of princely Appūti,
I am the servant.
Of Nīlanakkaṉ from Cāttamaṅkai by the sounding river,
I am the servant.
Of the servants of the noble Lord Naminanti,
I am the servant.
I am the poet Ārūraṉ, slave of our Father in Ārūr.

5
Of the servants of my master Campantaṉ
who worships nothing but the feet
of the Lord who wears in his hair
fragrant flowers swarming with humming bees
and the good *koṉṟai*'s honey-filled blossom,
I am the servant.
Of the servants of Kalikkāmaṉ, prince of the Ēyars,
I am the servant.
Of the servants of our Master Tirumūlaṉ,
I am the servant.
Of Taṇṭi who was blessed with vision, and of Mūrkkaṉ,
I am the servant.
Of Cōmāci Māṟaṉ of Ampar,
I am the servant.
I am the poet Ārūraṉ, slave of our Father in Ārūr.

6
Of Cākkiyaṉ who devoutly threw stones
at the feet of the Lord who shares his body
with Umā, whose lovely breasts are bound
with the breastcloth,
I am the servant.

Of generous Ciṟappuli of good fame,
I am the servant.
Of Ciṟuttoṇṭaṉ of Ceṅkāṭṭaṅkuṭi,
I am the servant.
Of Kaḻaṟiṟṟaṟivāṉ, generous as a showering cloud,
I am the servant.
Of the servants of Kaṇanātaṉ of Kāḻi-on-the-sea,
I am the servant.
Of Kūṟṟaṉ of the victorious spear, prince of Kaḷantai,
I am the servant.
I am the poet Ārūraṉ, slave of our Father in Ārūr.

7
Of all poets who shun crooked patrons,
I am the servant.
Of King Pukaḻ Cōḻaṉ who was slain in battle
at fertile Karuvūr field,
I am the servant.
Of the true devotee, Naraciṅka Muṉaiyaraiyaṉ,
I am the servant.
Of Atipattaṉ of wave-washed Nākai-on-the-sea,
I am the servant.
Of the servants of Kalikkampaṉ of the drawn bow,
who cut off enemies' arms,
Of Kaliyaṉ, and of Catti, the Variñcaiyar chief
with the hero's anklet,
I am the servant.
Of the servants of Aiyaṭikaḷ, King of the Kāṭavas,
I am the servant.
I am the poet Ārūraṉ, slave of our Father in Ārūr.

8
Of Lord Kaṇampullaṉ who worshipped
the feet of the Lord with the poison-stained throat
as his only shield, and of Kāri,
I am the servant.
Of the servants of "upright" Neṭumāṟaṉ
who won the battle of Nelvēli,
king who has mastered his mind and senses,
I am the servant.
Of the servants of Vāyilāṉ of ancient Mayilai,
where the red coral washed ashore by the sea
brightens the sky,
I am the servant.

Of Prince Muṉaiyaṭuvāṉ of the spear of war,
I am the servant.
I am the poet Ārūraṉ, slave of our Father in Ārūr.

9
Of the servants of Kaḻaṟciṅkaṉ, Kāṭava king,
sovereign protector of sea-girt earth,
I am the servant.
Of Prince Iṭaṅkaḻi with the flower garland,
and of the servants of Ceruttuṇai, King of Tañcai,
I am the servant.
Of Pukaḻttuṇai who meditated only on the golden feet
of the dancer who dances, making the snakes dance
on the tigerskin band at his waist,
I am the servant.
Of lordly Kōṭpuli of the victorious spear,
I am the servant.
I am the poet Ārūraṉ, slave of our Father in Ārūr.

10
Of all who worship Śiva as his devotees,
I am the servant.
Of those who sing only of the Lord,
I am the servant.
Of every man who meditates on Śiva,
I am the servant.
Of all who are born in holy Ārūr,
I am the servant.
Of men who thrice daily touch the Lord's holy image,
I am the servant.
Of sages who wear the sacred ash,
I am the servant.
Of all who seek the Lord's feet everywhere,
I am the servant.
I am the poet Ārūraṉ, slave of our Father in Ārūr.

11
Of renowned Pūcal of Niṉṟavūr, brahmin
who chanted the sacred Veda,
Of the noble queen with the beautiful bracelets,
and of Nēcaṉ,
I am the servant.
Of Ceṅkaṇ who ruled the world as King of the South,
I am the servant.

Of the Pāṇan̲ musician Tirunīlakaṇṭan̲,
I am the servant.
Those who delight in the song of devotion
sung by Ārūran̲, prince of holy Nāvalūr,
who loves Icaiñān̲i and Caṭaiyan̲,
true devotees of my Lord Aran̲'s feet,
will become lovers of our Father in Ārūr.

APPENDIXES AND GLOSSARY

APPENDIX A

Important Sacred Places in the *Tēvāram*

The following sacred places have five or more *Tēvāram* hymns dedicated to them.

C – Campantar; A – Appar; Cu – Cuntarar

Place	Total no. of hymns	No. of hymns by each saint
Cōḻanāṭu, North of the River Kaveri		
Aiyāṟu (Tiruvaiyāṟu)	18	C 5; A 12; Cu 1
Āṉaikkā (Tiruvāṉaikkā)	7	C 3; A 3; Cu 1
Chidambaram (Kōyil, Tillai)	11	C 2; A 8; Cu 1
Cīrkāḻi (under twelve names)	71	C 67; A 3; Cu 1
Iṉṉampar	5	C 1; A 4
Kaḻippālai	8	C 2; A 5; Cu 1
Maḻapāṭi	6	C 3; A 2; Cu l
Nāraiyūr (Tirunāraiyūr)	5	C 3; A 2
Neyttāṉam	6	C 1; A 5
Paḻaṉam	6	C 1; A 5
Veṇkāṭu (Tiruveṇkāṭu)	6	C 3; A 2; Cu 1
Cōḻanāṭu, South of the River Kaveri		
Ārūr (Tiruvārūr), 37 hymns for three shrines:		
Main shrine	34	C 5; A 21; Cu 8
Araneṟi	2	A 2
Paravaiyuṇ-maṇṭaḷi	1	Cu 1
Āvaṭuturai	8	C 1; A 5; Cu 2
Cōṟṟuttuṟai	6	C 1; A 4; Cu 1

Place	Total no. of hymns	No. of hymns by each saint
Iṭaimarutūr (Tiruviṭaimarutūr)	12	C 6; A 5; Cu 1
Kaṭavūr (or Kaṭaiyūr), 8 hymns for two shrines:		
Vīraṭṭam	5	C 1; A 3; Cu 1
Mayāṉam	3	C 1; A 1; Cu 1
Maṟaikkāṭu (Vedāraṇyam)	9	C 4; A 4; Cu 1
Nākaikkārōṇam	7	C 2; A 4; Cu 1
Nākēccaram (Tirunākēccaram)	6	C 2; A 3; Cu 1
Naḷḷāṟu (Tirunaḷḷāṟu)	7	C 4; A 2; Cu 1
Nallūr	5	C 3; A 2
Pukalūr, 9 hymns for two shrines:		
Main shrine	8	C 2; A 5; Cu 1
Varttamāṉīccaram	1	C 1
Valañcuḻi	6	C 2; A 3; Cu 1
Vīḻimiḻalai (Tiruvīḻimiḻalai)	24	C 15; A 8; Cu 1
Pāṇṭināṭu (Pāṇṭiya-nāṭu)		
Ālavāy (Maturai)	11	C 9; A 2
Naṭunāṭu (the macro-region between Cōḻanāṭu and the northern region of Toṇṭaināṭu)		
Āmāttūr	5	C 2; A 2; Cu 1
Aṇṇāmalai (Tiruvaṇṇāmalai)	5	C 2; A 3
Atikai (Tiruvatikai Vīraṭṭāṉam)	18	C 1; A 16; Cu 1
Mutukuṉṟam (Vṛddhācalam)	11	C 7; A 1; Cu 3
Toṇṭaināṭu		
Kacci (Kāñci, Kanchipuram), 17 hymns for five shrines:		
Ēkampam	12	C 4; A 7; Cu 1
Mēṟṟaḷi	2	A 1; Cu 1
Ōṇakāntaṉṟaḷi	1	Cu 1
Anēkataṅkāvatam	1	Cu 1
Neṟik kāraikkāṭu	1	C 1
Māṟpēṟu	6	C 2; A 4
Oṟṟiyūr (Tiruvoṟṟiyūr)	8	C 1; A 5; Cu 2

APPENDIX B

The Twenty-three *Paṇ* Scale-Types in the *Tēvāram*

Classical Tamil *Paṇ* Scale-Type	Carnatic *Rāga* Scale-Type (similar to the classical *paṇ*)
Cevvaḻi	Yadukula Kāmbodhi
Takkarākam	Kannada Kāmbodhi
Puṟanīrmai	Bhūpālam?
Pañcamam	Āhiri
Kāntāram	Hejjajji? Mohanam?
Naṭṭapāṭai	Harikāmbodhi or Nāṭṭaikkuṟiñci
Antāḷikkuṟiñci	Śailadeśākṣi or Sāmā
Paḻampañcuram	Śaṅkarābharaṇam
Mēkarākakkuṟiñci	Nīlāmbari
Kollikkauvāṇam	Sindhu Kannaḍa or Naṭa Bhairavi
Paḻantakkarākam	Suddha Sāvēri or Ārabhi
Kuṟiñci	Harikāmbodhi? Malahari?
Naṭṭarākam	(Śubha) Pantuvarāḷi
Viyāḻakkuṟiñci	Saurāṣṭram
Centurutti	Madhyamāvati
Takkēci	Kāmbodhi
Kolli	Sindhu Kannaḍa or Nauroj
Intaḷam	Neḷitapañcami
Kāntārapañcamam	Kedāra Gauḷa or Nārāyaṇa Gauḷa
Kaucikam	Bhairavi
Piyantaikkāntāram	Hejjajji
Cīkāmaram	Nādanāmakriyā or Māyāmālava Gauḷa
Cātāri	Pantuvarāḷi

NOTE: Appar's Tāṇṭakam hymns are sung in the *rāga* Harikāmbodhi.

APPENDIX C

Aṭṭavīraṭṭāṉam: The Sites of the Eight Heroic Deeds of Śiva

Site	*Deed*
(Tiruk-) Kaṇṭiyūr Vīraṭṭam	Śiva cut off one of the heads of Brahmā
(Tiruk-) Kōvalūr Vīraṭṭam	Śiva killed the demon Andhaka
(Tirup-) Paṟiyalūr Vīraṭṭam	Śiva destroyed Dakṣa's sacrifice
(Tiruk-) Kuṟukkai Vīraṭṭam	Śiva burned Kāma, god of Love
(Tiruv-) Atikai Vīraṭṭam	Śiva destroyed the three cities of the demons
(Tiru-) Vaḻuvūr Vīraṭṭam	Śiva flayed the elephant-demon Gajāsura, and danced with the flayed skin
(Tiruk-) Kaṭavūr Vīraṭṭam	Śiva saved the boy Mārkaṇḍeya by kicking Kāla, god of Death
(Tiru-) Viṟkuṭi Vīraṭṭam	Śiva destroyed the demon Jalandhara

APPENDIX D

Major Puranic Myths of Śiva in the *Tēvāram*

Different versions of the myths of Śiva can be found in the *Mahābhārata* and Sanskrit Purāṇas, such as the *Śiva*, *Liṅga*, *Vāmana*, and *Skanda* Purāṇas. The Tamil *Kanta purāṇam*, which presents the major myths of Śiva in their authoritative Tamil version, is much later than the *Tēvāram* hymns. I have not followed any one of the above accounts exclusively in the general summaries I provide here. Readers interested in details and variants and their relationship to the *mūrti*s (iconographic forms) of Śiva may consult the following books: for the Sanskrit, Wendy D. O'Flaherty, *Hindu Myths* (Penguin, 1975), and Stella Kramrisch, *The Presence of Śiva* (Princeton University Press, 1981); and for the Tamil in relation to the Sanskrit, volume 1 of M. A. Dorai Rangaswamy, *Religion and Philosophy of the Tēvāram* (University of Madras, 1958–1959). These are cited below by the authors' surnames and titles abbreviated as *HM*, *PS*, and *RPT*.

ŚIVA MANIFESTS HIMSELF AS THE FIERY *Liṅga*: LIṄGODBHAVA-MŪRTI

At the end of a cosmic era, Brahmā and Viṣṇu were arguing with each other, each claiming that he was the supreme deity and the creator of the universe. Suddenly a great column of light—a fiery *liṅga*—appeared before them. The two rival gods agreed that the one who first succeeded in finding the top or base of the immense column would be acknowledged by the other as the supreme Lord. Taking the form of a boar, Viṣṇu burrowed deep into the earth, while Brahmā, turning himself into a wild goose, flew up into space. The search proved to be futile, and the gods were forced to admit defeat. At this point, Śiva graciously revealed himself in the cosmic *liṅga* (see illus. 10) and, their pride humbled, Brahmā and Viṣṇu bowed to him and declared Śiva's supremacy. (O'Flaherty, *HM*, 137–41; Kramrisch, *PS*, 158–78. Dorai Rangaswamy, *RPT*, 196–209.)

THE DESTRUCTION OF THE THREE CITIES: TRIPURĀNTAKA-MŪRTI

Tārakākṣa, Kamalākṣa, and Vidyunmālin, the three sons of the demon Tāraka, once practiced austerities (*tapas*) and won the gift of immense power from Brahmā. According to this boon, the three demons would live for a thousand years in three invincible, moving cities or castles (*tripura*), wreaking destruction in the universe, and the castles could be destroyed only by a cosmic arrow that would merge them into one and set fire to them. Śiva Mahādeva alone could accomplish the task. At the end of the thousand years the gods, elements, and other cosmic forces became the various parts of the bow, the arrow, and Śiva's chariot. With Brahmā as his charioteer, Śiva went forth, shot the single arrow of fire, and destroyed the three cities. (O'Flaherty, *HM*, 125–37; Kramrisch, *PS*, 405–12. Dorai Rangaswamy, *RPT*, 304–22.)

ŚIVA SWALLOWS POISON AT THE CHURNING OF THE OCEAN: VIṢĀPAHARAṆA-MŪRTI

The gods and demons decided to churn the celestial ocean of milk in order to bring forth *amṛta* (ambrosia), the elixir of immortality. With Mount Mandara for their churning stick and the world-snake Śeṣa or Vāsuki for the rope, they began churning the ocean. To their dismay, the first substance to rise from the ocean was a black mass of Kālakūṭa, the world-poison. The frightened gods and demons appealed to Śiva Mahādeva to rescue them. Śiva at once seized the poison and drank it, retaining it in his throat, which turned blue-black on account of the poison. (O'Flaherty, *HM*, 274–80; Kramrisch, *PS*, 145–52; Dorai Rangaswamy, *RPT*, 262–71.)

RĀVAṆA TRIES TO LIFT KAILĀSA: RĀVAṆĀNUGRAHA-MŪRTI

Rāvaṇa, demon-king of Laṅkā, had acquired great power and was puffed up with pride. Flying about in his celestial car, he saw Mount Kailāsa, abode of Śiva in the Himalayas, and resolved to uproot it and transport it to his southern realm. When the arrogant demon tried to lift the mountain, Śiva, who was seated at ease with the Goddess and his retinue, simply laughed, and set his big toe on the mountain, crushing Rāvaṇa's ten heads and twenty shoulders. (See illus. 11.) Terrified, Rāvaṇa repented and sang hymns of praise for Śiva. The merciful god not only forgave the demon, but also gave him several boons. (Dorai Rangaswamy, *RPT*, 296–303.)

ŚIVA SEVERS ONE OF BRAHMĀ'S HEADS: BRAHMAŚIRAŚCHEDA-MŪRTI, BHAIRAVA, BHIKṢĀṬANA, KAṄKĀḶA-MŪRTI

In his terrifying persona as Bhairava, Śiva cut off, with the mere snap of a nail, one of the five heads of Brahmā, when the latter arrrogantly declared himself to be the supreme creator-god. Brahmā's skull stuck firmly to Bhairava's left palm. In order to expiate for the sin of cutting off a brahmin's head, Śiva had to take the *Kāpālika* vow of wandering all over the world as a naked beggar (see illus. 9), carrying the skull as his alms bowl, until the day it fell from his hand. As Bhikṣāṭana, the naked beggar, Śiva came to the Pine Forest (Dārukavana, where he shocked the sages with his lewdness and nudity and seduced their wives. At the end of a long confrontation with Śiva, the sages realized Śiva's greatness and worshipped the *liṅga* (phallus) that he let fall, as his sign (*liṅga*).

After his encounter with the sages, Śiva-Bhairava continued his wanderings and eventually reached the abode of Viṣṇu. When Viṣṇu's gatekeeper Viṣvaksena refused to let him in, Śiva impaled the guard on his trident and walked in with the corpse (as *Kaṅkāḷa-mūrti*). A conciliatory Viṣṇu offered his own blood to Śiva, but even vast streams of Viṣṇu's blood could not fill up Śiva's skull-bowl. It was only when Śiva reached the city of Vārāṇasī (Benares) that Brahmā's skull vanished from his hand. (O'Flaherty, *HM*, 141–54 [the Pine Forest myths]; Kramrisch, *PS*, ch. 9; Dorai Rangaswamy; *RPT*, 372–416.)

THE DESTRUCTION OF DAKṢA'S SACRIFICE: DAKṢĀRI-MŪRTI

The Prajāpati (progenitor) Dakṣa, father of Śiva's wife Satī, performed a great sacrifice to which he invited all the gods except his son-in-law Śiva. When Satī went to the sacrifice, Dakṣa insulted Śiva to her face. Unable to bear the insult, Satī immolated herself. Crazed with grief and anger, Śiva—as Vīrabhadra, or through the agency of Vīrabhadra—destroyed Dakṣa's sacrifice and mutilated the various gods who had come to the sacrifice. He cut off Dakṣa's head and replaced it with that of a goat. (O'Flaherty, *HM*, 118–25; Kramrisch, *PS*, 301–33; Dorai Rangaswamy, *RPT*, 323–36.)

ŚIVA BURNS KĀMA, GOD OF LOVE: KĀMĀRI-MŪRTI, DAKṢIṆĀMŪRTI

After the destruction of Dakṣa's sacrifice, Satī was reborn as Pārvatī or Umā, daughter of the mountain Himalaya. Meanwhile, Śiva withdrew from the world and sat in yogic meditation in a Himalayan forest. The gods sought to bring about the union of Śiva and Pārvatī, so that a powerful son born to them would eventually lead the army of the gods to victory over the demons. They asked Kāma, the god of Desire, to shoot a flower-arrow at Śiva as he sat in meditation, to make him fall in love with Umā. However, when Kāma aimed his arrow at Śiva, the god opened the fiery eye on his forehead and burned Kāma to ashes. In some versions of the myth, Kāma disturbs Śiva as he sits as *Dakṣiṇāmūrti* under a banyan tree (*āl*), discoursing on supreme wisdom to a group of sages. (O'Flaherty, *HM*, 154–59; Kramrisch, *PS*, 349–63; Dorai Rangaswamy, *RPT*, 337–42 [*Kāmāntaka*], 417–39 [*Dakṣiṇāmūrti*].)

THE SLAYING OF ANDHAKA: ANDHAKAVADHA-MŪRTI

The Goddess (Pārvatī) once crept up behind Śiva and playfully covered his three eyes with her hands. Immediately, the universe was plunged in darkness. Drops of sweat fell from Śiva's forehead, and a frightful creature was born from them. Since this demonic creature was blind, he was called Andhaka ("the blind one"). Andhaka performed extreme austerities and won a great boon from Brahmā: nothing and no one in the universe would be able to kill him until the demon lusted after a divine woman who was "a mother" to him. Drunk with power, Andhaka rampaged unchecked in the universe, until one day he coveted the goddess Pārvatī, whose playful act had been responsible for his birth. Andhaka fought a terrible battle with Śiva but was overcome in the end. Śiva impaled him on his trident and danced until the demon repented and begged to become Śiva's devotee. Śiva then turned him into his demon-attendant Bhṛṅgi. (O'Flaherty, *HM*, 168–72; Kramrisch, *PS*, 374–83; Dorai Rangaswamy, *RPT*, 369–71.)

ŚIVA KILLS THE DEMON JALANDHARA: JALANDHARĀSURA-SAṂHĀRA-MŪRTI

The demon Jalandhara was born when Śiva cast his rage, in the form of the fire from his eye, into the ocean. Jalandhara became king of the demons, married the chaste Vṛndā, but desired the goddess Pārvatī. In the course of his combat with Śiva over the Goddess, Śiva drew a great wheel (*cakra*) in the waters and challenged the demon to lift it above his head. When Jalandhara tried to do so, the wheel severed his head. Later Śiva gave the wheel to Viṣṇu to keep as his permanent attribute. (Kramrisch, *PS*, 388–94; Dorai Rangaswamy, *RPT*, 352–58.)

THE SLAYING OF THE ELEPHANT-DEMON: GAJĀSURA-SAṂHĀRA-MŪRTI

The demon Gajāsura, who had the form of an elephant (*gaja*), persecuted the gods. When he attacked Śiva and Pārvatī the Goddess was terrified, but Śiva effortlessly killed the demon and flayed his skin. He draped the skin, dripping with blood, as a cloak around him, and danced a dance of victory. (Dorai Rangaswamy, *RPT*, 343–51.)

ŚIVA RESCUES MĀRKAṆḌEYA FROM DEATH: KĀLA-SAṂHĀRA-MŪRTI

The childless sage Mṛkaṇḍu appealed to Śiva and won from him the boon of a son. However, Mārkaṇḍeya, the gifted son who was born to the sage, was given a life span of only sixteen years. Mārkaṇḍeya grew up as a great devotee of Śiva. As Mārkaṇḍeya was worshipping a *liṅga* of Śiva on the day that his life was destined to end, the god of Death (Yama or Kāla) himself came to take the boy's soul away, but Mārkaṇḍeya clung to the *liṅga* and cried out to Śiva. Śiva emerged from the *liṅga*, and kicked and killed Death. (See illus. 12.) Śiva revived Kāla only on the condition that the devout boy should receive the gift of immortality. (Kramrisch, *PS*, 165; Dorai Rangaswamy, *RPT*, 359–68.)

ARJUNA AND ŚIVA AS THE HUNTER: KIRĀTĀRJUNA-MŪRTI OR PĀRTHĀNUGRAHA-MŪRTI

The encounter between Śiva and the hero Arjuna is an important episode in the *Mahābhārata*. On behalf of the Pāṇḍava brothers, Arjuna went to the Himalayas and practiced great austerities in order to win from Śiva the infallible Pāśupata, the weapon that would help the Pāṇḍavas annihilate their enemies in war. Wishing to test the courage and dedication of the hero, Śiva appeared to him in the guise of a Kirāta (hunter), quarreled with him over a wild boar, and challenged him to combat. In the course of the combat, the god stripped the hero of all his weapons, but Arjuna continued to fight with his bare hands. Pleased, Śiva revealed himself and gave Arjuna the Pāśupata weapon. (Kramrisch, *PS*, 257–59; Dorai Rangaswamy, *RPT*, 281–85.)

ŚIVA RECEIVES THE GANGES IN HIS MATTED HAIR: GAṄGĀDHARA-MŪRTI

Bhagīratha, a member of the solar race of kings, performed severe *tapas* (austerities) in order to bring the celestial river Ganges down to earth and the nether world, so that her water would purify and sanctify the ashes of his ancestors, who had been burned to death by the anger of a sage. The Ganges was such a mighty river that the earth would not be able to withstand the full impact of her descent. At Bhagīratha's request, Śiva graciously held out his matted hair to catch the river as she descended, and softened her journey to earth. The Ganges became a permanent attribute of the god's hair. (Dorai Rangaswamy, *RPT*, 272–80.)

IN

MA

October

The Great and the

Imperial Delhi

Dawn

Listening to the Lute

Nationality

Plan

GLOSSARY

GLOSSARY

Only names and words that occur frequently in the poems and the introductory essay have been included in this glossary. Sanskrit terms have been identified by (S).

acai The basic metrical unit in classical Tamil poetry.

Āgama (S) Sacred texts treating ritual, iconography, and other subjects related to temples and image worship.

akam "Interior," "the inner part"; the genre of love poetry in classical Tamil (Caṅkam) literature.

Akattiyar Sanskrit "Agastya," a legendary sage and culture-hero of the Tamils.

akaval Standard meter of classical Tamil poetry of the Caṅkam era.

akṣa (S) Also *rudrākṣa* ("Rudra's [Śiva's] eye"). Tamil *akku*; seeds sacred to Śiva, worn by Śaiva devotees.

ālāpana (S) Form of improvisation used in elaborating a *rāga* scale-type in classical Indian music.

Āḻvār Tamil Vaiṣṇava poet-saint; the twelve Āḻvārs are the authors of the Tamil Vaiṣṇava hymns of the *Nālāyirat tivviyap pirapantam.*

Araṉ Sanskrit "Hara" ("the Seizer"), a name of Śiva.

Ari Sanskrit "Hari"; name of Viṣṇu.

Arjuna One of the five Pāṇḍava brothers, heroes of the *Mahābhārata* epic; through his devotion, wins Pāsupata weapon from Śiva.

aruḷ Divine grace, an important doctrine in Śaiva Siddhānta theology.

Aṟupattumūvar "The Sixty-three"; the sixty-three saints (Nāyaṉmār) of the Tamil Śaiva tradition.

aṭaṅkaṉmuṟai "The complete canon"; a term applied to the collection of the seven books of hymns composed by Appar, Campantar, and Cuntarar.

aṭiyār Devotee; "one who is at the feet (of the Lord)."

aṭṭamūrtti Sanskrit "Aṣṭāmūrti"; Śiva as he manifests himself in "eight forms": the five elements, the sun, moon, and the sacrificing priest.

Aṭṭavīraṭṭāṉam The sites of the Eight Heroic Deeds of Śiva in the Tamil region.

Ayaṉ Sanskrit "Aja" ("the unborn"), a name of Brahmā, the creator-god.

bhakta (S) Devotee; see *aṭiyār* and *toṇṭar*.

bhakti (S) Devotion to God.

Bhikṣāṭana (S) A mythic form of Śiva, in which he wanders as a beggar, with a skull for his alms bowl.

Brahmā (S) The Creator in the Hindu triad of cosmic gods.

brahmin Member of the priestly class in the Hindu system of four classes; the brahmin class ranks highest in the general hierarchy of classes.

camayakuravar The saints Campantar, Appar, Cuntarar, and Māṇikkavācakar as the "Preceptors" of the Tamil Śaiva tradition.

Caṅkam Classical period of Tamil civilization and literature.

cantāṉācāriyārkaḷ The "lineage" of fourteen teachers and authors of the Śaiva Siddhānta treatises.

Caṇṭīcar One of the sixty-three Tamil Śaiva saints.

cariyai Sanskrit *caryā*, service, one of the four ways of devotion in the Śaiva Siddhānta system.

Cēkkiḻār Author of the *Periya Purāṇam*, the lives of the sixty-three Tamil Śaiva saints.

cēl A fish.

Cēra One of the three ancient Tamil kingdoms or "lands"; the ruler of the Cēra kingdom.

cerunti *Ochna squarrosa*, a plant with yellow-orange flowers.

Cilappatikāram "Epic of the Anklet," Tamil epic of the late classical period.

cīr Metrical unit in classical Tamil poetry, a "foot" made up of *acai*s.

Civācāriyār A learned and initiated person in the Tamil Śaiva tradition, qualified to perform Āgamic rites.

Cōḻa One of the three ancient Tamil kingdoms; the ruler of the Cōḻa (or Chola) land.

erukku One of the flowers worn by Śiva.

etukai Rhyming or correspondence of the second syllable of the first words in the lines of a verse; a standard feature of much of Tamil verse.

gaṇa (S) Attendant of Śiva, usually a ghost, demon, or other spirit.

Gaṇeśa (S) Also known as Gaṇapati, lord of the *gaṇas*; elephant-headed son of Śiva and Pārvatī; remover of obstacles to success.

Gaṅgā (S) The river Ganges.

ghee Clarified butter; one of the "five products" of the cow.

gotra (S) Clan group tracing descent from one of the Vedic seers (ṛṣi).

icai Music; musical Tamil; genres associated with music in Tamil literature.

Īcaṉ Sanskrit Īśa, "the Lord"; a name of Śiva.

Kailāsa (S) Mountain, the abode of Śiva in the Himalayas.

Kāla (S) Also Yama, Yama-dharma-rāja; god of death.

kaḻal Ring of heroism or victory worn on the leg by heroes in classical Tamil civilization; foot.

Kali A meter in late classical and post-Caṅkam Tamil poetry.

Kāma (S) God of Love.

Kaṅkāḷa A form of Śiva, in which he carries a corpse or skeleton on his shoulder.

Kaṇṇappar The hunter-saint; one of the sixty-three Tamil Śaiva saints.

Kāpālika (S) Person who has undertaken a vow of begging with a skull as an alms bowl; a Śaiva sect.

Kapālin (S) "He who bears the skull"; a name of Śiva.

Kāraikkāl Ammaiyār Early Tamil Śaiva woman poet-saint.

karma (S) Tamil *viṉai* (act, deed); the law of action leading to effect and rebirth.

kaṭṭaḷai The rhythmic and musical mold in which the *Tēvāram* hymns are cast.

Kaveri Major river in Tamilnadu; also known as "Poṉṉi."

kāvya (S) Ornate poetry in the classical or "court" style.

kayal Type of fish.

keṇṭai Type of fish.

kiriyai Ritual service; one of the four types of activities undertaken toward liberation according to Śaiva Siddhānta theology.

kōṅkam *Cochlospermum gossypium*, a tree with yellow flowers.

koṉṟai Laburnum or cassia tree, the flower of which is sacred to Śiva.

koṭukoṭṭi A dance; also a kind of drum.

kōyil Temple; in classical Tamil, abode of a king.

kuravam *Webera corymbosa*, a shrub.

Kuṟiñci The *paṇ* musical mode appropriate to the kuṟiñci (hill) landscape.

kuṟiñci Conehead plant (Strobilanthus); the hill landscape in Caṅkam poetry.

kuruntam A kind of lime tree.

Kuṟuntokai One of the eight anthologies of classical Tamil poetry.

kuṟuntokai A classical Tamil meter. The *Tēvāram* poet Appar's *Kuṟuntokai* hymns are cast in this meter.

kūviḷam The flower of the *bilva* tree, sacred to Śiva.

liṅga (S) "Sign," phallus (as the male "sign"); symbol and aniconic image of Śiva.

Mahādeva (S) "The great god," name of Śiva.

Māl Also Tirumāl, Tamil name for Viṣṇu.

Māṇikkavācakar Tamil Śaiva saint; author of the *Tiruvācakam.*

mantra (S) Sacred chant; Vedic chant; the Vedas.

maṟai Veda, primary sacred text.

mattam Datura, a flower worn by Śiva.

mōṉai Correspondence of the initial sounds of several words within a line of Tamil poetry; a standard feature of Tamil verse.

muḻavam or muḻavu A kind of concert drum.

mullai Type of jasmine; the pastoral landscape in classical Tamil poetry.

mūrti (S) Tamil *mūrtti*; iconographic form of a divinity.

Murukaṉ Tamil hill-god, identified as Kumaraṉ (Sanskrit Kumāra) or Skanda, the son of Śiva.

mūvar The three poet-saints Appar, Campantar, and Cuntarar.

muyalakaṉ *Apasmārapuruṣa*, dwarf-demon of ignorance, on whom Śiva dances as Naṭarāja.

namaccivāya From Sanskrit "namaḥ śivāya," "salutation to Śiva"; the sacred *mantra* (chant) for Śaivas; see *pañcākṣara.*

ñānam Sanskrit *jñāna*, "wisdom," one of the four disciplines leading to liberation in Śaiva Siddhānta theology.

Naṭarāja (S) Lord of the Dance; Śiva as the cosmic dancer.

nāṭu Country, region, or realm; regional subdivision of the Tamil area.

Nāyaṉār One of the sixty-three saints of the Tamil Śaiva tradition. Plural Nāyaṉmār.

Nēricai A classical Tamil *paṇ* musical mode; a musical and poetic genre used by the *Tēvāram* poet Appar; verses in the nēricai meter.

neytal *Nymphaea stellata*, the dark lily; the seaside landscape in classical Tamil poetry.

ōtuvār Professional singer of hymns from the *Tēvāram* and other Tamil Śaiva texts at Śiva temples in the Tamil region.

Pallava Dynasty that held power in the Tamil region between the second and ninth centuries A.D.

paṇ Scale-type or mode in Tamil music of the classical age and the *Tēvāram* hymns.

pāṇar In the classical (Caṅkam) civilization, a musician who performs to the accompaniment of the *yāḻ*.

pañcākṣara (S) "The five sacred syllables": "namaḥ śivāya"; see *namaccivāya*.

pāṇi A classical song and dance genre, probably associated with religious themes.

pāṇṭaraṅkam One of Śiva's dances.

Pāṇṭiya Also "Pandyan"; one of the three ancient Tamil kingdoms.

paṟai A kind of drum.

paripāṭal A musical meter in late classical Tamil poetry.

pāśa (S) (Tamil *pācam*) "fetter," the bonds of karma in Śaiva Siddhānta philosophy.

paśu (S) The individual soul in Śaiva Siddhānta.

Pāśupata (S) A Śaiva sect; a celestial weapon won by Arjuna from Śiva.

Paśupati (S) "Lord of Souls (or Beasts)," a name of Śiva.

pati (S) "The Lord" in Śaiva Siddhānta; Tamil *pati*: a sacred place.

patikam In the Tamil Śaiva tradition, a devotional hymn, usually consisting of ten or eleven stanzas; a stanza from such a hymn.

paṭutam Type of dance.

Periya purāṇam Also *Tirut toṇṭar purāṇam*; see Cēkkiḻār.

pulaiyan̲ An outcaste or person of low caste, whose occupation involves handling unclean substances and objects.

pūjā (S) Ritual worship according to the Āgamas.

pur̲am "Exterior," dealing with war and public affairs; the "public" genre of classical Tamil poetry.

Purāṇa (S) Compendium of myths; a sacred text in Hinduism.

rāga (S) Scale-type in Indian classical music.

Rudra (S) Vedic god identified with Śiva.

rudrākṣa See *akṣa*

Śaṅkara (S) Name of Śiva.

Śatarudrīya (S) Section of chants in praise of Rudra in the Yajur Veda.

Śaiva (S) A worshipper of Śiva.

Śaiva Siddhānta (S) The philosophical and theological system of the Tamil Śaiva sect.

Śiva (S) "The auspicious"; the destroyer-god in the Hindu triad.

smṛti (S) Traditional sacred texts, distinguished from Vedic literature.

śruti (S) The Vedas, as eternal scripture without a human author.

stotra (S) Hymn in praise of a god; usually in Sanskrit.

takkai Type of drum.

tāla (S) Cycle of beats in Indian classical music.

tamil̲ The Tamil language; the three types of Tamil literature: prose and poetry, music, and drama.

Tāṇṭakam A hymn-type used by the *Tēvāram* poet Appar, set in the extended meter called *tāṇṭakam*.

tantra (S) Esoteric works related to the religion of the Āgamas; another word for Āgama.

Tirukkaṭaikkāppu "The sacred final protection," the signature verse with which Campantar ends his hymns.

Tirumūlar Author of the Tamil Śaiva text *Tirumantiram*.

Tirumur̲ai Primary canonical text in the Tamil Śaiva sect.

Tirut toṇṭat tokai The *Tēvāram* hymn in which Cuntarar names the Nāyan̲ārs.

Tiruviruttam A genre of hymns composed by Appar and other Tamil *bhakti* saints.

toṇṭar "Servants," devotees.

tuṭi Type of drum.

Umā Name of Pārvatī, the Goddess, spouse of Śiva.

Vaiṣṇava (S) Worshipper of Viṣṇu.

vaṇṇam Song with complex rhythms.

vaṉṉi *Prosopis spicigera*, the Suma tree.

vāram Type of song.

Veda (S) The four Vedas; see *śruti.*

Vellala Tamil "*vēḷālar*"; general term for a group of high-ranking non-brahmin castes in Tamilnadu.

vēṅkai The kino tree.

vimāṉa The tower of the Hindu temple.

vīṇā Stringed instrument.

viṉai See *karma.*

viruttam A style of singing the *Tēvāram* hymns; a Tamil meter.

Viṣṇu (S) The preserver-god in the Hindu triad.

yāḻ Ancient Tamil stringed instrument.

yogi (S) One who practices yoga.

yōkam Sanskrit *yoga*; meditative discipline, one of the four activities directed toward liberation in Śaiva Siddhānta theology.

BIBLIOGRAPHY

Tamil Texts, by Title

Note: The Tirunelveli South Indian Saiva Siddhanta Works Publishing Society has been abbreviated as SISSW Publishing Society.

Akattiyar tēvārat tiraṭṭu: Mūlamum uraiyum. With glossary and commentary by Kayappākkam Catāciva Ceṭṭiyār. Madras: SISSW Publishing Society, 1925. June 1976 edition.

Cilappatikāram: Mūlamum uraiyum. The *Cilappatikāram* of Iḷaṅkōvaṭikaḷ with the commentary of Pō. Vē. Cōmacuntaraṉār. Madras: SISSW Publishing Society, 1969. 1977 edition.

Cuntaramūrtti cuvāmikaḷ aruḷicceyta tēvārap patikaṅkaḷ (Periyapurāṇa muṟai). The Tēvāram Hymns of Saint Cuntaramūrtti. With a biographical essay and notes by A. Cōmacuntaram Ceṭṭiyār. Madras: Saiva Siddhānta Mahā Samājam, 1935. Cited in the notes as *Cuntaramūrtti Tēvāram.*

Kanta purāṇam. Śrī Kantapurāṇam. 2 volumes. Edited by A. Ramanathan. Retold by Rā. Sarasvati. Madras: Prema Press, 1974. 2nd edition, 1979.

Kāraikkāl ammaiyār patikaṅkaḷ. See *Patiṉorāṉ tirumuṟai.*

Kāvirit teṉkarait talaṅkaḷ. Madras: Tarumai Ātīṉam Center Worship Society Publication. Madras, 1965.

Nālāyirat tivviyap pirapantam. The Hymns of the *Āḻvārs.* Edition supervised by Aṇṇaṅkarācārya Svāmikaḷ. Madras: V. N. Devanathan, 1971.

Oṉpatām tirumuṟai. Tirumuṟai IX. Containing the *Tiruvicaippā* and *Tiruppallāṇṭu* of Tirumāḷikaittēvar and others. Tarumapuram: Tarumapuram Ātīṉam, 1969.

Paṉṉiru tirumuṟaip peruntiraṭṭu. An anthology of hymns from the Twelve Tirumuṟai. Edited by Pa. Irāmanāta Piḷḷai. Madras: SISSW Publishing Society, 1961. 1980 edition.

Paripāṭal: Mūlamum uraiyum. Paripāṭal, with the commentary of Pō. Vē. Cōmacuntaraṉār. Madras: SISSW Publishing Society, 1957. 1975 edition.

Patiṉorāṉ tirumuṟai. Tirumuṟai XI. Composed by twelve saints. With notes by Cu. A. Irāmacāmip pulavar. Madras: SISSW Publishing Society, 1971.

Periya purāṇam. Tiruttoṇṭar mākkatai (or: *Tirut toṇṭar purāṇam*) of Cēkkiḻār. With historical notes by Pa. Irāmanāta Piḷḷai and textual notes by Cu. A. Irāmacāmip pulavar. Madras: SISSW Publishing Society, 1970.

Periya purāṇam. Tirut toṇṭar purāṇam eṉṉum periya purāṇam: Cēkkiḻār aruḷic ceytatu. 6 volumes. Edited with a commentary by C. K. Subramaniya Mutaliyār. Kōyamuttūr Tamil Sangam, 1937–1953. Second edition.

Tēvāram. Volume One. Tirumuṟai I–III. *Tiruñāṉacampantar tēvārap patikaṅkaḷ.* Edited by Kayappākkam Catāciva Ceṭṭiyār. Madras: SISSW Publishing Society (Kaḻakam), 1927. 1973 edition. Cited in the notes as *Tēvāram* Kaḻakam edition.

Tēvāram. Volume Two. Tirumuṟai IV–VII. *Tirunāvukkaracar, Cuntaramūrtti tēvārap patikaṅkaḷ.* Edited by Kayappākkam Catāciva Ceṭṭiyār. Madras: SISSW Publishing Society (Kaḻakam), 1928–1929. 1973 edition. Cited in the notes as *Tēvāram* Kaḻakam edition.

Tēvāram. (*Paṇmuṟai*). Tirumuṟai I–VII. *Tiruñāṉacampantar, Tirunāvukkaracar, Cuntaramūrtti Tēvāram.* Published in seven volumes with commentary by various scholars. Tarumapuram: Tarumapuram Ātīṉam, 1953–1964. Cited in the notes as *Tēvāram* Ātīṉam edition.

Tēvāram: Hymnes Śivaïtes du pays tamoul. Volume I. *Ñāṉacampantar.* Edited by T. V. Gopal Iyer. General Editor: François Gros. Publications de l'Institut français d'indologie no. 68.1. Pondicherry: Institut français d'indologie, 1984. Cited in the notes as *Tēvāram* Pondicherry edition.

Tēvāram: Hymnes Śivaïtes du pays tamoul. Volume II. *Appar et Cuntarar.* Edited by T. V. Gopal Iyer. General Editor: François Gros. Publications de l'Institut français d'indologie no. 68.2. Pondicherry: Institut français d'indologie, 1985. Cited in the notes as *Tēvāram* Pondicherry edition.

Tirumantiram. Tirumuṟai X. The *Tirumantiram of Tirumūlar.* 2 volumes. With a commentary by Pa. Irāmanāta Piḷḷai and notes by A. Citamparaṉār. Madras: SISSW Publishing Society, 1942. 1975 edition.

Tiruvācakam and *Tirukkōvaiyār. The Tiruvācakam and Tirukkōvaiyār of Māṇikkavācakar.* Tirumuṟai VIII, with notes. Tarumapuram: Tarumapuram Ātīṉam, 1966.

Tiruviḷaiyāṭaṟ purāṇam. The Tiruviḷaiyāṭaṟpurāṇam of Parañcōti Muṉivar. With a glossary. Madras: SISSW Publishing Society, 1931. 1979 edition.

Umāpaticivam tēvāra aruḷmuṟait tiraṭṭu. With the commentary of Pa. Irāmanāta Piḷḷai. Madras: SISSW Publishing Society, 1961.

Vāḻkkaiyil tirumuṟaikaḷ (The Tirumuṟai Texts in Life). Edited by Ce. Cuntaraṉ. Madras: Puracait Tiruneṟik Kaḻakam, 1973.

Secondary Sources in Tamil, by Author

Bhāskarat Toṇṭaimāṉ, To. Mu. *Vēṅkaṭam mutal kumari varai*. 4 volumes. Tirunelveli: S. R. Subramaniya Pillai, 1960–1967. Reprint, 1967.

Ceṅkalvarāya Piḷḷai, Va. Cu. *Tēvāra oḷineṟi: Campantar*. 2 volumes. Madras: SISSW Publishing Society, 1946, 1950. Reprint, 1963.

———. *Tēvāra oḷineṟi: Cuntarar*. Madras: SISSW Publishing Society, 1963.

Cuppiramaṇiya Piḷḷai, Ta. *Civastala mañcari*. Madras: Tiruppati Shri Mahantu Press, 1931. 3rd edition.

Cuppu Reṭṭiyār, Na. *Toṇṭai nāṭṭut tiruppatikaḷ*. Tirunelveli: S. R. Subramaniya Pillai, 1973.

———. *Pāṇṭi nāṭṭut tiruppatikaḷ*. Tirunelveli: S. R. Subramaniya Pillai, 1977.

Irācamāṇikkaṉār, Mā. *Periya purāṇa ārāycci*. Madras: Pāri Nilaiyam, 1948. 3rd edition, 1978.

Irāmanātaṉ Ceṭṭiyār, Lē. Pa. Ka., ed. *Paṉ ārāycciyum ataṉ muṭivukaḷiṉ tokuppum*. Compiled by Pe. Tūraṉ. Madras: Tamiḻ Icaic Caṅkam, 1974.

Kaliyāṇacuntara Tēcikar, A. "Tarumaiy ātīṉak kuruparamparai varalāṟu." *Makākumpāpiṣēka Viḻā Malar*, 338–466. Tarumapuram: Vaidyanāthasvāmi Devasthānam, 1970.

Murukavēḷ, Na. Rā. *Meykaṇṭa nūlkaḷiṉ vāḻviyal uṇmaikaḷ; tirumuṟaikaḷiṉ ciṟappu*. Tirukkaḻukkuṉṟam: Kurukulam, 1973.

———. *Tirumuṟaic ceḻumalar: Tokuppum viḷakkamum*. Kārttikai Tīpam publication. Madras: Kāraṇīśvarar Temple, Caitait Tēvāra Capai, 1975.

Naṭēca Kavuṇṭar, Ku. *Appar varalāṟṟarāycciyum tēvārat tiṟaṉāyvum*. Madras: SISSW Publishing Society, 1972.

Samy, B. L. *Caṅka ilakkiyattil ceṭikoṭi viḷakkam*. Madras: SISSW Publishing Society, 1967. 1982 edition.

———. *Caṅka ilakkiyattil puḷḷiṉa viḷakkam*. Madras: SISSW Publishing Society, 1976.

Subramaniyam, Nīlāmbāḷ, ed. *Āḻvārkaḷum nāyaṉmārkaḷum*. Madras: Jayashree, 1966.

Turaicāmip Piḷḷai, Auvai Cu. *Caiva ilakkiya varalāṟu (ki. pi. 7 mutal 10-m nūṟṟāṇṭu varai)*. Annamalainagar: Annamalai University, 1958. 2nd edition, 1978.

Veḷḷaivāraṇaṉ, Ka. *Paṉṉiru tirumuṟai varalāṟu: Mutal ēḻu tirumuṟaikaḷ*. Annamalainagar: Annamalai University, 1972.

Vipulānanta Cuvāmikaḷ. *Yāḻnūl: A Treatise on Ancient Tamil Music*. Tanjore: Karantai Tamil Sangam, 1974.

Works in Other Languages

Agrawala, V. S. *Śiva-Mahādeva*. Varanasi, 1966.

Appadurai, Arjun. *Worship and Conflict under Colonial Rule: A South Indian Case*. Cambridge South Asian Studies 27. Cambridge: Cambridge University Press, 1981.

Apte, V. S. *The Practical Sanskrit-English Dictionary*. 3rd edition, revised and enlarged. Delhi: Motilal Banarsidass, 1965. First published 1912.

Balasubrahmanyam, S. R. *Early Chola Temples*. Delhi: Orient Longman, 1971.

———. *Middle Chola Temples*. Delhi: Thomson Press, 1975.

———. *Later Chola Temples*. Delhi: Mudgala Trust, 1979.

Barrett, Douglas. *Early Cōḻa Architecture and Sculpture, 866–1014*. London: Faber, 1974.

Bhandarkar, R. G. *Vaiṣṇavism, Śaivism and Minor Religious Systems*. Strasbourg: Karl J. Trübner, 1913.

Carpenter, J. Estlin. *Theism in Medieval India*. 1921. Reprint. Delhi: Munshiram Manoharlal, 1977.

Chatterji, J. C. *Kashmir Shaivism*. Srinagar, 1914.

Chidambaranatha Chettiar, A. *Advanced Studies in Tamil Prosody*. Annamalainagar: Annamalai University, 1977.

Clothey, Fred W., and J. Bruce Long, eds. *Experiencing Śiva: Encounters with a Hindu Deity*. Columbia, Mo.: South Asia Books, 1983.

Coomaraswamy, Ananda K. "The Dance of Shiva." In *The Dance of Shiva: Fourteen Indian Essays*, 66–78. New York: Noonday Press, 1957. Revised ed. 1962.

Courtright, Paul. "On This Holy Day in My Humble Way: Aspects of Pūjā." In *Gods of Flesh, Gods of Stone*, 33–50. *See* Waghorne and Cutler 1985.

Curtis, J.W.V. "Space Concepts and Worship Environment in Śaiva Siddhānta." In *Experiencing Śiva*, 87–101. *See* Clothey and Long 1983.

Cutler, Norman Joel. *Songs of Experience: The Poetics of Tamil Devotion*. Bloomington: Indiana University Press, 1986.

Daniélou, Alain. *Vedic Recitation and Chant: The Music of India*. Record no. 6. UNESCO collection, *A Musical Anthology of the Orient.* Kassel/Basel: Bärenreiter.

Devasenapathy, V. A. *Śaiva Siddhānta.* Madras: University of Madras, 1958.

———. *Of Human Bondage and Divine Grace.* Śivajñāṉa Siddhiyār Endowment Lectures, 1959. Annamalainagar: Annamalai University, 1963.

Dhavamony, Mariasusai. *Love of God according to Śaiva Siddhānta: A Study in the Mysticism and Theology of Śaivism.* Oxford: Oxford University Press, 1971.

Dorai Rangaswamy, M. A. *The Religion and Philosophy of Tēvāram; with Special Reference to Nampi Ārūrar (Sundarar).* 4 volumes in 2 books. Madras: University of Madras, 1958–1959.

Eck, Diana L. *Darśan: Seeing the Divine Image in India.* Chambersburg, Pa.: Anima Books, 1981.

Eliade, Mircea. *The Sacred and the Profane: The Nature of Religion.* Translated from the French by Willard R. Trask. New York: Harper & Row, 1959.

Filliozat, Jean. "The Role of the Śaivāgamas in the Śaiva Ritual System." In *Experiencing Śiva,* 81–86. *See* Clothey and Long 1983.

Fuller, Charles J. *Servants of the Goddess: The Priests of a South Indian Temple.* Cambridge: Cambridge University Press, 1984.

Gargi, Balwant. *Folk Theater of India.* Seattle: University of Washington Press, 1966.

Gerow, Edwin. *A Glossary of Indian Figures of Speech.* The Hague: Mouton, 1971.

Gonda, Jan. *On Names and the Name of God in Ancient India.* Verhandelingen der Koningklijke Nederlandse Akademie van Wetenschappen. Letterkunde. Nieuwe Reeks, vol. 75, no. 4. Amsterdam, 1970.

———. *Medieval Religious Literature in Sanskrit.* A History of Indian Literature. Volume II, fasc. 1. Wiesbaden: Otto Harrassowitz, 1977.

———. "The Śatarudrīya." In *Sanskrit and Indian Studies,* 75–91. *See* Nagatomi et al. 1980.

Government of India Census 1961. Volume IX: Tamil Nadu. Part XI–D: Temples of Tamil Nadu. Volume VII (i): Thanjavur. By K. Chockalingam. Thanjavur Temples, 1971.

Hardgrave, Robert L. *The Dravidian Movement.* Bombay, 1965.

Hardy, Friedhelm. "Ideology and Cultural Contexts of the Śrīvaiṣṇava Temple." In *South Indian Temples,* 119–51. See Stein 1978.

———. *Viraha-Bhakti: The Early History of Kṛṣṇa Devotion in South India.* Delhi: Oxford University Press, 1983.

Hart, George L., III. *The Poems of Ancient Tamil: Their Milieu and Their*

Sanskrit Counterparts. Berkeley: University of California Press, 1975.

———. "The Nature of Tamil Devotion." In *Aryan and Non-Aryan in India*, edited by Madhav M. Deshpande and Peter E. Hook, 11–33. Michigan Papers on South and Southeast Asia, no. 14. Ann Arbor Center for South and South East Asian Studies, 1979.

———. *Poets of the Tamil Anthologies: Ancient Poems of Love and War*. Princeton Library of Asian Translations. Princeton: Princeton University Press, 1979.

———. "The Little Devotee: Cēkkiḻār's Story of Ciṟuttoṇṭar." In *Sanskrit and Indian Studies*, 217–36. *See* Nagatomi et al., 1980.

Heifetz, Hank, trans. and ed. *The Origin of the Young God: Kālidāsa's Kumārasaṃbhava*. Translated, with annotation and an introduction. Berkeley: University of California Press, 1985.

Herbert, George. "Jordan (1)" and "Jordan (2)." In *Seventeenth Century Prose and Poetry*, edited by Alexander M. Witherspoon and Frederick J. Warnke, pp. 849, 854. New York: Harcourt Brace and World, 1929. 2nd edition, 1963.

Hopkins, Thomas J. *The Hindu Religious Tradition*. Encino, Calif.: Dickenson, 1971.

Ingalls, Daniel H. H. *An Anthology of Sanskrit Court Poetry: Vidyākara's Subhāṣitaratnakoṣa*. Harvard Oriental Series, vol. 44. Cambridge: Harvard University Press, 1965.

———. "Kālidāsa and the Attitudes of the Golden Age." *Journal of the American Oriental Society* 96, no. 1 (January–March 1976): 15–26.

Jackson, William J. "Tyāgarāja: Musician Saint of South India." Ph.D. diss., Harvard University, 1984.

Kailasapathy, K. *Tamil Heroic Poetry*. Oxford: Oxford University Press, 1968.

Karavelane, trans. *Chants dévotionnels tamouls de Kāraikkālammaiyār*. Edited and translated by Karavelane. Publications de l'Institut français d'indologie, no. 1. New edition. Pondicherry, 1982.

Kingsbury, F., and G. E. Phillips. *Hymns of the Tamil Śaivite Saints*. The Heritage of India Series. Calcutta: Association Press; London: Oxford University Press, 1921.

Kramrisch, Stella. *The Hindu Temple*. Calcutta: University of Calcutta, 1946. 2 volumes. Reprint. Delhi: Motilal Banarsidass, 1976.

———. *Manifestations of Śiva*. Philadelphia: Philadelphia Museum of Art, 1981.

———. *The Presence of Śiva*. Princeton: Princeton University Press, 1981.

Long, J. Bruce. "Rudra as an Embodiment of Divine Ambivalence in the

Śatarudrīya Stotram." In *Experiencing Śiva*, 103–28. *See* Clothey and Long 1983.

Lord, Albert B. *The Singer of Tales*. London, 1960.

Lorenzen, David N. *The Kāpālikas and Kālāmukhas: Two Lost Śaivite Sects*. Berkeley: University of California Press, 1972.

Mahalingam, T. V. *Kāñcīpuram in Early South Indian History*. New York: Asia, 1969.

Miller, Barbara Stoler. *Love Song of the Dark Lord: Jayadeva's Gītagovinda*. New York: Columbia University Press, 1977.

———. "Kālidāsa's Verbal Icon: Aṣṭāmūrti Śiva." In *Discourses on Śiva: Proceedings of a Symposium on the Nature of Religious Imagery*, edited by Michael W. Meister. Philadelphia: University of Pennsylvania Press, 1984.

———, ed. and trans. *Theater of Memory: The Plays of Kālidāsa*. New York: Columbia University Press, 1984.

Nagatomi, Masatoshi, B. K. Matilal, J. M. Masson, and E. C. Dimock, Jr., eds. *Sanskrit and Indian Studies: Essays in Honor of Daniel H. H. Ingalls*. Dordrecht: D. Reidel, 1980.

Narayana Ayyar, C. V. *Origin and Early History of Śaivism in South India*. Madras: University of Madras, 1939. Reprint, 1974.

Narayanan, Vasudha. "Arcāvatāra: On Earth As He Is in Heaven." In *Gods of Flesh, Gods of Stone*, 53–66. *See* Waghorne and Cutler 1985.

Natarajan, B. *The City of the Cosmic Dance: Chidambaram*. Southern Art Series 2. Delhi: Orient Longman, 1974.

Nilakanta Sastri, K. A. *The Cōḻas*. 2nd edition, revised. 2 volumes in 1. Madras: University of Madras, 1955.

———. *Development of Religion in South India*. Madras: Orient Longmans, 1963.

———. *The Culture and History of the Tamils*. Calcutta: Firma K. L. Mukhopadhyay, 1964.

O'Flaherty, Wendy Doniger. *Asceticism and Eroticism in the Mythology of Śiva*. Oxford: Oxford University Press, 1973.

———. *Hindu Myths: A Sourcebook Translated from the Sanskrit*. With an introduction. Harmondsworth: Penguin Books, 1975.

Parry, Milman. *Les Formulas et la métrique d'Homère*. Paris, 1928.

Peterson, Indira. "Singing of a Place: Pilgrimage as Metaphor and Motif in the *Tēvāram* Hymns of the Tamil Śaivite Saints." *Journal of the American Oriental Society* 102, no. 1 (January-March 1982): 69–90.

———. "Lives of the Wandering Singers: Pilgrimage and Poetry in Tamil Śaivite Hagiography." *History of Religions* 22, no. 4 (1983): 338–60.

Peterson, Indira. "The *kṛti* as an Integrative Cultural Form: Aesthetic Experience in the Religious Songs of Two South Indian Composers." *Journal of South Asian Literature* 19, no. 2 (Fall-Winter 1984): 165–79.

———. "Sanskrit in Carnatic Music: The Songs of Muttusvāmi Dīkṣita." *Indo-Iranian Journal* 29 (1986): 183–99.

———. "In Praise of the Lord: The Image of the Royal Patron in the Songs of Saint Cuntaramūrtti and the Composer Tyāgarāja." In *Patronage in Indian Culture*, edited by Barbara Stoler Miller. Princeton: Princeton University Press, forthcoming.

Pope, G. U. *The Tiruvāçagam or 'Sacred Utterances' of the Tamil Poet, Saint and Sage Māṇikkavāçagar. Tamil Text, Translation etc.* Oxford: Clarendon, 1900. Reprint. Madras University, 1970.

Powers, Harold S. Essay I ("The region, its music and music history") and II ("Theory and practice of classical music) under "India, Subcontinent of." In *The New Grove Dictionary of Music and Musicians*, edited by Stanley Sadie. Vol. 9, 69–141. London: Macmillan, 1980.

Raghavan, V. *The Indian Heritage: An Anthology of Sanskrit Literature.* Bangalore: Indian Institute of World Culture, 1956.

Ramamurti, Rajam. "On the Themes of Divine Immanence and Localization." *Tamil Civilization*, Quarterly Research Journal of the Tamil University, Thanjavur (September 1983): 73–76.

Ramanujan, A. K. *The Interior Landscape: Love Poems from a Classical Tamil Anthology.* UNESCO collection of representative works. Bloomington: Indiana University Press, 1967. Midland edition, 1975.

———. "Form in Classical Tamil Poetry." In *Symposium on Dravidian Civilization*, edited by Andrée F. Sjoberg. 73–105. Publication no. 1, Asian Series, Center for Asian Studies, University of Texas at Austin. General editors: Edgar C. Polomé et al. Austin and New York: Jenkins, 1971.

———. *Speaking of Śiva.* Baltimore: Penguin, 1973.

———. *Hymns for the Drowning: Poems for Viṣṇu by Nammāḻvār.* Princeton: Princeton University Press, 1981.

———. *Poems of Love and War: From the Eight Anthologies and the Ten Long Poems of Classical Tamil.* New York: Columbia University Press, 1985.

Ramanujan, A. K., and Norman Cutler. "From Classicism to Bhakti." In *Essays on Gupta Culture*, edited by Bardwell L. Smith, 177–94. Columbia, Mo.: South Asia Books, 1983.

Shulman, David D. *Tamil Temple Myths: Sacrifice and Divine Marriage in the South Indian Śaiva Tradition.* Princeton: Princeton University Press, 1980.

Sivaramamurti, C. *Naṭarāja in Art, Thought and Literature.* Delhi: National Museum, 1974.

———. *Śatarudrīya: Vibhūti of Śiva's Iconography.* Delhi: Abhinav, 1976.

Sivaraman, K. *Śaivism in Philosophical Perspective: A Study of the Formative Concepts, Problems and Methods of Śaiva Siddhānta.* Delhi: Motilal Banarsidass, 1973.

Smith, Wilfred Cantwell. "The Study of Religion and the Study of the Bible." *Journal of the American Academy of Religion* 34, no. 2 (1971): 131–40.

Somasundaram, P. S. *Tirujñāṉasambandhar: Philosophy and Religion.* Madras: Vani Pathippakam, 1986.

Soundara Rajan, K. V. *South Indian Temple Styles.* Delhi: Munshiram Manoharlal, 1972.

Spencer, George W. "The Sacred Geography of the Tamil Shaivite Hymns." *Numen* 17 (1970): 232–44.

Staal, J. Frits. "Sanskrit and Sanskritization." *Journal of Asian Studies* 22, no. 3 (May 1963): 261–75.

Stein, Burton. *Peasant State and Society in Medieval India.* Delhi: Oxford University Press, 1980.

———. *South Indian Temples: An Analytical Reconsideration.* Delhi: Vikas, 1978.

Subramaniam, T. N., ed. *South Indian Temple Inscriptions.* 3 volumes. Madras Government Oriental Series no. 157. Madras: Government Oriental Manuscripts Library, 1955–1957.

Subrahmaniya Pillai, G. "Introduction and History of Śaiva Siddhānta." In *Collected Lectures on Śaiva Siddhānta: 1946–1954.* Tiruppanandal Endowment Lectures, Lecture 1. Annamalainagar: Annamalai University, 1965.

Subramanyan, S. *The Commonness in the Metre of the Dravidian Languages.* Research Project Publication no. 22. Trivandrum: Dravidian Linguistics Association, 1977.

Suddhananda Bharati, Yogi. *The Grand Epic of Saivism.* Tirunelveli/Madras: SISSW Publishing Society, 1970.

Tamil Lexicon. 6 volumes and supplement. Madras: University of Madras, 1936.

Turner, Victor. *The Ritual Process: Structure and Anti-Structure.* Chicago: University of Chicago Press, 1969.

Vatsyayan, Kapila. *Traditional Indian Theater: Multiple Streams.* New Delhi: National Book Trust, 1980.

Venkatachari, K.K.A. *The Maṇipravāla Literature of the Śrīvaiṣṇava Ācāryas: 12th–15th Century A.D.* Anantacharya Research Institute Series no. III. Bombay: Anantacharya Research Institute, 1980.

Venkataramanayya, N. *An Essay on the Origin of the South Indian Temple*. Madras: Methodist Publishing House, 1930.

Waghorne, Joanne P., and Norman Cutler, in association with Vasudha Narayanan, eds. *Gods of Flesh, Gods of Stone: The Embodiment of Divinity in India*. Chambersburg, Pa.: Anima, 1985.

Warder, A. K. *Indian Kāvya Literature*. Volume 3. Delhi: Motilal Banarsidass, 1977.

Yocum, Glenn E. "Shrines, Shamanism and Love Poetry: Elements in the Emergence of Popular Tamil Bhakti." *Journal of the American Academy of Religion* 41, no. 1 (March 1973): 3–17.

———. "Sign and Paradigm: Myth in Tamil Śaiva and Vaiṣṇava *bhakti* Poetry." In *Structural Approaches to South India Studies*, edited by Harry M. Buck and Glenn E. Yocum, 184–206. Chambersburg, Pa.: Anima Books, 1974.

———. *Hymns to the Dancing Śiva: A Study of Māṇikkavācakar's Tiruvācakam*. New Delhi: Heritage, 1982.

Young, Katherine K. *Beloved Places (Ukantaruḷiṉanilaṅkaḷ): The Correlation of Topography and Theology in the Śrīvaiṣṇava Tradition of South India*. Delhi: Motilal Banarsidass, 1984.

Younger, Paul. "Singing the Tamil Hymn book in the Tradition of Rāmānuja: The *Adyayanotsava* Festival in Śrīraṅkam." *History of Religions* 20, no. 2 (February 1982): 272–93.

Zelliot, Eleanor. "The Medieval Bhakti Movement in History: An Essay on the Literature in English." In *Hinduism: New Essays in the History of Religions*, edited by Bardwell L. Smith, 143–168. Leiden: E. J. Brill, 1976.

Zvelebil, Kamil V. *The Smile of Murugan: On Tamil Literature of South India*. Leiden: E. J. Brill, 1973.

———. *Tamil Literature*. In *A History of Indian Literature*. Jan Gonda Volume X, fasc. 1. Wiesbaden: Otto Harrassowitz, 1974.

———. *Tamil Literature*. In *Handbuch der Orientalistik*. Zweite Abteilung, *Indien*. Edited by Jan Gonda. Band 2: *Literatur und Bühne*, Abschnitt 1. Leiden/Cologne: E. J. Brill, 1975.

INDEX OF POEMS

The poems are numbered according to the Kaḻakam edition of the *Tēvāram*.

GENERAL INDEX